The Portrait of an Artist as a Pathographer

On Writing Illnesses and Illnesses in Writing

Edited by

Jayjit Sarkar
Raiganj University, India

Jagannath Basu
Sitalkuchi College, India

Series in Literary Studies

VERNON PRESS

Copyright © 2022 by the authors.

All rights reserved. No part of this publication may be reproduced, stored in a retrieval system, or transmitted in any form or by any means, electronic, mechanical, photocopying, recording, or otherwise, without the prior permission of Vernon Art and Science Inc.

www.vernonpress.com

In the Americas:	*In the rest of the world:*
Vernon Press	Vernon Press
1000 N West Street, Suite 1200	C/Sancti Espiritu 17,
Wilmington, Delaware, 19801	Malaga, 29006
United States	Spain

Series in Literary Studies

Library of Congress Control Number: 2020952102

ISBN: 978-1-64889-369-8

Also available: 978-1-64889-064-2 [Hardback]; 978-1-64889-271-4 [PDF, E-Book]

Cover design by Vernon Press. Cover image by photosforyou from Pixabay.

Product and company names mentioned in this work are the trademarks of their respective owners. While every care has been taken in preparing this work, neither the authors nor Vernon Art and Science Inc. may be held responsible for any loss or damage caused or alleged to be caused directly or indirectly by the information contained in it.

Every effort has been made to trace all copyright holders, but if any have been inadvertently overlooked the publisher will be pleased to include any necessary credits in any subsequent reprint or edition.

To artists, pathographers, and everyone in-between.

Table of contents

	Preface	*ix*
	Introduction	*xi*
	I. European Literary Pathographies	*1*
Chapter 1	**The Gift of Chains: Atopic Violence and Embodied Community in Aeschylus's *Prometheus Bound***	3
	Anda Pleniceanu *Western University in Ontario, Canada*	
Chapter 2	**Pathography of Man and Evil in Joseph Conrad's *Heart of Darkness***	19
	Nina Muždeka *University of Novi Sad, Serbia*	
Chapter 3	**Care, Pig!: The Abject Caregiver in Beckett's Plays**	33
	Gabriel Quigley *New York University, USA*	
Chapter 4	**"But of course Rachel's illness is quite different": Reconfiguring the 'Medical' and 'Illness' in Virginia Woolf's *The Voyage Out***	49
	Chloe Leung *University of Edinburgh, UK*	
Chapter 5	**"Between Horror and Hunger": Reflections on the Medical Poems of Miroslav Holub**	65
	Anik Sarkar *Salesian College, India*	

Chapter 6	**"I am God in a body":** *The Diary of Vaslav Nijinsky* **as Initiation into Psychosis**	81
	Jamil Ahmed *Middlesex University, UK*	
Chapter 7	**Doctor, Soldier, Writer: António Lobo Antunes as Portugal's Pathographer**	95
	Ricardo Rato Rodrigues *Uniwersytet Marii Curie-Skłodowskiej w Lublinie, Poland*	
	II. American Literary Pathographies	*111*
Chapter 8	**"To Him Who Wants It!": Understanding William Carlos Williams' Pathography**	113
	Seunghyun Shin *University of Vermont, USA*	
Chapter 9	**Lesbianism, Disability, and Pain: Shirley Jackson's** *We Have Always Lived in the Castle* **as a Pathography**	127
	Tatiana Prorokova-Konrad *University of Vienna, Austria*	
Chapter 10	**"The struggle to Breathe": Narrating the Sick Body in Lorrie Moore's Short Stories**	143
	Nadia Boudidah Falfoul *University of Kairouan, Tunisia*	
Chapter 11	***Taking Turns*** **in Writing Pain: Comics' Approximation of Pathography**	159
	Victoria Lupascu *University of Montréal, Canada*	
	III. Literary Pathographies of the World	*175*
Chapter 12	**Wopko Jensma as a Pathographer: The Interface between Poetry and Schizophrenia**	177
	Ayub Sheik *University of KwaZulu-Natal, South Africa*	

| Chapter 13 | ***The Black Book*** **as Pathography: Romancing Disease and Decay in the Late Ottoman Empire** | 193 |

Meltem Gürle
University of Cologne, Germany

| Chapter 14 | **Dis-eases of the Heart Cured by Magic: Heian *Onmyōji* in Yumemakura Baku's Popular Japanese Fiction** | 211 |

Amy W. S. Lee
Hong Kong Baptist University, Hong Kong

| Chapter 15 | **Writing Illness: Morbid Humour as a Strategy to Cope with Disease and Pain in Zimbabwean Literature** | 227 |

Nhlanhla Landa, Sindiso Zhou
University of Fort Hare, South Africa

| Chapter 16 | **"Back from the Shades of Death": The Pleasures and Pains of Convalescence in the Nineteenth-Century City** | 245 |

Edward Grimble
Lancing College, UK

| Chapter 17 | **The Lessons (Not) Learned: Literary Bioethics and Biopolitics from Stoker to Atwood** | 267 |

Ronja Tripp-Bodola
Louisiana State University, USA

| | *Coda: "How is the pain?"* | *285* |

Mohona Banerjee
Amity University, Noida, India

| | *Notes on Contributors* | *287* |

| | *Index* | *291* |

Preface

This volume, following an invitation from the Commissioning Editor at Vernon Press, was conceived during Covid-19 pandemic and materialised when the world was still trying to grapple with the "new normal". Perched with a sense of anxiety, both individual and collective, we instantaneously felt the prospective importance of a project like this. A volume such as this, with its focus on pathography as world literature, was rarely thought of to date and that too through the exploration of such varied, hitherto unknown, interconnections between medical humanities and literary studies. Just as "illness" is a rupture in the holistic emblem of mind-body, self-other, and time-space, this volume too aspires to break that sweet canonical "whole" which literary studies often indulge in. We believe that world literature needed a project such as this one, so that it may evoke an alternative narrative (for example, that of pathography) and, more importantly, an alternative modernity (of a reclusive, withdrawn, ill self). Such other(s) of the canon or other-canons are necessary to continue the dialectic at play; it is a replenishment such as illness which can provide us with a new meaning of health, and everything health entails: social, political, cultural and obsiviously corporeal. No wonder, scholars from different parts of the world connected with this project, and ventured to see the "new light" that one often visualizes at the other side of illness. The more severe the illness is, the profound is the desire to see the light. Perhaps the pandemic caused by Covid-19 evoked such a collective anxiety (or an illness) within all of us; and this resulted in the birth of *The Portrait of an Artist as a Pathographer*. This book is thus about that "new light" that exists on the other side of pain, suffering and illness. It is this collective desire that brought us all together and made us complete this volume. In thinking (with) illness, the work tries to address two overarching questions: firstly, how to *write* illness and secondly, how to *read* illness in writing?

The emotional yet challenging experience of putting everything together in *The Portrait* is worth unfolding. It comprised of scholars from across the globe: Ayub Sheik, Meltem Gürle, Seunghyun Shin, Nadia Boudidah Falfoul, Gabriel Quigley, Amy W S Lee, Jamil Ahmed, Anda Pleniceanu, Chloe Leung, Tatiana Prorokova-Konrad, Nina Muždeka, Victoria Lupascu, Nhlanhla Landa, Sindiso Zhou, Edward Grimble, Ronja Tripp-Bodola, Anik Sarkar and Ricardo Rato Rodrigues. We thank them wholeheartedly for bearing with us, our requirements, which at times was quite demanding, and for meeting our deadlines. It was inspiring to work with all of them and hopefully, we would come up with something more challenging in the near future. It is always a pleasure to have friends such as Prof. Elizabeth Outka of the University of

Richmond, Virginia, Prof. Sangeeta Ray of the University of Maryland, and Prof. Priya Menon of Troy University, Alabama who have shown their tremendous support throughout this project. We would also like to thank Mohona Banerjee, one of our brightest students, who has voluntarily agreed to share her poem for the Coda: "How is the pain?" Last but not the least, we would like to offer our earnest gratitude to the team at Vernon Press for believing in us and helping us through this journey.

Jayjit Sarkar
Jagannath Basu

India
27 August 2020

Introduction

> I record symptoms as I see'em. I advise no remedy. I don't even draw the disease usually. Temperature 102$^{3/8}$, pulse 78, tongue coated, etc., eyes yellow, etc.
>
> — Ezra Pound to William Carlos Williams
> *Selected Letters*

Illness *is* Philosophy

To philosophise is to learn how to die. To philosophise is to learn how to be ill (Carel 1995, 8).

Illness *is* philosophy. There is an inherent problem in introducing a thought like illness with the verb "is" as it entails presupposition— the very natural attitude it is against. It is this "image" in the image-of-thought with which a thought fixates itself and becomes dogmatic. Illness is, what Deleuze ([1968] 2004) would call, an act of thought without image— or perhaps, more appropriately, another image-of-thought "that takes its point of departure not in a point— a point that does not have any spatial extension, nevertheless the whole world hinges on it— but rather in a line" (Abrahamsson 2018, xxi). Illness is in fact philosophy without the usual pre-philosophical fixed points and predetermined contours.

A flow is always silent, disruption noisy. Illness is the Event[1] within the homogeneous, empty time[2] of health and what we call the "everyday, every day" of health— a continuous flow of time where one moment is not distinguishable from another. The homogeneous, empty time of health is an uninhibited linear "flow" which simply passes in silence but never enlivened. Illness, on the other hand, is a rupture in the dominant ideology of health; and "rupture," for Derrida, is not only a rupture, a break, but also a redoubling. It leads to a rupture; and *is* a rupture. It presence (*parousia*) itself all of a sudden, and with it surfaces (Badiou's) the "inconsistent multiplicity", the "other," which was hitherto excluded by the dominant ideology. Illness is the excluded "post-" which comes *before* the "whole" of the health. The former is the déjà, the already, of health. The dissemination of the ideology of health as a "whole" is, therefore, an act of exclusion, a majoritarian de-cision (from the Latin *de* + *caedere*, meaning "to cut off"), of the noise of the inconsistent multiplicity. The ideology of health is *in* the flow, in the circulation; illness is a break in that "dynamic experiential field of meanings" (Aho 2017, 121). Like any other rupture, it calls for an unpremeditated understanding of both the being and the world around. Illness, like health, is a phenomenological condition, a particular way of being-in-the-world and being-with-the-world but unlike health, it throws at us a different and a newer understanding which is not dictated by some pre-reflective involvement with the world. It is being-other than "being as being." The noise of illness is a sudden disruption in the silence of health. Illness is *in* the middle; and *is* the middle as it is in-between two immediate conditions of health — between retrospective and prospective health. And, as Michel Serres (1982) claims, the middle is always "noisy."

Illness is a rupture in the "flow" of being-with-the-world; it is a disruption in the "flow" of the body's ex-sistence in the world. More than the "what is" in ill, we are therefore more interested in the "how to *be*" in illness. It is a particular way of "there-being" which is different from "there-being" of health. The former is more reflective and "deeper". Illness— and the now-ness and here-ness of illness— are ruptures in the continuum of lived-time and lived-space. It is Badiou's *hasardeux* (haphazard) and *surgissement* (eruption). The horizon or the field of health, as it stretches in time and space, is marked by the horizontality. An ill being's involvement-ality, on the other hand, is vertical as it involves "deepening". One either moves "up" or "down" in illness and never forward or backward. Either the effects would be transcendental, for example, in John Keats and Virginia Woolf, or to "remain earthly" (Nietzsche's phrase). It is in this sense inextensible— quite contrary to the body in health which "stretches out", in time, in space, to the other, to the world. It feels like "stone" or rather Molloy's "extraordinary hazard" of sucking the same four stones: of "only sucking four, always the same, turn and turn about" in "impeccable succession" (Beckett 1955, 64). While hinting at his condition similar to what we are arguing as illness, of being ill in the world, Molloy in his monologue says: "And deep down it was all the same to me whether I sucked a different stone each time or always the same stone, until the end of time. For they all tasted exactly the same" (69).

This failure of the "general circulation": the "general circulation of the stones from pocket to pocket" in Molloy's case is reminiscent of the condition of "-ness" of ill, of to-be-with-illness in the world. The currency of health— the flow— remains invalid during illness. "Serious illness", as Arthur Frank points out "is a loss of the "destination and map" that had previously guided the ill person's life...." (1995, 1) The map, the "method", of health is wrecked by the "haphazard" of illness. The latter is a method in itself. It has its own grammar. The more Molloy tries to methodise his effort, the more (extraordinarily) hazardous the effort becomes.

The *poeisis*— the act of coming into being— of illness has a "secret" which resists hermeneutics— the secret which withstands the trained gaze, the "scope", of the stethoscope and microscope— the interpreting tools of medical practitioners. It resists becoming a disease, becoming interpretable. As Arthur Kleinman explains, "Disease is what practitioners have been trained to see through the theoretical lenses of their particular form of practice" (1988, 5). Illness is "form-less"; the moment an illness is given a "form", it ceases to remain an illness and becomes a disease. It has a sort of what Aristotle would call "impotentiality" or "potentiality-not-to-be" which resists any kind of actualisation. The potentiality (*dunamis*) of illness lies in its impotentiality (*adunamis*): that is, to remain independent of the *praxis* of medical wisdom. Pathography is not an illness actualised. It is in no way an actualisation of illness; it is not an "act" where things are actualised but an attempt of keeping the "secret" a secret, and potentiality to be potentiality "to-come" (*avenir*). The other brushes "withagainst" (Cixous' portmanteau word) the self in illness. In disease, the self is overwhelmed by and, at many times, becomes the other.

An illness, as opposed to a disease, is incommensurable in medical terms. In this sense, it is not real, as according to the "peculiar dogma" of medical science, "only what is measurable is real" (Aho 2018, xv). It is Badiou's "supernumerary", an other/Other, inassimilable to the dominant ideology. It is generally voluntary or involuntary responses/signals which we give to ourselves and the world around in a sort of "metalanguage" that something somewhere is not quite right. It is a sort of *ur*-language of *ur*-civilization or what Wittgenstein would call "the primitive, the natural expressions of the sensations" (Bourke 2014, 5). All illnesses may or may not turn out to be a disease; the latter is a sort of categorization, diagnosis followed by prognosis, based on existing medical episteme. An illness, on the other hand, is very difficult to locate and describe as it defies any form of causality: it is what Anatole Broyard calls "a series of disconnected shocks" (Hawkins 1999, 2). Disease is geometrical, illness topological. The journey of an illness becoming a disease— with all the medical paraphernalia— is also a journey of a sufferer becoming a patient. It is only after its fair share of "violence" and "initiation rituals" that the journey is consummated. Similar to the process called civilization where the ultimate goal is the production of the civilized, society and individual, medicalisation is also a process towards being medicalised. And, to be medicalised is to be "stripped of every right", agency or autonomy (Agamben 1998, 183). Illness resists such medicalisation; disease is when illness is somehow lost in the process. Both the system and the subject are formed with this act of violence— with an exclusion of illness and followed by an unconditional surrender to the "sovereign" medical system whose "fundamental activity" is to produce "bare life": a form of biological reductionism (Ibid., 181). The ontological disposition of being ill undermines language in general, whether it is the language of ethnoscientific epistemology or the more mundane phenomenological exchanges. It is this deficiency or the inherent lack in the language itself that makes us re-turn towards literary works which over the years have been able to capture in some way this cryptic language and present before us a tradition of "writing pain" (*pathos* + *graphia*). The biological reductionism of medical science, of reducing one to mere biological fact of life, the logic of the numbers, is antithetical to the possibilities and potentialities of being ill. Illness, on the other hand, entails phenomenological reduction. It is Husserlian *epoché* but with a difference: "it can challenge the prevalent pre-reflective and metaphysical discourses and can become an embodied "philosophical gate" through which horizons of understanding and new philosophical encounters can be expanded and established" (Sarkar 2019, 42); it brackets out the natural attitude and brings forth a critical attitude but unlike *epoché* or any other philosophical interrogation, illness is non-volitional and painful. Notwithstanding this involuntary entanglement with pain and suffering, illness can still be seen as a philosophical mode, as a form of *phronesis*— Aristotle's word for "practical wisdom" in *Nicomachean Ethics*. Illness as *phronesis*, quite naturally then is different from other forms of modern medical knowledge, that of *techné* and *episteme*. To philosophise is to learn how *not* to be healthy. To philosophise, as Havi Carel (1995) points out, is to learn how to be ill.

The mind rules the kingdom of health. The realm of illness, even in the case of mental illness, is the realm of the body. It generates a distance and *is* a distance (from the Old French *destance* meaning "discord") between, the hitherto indistinguishable, lived-body (*leib*) and the corporeal body (*körper*). Even in illnesses which are primarily considered to be of the mind, the sickness, as in Kafka's "The Penal Colony," is also inscribed on the body. Just like how the hammer vanishes in hammering, taking a cue from Heidegger, the body too vanishes in bodying-forth, in "ek-stasis". The body disappears in health; in illness it re-surfaces. One can feel its weight as it tries to enforce itself upon the world. The mind which is wrecked and gets drowned in the water of illness, re-surfaces as the body. The hitherto absent body of health re-appears or rather dys-appears in illness. This dys-appearance entails a principle where, as Drew Leder points out, "the body appears as thematic focus, but precisely as in a *dys* state— *dys* is from the Greek prefix signifying 'bad,' 'hard,' or 'ill,' and is found in English words such as dysfunctional" (1990, 84). The flow is disrupted and like in any other noisy dysfunctional family, one's "tacit sense of feeling connected and 'at home' is replaced with the uncanniness of feeling 'un-homelike'" (Aho 2017, 121). One becomes then at dys-ease with the world around. The "in-the-world" and "with-the-other" of health is dys-placed and re-placed, a deterritorialization followed by reterritorialization, in the kingdom of ill or what Virginia Woolf calls in *On*

Being Ill "undiscovered countries". It is for the same reason that illnesses are often associated with journeys and (mis)adventures, without fixed points of departure and arrival. Therefore, if health is home, to be ill is to be away from home, *far* away from home, or not being able to be at home (Svenaeus 2000, 9). The intensity of illness depends upon this distance. When one is at home, one does not realise what it is to be at home; it is this distance from home, from health, which makes one realise what it means to be at home, in health.

The task of a wounded storyteller (Frank 1995) is to reterritorialize the already deterritorialized psychosomatic condition and restore some "form" of order to the chaos and some "form" of voice to the noise of illness. Unlike medical science which tries to impose some order into the chaos from outside, a pathography is where the order evolves from within. The latter is what Deleuze, borrowing a term from James Joyce, would call "chaosmos". A "pathography" (Hawkins 1999), along with what Arthur Klienman (1988) calls "illness narrative" and Rita Charon (2006) calls "narrative medicine" is about giving "form" to something which is seemingly "formless": the pain, the suffering, and the anxiety which come with illness. To put it in narrative is to give it order, and some form of causality. Anne Hunsaker Hawkins writes: "The task of the author of a pathography is not only to describe this disordering process but also to restore to reality its lost coherence and to discover, or create, a meaning that can bind it together again" (1999, 3).

A sufferer speaks in terms of illness; the physician understands the same in terms of disease. Therefore, a pathographer often maintains that "fine balance" between the lived reality of the sufferer and the *realbodypolitik*, that is, the scientific reality of modern medical dispositif. It is about finding a "balance" at the site of loss, of the erstwhile "balance" (called health). It is also about finding a "balance" between two subjects and their respective reductionisms: one, that of phenomenological reductionism of the sufferer and the other, that of techno-scientific reductionism of the physician. The subject (the ill) here, is also an object (the patient) of medical treatment. Because there is no "pure" illness, our illnesses more often than not overlap with the contemporary discourses of medical *techné*. An illness narrative, therefore, is also this balancing act between the subjective impulses and the objective know-how; between "care" (Heideggerian *sorge*) and cure; and between illness and disease. If illness entails contraction of time and space, then an illness narrative is about spacing and timing: a mode of "worldling" in the face of chaos and disorder. "The medical report" as Hawkins points out "is usually composed of brief statements about present symptoms and body chemistry whereas a pathography is an extended narrative situating the illness experience within the author's life and the meaning of that life" (13). Pathography is *not* medical history; it is an alternate historiography of the body in pain— and at the same time it is also not free from medical history altogether. Though not necessarily overwhelming, the narrative one finds in medical history— the history written from the *above*— tends to influence the trajectory of one's journey into the night of illness, albeit in different degrees. There is, hence, no "pure" illness or "pure" pain. "In other words", as Joanna Bourke points out "a pain event possesses what philosopher Paul Ricoeur called, a "mine-ness." In this way, the person *becomes* or *makes herself into* a person-in-pain through the person of naming" (2014, 5). Illness is continuously negotiated and re-negotiated; it is christened as "disease" in the realm of medicine and as "sickness" in the realm of society. The former, therefore, should at all times be understood in its relational ontology. Disease is monadic, illness nomadic. But then, as Beth Torgerson notes in her introduction to *Reading the Brontë Body*, "The term 'illness' is fundamentally more useful for the purposes of literary analysis since it can incorporate the concept of 'disease' within it" (2005, 4). The task of a pathographer then, among many things, is to capture such fleeting and floating moments of being ill, being diseased, and being sick. The task of a pathographer is also to give an account of one's close encounter with those ill, diseased and/or sick.

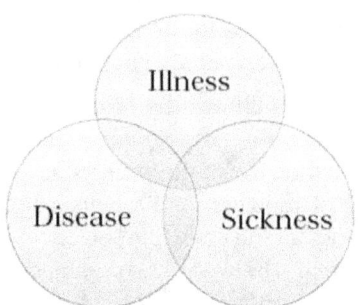

Hawkins classifies pathography, the act of writing pain, into three categories: testimonial pathographies, angry pathographies and pathographies advocating alternative modes of treatment. She calls pathography as "a form of autobiography or biography that describes personal experiences of illness treatment, and sometimes death" (1999, 1). But, unlike Hawkins, we have expanded this definition of pathography to include those who are writing pain from the other side of the spectrum: the pathologists, immunologists, caregivers and physicians who are trying to put into narrative their phenomenological and epistemological, and most of the time, banal experiences of dealing with the diseased. We have, taking a cue from Ann Jurecic, broadened the spectrum of understanding illness and particularly understand this form of life writing: of how "writers compose illness and how readers receive the accounts" (Jurecic 2012, 2) from different lived vantage points. Such imaginative pathographical accounts are different from the hegemonic medical historiography in the sense that the emphasis here is more on the lived-experience and less on the mimetic adroitness. As opposed to the medical history of the patient where he/she is no more than an *object* of study, the poems of William Carlos Williams and Miroslav Holub, for example, help us attain a deeper understanding and a certain degree of empathy towards the suffering subject. Such narratives by pathologists challenge and subvert the binaries such as subject/object, active/passive, voice/silence, agency/non-agency looming large in an otherwise highly stratified sphere of modern medicine.

The Portrait of an Artist as a Pathographer

Focusing on the various intersections between illness and literature across time and space, the chapters in this volume seek to understand how ontological, phenomenological and epistemological experiences of illness have been dealt and represented in literary writings and literary studies. In this volume scholars from across the world have come together to understand how pathological condition of being ill (the sufferers), as well as the pathologists dealing with the ill (the healers and caregivers) have shaped literary works. The language of medical science, with the jargon and the language of the everyday, with the emphasis on utility prove equally insufficient and futile in capturing the pain and suffering of illness. It is this insufficiency and futility that makes us turn toward the canonical works of Joseph Conrad, Samuel Beckett, William Carlos Williams, Virginia Woolf, Kazuo Ishiguro, Miroslav Holub as well as the non-canonical António Lobo Antunes, Yumemakura Baku, Wopko Jensma and Vaslav Nijinsky. The volume helps in understanding and capturing the metalanguage of illness while presenting before us the tradition of "writing pain." With the attempt of expanding the definition of pathography to include those who are on the other side of pain, the essays in this collection seek to portray the above-mentioned pathographers as artists— turning anxiety and suffering of illness into art form. Looking deeply into such creative aspects of illness, the volume also tries to evoke the possibility of pathography as world literature.

The seventeen chapters in the volume have been divided into three broad sections: European Literary Pathographies, American Literary Pathographies and Literary Pathographies of the World. The first section "European Literary Pathographies" discusses Aeschylus' *Prometheus Bound*, Joseph Conrad's *Heart of Darkness*, Samuel Beckett's select plays, Virginia Woolf's *The Voyage Out*, the select poems of Miroslav Holub, the diary of Vaslav Nijinsky, and the works of António Lobo Antunes. The second section "American Literary

Pathographies" discusses the select poems of William Carlos Williams, Shirley Jackson's *We Have Always Lived in the Castle,* Lorrie Moore's short stories and MK Czerwiec's graphic memoir *Taking Turns: Stories from HIV/AIDS Care Unit 371:8.* And the final section "Literary Pathographies of the World" brings together the discussions on the South Africa poet Wopko Jensma, the Ottoman-Turkish novella Suat Derviş' *The Black Book,* Yumemakura Baku's fiction from Japan, and the Zimbabwean NoViolet Bulawayo's novel *We Need New Names.* In this section, Edward Grimble's chapter highlights the figure of the convalescent in the nineteenth-century and the early twentieth-century literature: Baudelaire, Poe, Dickens, Whitman and others; and Ronja-Tripp Bodola's chapter discusses literary bioethics and biopolitics in works like Bram Stoker's *Dracula,* Aldous Huxley's *Brave New World* and *Brave New World Revisited,* Samuel Beckett's *Malone Dies* and Margaret Atwood's *The Handmaid's Tale.*

In the first chapter, "The Gift of Chains: Atopic Violence and Embodied Community in Aeschylus' *Prometheus Bound*" Anda Pleniceanu explores the theoretical implications of the ancient myth of Prometheus, as written by Aeschylus in his tragedy *Prometheus Bound,* using the concepts of Walter Benjamin's violence as law-preservation, Roland Barthes's atopia, and Roberto Esposito's community and immunity. To begin with, the chapter resists a straightforward interpretation of the myth, according to which Zeus, the tyrannical new ruler of Olympus, tortures Prometheus for his human-loving ways in order to firmly establish his authority over both heaven and earth. Instead, Pleniceanu interprets Prometheus' role as intermediary in the gifting of arts and means of classification of the world that the humans receive. Prometheus himself is unclassifiable— vulnerable like a human yet immortal and all-knowing— though he is still at the centre of the circulation of the gift. What complicates the matter is the immunological paradigm, which leads to an understanding of the violence and suffering displayed in the characters' speeches as the work of the negative, which Prometheus carries forth as protection for both godly and human realms. Without focusing on Prometheus as a hero, Pleniceanu argues that the *immunus* is not one of personal and individual choice but rather a contingent one: Prometheus has no choice but to pass the gift and endure the violence constitutive of law-preserving. Then, she goes on to connect Prometheus' role with that of Io, the cow-horned maiden whose situation is entirely oppositional to that of Prometheus in spite of their shared sufferings in the play, and show how Prometheus' legacy, and with it, the immunisation of community, continues through Io into the world.

Health and illness, indeed, form an integral part of Conrad's *Heart of Darkness,* not only on the thematic level, but also on the structural level. The

Introduction xix

whole journey of Marlow, the narrator, into "the heart of darkness", was undertaken as a result of agent Kurtz's mysterious illness. The narrative that recounts the journey follows the trajectory not only in terms of geography (Marlow's movement along the river), but also in terms of gathering information about Kurtz's illness and organising them into a system of meaning. In this respect, it can be read as a pathography, but a pathography that comes second-hand— both in terms of the temporal organisation (because the illness has already developed) and in terms of the narrative voice that recounts it (this voice gathers all the information about the illness prior to actually meeting the ill person). The pathographer in this case is neither the person suffering the illness, not the care-taker, but acts as a sort of detective who not only has the task of presenting the illness, but also identifying and uncovering it first. Through linking the mysterious illness with the specific historical moment, the absent protagonist's illness also turns into an illness more widely conceived of— an illness of an era, an illness of the times, an illness of philosophy and ideology. The aim of this chapter by Nina Muždeka, "Pathography of Man and Evil in Joseph Conrad's *Heart of Darkness*," is to analyse the physical and mental illness in *Heart of Darkness*, focusing on its development and the second-hand depiction of this development, taking into account the wider criticism of the times and its colonial practices.

The next chapter, "Care, Pig!: The Abject Caregiver in Beckett's Plays" examines Samuel Beckett's narratives of caregiving in *Waiting for Godot* and *Endgame* and reflect how caregiving labour is removed from the dialectic of recognition that late capitalist society has instrumentalised in the ongoing exploitation of caregivers. Over the past few decades, theorists and activists such as Silvia Federici and Nancy Fraser have drawn attention to the ways in which caregivers are dually needed for maintaining the social texture as well as continually exploited because of their exceptionalism from capitalist rubrics of value. Theorists such as Rosemarie Garland-Thomson and Eva Feder Kittay have demonstrated that disability contexts in particular show how the labour of caregiving is rendered exceptional from other kinds of labour which, while also exploited, are at least legible as labour within a capitalist schema. Following from Garland-Thomson, Feder Kittay, and others, Gabriel Quigley argues that the exploitation of caregivers can be reduced to the problem of recognition, in which the radical exploitation of caregivers is made possible by the ongoing failure to recognise caregiving labour *as* labour. Given the ways that both Lucky and Clov perform caregiving without the recognition of this labour or their needs, Quigley claims that the caregiving relationships in *Waiting for Godot* and *Endgame* stage precisely the contradiction materialising at the juncture of capitalism and care. This chapter examines the impoverished status of Beckett's caregivers in what Michael Davidson has identified as a "dialectics of disability" in Beckett's oeuvre, contending that the recognition of illness combined with the un-recognition of caregiving labour in *Waiting for Godot* and *Endgame* reflect the social demand for caregiving combined with society's failure to recognise caregivers as members of society.

Scholarship on Woolf and medicine is replete with how illness feeds her genius, or how depression perpetuates the melancholic aesthetic of her prose. Chloe Leung, however, is more interested in the very system that generates such positive-negative dichotomy about illness narratives in her chapter entitled "'But of course Rachel's illness is quite different': Reconfiguring the 'Medical' and 'Illness' in Virginia Woolf's *The Voyage Out*". Moving away from the popular example of *Mrs. Dalloway*, this chapter explores how Woolf's debut novel *The Voyage Out* (1915) reshapes the notion of the "medical" and "illness". Although the novel is often dismissed as pre-modernist and juvenile, canny readers will not overlook how the novel prefigures some of her more "mature" consciousness representations and its complex treatment of illness. The chapter argues that "illness" in the novel outstrips the medical sense of the word. Drawing from disability studies, Leung argues that *Voyage* interrogates a normative and medical understanding of illness. If medicine cannot fully explain the connotations of "illness", Woolf's novel suggests other possibilities of how "illness" could manifest outside biomedicine. Focusing on the metaphor and language of pain, Leung explores how "illness" functions as a symptom of our thwarted desire to communicate anti-discursive phenomenon in both social and clinical contexts. She concludes by contending that Woolf's novel adopts a rigorous hermeneutic ambiguity that endorses an epistemic generosity in configuring approaches to therapeutic practice.

A "curious mixture", poet-immunologist Miroslav Holub is unusual in his approach to poetry. As a man of reason, it may seem that Holub resists romantic impulses, while on the contrary, he relishes it with a scientific temperament. His juxtapositions of the real and the impossible give way to metaphors that he uses as a hypothesis: an instrument for testing experience through conjecture and experiment. Because of his belief that there exists in science, a wide body of imagination, away from all-encompassing theories and laboratory work, Holub is able to conjure abstractions that speak of human and non-human conditions, such as war, illness, suffering, pain, childhood and monotony; meanwhile, also alluding to pathological, medical and physical theories. Starting from Ancient Greece, to the Enlightenment, the West had been obsessed with the larger structures: the universe, planets, cosmos and God to understand the mechanics of how the world functions. But with the invention of the microscope, the discovery of atoms and enquires into genetics, the paradigm shifted from macro to the micro. We were less keen to look for meaning hidden in the folds of the greater cosmic order and instead turned towards the world of quantum particles, atoms, DNA and microorganisms, where understanding the smallest components and their structures would determine how larger societal order and civilizations come into being or operate. Holub's medical poems take on a similar rapport, where looking at life underneath the microscope, he is able to construct metaphors that comment on society at large. The chapter "'Between Horror and Hunger': Reflections on the Medical Poems of Miroslav Holub" by Anik Sarkar seeks to analyse the poems of Holub that deal with the "alternating rhythms of cosmological expansion and microscopic contraction" (Ling 1974, 506) uncovering his pathographical, aesthetical, social and political commentary while closely looking at his "nano-poetics."

The Diary of Vaslav Nijinsky is a rare thing— a writing which is synchronous to his initiation into psychosis. Written before his hospitalisation, the diary represents an account unhindered by an interpretive psychological framework, now commonplace. Instead, the diary reads like dance notation with its swishes, swirls and rigid stances. For Nijinsky, words were lacklustre in comparison to dance, as a form of expression. Although the diary mentions very little about dance, his rhythmic style of writing suggests that it is to be read in the embodied way that Nijinsky expressed himself— like a dance. If this is the case, then perhaps there has been an injustice from previous interpretations of his writing, focusing on the tautologies and non-sequiturs. Eschewing this popular form of exploration, Jamil Ahmed in this chapter, "'I am God in a body': *The Diary of Vaslav Nijinsky* as Initiation into Psychosis," demonstrates how Nijinsky gives us insight into his alienation from the world, through his embodied autopathography, documenting his slow retreat from the storehouse of everyday meaning.

This next chapter by Ricardo Rato Rodrigues, entitled "Doctor, Soldier, Writer: António Lobo Antunes as Portugal's Pathographer," tries to explore António Lobo Antunes, one of the major voices in Portuguese literature of the second half of the 20th century, through his unique biographical trajectory crucially imbued in his novels and chronicles, thus providing a mapping of the mental and physical suffering of human beings. A psychiatrist by training, Lobo Antunes has also participated in the Colonial War that opposed Portugal and its African colonies. Both experiences (as doctor and soldier) are central to his literature and its articulation of the multiplicity of illnesses affecting Portuguese society post-1974. Ranging from an initial trilogy in which post-traumatic stress disorder and other mental afflictions are explored in a compassionate and encompassing way, to his own autobiographical experiences (with PTSD, etc.), the author's oeuvre is particularly attuned to the pathological suffering of human beings. Moreover, it is not only an ethical preoccupation with illness that feeds Lobo Antunes' writing momentum, but a deep engagement with the universal questions about what it means to be human, with death and with the body and the mind. Even in terms of language, his writing shows an attention to the medical dimension of the world at large, sometimes as an ironic attack towards an ill society, and sometimes in a compassionate understanding of human misfortunes.

The first chapter in "American Literary Pathagraphies" section "'To Him Who Wants It!': Understanding William Carlos Williams' Pathography" explores the short stories, poetry and prose of William Carlos Williams' that engage with the interplay between medicine and literature. The central aim here is to demonstrate Williams' anti-modernist impulse in poetic projects, which were inspired by his own medical practice, while attempting to provoke a meaningful dialogue with townspeople both as a modernist poet and a physician. In illuminating how medical practice has driven the anti-modernist impulse in his experimental poetics, the research ultimately discusses how Williams' empathy clashed with his professionalism, and therefore, portrays his work as pathography. The interplay of medicine and poetry in his writing supplements the reshaping of pathography in literary studies through portraying as a pathographer of the local streets in New Jersey. He was always prepared to ask his patients and readers to maintain the hope of effective communication and productive human relationships in modern America. Taking his poetry as an exemplary synthesis of poetry and medicine, the chapter illustrates how Williams presented a vision of poetry as a uniquely positioned medium for communicating with patients who had physical, mental, and psychological pain. To make this argument, Seunghyun Shin first discusses how pathography is defined in literary studies; and after reshaping pathography in literary studies as "the language of pain," Shin refers to Williams' short stories that reveal his empathy clashing with his profession as a physician. By the end, the chapter shows how the writing of poetry was cathartic to Williams as a pathographer and how medical practices shaped his poetry to satisfy the pathographic fever to understand the language of pain of his patients.

The next chapter focuses on Shirley Jackson's novel *We Have Always Lived in the Castle*. Written in 1962, the work reflects the debilitating influence of patriarchy on women. Examining two main female characters, the sisters Merricat and Constance, from the perspective of disability studies and queer studies, Tatiana Prorokova-Konrad demonstrates how the novel reflects the discriminating nature of patriarchy on women, particularly lesbian women with disabilities. The chapter "Lesbianism, Disability, and Pain: Shirley Jackson's *We Have Always Lived in the Castle* as a Pathography" argues that the sisters' gender, sexual orientation, and disability intersect in the novel, showcasing female oppression during the times of patriarchy in the mid-twentieth century U.S. from a very specific perspective, thereby helping reinforce the perverse nature of patriarchy. Love plays an important role in the novel, as it is with the help of love that the women can withstand homophobia and ableism. At the same time, their love, as this chapter claims, is viewed as "perverse" and "abnormal" by the villagers, which results in the two characters' complete isolation from society. They choose to never leave the house again. This, Prorokova-Konrad argues, is a response to the hatred towards queer individuals and people with disabilities. It is through the issues of love, disability, and queerness that she explores Jackson's novel as a powerful illustration of how society discriminated against and publicly humiliated lesbian and/or disabled women.

The attraction of the "medical" body, its diseases and diagnoses, its pain and strain, as a subject of narrative interest has gained critical and literary ground in the last three decades. Yet, amidst this compelling desire to "write the sick body" and to "read the wound," lies a challenging urge to express and address the questions of meaning and suffering. Simultaneously, invoking and revoking expectations of narrative pleasure through the spectre of communicating pain, illness narratives proliferate through the ambiguous and problematic exploration of the ailing body and/ or mind as a reflection of culture, society, and consciousness. The chapter "'The struggle to Breathe': Narrating the Sick Body in Lorrie Moore's Short Stories" by Nadia Boudidah Falfoul seeks to explore the great potential that literature possesses to inscribe and shape the cultural meanings and experience of illness, pain, and suffering. Through a narratological and postmodernist reading of two of Lorrie Moore's collections of short fiction [*Like-Life* (1986) and *Birds of America* (1998)], the chapter contemplates "the seductive entrance of disease into language" and focuses on several ways in which "illness narratives" and "narratives of illness" represent a socio-cultural symptom and symbol of traumatic Post/modernity, thereby offering the medical and literary fields a new perspective into art and science, storytelling and medicine. The discourse of illness challenges and transcends our sense of time, space, continuity, causality, and even language since Pain, as Elaine Scarry asserts, "does not simply resist language but actively destroys it" (1985, 4).

The chapter by Victoria Lupascu, "*Taking Turns* in Writing Pain: Comics' Approximation of Pathography," considers the relationship between pathography and the comics genre to examine the ways in which visual representations of illnesses, from the healers' and caregivers' perspective, produce a plurivalent emotional vocabulary for understanding illnesses and grief. She focuses on MK Czerwiec's comic book *Taking Turns: Stories from HIV/AIDS Care Unit 371* and Stella Bruzzi's theorization of approximation as an epistemological tool that highlights a historical fact and "insert[s] it into a narrative, not in order to be collapsed into fiction, but to co-exist in collision with it." As a nurse in an HIV/AIDS special care unit in the 1990s, MK Czerwiec embodies both the professional caregiver and the healer from a biomedical perspective, and redefines the concept of boundaries between these roles and the sufferers. By negotiating these two positions, Czerwiec is at a unique junction, portrayed by unbalanced panels and interplay between text and visual representations of patients, and *approximates* the urgency of the epidemic with the slow development of ubiquitous grief in relation to HIV/AIDS in sufferers, healers and caregivers. Lupascu claims that the tension between fiction and reality in pathography is firmly apparent in comics such as *Taking Turns* where approximation becomes an underlining hermeneutical means of writing one's own and other's pain. Moreover, this chapter contends that comics show the boundaries of language and expand them through colour usage, pagination, panelling and create the physical space for formative silences necessary for the co-existence of illnesses and care. In this expansion that fuels pathography, comics produce epistemological and hermeneutic changes in traditional literary perceptions of illnesses, specifically in relation to HIV/AIDS, by imagining alternative modes of expression and understanding of the epidemic's, and illnesses' phenomenological valences.

Wopko Jensma's use of neologisms, portmanteau words, fragmentation and experimental topography has often resulted in a private idiomatic language that was seemingly incomprehensible. This difficulty has provoked widely divergent views ranging from accolades to criticism that he had finally "lost it", of being "schizophrenic" and that his poetry was nothing more than confused ramblings of a madman. Jensma's poetry of bizarre pathological motifs and speakers dispersed across multiple subjectivities is a chronicle of personal devastation rooted in the volatile chapter of South Africa's racist past. Image, diction and narrative coalesce in dissonant aesthetic strategies to express the anguish and psychological annihilation emanating from human degradation and despair borne of poverty and political disenfranchisement. Overwhelmed by a repressive society, racism and insidious materialism, the conflicted speakers in Jensma's poetry retreat into interior psychological spaces and the perpetration of pathological acts of self-harm or sadomasochism in response to the bizarre, Orwellian conditions of apartheid existence. The multiple voices which emerge are a startling polyphony of alienation, pathological hate, helplessness and sadomasochism. These voices express the hostility, oppression and suffering which characterised the apartheid state as well as personal torment and anguish. What is especially intriguing is the uncanny coincidence between Jensma's poetry and the aberrations that present in schizophrenia. Themed by suspicion of persecution, self-mutilation, alienation, hallucinations and manic delusions, Jensma's poetry appropriates the pathological resources of schizophrenia in a surreal critique of racial disenfranchisement and economic oppression. The first chapter in "Literary Pathographies of the World" by Ayub Sheik, "Wopko Jensma as a Pathographer: The Interface between Poetry and Schizophrenia," posits that Jensma's experimental discourse was also influenced by his affliction from schizophrenia which permeated his work. This is manifest in the use of asocial dialects with highly personal idioms, approximate phrases, discordant syntax and substitutes which make his language extremely difficult to follow at times.

Born to an aristocratic family in Istanbul at the turn of the century and having received an education in French and German, Suat Derviş was one of the leading women writers of her time. Although, she is mostly known for her later novels written in the genre "social realism", her first novella *Kara Kitap* [*The Black Book* (1921)] remains as one of the finest examples of decadent literature in Ottoman-Turkish literature with its gloomy setting, dark theme of illness, and characters at the brink of madness. Relying on Matei Calinescu's approach that views literary decadence identical with the ideology of progress and on Paul Bourget's treatment of the decadent style as a symptom of cultural breakdown and decay, the chapter "*The Black Book* as Pathography: Romancing Disease and Decay in the Late Ottoman Empire" by Meltem Gürle reads Derviş' portrayal of disease, decay and death (and the artistic expression she finds to convey these themes) in *The Black Book* in connection with the social and cultural climate of the late Ottoman Empire. In this short novella, where she tells the story of the fall of an aristocratic family through the perspective of a young woman dying of a mysterious disease, Derviş combines the high and the low literature, the philosophical and the popular, and composes a piece that reflects the consciousness of the increasingly weak and decadent Ottoman Empire at the turn of the century.

Japanese popular fiction writer Yumemakura Baku created a fiction series called *Onmyōji* in the late 1980s, which features the historical court astrologer Abe no Seimei (921-1005), and a courtier of royal blood, Minamoto no Hiromasa (918-980), historically a reputed musician. An *onmyōji* in the Japanese court had the responsibility to assist the Emperor in all important matters of the state, by choosing the most auspicious dates, and preparing proper rituals during the festivals. Abe no Seimei was one of the most famous *onmyojis* throughout Japanese history, and this fiction series translates his famed divination power into a more analytical understanding of the human heart and its complex desires. The fiction series is set at the Heian period (794-1185), one of the most glorious periods of cultural and artistic development in Japan. The stories depict courtiers as well as ordinary citizens coming to seek Abe no Seimei's help when they encountered inexplicable illnesses or suspected intervention from beyond the human world. Adapting the form of modern detective stories, Yumemakura Baku portrays Seimei and Hiromasa as a quasi-Holmes-and-Watson partnership in uncovering the causes of illnesses in these troubled characters. These magical adventures across various worlds of existence juxtapose what is visible in the material world with what cannot be seen in the psychological and emotional realms of the human experience, and package those as Abe no Seimei's "magic." In actual fact, the solutions that the court *onmyōji* proposed to his clients were but advice to look into their hearts and acknowledge the reality of their desires and fears. The chapter "Dis-eases of the Heart Cured by Magic: Heian *Onmyōji* in Yumemakura Baku's Popular Japanese Fiction" by Amy W S Lee reads a few of the stories in the series as diagnosis of contemporary illnesses, when the characters were made to face their unfulfilled desires, repressed fears, and challenged sense of identity by the court *onmyōji*, to bring them back to a more comfortable condition with themselves.

The chapter "Writing Illness: Morbid Humour as a Strategy to Cope with Disease and Pain in Zimbabwean Literature" by Nhlanhla Landa and Sindiso Zhou explores how disease and un-wellness in Zimbabwe are subjects of ridicule in NoViolet Bulawayo's *We Need New Names*. Guided by the Freudian concepts of the overt expression of the covert state of the unconscious mind, the chapter does an interpretive analysis of *We Need New Names* to show that Zimbabweans, having endured pain and illness for a long time due to a conspiracy of many issues such as politics, deteriorating economy and a poor health system, resort to morbid humour to cope. Bulawayo expertly fuses the subject of disease, specifically HIV and AIDS, and child play to paint a grim picture of the broader socio-economic and socio-political issues bedeviling the post-colonial state in Zimbabwe. She deploys grotesque humour and laughter as coping and resilience strategies to salve postcolonial wounds, disease and pain that stand in the way of everyday survival.

"There are many excellent books" as Rev. Robert Milman asserts in his 1865 examination of the spiritual and religious state of convalescing, "for the sick whilst they are ill. I have, myself, felt a want of a distinct and separate book for those who are recovering." His views could be extended to literary scholarship more broadly. Edward Grimble in the chapter "'Back from the Shades of Death': The Pleasures and Pains of Convalescence in the Nineteenth-Century City" re-examines the precarious, peculiar and intellectually provocative state of convalescence as examined by nineteenth and early twentieth-century writers. Inhabiting a hinterland between not only illness and wellness but also isolation and sociability, the recovering subject provides a vitally important way of examining the relationship between the private and public aspects of metropolitan life: how the city, its streets, and its crowds are encountered and experienced by the individual. Sustained study of the convalescent across a number of urban texts permits the uncovering of one of the marginalised "doubles" of the ubiquitous *flâneur*, a figure who has become amorphous through endless reformulation and reshaping. The cities of Baudelaire, Poe, Dickens, Whitman and others are populated by these liminal figures whose experiences of the metropolis are fuelled by the convalescent's unique combination of curiosity, child-like wonder at the urban spectacle, acute susceptibility to impressions, mental and pedestrian febrility, and mania.

The final chapter "The Lessons (Not) Learned: Literary Bioethics and Biopolitics from Stoker to Atwood" discusses biopolitics and bioethics as a broader epistemological framework that transverses a number of topics discussed in this collection. It takes a look at narratives, from Stoker's *Dracula* to Atwood's *The Handmaid's Tale*, and traces bioethics and the Foucauldian concept of biopolitics in these narratives to argue that these concepts are at the core of the literature/medicine interactions in the long twentieth-century. In this chapter, Ronja Tripp-Bodola offers an exemplary overview that illustrates the overarching socio-political take of literature, biopolitics and bioethics and the various ramifications for contemporary bio-social concerns. She contributes to the discussion of literature's importance to the field of medical humanities and argues for an integration of literary biopolitics into medical education.

Bibliography

Abrahamsson, Christian. *Topoi/Graphein: Mapping the Middle in Spatial Thought*. Lincoln & London: University of Nebraska Press, 2018.

Agamben, Giorgio. *Homo Sacer: Sovereign Power and Bare Life*. Trans. Daniel Heller-Roazen. Stanford: Stanford University Press, 1998.

Aho, Kevin. "A Hermeneutics of the Body and Placein Health and Illness". In *Place, Space and Hermeneutics*, edited by Bruce B. Janz, 115-26. Berlin: Springer International Publishing, 2017.

Aho, Kevin, ed. *Existential Medicine: Essays on Health and Illness*. London: Rowman & Littlefield, 2018.

Badiou, Alain. *Being and Event*. Translated by Oliver Feltham. London: Continuum Books, 2006.

Beckett, Samuel. *Three Novels: Molloy, Malone Dies, The Unnamable*. New York: Grove Press, 1955.

Benjamin, Walter. "Theses on the Philosophy of History." In *Illuminations*, 253-64. Translated by Harry Zohn. New York: Schocken Books, 1968.

Bourke, Joanna. *The Story of Pain: From Prayer to Painkiller*. New York: Oxford University Press, 2014.

Carel, Havi. "The Philosophical Role of Illness". *Metaphilosophy* 45 (1995): 20-40.

Charon, Rita. *Narrative Medicine: Honoring the Stories of Illness*. New York: Oxford University Press, 2006.

Deleuze, Gilles. *Difference and Repetition.* London: A&C Black, 2004.

Frank, Arthur W. *The Wounded Storyteller: Body, Illness, and Ethics.* Chicago: The University of Chicago Press, 1995.

Hawkins, Anne Hunsaker. *Reconstructing Illness: Studies in Pathography.* Indiana: Purdue University Press, 1999.

Jurecic, Ann. *Illness as Narrative.* Piitsburgh: University of Pittsburgh Press, 2012.

Klienman, Arthur. *The Illness Narratives: Suffering, Healing & the Human Condition.* The US: Basic Books, 1988.

Leder, Drew. *The Absent Body.* Chicago: The University of Chicago Press, 1990.

Ling, Amy. "The Uni(que)verse of Miroslav Holub." *Books Abroad* 48, no. 3 (1974): pp. 506-11. Accessed June 18, 2020. doi:10.2307/40128700.

Sarkar, Jayjit. *Illness as Method: Beckett, Mann, Woolf, and Eliot.* Wilmington, DE: Vernon Press, 2019.

Scarry, Elaine. *The Body in Pain: The Making and Unmaking of of the World.* New York: Oxford University Press, 1985.

Serres, Michel. *The Parasite.* Baltimore: The Johns Hopkins University Press, 1982.

Svenaeus, Fredrik. *The Hermeneutics of Medicine and the Phenomenology of Health.* Dordrecht: Kluwer, 2000.

Torgerson, Beth E. *Reading the Brontë Body: Disease, Desire, and the Constraints of Culture.* New York: Palgrave Macmillan, 2005.

Notes

[1] Alain Badiou, *Being and Event* (London: Continuum Books, 2006).

[2] Walter Benjamin, "Theses on the Philosophy of History," in *Illuminations* (New York: Schocken Books, 1968), 253-264.

I.
European Literary Pathographies

Chapter 1

The Gift of Chains: Atopic Violence and Embodied Community in Aeschylus's *Prometheus Bound*

Anda Pleniceanu

Western University in Ontario, Canada

Abstract: This chapter explores the theoretical implications of the ancient myth of Prometheus, as written by Aeschylus in his tragedy *Prometheus Bound*, using the concepts of Walter Benjamin's violence as law-preservation, Roland Barthes's *atopia*, and Roberto Esposito's community and immunity. First, the chapter resists a straightforward interpretation of the myth, according to which Zeus, the tyrannical new ruler of Olympus, tortures Prometheus for his human-loving ways to firmly establish his authority over both heaven and earth. Instead, I seek to interpret Prometheus's role as intermediary in the gifting of arts and means of classification of the world that the humans receive. Prometheus himself is unclassifiable—vulnerable like a human yet immortal and all-knowing—though he is still at the centre of the circulation of the gift. What complicates the matter is the immunological paradigm, which leads to an understanding of the violence and suffering displayed in the characters' speeches as the work of the negative, which Prometheus carries forth as protection for both godly and human realms. Without focusing on Prometheus as a hero, I argue that the *immunus* is not one of personal and individual choice but rather a contingent one: Prometheus has no choice but to pass the gift and endure the violence constitutive of preserving the law. Then, I connect Prometheus's role with that of Io, the cow-horned maiden whose situation is entirely opposite to that of Prometheus in spite of their shared sufferings in the play, and show how Prometheus's legacy, and with it, the immunisation of community, continues through Io into the world.

Keywords: Prometheus, *atopia*, Esposito, immunity, violence, community.

* * *

"We have come to a distant region of the earth / the Scythian wilderness where no mortals live" (Aeschylus *Prometheus Bound*, lines 1–2)—so proclaims Kratos (Ancient Greek for "power"), Zeus's agent, carefully overseeing that the absent tyrant's orders, to shackle Prometheus to the rock, are followed through. The language of these first lines is extraordinarily expressive, presenting with clarity and dramatic imagery the geographical and narrative circumstances of the play as well as the main affective drives that will unfold and intensify in the dialogues that follow. Kratos and Bia (Ancient Greek for "force") are Zeus's policemen, while Hephaestus, Zeus's son, is the Greek god of fire and Olympus's blacksmith, who, against his own will, is binding Prometheus, the rogue benefactor of mankind, in adamantine fetters—"in chains of adamant, bonds he cannot break" (6)—on the craggy rocks of a desolate land beyond the Black Sea, the limit of the Greek world.

For the Ancient Greeks, Prometheus's place of bondage is a "no-where," or *a-topos* (ἄτοπος, literally a non-space, also used to mean "strange," "absurd," or "extraordinary"). Roland Barthes used the notion of atopia—a variation of the same notion of non-place—to designate the singular and the unique, that which is unclassifiable by the categories that are normally available to common speech (Barthes 1977, 34). Atopia is marked equally by a certain originality as well as obscurity, and, being unclassifiable, it resists the authority of transparent social discourse. For Barthes, atopia is the lover's innocence, a quality of otherness that "cannot be imprisoned in any stereotype" (34), yet it should not be interpreted as a passive quality: the innocence of the atopic refuses being classified by language, social norms, and the legal terms, therefore placing the atopic beyond the power of the Law. Barthes asks, "Is not the innocent party unclassifiable (hence suspect in every society, which 'knows where it is only where it can classify Faults)?" (35). The threat that atopia poses is discursive by being outside of discourse: it is the uncontrollable and the unproductive in a context where productivity is the equivalent of the familiar and the classifiable. As such, atopia is not the resisting revolutionary; rather, it is the slippery wanderer, the odd unconquerable, the stubborn outsider—the ungovernable one.

"Atopia is superior to Utopia (utopia is reactive, tactical, literary, it proceeds from meaning and governs it)" (Barthes 1975, 49). Utopia is the reverse of the current world; it is a classifiable realm that is used to criticize and highlight the faults of the system which it opposes. Atopia is not a model, being neither negative nor positive. It is the unknown within the existing world, the

"Scythian wilderness" (Aeschylus, 2) and the "wintry chasm" (16). Consequently, atopia is uncomfortable and dangerous for authority and the Law, which seeks to make everything knowable. The sins that Prometheus is charged with by the absent Zeus are conferring fire, "the origin of every art" (Aeschylus, 8), to mortals, as well as the contemptible habit of loving humans (φιλανθρώπου τρόπου; Aeschylus, 11, 28)—accusations that are repeated, in different ways, many times throughout the play. However, it is unclear why Prometheus is punished so harshly, being not only shackled but perpetually tortured; the form of torture, well-known to us due to centuries of aesthetic depictions, was announced by Hermes at the end of the play: Prometheus's flesh was rendered asunder and his liver eaten by an eagle, only to regenerate and then be eaten again, night after night. It is quite confusing why, of all the gods, Zeus would consider love for mankind to be such a contemptible crime, seeing that Zeus himself was not only the protector of mankind but was known to frequently fall in love with mortal women (one of which, Io, makes a significant appearance at Prometheus's atopos in the second half of the play). Could it be that Prometheus became too unclassifiable to be tolerated—too involved with humans (far beyond the occasional tryst!) to be godly, yet still immortal; neither one of us nor one of them?

In his essay "Critique of Violence" (1972), Walter Benjamin argued that both natural and positive law, the main operating systems of law in society, conceive violence as a justified means when used for just ends (237–238), meaning that the use of violence for a just cause is not regarded as problematic by the citizens of the modern state. Natural law is also strengthened by the Darwinian thesis of natural selection, which considers the use of violence to be "appropriate" for natural ends (237). In short, natural law legitimates violence in relation to ends. Seemingly in contrast with natural law, positive law views violence historically, in terms of its means—is this or that violent act precedented or not? Benjamin's commentary on the two types of law acknowledges that, since ends call for the submission to the violent means used by the state, the distinction between just and unjust ends does not hold; by the same logic, means function according to the ends that are pre-established. For Benjamin, the compulsory violence of the state, which serves as a means to all its ends, and therefore the means through which the state exhibits its power, is represented by the institutions of the military and the police.

Before Benjamin, Hobbes and Machiavelli had already acknowledged military force as constituting the core of the state's power; Benjamin only made the necessary connection between legal ends and violent means: law-making and law-preserving look exactly the same when related to the concrete use of violence in the state because law-making *is* law-preserving. Similarly, the use of police force by the state is an unavoidable feature of law preservation, usually marking the moment when the legal system cannot, on its own, attain the ends that it aims at: "It follows . . . that all violence as a means, even in the most favourable case, is implicated in the problematic nature of law itself" (288). Thus, according to Benjamin's conception of violence, Prometheus's punishment has to be understood as law-preserving: a justified use of violence for the ends that are pre-established. But what are those ends exactly? We are not told because they are not clear—as is often the case, the ends of the Law remain obscure. What we are told at the beginning of the play is that Zeus's power is new and therefore harsher: "Zeus is not to be won over. / He is harsh, as all those new to power are harsh" (37–38). Later on, the political (mythical) background of the play, well-known to the Greek audiences of Aeschylus's time, is explained, in abridged and dramatized manner, by Prometheus himself in the latter's lament to the Chorus (186–241). The story is one of betrayal and broken familial and social bonds, leading to the tyranny of Zeus's rule and the violence of the punishment, which is ongoing and supposed to end at an uncertain time in the far future, though the legacy of violence continues even after Prometheus is set free, as we will see.

The context of *Prometheus Bound* is one of political change and unrest—a setting that, in fact, is representative of all of Greek literature and especially tragedy. The means employed by power are only justified abstractly from the point of view of a lord who is not present. Prometheus's charge is ambiguous from the moral standpoint of Greek laws. As Anthony C. Yu pointed out in his article "New Gods and Old Order: Tragic Theology in the 'Prometheus Bound'" (1971), "no moral justification can be found for the treatment of Prometheus, because that punishment is the payment of evil for good, and the severity of the penalty far exceeds the weightiness of the crime" (34). Meanwhile, the violence and suffering are expressed in clear terms from the beginning of the play. Those present and responsible for guaranteeing the means of Zeus's justice are the two policemen of Olympus who urge Hephaestus to do his job and shackle the victim, Prometheus. The police violence that, in Benjamin's account, is part of the ongoing process of reproducing violence in the state is embodied in the representatives of Zeus's cruel power, but Zeus himself is not present, just as Law for Benjamin is not fully actualized in the state. Zeus cannot be confronted as Power in the state also cannot be confronted, being slippery, ambiguous, and eternally receding. However, we can decipher, in Aeschylus's play, the mythical legacy whereby "violence brings at once guilt and retribution" (Benjamin 1972, 297), where lawmaking is at once bloody law-preserving, demanding constant sacrifice, and the helplessness of the subjects (the mortals, in the case of the Greek myth) is guaranteed and maintained by the whole system of lawmaking and law-preserving. Zeus has no reason to punish Prometheus, for mortals are not his enemies. Moreover, Zeus is already in power, while the human world is vulnerable and, most importantly, ephemeral, mortal. There is no guilt inherent in Prometheus's actions, which is to say that he is most guilty, for law-preserving pre-emptively inoculates guilt and sin into the institutions and structures of the world.

The interpretation of Zeus as Tyrannos, representative of harsh Law and Power, is in line with the dominant interpretation of the Promethean myth, according to which Prometheus is the hero of humankind, a deeply subversive figure who dares to speak truth to power and who is crushed for it, with the Heaven's police sent to carry out the deed. Prometheus is said to represent resilience and the struggle for human rights (Amnesty International, 2011) and the power of suffering and human resilience in the face of despotic authority (Roberts 2012, 23). However, the following question arises: if Zeus's power is new and his thirst for violence so great, then why does he choose to punish Prometheus in the *distant* Scythian land, the unclassifiable rock at the margins of the Greek world, the atopos? Why not punish the insubordinate Titan in Olympus, for all to see, in order to instil fear and inspire guilt for those who are, morally or emotionally, on Prometheus' side? Why create an atopia where Prometheus' story can be told and passed on, where his legacy can carve its path through the tragic and heroic future of Io's descendants?

In a sense, Prometheus' atopos in Aeschylus's play is the opposite of the panopticon: Prometheus is out of sight but fore-knowing, as his name suggests. He knows both future and past, he knows what is in store for the seemingly all-powerful Zeus, and for himself too. As he expresses in his first speech, "But what am I saying? Since I know what will be / in all its particulars, no pain can surprise me" (107–108). Prometheus, although imprisoned and in agony, is immortal and more knowledgeable than all the gods and humans. Knowledge is at the core of the situation in which Prometheus finds himself: not only is he gifted with knowing the future, but it is mentioned that Prometheus, with the gift of fire, taught mortals how to read their world (through divination) and how to use the world of objects for their world (their τέχνη), though he has also taken away a type of knowledge from the mortals, the knowledge of their own death. In fact, this is the first gift to humans that Prometheus himself mentions, before fire, in his conversation with the Chorus of Oceanides, the liquid forces that side with Prometheus: "I stopped mortals from envisioning their death" (Aeschylus, 273). His gift, therefore, starts with the subtraction of knowledge. Aeschylus's staging of the play cannot be more suggestive: an immobilised, all-knowing hero, able to grant and withdraw knowledge, is at the centre of the stage (while being in atopia), with the rest of the characters revolving around him and his suffering at the hands of an absent tyrant.

Prometheus cannot move, so all the focus is on what he says during the play: on discourse. His Scythian rock, a non-space—atopia—is the neutral space whence discourse is arranged, a place that is the origin of the ordered world as we know it, where the gift of knowledge and naming comes from, where the control of the land, sea, and sky originates from, but it is also a place of suffering, a "wintry sea of ruinous agony" (Aeschylus, 754). Prometheus's atopia is where the mapping of the world happens and the future is told to those who listen, like Io, the maiden courted by Zeus, transformed into a cow-horned maiden by Hera's jealousy, and recognized by Prometheus as "the gadfly-driven daughter / of Inachus" (602). Io receives the map of her travels from Prometheus, a map which can also be seen as a guide or instruction of the path she must walk on in order to establish the line of descendants that will provide relief from suffering, for herself and also for Prometheus, who, as prophecy has it, will be unchained by Heracles, a distant descendant of Io.

Io, in Aeschylus's play, is the antithesis of Prometheus: she is a mortal woman, and Prometheus is an all-knowing immortal; she is unknowing of the future and ignorant concerning the direction of her current wanderings, while Prometheus knows only too well where he is and what his fate is going to be. Io is doomed to wander the earth without rest while being followed and stung by the gadfly, the shape taken by Argus Panoptes, the giant with hundred eyes (πανόπτης means literally "all-seeing"), Hera's servant who was instructed to watch Io at all times. Io, therefore, lives with the panopticon monitoring her at all times, she has no peace and cannot escape her fate, which befell her not through her own doing but due to Zeus's desire. She enters the stage, following the Oceanides' stasimon, approaching Prometheus' rock, with shrieks of pain and terror:

> It stings me again. I am wretched. Aah, the gadfly,
> the ghost of earthborn Argus.
> Get him away. Oh no. The terror. I see him,
> the herdsman with countless eyes.
> He and his shifty look keep pace with me.
> He died but the earth does not cover him;
> he comes from below to hunt me in my pain,
> and drives me starving along the sandy shore. (571–580)

The recognisable aspect of Io's story is that she is a woman, suffering for the desire that she has attracted unknowingly, enduring the pain that the attention of power has inflicted upon her. Although she is a mortal, she is at the confluence of the godly and human worlds: she represents the pain and lack that desire originates from. Prometheus, on the other hand, is a Titan, unable to move due to his adamantine fetters (ἀδαμαντίνων δεσμῶν), suffering at the hands of power but able to keep intact his strength, coherence, and, more importantly, his defiance. Io goes around the world in pain, while the world revolves around Prometheus's suffering. Io often becomes incoherent during her speeches and at the end of her scene, when she receives the map of her future wanderings, she leaves the stage frenzied with madness:

> On, on, on, on!
> Again wrung by pain,
> on fire with the madness
> that beats on my mind,
> stung by the gadfly,
> a barb no man forged.
> My heart kicks my chest
> in fear, my eyes roll.
> The fierce breath of frenzy
> drives me off course.
> I can't govern my tongue.
> Troubled words strike at random
> on the waves
> of hateful disaster. (880–893)

The disease that Io carries with her takes apart the world of discourse, of classification, while Prometheus originates discourse and categorization with his gift of the human arts. Prometheus's role as the speaker of truth and the facilitator of civilization is emphasized throughout the play. He is warned by the Chorus, Ocean, and Hermes to keep quiet in order to not anger Zeus more, but Prometheus insists that "it hurts [me, Prometheus] even to speak about these things, / but it hurts to keep quiet" (225–6). Ocean insists: "this is the result, / Prometheus, of your too boastful speech" (349–350) and "Keep yourself quiet and don't talk out of turn; / or don't you know—since you're so very wise— / that a foolish tongue will have to pay a price?" (358–360). However, the truth that Prometheus tries to impart in his scene with Ocean is that his situation is not a matter of choice as he is not master of the knowledge he yields. The picture of the world he paints with every speech, although wrought by his own suffering, which has, curiously, a humanizing effect, is a world where categories of knowledge are necessary but unstable since it is not the case that one is in charge of them: "Don't think it's delicacy or stubbornness / that keeps me quiet: my knowledge eats my heart / as I see myself mistreated in this way" (51–53). In the same speech, he continues with the story of the humans devoid of such knowledge of categories: "they saw but seeing was no use; / they heard but didn't hear. Like shapes in dreams, / they passed long lives in purposeless confusion" (462–464).

Prometheus imparts the knowledge that allows the shaping of the world, the ordering of all things. However, he is clear that this same art does not rule the world, for "[a]rt is far weaker than necessity" (525), necessity that is ruled over by another set of divine creatures (or, rather, concepts): "the triple Fates and the Furies who remember" (527). Thus, the no-place where Io and Prometheus meet, in their antithetical expressions, the atopia where contrasting semantic fields meet and where power is both enforced with harshness and challenged with inflexibility, is the place of suffering that at all times deforms the clear path of classification and interpretation. A parallel with Foucault's (1966) analysis of Borges's fictional Chinese encyclopaedia is fitting: "the mythical homeland Borges assigns to that distortion of classification that prevents us from applying it, to that picture that lacks all spatial coherence, is a precise region whose name alone constitutes for the West a vast reservoir of utopias" (xx). Atopia challenges utopia in that it does not allow for the affective and anticipatory investment in a place that is better than the present world but challenges the very fabric of the world, the perceived reality, the common sense that we rely on, the coherence of all ordering schemes. The atopia of the Scythian wilderness is such a "mythical homeland" that confronts the subject-grounded empirical systems of ordering according to similarities and differences and challenges the common ground for establishing a preliminary criterion of representation. This, moreover, is the case especially when pain and suffering, distorting all perception, are brought into the picture (in our case, onto the scene). As such, atopia represents the "loss of what is 'common' to place and name" (xx).

The Gift of Community: Prometheus and Io

Roberto Esposito traces the origin of the term "community" to the Latin word *communitas*, which is composed of two elements: *cum*, "with," and *munus*, which has the complex connotation of "gift," "obligation," "office," or "law" (Esposito 1998, 4-5). Esposito focuses on the *munus* rather than the *cum* portion of the etymological root in interpreting the signification of community, which is to say that he focuses on the ambiguity of the gift/law relation rather than on the togetherness or the common-ness of the term (Esposito 2013). For Esposito, the *munus* "is the gift that one gives because one must give and because one *cannot not* give" (1998, 5). It is, therefore, the obligation that the gift puts in circulation that is at the core of this term:

> Although produced by a benefit that was previously received, the *munus* indicates only the gift that one gives, not what one receives. All of the *munus* is projected onto the transitive act of giving. It doesn't by any means imply the stability of a possession and even less the acquisitive

dynamic of something earned, but loss, subtraction, transfer. It is a "pledge" or a "tribute" that one pays in an obligatory form. The *munus* is the obligation that is contracted with respect to the other and that invites a suitable release from the obligation. The gratitude that demands new donations. *Munus*, in this sense, and even more *munificus*, is he who shows the proper "grace," according to the equation of Plautus' *gratus-munus*: giving something that one can not keep for oneself and over which, therefore, one is not completely master. (Esposito 1998, 5)

Regarding Prometheus' gift to the humans, Aeschylus does not discuss the origin of the gift, probably because it does not serve the purpose of the play. The Promethean myth is regarded by many (notably by Plato in *Protagoras*) as the origin of the community-constituting gift. Due to the forgetfulness of his brother, Epimetheus, to distribute the gifts granted by Zeus to mankind, Prometheus has to compensate and steal fire from its guardian, Hephaestus—the same god who, against his own will, had to bind Prometheus to the Scythian rock in Aeschylus's play. Therefore, the gift that Prometheus grants to the mortals has its origins in lack. Humans are bound together in community not because of their artificial, constructive decision, by their practical, craft-making ways, which would mean that they possessed and developed the natural ability to develop the world in voluntary unity with others; rather, they are bound together by "honors to which they have no right" (Aeschylus, 32–3). Without the gift, as Prometheus himself explains to Ocean, "mortals saw but seeing was no use; / they heard but didn't hear. Like shapes in dreams, / they passed long lives in purposeless confusion" (462–3). There follows a list of all the gifts granted by Prometheus, whereby humans can master their environment, govern their changing setting, read the signs, work the land, and be in community with each other. But for Prometheus, the arts and knowledge whose transfer he is responsible for cannot help him escape his fate. Moreover, the gifts are not in Prometheus's possession; he teaches, he transfers the knowledge, he enlightens mortals, he brings them together but he cannot use the crafts they have, for instance in freeing himself. As the Chorus observes after a long list of gifts, Prometheus is "like a bad physician / who has fallen ill, you lose heart, and don't know / how to find out what drugs will cure your sickness" (487–9).

Although *Prometheus Bound* is seemingly a play about the conflict between two gods, where one is overcome by the power and force of another's law and, as a result, ends up immobilized on a rock in a remote corner of the world, we learn that he is also the powerful forethinker who is able to gift and withhold knowledge. Prometheus is the one who puts into circulation the *munus*, the system of obligation and laws and, while his vulnerable condition in the play constitutes the emphasis of many laments, he is the only one, in fact, who can be outside of the obligation that the *munus* creates: he is merely the mediator of the gift, not the originator, neither of the things he gives nor of the mortals' originary lack which he makes up for. The community that Prometheus brings about is not common property; it is related not to the proper but to praxis—to that which humans can do together.

So, then, why is Prometheus tortured? Is he not the symbol of the suffering benefactor of humanity, the originator of human rights, the father of community? Moreover, why is Zeus's police present at the Titan's punishment, why is the machinery of law-preserving present in full uniform? The Latin word *delinquere* (from *linquō* – "to quit," "to leave behind" but also "to be in want") points to the original crime which community is tied to: the crime associated with "the breach, the trauma, the lacuna out of which we originate. Not the Origin but its absence, its withdrawal" (Esposito 1998, 8). As noted previously, atopia is a place of both structuring and of destructuring the classificatory system of the world—the place where loss and lack are emphasized, along with the knowledge that grants both gods and mortals consciousness of the world. The picture that all the elements uncovered through Aeschylus' hero paint is emphatically of a structure that stands outside of subjectivity. The choice of the individual is often emphasized as a negative concept—only the arrogant are under the impression that they have any choice in how their fate unrolls. What brings the community together, as we saw above, is the *munus*—the obligation or acting with the others, of being exposed to otherness, of keeping the gift in circulation. The impersonal of fate or necessity, so important for Greek myth, is that which unbinds, destructures the obligation of community. The impersonal, in its manifestation, is the *immunus*, in dialectical relation with the community:

> If *communitas* is what binds its members in a commitment of giving from one to the other, *immunitas*, by contrast, is what unburdens from this burden, what exonerates from this responsibility. In the same way that community refers to something general and open, immunity – or immunization – refers to the privileged particularity of a situation that is defined by being an exception to a common condition. (Esposito 2013, 84)

Immunisation is that through which the community (*cum-vivere*) can take shape out of the individualised fear of the other. The immunus is one who, contrary to the munus, has no office and is the exception to the debt that binds community. The one who is at the heart of this lack (*delinquere*) is absolved, relieved from their office and function in society. The immune is outside of the circulation of the gift, which makes them both privileged and an outcast. In medical terms, which "immunization" immediately sends to, the protection that the immunus provides relies both on the element's similarity and opposition to the organism. What protects the organism is also that which negates it. Immunitary protection involves neutralizing the element that negates—not completely rejecting, nor completely incorporating and treating it as one of the individuals constituting the structure but through "exclusionary inclusion or exclusion by inclusion" (Esposito 2002, 8). This is the principle that the inoculation of the virus, known as the controversial vaccine, is based on. Esposito uses here the Hegelian formula of the negation of negation, though instead of working towards an affirmative resolution and sublation, he focuses on maintaining the tension at the heart of the dialectic. In that sense, his is a negative dialectic, where the synthesis is never realized but, instead, the cure is ongoing and the negative is always necessary to the continuation of the structure of life. For Esposito, there is no originary wholeness, as we saw. Moreover, by applying the logic of the immunitary protection, the foreign, the adversary of life, is always present and needs to remain as such. In physical terms, life's "salvation thus depends on a wound that cannot heal, because the wound is created by life itself" (8). Death, the element most hostile to life, must be incorporated in order to be deferred.

If immunus is that which embodies the negative in order to protect life from contagion or relieve it from its own burden of the gift, it cannot be completely outside of the world nor internal to it either: it has to be contained and operative in its role of protection. Prometheus's atopic exile represents his position in relation to both worlds, the godly and the human: he is immortal, though excluded from Olympus, and he is the mortals' benefactor, while not one of them. In terms of the immunitary paradigm, the law-preserving violence that Prometheus is subjected to is the violence that the law must generate in order to keep violence away from the community. For Zeus and the structures of power in Olympus, the only way to incorporate the threat that Prometheus poses is to contain him. Moreover, the humans are outside of the Olympic realm, they are the other, therefore moving the human element inside the structure, albeit in a non-place, a position exonerated from office, which allows it to be productive in its negation. In a sense, the offences that Prometheus is charged with are circumstantial: it is not that human life in itself threatens the gods but rather, in order to prevent any future moment of transgression, mortals, along with their benefactor, are guilty.

For mortals and immortals alike, living is circumscribed within the law-preserving mechanisms, which operate by passing the condemnation before the delinquency appears in order to prevent the crime. In sacrificial terms, the victim needs to be deprived of life in order for life to be preserved. This operation is bound to be continuous and violence is normalized as part of the law. Instead of seeing, on the one hand, the violence of Zeus Tyrannos and, on the other, the proliferation of life on Earth without the divine law, the two have to be integrated, as they are in dialectical relation at all time. Prometheus, the neutral element, exempt from his duties in Olympus, is the immunus who keeps the two sides connected while also resisting a strict categorization of the mythical elements. Generating guilt while mapping the world for Io to continue his legacy of immunity, Prometheus is constantly involved in the work of the negative. He is the element that maintains communication (albeit in violent terms) between the human and the godly, between self and other, inside and outside. He is the healer who cannot heal himself, the bearer of the gift who takes on the violence that protects both the godly and human realms.

Moreover, while circulating the gift of the arts that organize human life, he always points to forces greater than humans, greater than himself and Zeus too. In Greek myth, violence and Fate are intertwined, while life is always referred to as guilty, burdened, and wretched. All beings are at the hands of Fate. In the case of Prometheus, there are no clear reasons why he chooses to help the humans, though the violence of his punishment and his suffering guarantee the continuation of his work of helping humans. The gift of the arts that he passes on would no longer circulate, obliging and gluing the community in its praxis of structuring the world, if not accompanied by the continuous suffering generated in order to protect from suffering. Violence points to that which is both danger and protection—it points to the lack that constitutes the origin of life and of humanity. Thus, violence and desire go hand in hand, if desire is that which is constituted by absence and loss.

Prometheus is not the only one doing the work of the negative in *Prometheus Bound*—Io, on the mortal side of the immunological paradigm, is marked in the most striking sense by the violence of the gods and by her condition of a young woman who attracts the desire of a god. Her sickness, an expression of the constant violence inflicted by Argos's ghost, the agent of Hera, as well as the very reason for her suffering— the unwanted desire of Zeus— point to her as the sacrificial victim of the generations to come. Io embodies the *pharmakon*: the scapegoat is invested with all the sexual violence (both masculine and feminine) that the community wishes to be protected from. As noted above, in her wanderings, Io meets Prometheus in the atopia of his punishment and receives the story of her future. In her article "Io in the Prometheus Bound: A Coming of Age Paradigm for the Athenian Community" (1999), Phyllis B. Katz argues that Io's disease is a metaphor for the coming-of-age process in Ancient Greece for young women, who were usually married early on in their teens, shortly after reaching menarche. The hysteria-like imagery used in the Io episode of Aeschylus' play, argues Katz, parallels the rites of passage whereby young women are initiated into the life of a mature woman and depicts Io "as if she is suffering from an illness for which the prescribed cure is marital intercourse and pregnancy" (131).

The episode of the tragedy where Io's future is mapped out by Prometheus, as well as the medical and social records of the time that describe the rites of passage for young women in Ancient Greece, do provide ground for such an argument. For example, in Prometheus' last speech containing the story of Io's future, after laying out an intricate map of Io's travails throughout the world, he describes the touch that frees Io from her suffering: "There Zeus will bring you to your senses, with / a gentle touch, a hand you need not fear. / Your son, dark Epaphus, born from that touch / and named for it, will harvest all the land / irrigated by the broadly flowing Nile" (Aeschylus, 852–856). Epaphus (from ἐπαφάω, "to touch lightly") is the fruit of the young girl's maturation process and of her pregnancy and childbirth by Zeus, whose desire, as we have seen, is also the cause of her pain. Although this interpretation is grounded in textual evidence, there is a dimension that is missing, namely the immunological one. It is not that Io is completely relieved from pain when Zeus mates with her; rather, the inoculation that she embodies is passed on to her descendants. There is also an immunological focus on the body, which is carried forward into the body politic (in the society that myth presents after the event of the play). A focus on the pain of the diseased maiden, where her sufferings, more than those of the all-knowing Prometheus, especially as she is hardly knowing of her own surroundings, lead to a focus on the flesh which is not available through the description of Prometheus' sufferings. The insistence on her absolute ravaging through countless ordeals leads to the opposite: a disembodiment, a flesh-made-bare situation. It is as in the case of a malady: the body can only get better after the disease takes over completely. The flesh can only regenerate after it completely degenerates (Esposito 2002, 118). The disembodied entity exposes the lack of wholeness, the constitutive difference which forms the body: the impossibility of a complete and total unity in individuality. As such, another meaning of the Io myth is revealed: her body is the original *munus*, the gift constituting the common, while the violence bestowed on her acts as an immunitary disembodiment.

If we see Io as the *munus*, another gift that Prometheus mediates and maps the world for (or through?), the generations that follow carry on the inoculation that Io brings into the world, the gift that Io gives the community in order to maintain the immunity paradigm. As Prometheus announces at the end of his speech, one of Io's descendants, Heracles, will be responsible for his unchaining: "It would take too long to set it out in detail, / but from this seed, a brave man will be born, / famed for his bow, and he will rescue me" (873–5). However, if we do follow the myth closely, we find that Heracles, besides being the famous hero he is known to be, meets his death in a gory episode after, due to a mistake, his wife hands him the cloak poisoned by the centaur Nessus, whom Heracles had killed. The episode appears in Sophocles' *Trachinian Women*, where Heracles' descent is described in all the details and where the hero, who was previously considered to be the saviour and protector of the community, is exposed in all his grotesque, bestial violence. In this case, the violence spills over and the immunitary paradigm turns into an auto-immune system, which passes the threshold needed for it to act as protection for the community and turns destructive. Heracles is known for his twelve labours, all of which involve killing violent mythical creatures placed outside the ordered human realm. The violence he uses in these acts is already a compensation for an earlier episode of madness, where his viciousness is out of bounds and he ends up killing his sons. As reparation, he undergoes the trials, adding to the existing order of the mortal world and separating the beastly chaos from human order. Nessus, the centaur that Heracles kills for inappropriately touching his wife, Deianira, is part of the same feral world as the beasts killed in the labours and through his blood, Heracles becomes contaminated with a violence that cannot be contained—an auto-immune reaction that turns against the very structure it is protecting. As Esposito notes, "if his poisoned arrow brings the community contagion to an end, Nessus's shirt responds with an additional, final contagion: it communicates to whoever comes into contact with it a contagion that is impossible to be immunized against, because it is the poisoned product of immunization itself" (2002, 44–5). Seen in the larger context, Heracles is already carrying the legacy of immunisation, passed down through Prometheus to Io. The line of the immunus continues, this time through Heracles' bow with poisoned arrows, which he gifts, before his death, to a Greek hero known for his participation in the Trojan war, whose story is told by Sophocles in a play by the same name as its hero—*Philoctetes*.

In this story, the hero's environment resembles the barrenness of the Promethean Scythian wilderness: Philoctetes is exiled on a deserted and desolate island named Lemnos because he was, accidentally, bitten by a snake. Much of the play focuses on Philoctetes' excruciating pain, while two other Greek heroes, Odysseus and the young Neoptolemus, attempt to rob him of his bow, without which the Greek army cannot win the Trojan War. Philoctetes is rarely coherent in the play and often faints due to the excruciating pain that he experiences. Though suffering only due to a lesion on his leg, Philoctetes is completely reduced to his body, and his body to a wound. The wound, a mark of an encounter with the other, the chaos of the unrestrained natural world, takes over as that which cannot heal, which life relies on for survival. In this discussion of the legacy of the immunus, passed on from Prometheus, through Io, to the world, we can see how the focus shifts, gradually, on the object that maintains the immunity paradigm: the bow, the wound, the *technē*, which attest, once more, that the gift, which brings us together through lack and loss, is never ours, as our self is never self.

References

Aeschylus. 2012. *Prometheus Bound*. Translated by Deborah H. Roberts. Massachusetts: Hackett Publishing Company.

Amnesty International. 2011. "Prometheus Bound: Connecting the Arts and Human Rights." Accessed July 20, 2020. https://www.amnestyusa.org/the-prometheus-project-connecting-the-arts-and-human-rights/.2011

Barthes, Roland. 1975. *Roland Barthes*. Translated by Richard Howard. Berkley: University of California Press.

———. 1977. *A Lover's Discourse*. Translated by Richard Howard. London: Penguin Books.

Benjamin, Walter. 1972. "Critique of Violence." In *Selected Writings*, edited by Michael W. Jennings, 236–253. Cambridge, Massachusetts: Harvard University Press.

Esposito, Roberto. 1998. *Communitas: The Origin and Destiny of Community*. Translated by Timothy Campbell. Stanford: Stanford University Press.

———. 2002. *Immunitas: The Protection and Negation of Life*. Translated by Zakiya Hanafi. Cambridge, UK: Polity Press.

———. 2013. "Community, Immunity, Biopolitics." *Angelaki: Journal of the Theoretical Humanities* 18, no. 3: pp. 83–91.

Foucault, Michel. 2001. *The Order of Things: An Archaeology of the Human Sciences*. London: Routledge.

Katz, Phyllis B. 1999. "Io in the *Prometheus Bound*: A Coming of Age Paradigm for the Athenian Community." *Bucknell Review* 43, no. 1: pp. 129–147.

Roberts, Deborah H. 2012. "Introduction." In *Prometheus Bound*, 8–24. Massachusetts: Hackett Publishing Company.

Yu, Anthony C. 1971. "New Gods and Old Order: Tragic Theology in the 'Prometheus Bound'." *Journal of the American Academy of Religion* 39, no. 1: pp. 19–42.

Chapter 2

Pathography of Man and Evil in Joseph Conrad's *Heart of Darkness*

Nina Muždeka

University of Novi Sad, Serbia

Abstract: "Men who come out here should have no entrails", says the manager of the first outpost in Joseph Conrad's 1899 novella, *Heart of Darkness*, referring to the general health of agents on the Dark Continent. Indeed, health and illness form an integral part of the novella, not only on the thematic level, but also on the structural level. The whole journey of Marlow, the narrator, into "the heart of darkness" was undertaken as a result of agent Kurtz's mysterious illness. The narrative that recounts the journey follows the trajectory not only in terms of geography (Marlow's movement along the river), but also in terms of gathering information about Kurtz's illness and organising them into a system of meaning. In this respect, it can be read as a pathography, but a pathography that comes second-hand— both in terms of the temporal organisation (because the illness has already developed) and in terms of the narrative voice that recounts it (this voice gathers all the information about the illness prior to actually meeting the ill person). The pathographer, in this case, is neither the person suffering the illness nor the caretaker, but acts as a sort of detective who not only has the task of presenting the illness but also identifying and uncovering it first. Through linking the mysterious illness with the specific historical moment, the absent protagonist's illness also turns into an illness more widely conceived of – an illness of an era, an illness of the times, an illness of philosophy and ideology. The aim of this chapter is to analyse the physical and mental illness in *Heart of Darkness*, focusing on its development and the second-hand depiction of this development, taking into account the wider criticism of the times and its colonial practices.

Keywords: Man, evil, Pathography, illness, Africa, darkness.

***

Introduction: Conrad, the Congo, and Disease

Joseph Conrad's 1899 novella *Heart of Darkness* was his own favourite: in a letter from December 1902 he called it "my pet" (Goonetilleke 2003, 7). A literary classic and a staple on the literature studies reading lists, it is also Conrad's "first profound work" (Spittles 1992, 62) — one that challenges, engages and stimulates both the literary and academic audiences. Most commonly— and justifiably— read as a commentary on imperialism, colonialism and racism of the 19th century, it is also, in a more universal interpretation, a cautionary tale of all exploitation under the guise of supposed civilization. Due to its specific narrative structure and an ironic detachment it provides, Marlow's yarn is never fully explained, so that interpretive possibilities of the novella indeed remain numerous. However, though it presents a terrifying account of one man's journey to the deepest and darkest recesses of both nature and human soul, *Heart of Darkness* is rarely read as a narrative of illness, which is what I propose to do.

Adopting Anne Hunsaker Hawkins' definition of pathography, I read *Heart of Darkness* not as one but as a series of pathographies, including narratives of Kurtz's mental and physical illness, imperialism and colonialism as illness of the times, the narrative of human evil as an illness, and Marlow's journey to Africa and upstream on the Congo river which ultimately leads to a narrative of Marlow's own illness. The most dominant of these are two: that of gradual dismantling of Kurtz's mind, and that of human evil facilitated by all the pretenses of imperialism. These two narratives run in parallel, and in both instances, Marlow's role is the role of a secondhand chronicler and secondhand biographer— until the moment he personally begins to experience the changes he witnesses around him.

As Martin Bock writes in his chapter on disease and medicine in Conrad's life, "Disease and doctors were Conrad's lifelong companions" (2009, 124). Moreover, illness for Conrad seems to be inextricably connected to life at sea. As Brian Spittles writes in *Joseph Conrad: Text and Context*, the illnesses Conrad's characters endure in *The Nigger of the 'Narcissus'* and *The Shadow-Line* "were both manifestations of humanity's unequal struggle against an apparently hostile fate, and an accurate record of the hardships of a seaman's life" (1992, 16). Marlow's journey up the Congo River, in *Heart of Darkness*, was modelled on Conrad's eight-month-long personal experience, including that of disease. As a man of the sea himself, in 1890, he acquired a three-year appointment in the Belgian Congo, from which he returned in 1891, suffering from "dysentery and probably malaria" (Bock 2009, 124). In addition to having influenced his change of career, this experience left Conrad with long-lasting medical consequences, including "neuralgic pains, touchy digestion, familial gout, rotten teeth and susceptibility to influenza and nervous breakdown" (Bock 2009, 124). In May 1891, in one of his letters from Africa, Conrad wrote:

> What makes me rather uneasy is the information that 60 per cent. of our Company's employees return to Europe before they have completed even six months' service. Fever and dysentery! There are others who are sent home in a hurry at the end of a year, so that they shouldn't die in the Congo. God forbid! It would spoil the statistics which are excellent, you see! In a word, it seems there are only 7 per cent who can do their three years' service. (*The Collected Letters*, 20)

Conrad incorporated this factual reality into his 1899 novella, depicting the Congo as a domain not only of impenetrable darkness, but also sickness and death. Following Anne Hunsaker Hawkins' distinction between a disease and an illness— where a disease designates a purely medical condition that would be the subject matter of a medical report or a case study, and an illness includes a patient's personal, psychological perspective and is therefore presented in the form of a pathography— I argue that Conrad, in *Heart of Darkness*, did not depict diseases only, but more importantly illnesses.

Kurtz's Illness and the Generic Traits of Pathography

Writing about pathography as a literary genre and treating it as an account of one's own or other person's journey through an illness, Anne Hunsaker Hawkins treats it as "a subgenre of autobiography" (1999, 3). She applies the same generic category even to those accounts that are "technically biographies" because "they are as much autobiographical accounts of the author's experience as witness as they are biographical accounts of another's illness and death" (3). *Heart of Darkness* almost perfectly corresponds to this definition— whether understood as an account of an illness of the times or of the person, the novella presents the literary autobiographical experience of Charlie Marlow, who on his journey upstream on the Congo River first learns about this extraordinary person, Kurtz, and later of his illness.

Following the requirements of a work of biography, Marlow seems to be eager to provide as many biographical details about Kurtz as possible and plausible in his situation. His biography of Kurtz is composed of the bits and pieces he picked up along the way, from the several people he encountered in the Congo who could provide some information on this mysterious person that nevertheless keeps cropping up. Structurally speaking, the portrait of Kurtz is composed twice: for Marlow, it emerges parallel to the progression of his journey, and for the listeners of Marlow's story aboard the *Nellie*— and for the readers alike— parallel to the progression of Marlow's subsequent narrative. Though the details gradually amass, the portrait of Kurtz never emerges as it would in a jig-saw puzzle narrative: the biography remains as elusive as any other substance in Marlow's account. Kurtz was a first-class agent, an excellent ivory trader, the chief of the Inner Station, a journalist, a great musician, a poet, a prospective politician, a man of many talents— yet, as Marlow admits: "to this day I am unable to say what was Kurtz's profession, whether he ever had any— which was the greatest of his talents. I had taken him for a painter who wrote for the papers, or else for a journalist who could paint—but even the cousin (who took snuff during the interview) could not tell me what he had been—exactly. He was a universal genius [...]" (Conrad 2006).

By all accounts, whatever his true profession, Kurtz was "a prodigy", "an emissary of pity and science and progress, and devil knows what else" (Conrad 2006). Yet for Marlow, for the majority of his journey and for the majority of his pathography, the figure of Kurtz remains insubstantial: "I had heard Mr. Kurtz was in there. I had heard enough about it, too— God knows! Yet somehow it didn't bring any image with it— no more than if I had been told an angel or a fiend was in there. I believed it in the same way one of you might believe there are inhabitants in the planet Mars" (Conrad 2006).

Hawkins emphasizes the matter of perspective and attitude towards both the subject and the subject matter as one of the genre-defining criteria of pathographies. Instead of deploying a disinterested or objective perspective, pathographies are "almost always written by someone with a close relation to the ill person who is the book's subject", thus overriding "the conventional boundaries of self and other or biographer and subject" (1999, 3). Marlow's lack of a clear vision of the subject of his pathography does not entail detachment. Though he is not a member of the family nor the care-giver, Marlow is nevertheless closely attached to Kurtz and his perspective is far from disinterested. Under the attacks on Kurtz on the part of the manager of the Central Station and his uncle, the leader of the Eldorado Exploring Expedition, he soon feels obliged to side with Kurtz. His attachment might be founded on the premise of the shared character, shared ideas and ideals, perhaps. However, the foundation of this camaraderie remains as indefinable as the rest of Marlow's narrative. After finding Kurtz, his loyalties— as well as his preferences— become obvious: "I found myself lumped along with Kurtz as a partisan of methods for which the time was not ripe: I was unsound! Ah! but it was something to have at least a choice of nightmares" (Conrad 2006).

Writing about the ways in which people frame the narratives of illness, Hawkins uses the term "myth" and lists the myths of death and rebirth, battle, and journey as the most common ones. The myth of journey as a framing device functions particularly well in Conrad's novella. This journey, however, is both literal and metaphorical and functions simultaneously as a structural device. Each stage of Marlow's itinerary brings new information on Kurtz, his life and his illness, and with these pieces of information Marlow's interest is initially piqued and his attachment later formed. When Marlow first hears of Kurtz, there is no mention of any illness on his part. On the contrary, Kurtz appears to be the embodiment of energy and efficiency, "a very remarkable person", "at present in charge of a trading-post, a very important one, in the true ivory-country, at 'the very bottom of there'", who "sends in as much ivory as all the others put together" and who "will go far, very far" (Conrad 2006). This information is divulged, however, in the atmosphere of illness and impending death, in a hut where "a sick man (some invalid agent from upcountry)" (Conrad 2006) lies and moans. These circumstances undoubtedly serve as an omen, foreshadowing Kurtz's own illness and death, and tracing the pattern applicable to the majority of those who come to the Congo. It is only from the manager of the Central Station, who himself is never ill, that Marlow learns that "the situation was 'very grave, very grave'" and that "a very important station was in jeopardy, and its chief, Mr. Kurtz, was ill" (Conrad 2006).

Parallel to the progress of his journey, Marlow's interest and attachment to the object of his search intensifies. While at the Central Station, Marlow is still not very interested in Kurtz, who was "just a word" to him. His interest amounts to the level of curiosity, as he wanted to see what this extraordinary person, of whose various talents everyone was convinced, would amount to. He appears "to see Kurtz for the first time" when he learns about how he attempted to return from the Inner Station, but changed his mind: "It was a distinct glimpse: the dugout, four paddling savages, and the lone white man turning his back suddenly on the headquarters, on relief, on thoughts of home— perhaps; setting his face towards the depths of the wilderness, towards his empty and desolate station. I did not know the motive" (Conrad 2006). At the same time, the pathography of Kurtz's illness progresses, since Marlow also learns that Kurtz had been very ill in the past and had recovered imperfectly. Upon leaving the Central Station, Marlow is "rather excited at the prospect of meeting Kurtz very soon" (Conrad 2006). From that point on, for him, the river and the steamboat "crawled towards Kurtz - exclusively" (Conrad 2006).

The task of pathographer includes chronicling of impediments and disappointments on the perceived journey through an illness. Likewise, Marlow's fascination with Kurtz soon turns into frustration: "The approach to this Kurtz grubbing for ivory in the wretched bush was beset by as many dangers as though he had been an enchanted princess sleeping in a fabulous castle" (Conrad 2006). His extreme disappointment, upon thinking that Kurtz must be already dead, reinforces the sense that he "had been striving after something altogether without a substance" (Conrad 2006). When he finally physically meets Kurtz, the image of illness is striking and powerful:

> He looked at least seven feet long. His covering had fallen off, and his body emerged from it pitiful and appalling as from a winding-sheet. I could see the cage of his ribs all astir, the bones of his arm waving. It was as though an animated image of death carved out of old ivory had been shaking its hand with menaces at a motionless crowd of men made of dark and glittering bronze. I saw him open his mouth wide—it gave him a weirdly voracious aspect, as though he had wanted to swallow all the air, all the earth, all the men before him. (Conrad 2006)

The only character who can be ascribed the role of a caretaker is the Russian, the Harlequin, a man in colourful patched clothes, the owner of a sailor's manual in English. In his own words, he nursed Kurtz for three years and through two illnesses, defending him and saving him – though ultimately not from himself. His respect for Kurtz is blinded. Upon Marlow's claim that Kurtz must be mad— having lived as a chief of the tribe of natives in a hut surrounded with staked human skulls— the Russian protests indignantly. As for Kurtz's physical health, the Harlequin readily admits to its bad state, having nursed Kurtz, who was lying helpless, until Marlow's arrival.

After finding Kurtz— the moment which, as an event, represents both the furthest point of navigation and the culminating point of Marlow's experience— the journey back unfolds at "twice the speed of our upward progress" (Conrad 2006). It also retains its structural relevance for the development of the action, since parallel to the movements of the steamboat, Kurtz's life is "running swiftly, too, ebbing, ebbing out of his heart into the sea of inexorable time" (Conrad 2006).

A Pathography of Evil: The Illness, the Darkness, the Madness

Just as it is true that Marlow's journey was modelled on Conrad's own journey in the Congo, it is also true that the whole situation sprang from a particular historical moment. Following the Berlin Conference of 1884-85 and the divvying up of Africa amongst European colonial powers, the Congo Free State was established in 1885 as independently owned and ruled by King Leopold II of Belgium (Goonetilleke 2003, 9). Marlow's statement that "going up that river was like travelling back to the earliest beginnings of the world" (Conrad 2006) can also incorporate travelling back to the roots of the mysterious illness that he encounters since the beginning of his journey. Ever since the opening of the novella, an atmosphere of doom, anxiety and illness— both of people and an era— haunts the narrative. Even before he reaches the mouth of the Congo

River, Marlow witnesses meaningless violence, purposeless actions and waste of resources and human lives. Indeed, the value of human life is minimal: "In a few days, the Eldorado Expedition went into the patient wilderness, that closed upon it as the sea closes over a diver. Long afterwards, the news came that all the donkeys were dead. I know nothing as to the fate of the less valuable animals" (Conrad 2006).

Conrad's damnation of the colonial pretense of bringing progress, development and modernization is obvious in a vignette of Marlow's meeting with a drunk man in charge of the upkeep of the road through the jungle: "Can't say I saw any road or any upkeep, unless the body of a middle-aged negro, with a bullet-hole in the forehead, upon which I absolutely stumbled three miles farther on, may be considered as a permanent improvement" (Conrad 2006). Though *Heart of Darkness* is set in the Belgian Congo, Conrad's criticism is not exclusively directed at Belgium, nor is England entirely excused. The presence of rifles such as Martin-Henrys and Winchesters alludes to the involvement of other forces as well, and Africa is seen as a plundered playground of various European colonial forces. Symbolically, Kurtz himself is seen as the product not of one nation, but of entire Europe: "The original Kurtz had been educated partly in England, and— as he was good enough to say himself— his sympathies were in the right place. His mother was half-English, his father was half-French. All Europe contributed to the making of Kurtz" (Conrad 2006).

"Men who come out here should have no entrails" (Conrad 2006), says the manager of the Central Station, referring to the general health of agents on the Dark Continent. In the Congo, European people are getting sick at a quick rate: "But the rest—oh, my goodness! All sick. They die so quick, too, that I haven't the time to send them out of the country— it's incredible"! (Conrad 2006) However, Europeans in Africa are not burdened only by disease. While Chinua Achebe famously— and wrongly— criticized Conrad for reducing Africa "to the role of props for the break-up of one petty European mind" (Simmons 2009, 86), much closer to the truth would be to read Africa not as a mere exotic backdrop but as a domain of socially unrestrained behaviour of the Europeans. For Marlow, Kurtz's mental illness is closely linked to the wilderness and to the darkness: "The wilderness had patted him on the head, and, behold, it was like a ball— an ivory ball; it had caressed him, and— lo! — he had withered; it had taken him, loved him, embraced him, got into his veins, consumed his flesh, and sealed his soul to its own by the inconceivable ceremonies of some devilish initiation" (Conrad 2006).

Similar to William Golding's *Lord of the Flies*, the wilderness does not equal evil— it just helps the innate human potential for evil to surface, due to the lack of social structures that would impose social order. If the prolonged periods of time spent in the wilderness can "disorientate the European, stripping off the veneer of civilization", then I would argue that it is not "an underlying madness" (Spittles1992, 21) that is revealed, but a mindless capacity for evil akin to that rearing of its ugly head on Golding's desert island. In Marlow's interpretation, the following is a summary of civilization and the anchor it provides:

> You can't understand. How could you?—solid pavement under your feet, surrounded by kind neighbours ready to cheer you or to fall on you, stepping delicately between the butcher and the policeman, in the holy terror of scandal and gallows and lunatic asylums—how can you imagine what particular region of the first ages a man's untrammeled feet may take him into by the way of solitude—utter solitude without a policeman— by the way of silence— utter silence, where no warning voice of a kind neighbor can be heard whispering of public opinion? These little things make all the great difference. When they are gone you must fall back upon your own innate strength, upon your own capacity for faithfulness. (Conrad 2006)

In her essay *Illness as Metaphor*, Susan Sontag writes about "the analogy between disease and civil disorder", as well as the fact that "Illnesses have always been used as metaphors to enliven charges that a society was corrupt or unjust" (1997, 72). Marlow's narrative does bring to mind "the age-old connection between physical pathology and an ailing society" (Novillo-Corvalán 2015, 16), but here is where Conrad turns the table on the reader: he does not offer the promise that the treatment of the illness will restore the health of the society, nor does he claim that the society within which the illness occurs is the one that is indeed ill. Kurtz succumbs not to the power of the darkness outside of him, hiding at some impenetrable reaches of the jungle, or among the black bodies huddled at the river banks. He succumbed to the power of the darkness within, the one that lies dormant irrespective of the skin tone:

> I tried to break the spell—the heavy, mute spell of the wilderness— that seemed to draw him to its pitiless breast by the awakening of forgotten and brutal instincts, by the memory of gratified and monstrous passions. This alone, I was convinced, had driven him out to the edge of the forest, to the bush, towards the gleam of fires, the throb of drums, the drone of weird incantations; this alone had beguiled his unlawful soul beyond the bounds of permitted aspirations. (Conrad 2006)

And it is precisely in these "permitted aspirations" that one sees the effect of the society and social institutions. In renouncing the laws that apply to ordinary men, Kurtz makes it impossible for Marlow to appeal to him in the name of anything— for "there was nothing either above or below him", for "he kicked himself loose of the earth" (Conrad 2006). When Marlow hunts for Kurtz, who escaped from the steamboat and apparently attempted to return to the jungle, he clearly states that he is not arguing with a lunatic, that his intelligence was perfectly clear, adding: "But his soul was mad. Being alone in the wilderness, it had looked within itself, and, by heavens! I tell you, it had gone mad." Faced with the wilderness, Kurtz was left with "no restraint, no faith, and no fear"— and his soul struggled blindly with itself (Conrad 2006). It is this lack of restraint, which made Kurtz "hollow at the core", that Marlow sees as an explanation of Kurtz's demise and his surrender to the powers of the darkness within. Simultaneously, this restraint is, in Marlow's view, a panacea and an antidote against the wilderness-induced horrors of the human soul.

Kurtz came out to the Congo equipped with noble ideas: "Each station should be like a beacon on the road towards better things, a centre for trade of course, but also for humanizing, improving, instructing" (Conrad 2006). In Marlow's words, soon enough "powers of darkness claimed him for their own" (Conrad 2006). Lying on his deathbed, Kurtz appears to be haunted by shadowy images of his accomplishments: "My Intended, my station, my career, my ideas" (Conrad 2006). His emotions are described as heightened, as diabolic, unearthly, and primitive, and the expressions of "somber pride, of ruthless power, of craven terror – of an intense and hopeless despair" all mix on his face (Conrad 2006). The sinister force that rendered him such is described as "a mournful gloom", "implacable force brooding over an inscrutable intention", and "a flabby, pretending, weak-eyed devil of a rapacious and pitiless folly" (Conrad 2006). Jeffrey Berman posits that, on a metaphysical level, this force is associated with "chaos, purposelessness, lack of structure", and on a psychological level "with lust, savagery, appetitiveness" imbued with "impalpable passivity which effects destruction through silent fatigue" (1977, 55). Without the shelter of familiar social structures that would keep the unknown at bay, to Conrad's protagonists illness comes as a physical, bodily literalisation of what they are not equipped to deal with, despite all their potentially and/or seemingly noble intentions.

Marlow's Illness: An Auto-Pathography

Although at the very opening of the novel Marlow is not presented as a picture of health, but rather— with his "sunken cheeks, a yellow complexion" and "an ascetic aspect" (Conrad 2006) — brings forth the association of illness, it is not his health that is at the core of the novella. The pain with which Marlow writes, and narrates in his yarn, is not only mysterious and elusive, but also omnipresent and unavoidable. It haunts the narrator even before the onset of his adventure and reveals itself through a series of bad omens Marlow encounters while executing preparations for the journey. On the Continent, in white sepulchral city where the central offices of the Company are, Marlow is met by two women, clad in black, one of which is knitting black wool. Resembling witches, uncanny and fateful, to Marlow, they looked as if they were "guarding the door of Darkness, knitting black wool as for a warm pall, one introducing, introducing continuously to the unknown" (Conrad 2006). The doctor who examines Marlow introduces the topic of mental illness, of mental anguish awaiting those who embark upon such a journey. While measuring Marlow's cranium and inquiring about any history of madness in his family, he adds that he never gets to see people who come back from Africa, and that the changes, at any rate, occur inside. And indeed, when in Africa, Marlow will feel himself "become medically interesting" as he starts to succumb to the enchanting power of the darkness.

Marlow is for a long time able to avoid the destiny of other Europeans due to the everyday tasks he has to perform: "When you have to attend to things of that sort, to the mere incidents of the surface, the reality— the reality, I tell you— fades. The inner truth is hidden— luckily, luckily. But I felt it all the same; I felt often its mysterious stillness watching me at my monkey tricks..." (Conrad 2006). Ultimately, Marlow does reach the point of his own physical illness. Unlike the pathography of his mental changes, or of his siding with Kurtz, this pathography is a brief one. The pilgrims buried Kurtz in a muddy hole, "And then they very nearly buried me", professes Marlow almost casually. Of his own wrestling with death, Marlow says:

> It is the most unexciting contest you can imagine. It takes place in an impalpable greyness, with nothing underfoot, with nothing around, without spectators, without clamour, without glory, without the great desire of victory, without the great fear of defeat, in a sickly atmosphere of tepid scepticism, without much belief in your own right, and still less in that of your adversary. (Conrad 2006)

And here, Marlow finds a divergence point not only from Kurtz's destiny, but from belonging to the clan the two of them supposedly formed. While Kurtz's last words came as an ultimate curse, an ultimate judgment pronounced on all of the mankind ("The horror! The horror!"), he at least had something to say and he said it. "I found with humiliation that probably I would have nothing to say" (Conrad 2006), admits Marlow. Yet he uses his experience of physical illness as a basis to better understand Kurtz: "Since I had peeped over the edge myself, I understand better the meaning of his stare, that could not see the flame of the candle, but was wide enough to embrace the whole universe, piercing enough to penetrate all the hearts that beat in the darkness. He has summed up – he had judged" (Conrad 2006).

Even when the apparent physical illness is over and Marlow is safely back in Europe, in a sepulchral city whose streets are full of people both blessedly and foolishly ignorant of any darkness lurking within and without them, he is not healthy. He roams the streets going about his business but grins "bitterly at perfectly respectable persons" (Conrad 2006), and the excuse for such "inexcusable" behaviour finds in the physical fact that his "temperature was seldom normal in these days" (Conrad 2006). Linking the physical and the mental, he declares that it was his "imagination that wanted soothing", not his strength (Conrad 2006).

Writing about the unifying elements of different kinds of pathographies, Hawkins focuses on a common motive, or purpose— "the need to communicate a painful, disorienting, and isolating experience" (10). Upon returning to Europe, Marlow indeed feels isolated, disconnected from and different than an ordinary man. For him, uninitiated denizens of the safe and ordered civilized world "were intruders whose knowledge of life was to me an irritating pretence, because I felt so sure they could not possibly know the things I knew" (Conrad 2006). "Metaphors of travel and entry into the strange world" (Brody 2002, 90), used by the journey myth utilized by pathographies, for Marlow, are not just metaphors but literal experiences which he is unable to shake off. If, as Brody interprets Hawkins, a pathography is indeed used "to construct a framework of meaning to understand and thereby to control a frightening experience" (2002, 90), it is questionable to what extent Marlow's pathography serves this purpose. "I am not trying to excuse or even explain – I am trying to account to myself for – for – Mr. Kurtz – for the shade of Mr. Kurtz" (Conrad 2006), says Marlow, confirming the potentially cathartic dimension of the narrative of illness but also doubting his success at the endeavour. In his need to tell others of his traumatic, yet transformative experience, Marlow can be seen to resemble Coleridge's Ancient Mariner. Here also might lie an interpretation of Conrad's statement that "perhaps true literature […] is something like a disease which one feels in one's bones, sinews, and joints" (*The Collected Letters* 2:368, qtd. in Bock 2009, 130).

Marlow's experience in the Congo is one that is hard to comprehend, one so divorced from the usual European everyday reality at the time. The chosen narrative structure adds to this impression: Marlow's initial experience is retold by an older Marlow, so it is refracted through the prism of his subsequent years and experiences. This story is then told to the readers by an unnamed narrator, one of the group of people gathered on board the cruising yawl *Nellie*, waiting for the tide to turn, so that it is additionally filtered and altered. The narrative within a narrative structure provides "deliberate thematic ambiguities, a critical historical perspective" (Spittles 1992, 62) and means that nothing is to be taken for granted, that the core of the yarn is perhaps even more elusive than in Marlow's original experience which itself was not definitive and explicated.

It would be all too easy, therefore, to equate Conrad's oppositions of white/black and light/darkness with the binaries health/illness and life/death which are generally found in pathographies. Though the Dark Continent does indeed mean illness and death for many white people that come there, Conrad introduces a reversal of this perspective by depicting death and decay that white men's exploitation under the guise of civilizing brings to the black people. The Congo, thus, does not equal illness and death— on the contrary, mindless destruction is brought to it by the Europeans coming to plunder for profit. The question of Kurtz's victimhood or villainess is constructed along the similar lines.

Yet, as a testimony of illness, *Heart of Darkness* abides by the rules set out for the literary genre of pathography. The narrative that recounts the journey follows the trajectory not only in terms of geography (Marlow's movement along the river), but also in terms of gathering information about Kurtz's illness and organizing them into a system of meaning. In this respect, it can be read as a pathography, but a pathography that comes second-hand— both in terms of the temporal organization (because the illness has already developed) and in terms of the narrative voice that recounts it (this voice gathers all the information about the illness prior to actually meeting the ill person). The pathographer in this case is neither the person suffering the illness, not the care-taker, but acts as a sort of detective who not only has the task of presenting the illness, but also identifying and uncovering it first. Through linking the mysterious illness with the specific historical moment, the absent protagonist's illness also turns into an illness more widely conceived of— an illness of an era, an illness of the times, an illness of philosophy and ideology.

References

Berman, Jeffrey. 1977. *Joseph Conrad: Writing as Rescue.* New York: Astra Books.
Bock, Martin. 2009. "Disease and Medicine". In *Joseph Conrad in Context*, edited by Allan Simmons, 124 – 131. Cambridge: Cambridge University Press.
Brody, Howard. 2003. *Stories of Sickness.* Oxford: Oxford University Press.
Conrad, Joseph. 2006. *Heart of Darkness.* The Project Gutenberg e-book. http://www.gutenberg.org/cache/epub/526/pg526.html
Goonetilleke, D.C.R.A. 2003. "Preface." In *Joseph Conrad, Heart of Darkness*, edited by D.C.R.A. Goonetilleke, 7 – 9. Peterborough: Broadview Press.

Hawkins, Anne Hunsaker. 1999. *Reconstructing Illness: Studies in Pathography.* West Lafayette: Purdue University Press.

Novillo-Corvalán, Patricia, ed. 2015. *Latin American and Iberian Perspectives on Literature and Medicine.* New York: Routledge.

Simmons, Allan, ed. 2009. *Joseph Conrad in Context.* Cambridge: Cambridge University Press.

Sontag, Susan. 1997. *Illness as Metaphor.* New York: Farrar, Straus, and Giroux.

Spittles, Brian. 1992. *Joseph Conrad: Text and Context.* London: Macmillan.

Chapter 3

Care, Pig!: The Abject Caregiver in Beckett's Plays

Gabriel Quigley

New York University, USA

Abstract: This chapter examines Samuel Beckett's narratives of caregiving in *Waiting for Godot* and *Endgame* in order to reflect how caregiving labour is excepted from the dialectic of recognition that the late capitalist society has instrumentalised in the ongoing exploitation of caregivers. Over the past few decades, theorists and activists such as Silvia Federici and Nancy Fraser have drawn attention to the ways that caregivers are dually needed for maintaining the social texture as well as continually exploited because of their exceptionalism from capitalist rubrics of value. Theorists such as Rosemarie Garland-Thomson and Eva Feder Kittay have demonstrated that disability contexts, in particular, show how the labour of caregiving is rendered exceptional from other kinds of labour which, while also exploited, are at least legible as labour within a capitalist schema. Following Garland-Thomson, Feder Kittay, and others, I argue that the exploitation of caregivers reduces to a problem of recognition, in which the radical exploitation of caregivers is made possible by the ongoing failure to recognise caregiving as labour. Given the ways that both Lucky and Clov perform caregiving without recognition of this labour or their needs, I claim that the caregiving relationship in *Waiting for Godot* and *Endgame* stage precisely the contradiction materialising at the juncture of capitalism and care. This chapter thus examines the impoverished status of Beckett's caregivers in what Michael Davidson has identified as a "dialectics of disability" in Beckett's oeuvre, contending that the recognition of illness combined with the unrecognition of caregiving labour in *Waiting for Godot* and *Endgame* reflect the social demand for caregiving combined with society's failure to recognise caregivers as members of society.

Keywords: Capitalism, recognition, abject, illness, labour, care, disability.

* * *

Before Pozzo gives his speech in Samuel Beckett's *Waiting for Godot*, he asks "is everybody looking at me? [*He looks at* LUCKY, *jerks the rope.* LUCKY *raises his head.*] Will you look at me, pig! [LUCKY *looks at him.*] Good."[1] Pozzo's demand for unreciprocated recognition in this exchange reflects the asymmetry that structures his relationship to Lucky, but it also evokes the non-recognition afforded to caregiving labour in contemporary society. Care has become a central topic in recent political and academic debates, as more activists and scholars draw attention to the deep neglect afforded to individuals working in caregiving roles. By staging the asymmetrical distribution of care between caregivers and dependents, Beckett's plays *Waiting for Godot* and *Endgame* underscores a contradiction at the heart of what recent care theorists have identified as capitalism's "crisis of care."

In their introduction to the recently published special issue of *Social Text* titled "Radical Care: Survival Strategies for Uncertain Times," editors Hi'ilei Julia Kawehipuaakahaopulani Hobart and Tamara Kneese define care as "a relational set of discourses and practices between people, environments, and objects that approximate what philosophers like Adam Smith and David Hume identify as 'empathy,' 'sympathy,' or 'fellow feeling.' Theorized as an affective connective tissue between an inner self and outer world, care constitutes a feeling with, rather than a feeling for, others."[2] Hobart and Kneese observe that this definition of care can, however, mean different things to different social agents:

> On the one hand, self-care is both a solution to and a symptom of the social deficits of late capitalism, evident, for example, in the way that remedies for hyperproductivity and the inevitable burnout that follows are commoditized in the form of specialized diets, therapies, gym memberships, and schedule management. On the other hand, a recent surge of academic interest in care and its metonyms across multiple disciplines and subfields through recent or forthcoming volumes, symposia, conference panels, and keynote addresses...considers how our current political and sociotechnical moment sits at the forefront of philosophical questions about who cares, how they do it, and for what reason.[3]

As Hobart and Kneese point out, care has become one of late capitalism's keywords, which keeps the tracks of consumption and the labour required to produce commodities well-oiled. But care has also become a locus of anti-capitalist analysis and activism, especially in relation to society's reliance on what many theorists have referred to as "social reproduction," the glue that holds together the fabric of belonging and posterity. From this perspective, the extension and exploitation of caregiving are questions that are fundamentally intertwined with the struggle for justice, as Angela Davis has recently observed: "what counts as radical have changed over time. Self-care and healing and attention to the body and the spiritual dimension— all of this is now a part of radical social justice struggles."[4]

Current debates about care owe much to Silvia Federici's 1975 "Wages Against Housework," which foregrounds care's dual identity as both a site of exploitation and a fulcrum for anti-capitalist resistance. Federici states,

> the wage gives the impression of a fair deal: you work and you get paid, hence you and your boss are equal; while in reality the wage, rather than paying for the work you do, hides all the unpaid work that goes into profit. But the wage at least recognizes that you are a worker, and you can bargain and struggle around and against the terms and the quantity of that wage, the terms and the quantity of that work.[5]

The demand for wages, Federici argues, is not reducible to a demand for compensation— rather, it is the demand that women's work be legible as work, and therein lies its revolutionary potential:

> wages for housework, then, is a revolutionary demand not because by itself it destroys capital, but because it attacks capital and forces it to restructure social relations...To say that we want money for housework is the first step towards refusing to do it, because the demand for a wage makes our work visible, which is the most indispensable condition to begin to struggle against it, both in its immediate aspect as housework and its more insidious character as femininity.[6]

Federici goes on to point out that feminist struggle, which is indissociable from anti-capitalist struggle, is futile unless housework first gains the paltry honorific of "work." At the heart of this work is caregiving, which she conceives as the uncompensated labour that fills in the physiological and psychological deficits of labour that are structurally reproduced by the inflation of demand in a capitalist economy. She thus defines care as "this peculiar combination of physical, emotional and sexual services that are involved in the role women must perform for capital that creates the specific character of that servant which is the housewife.... It is not an accident that most men start thinking of getting married as soon as they get their first job...having somebody at home who takes care of you is the only condition not to go crazy after a day spent on an assembly line or at a desk."[7]

Nancy Fraser expands upon Federici by identifying what she sees as a care-shaped crisis in the economic structure of late capitalism. In "Contradictions of Capital and Care," Fraser refers to the work of theorists such as Federici, Lise Vogel, and Christine Delphy by invoking their concept of "social reproduction:"

> non-waged social-reproductive activity is necessary to the existence of waged work, the accumulation of surplus value and the functioning of capitalism as such. None of these things could exist in the absence of housework, child-rearing, schooling, affective care and a host of other activities which serve to produce new generations of workers and replenish existing ones, as well as to maintain social bonds and shared understandings.[8]

Federici argues that capitalism reproduces the illusion of sustainability by drawing on (and refilling) the reservoirs of gender conventions, such that the costs of care work are sutured to the rhythms of nature. Fraser provides the economic explanation for why care work is thus transformed, stating that "every form of capitalist society harbours a deep-seated social-reproductive 'crisis tendency' or contradiction: on the one hand, social reproduction is a condition of possibility for sustained capital accumulation; on the other, capitalism's orientation to unlimited accumulation tends to destabilize the very processes of social reproduction on which it relies."[9] Because the commodity form involves the constant inflation of demand, the price of a commodity is always in excess of its production cost. Capitalism compensates for the deficit thus incurred by, in Fraser's words, "free riding" on "activities of provisioning, care-giving and interaction that produce and maintain social bonds although it accords them no monetized value and treats them as if they were free. Variously called 'care', 'affective labour' or 'subjectivation', such activity forms capitalism's human subjects."[10] Care is the free labour that is used to routinely remedy the labour debt incurred by a capitalist economy, and as such it does not even rise to the level of exploitation; care is the radical exception to exploitation that allows for exploitation to continue in capitalist society.

Disability Studies provides a useful register for analyzing the role of bodies in capitalism's reliance on care work. Within the framework of disability, care is not reducible to the object of exchange between husband and wife, as it is in analyses of care that take the domestic sphere for its blueprint or paradigm. While the roles of caregiver and dependent have undoubtedly been shaped by heteronormative domesticity, physiological and psychological factors also inform the terms of this relationship. Tobin Siebers distinguishes disability from impairment, describing impairment as a physical or cognitive inability and disability as an incongruence between a built environment and a person's body or mind. The constitutive publicity of disability thus pushes its concept beyond domestic privacy, to the extent that "disability is not a physical or mental defect but a cultural and minority identity."[11] Disability is the static accrued by bodies and minds rubbing up against the infrastructural manifestation of societal expectations. Siebers thus discerns an ideology of ability at work in contemporary society that "defines the baseline by which humanness is determined, setting the measure of body and mind that gives or denies human status to individual persons. It affects nearly all of our judgments, definitions, and values about human beings, but because it is discriminatory and exclusionary, it creates social locations outside of and critical of its purview."[12] Rosemarie Garland-Thomson argues that this baseline is decided in reference to "the normate": "the corporeal incarnation of culture's collective, unmarked, normative characteristics."[13] As Garland-Thomson observes, rather than being "normal" in the real, the normate must in fact always exceed what bodies and minds can really do. With the concept of the normate in mind, I argue that the ideology of ability is complicitous with capitalism in ways that resonate with Fraser's analysis, since the labour that capitalism demands is always in excess of what bodies and minds can actually do. Like the normate, the ideal labourer is extrahuman. Analogous to how the work of wives continually fills in the gaps between the demand for social productivity and the husband's work, the work of disability caregivers continually fills in the gaps between the demand for social productivity and bodies and minds as they really are.

Garland-Thomson and Disability Studies scholar Eva Feder Kittay oppose the kind of care that capitalism requires to a kind of care that we all need in common. Garland-Thomson argues that all bodies need care in virtue of its essential finitude, stating that

> although our modern collective cultural consciousness denies vulnerability, contingency, and mortality, disability insists that our bodies are dynamic, constantly reformed by the call and response between flesh and world...Our bodies need care; we need assistance to live; we are fragile, limited, and pliable in the face of life itself...What we call disability is perhaps the essential characteristic of being human.[14]

Garland-Thomson here touches on a contradiction in society's standards of ability that parallels the structure of capitalism's care crisis, since the ideology of ability is both sustained by care and effaces it. Garland-Thomson's claim resonates with many recent Disability Studies perspectives, but it is especially responsive to Feder Kittay's argument that the ideology of ability reflects how liberalism's espousal of autonomy repudiates the fact of human dependency. Feder Kittay's "dependency critique of equality" challenges contemporary society's valorization of autonomy by drawing attention to both our fundamental dependency on others as well as the fact that care relations are rendered asymmetrical by contemporary social organization. For Garland-Thomson and Feder Kittay, care has two aspects: on the one hand, it is both the residue and fuel of today's ideology of ability, which leads to its asymmetrical distribution; on the other hand, it is what makes us human. Departing from feminist care scholarship, Garland Thomson asserts that "a feminist disability studies complicates both the feminist ethic of care and liberal feminism in regard to the politics of care and dependency"[15] by advancing a practice of care that responds to universal human finitude rather than the manufactured lacks of late capitalist society.

Central to such an ethic of care is a recognition of the caregiver's need for care. According to Feder Kittay, liberalism's ideal of autonomy produces an asymmetrical concept of care that is bound to the exchange between a caregiver and a care recipient. The asymmetry of this relationship props up liberalism's ideal of autonomy by presenting the caregiver as "independent" to their dependent, thus effacing the caregiver's own claim to care. This prompts Feder Kittay to ask, "what about the obligations owed to the dependency worker? Who is to care for the caregiver? How are her needs to be recognized?"[16] Contrary to the illusion of autonomy that a society based on liberal values assigns to its caregivers, "Those who give care will frequently find that the burdens are substantial. Often, caregiving is carried out by family members at great cost to themselves, financially, medically, and professionally. Paid caregivers are generally poorly paid, and the work lacks high social status."[17] Feder Kittay goes on to point out that

> Dependency work may be familial and unpaid or waged labour, but wherever it is found, it is largely carried out by women, and not infrequently by women (and sometimes men) who are marginalized by virtue of race and class. In spite of the time, energy, and resources, both material and emotional, both social and individual, that dependency care requires – in spite of the importance in our lives of the relations we have with those upon whom we have depended and who depend upon us – dependency concerns rarely enter in philosophical and political discussions.[18]

Rather than trying to discourage caregiving or eclipse the dependency felt by the dependent, Feder Kittay draws attention to the vulnerabilities of the caregiver in order to shed light on the fact of human interdependency. Whereas the liberal justification for care is tied to the principle that dependency is produced by a descent from a prior state of equally assigned autonomy, Feder Kittay proposes "an equality wherein the condition of its possibility is the inevitability of human interdependence: The interdependence which is featured both literally and metaphorically in the aphorism that we are all some mother's child."[19] By depriving housewives and caregivers of the care that they need, contemporary society perpetuates an asymmetrical model of care relationships that keeps both capitalism and liberal values afloat.

Although Federici, Fraser, Garland-Thomson, and Feder Kittay address the topic of care from different perspectives, their analyses point towards a debt in contemporary society. This debt is continually filled by the free or underpaid labour of caregivers that never rises to the level of being recognized as such. In "On Elder Care Work and the Limits of Marxism," Federici claims that caregivers form an "underclass," stating that

> the crisis of elder care, whether considered from the viewpoint of the elders or their care providers, is essentially a gender question. Although increasingly commodified, most care work is still done by women and in the form of unpaid labour that does not entitle them to any pension...Paid caregivers too, as we have seen, are affected by the devaluation of reproductive work, forming an 'underclass' that still must fight to be socially recognized as workers.[20]

She draws attention to the example of "home care workers in the United States [where] nearly half must rely on food stamps and other forms of public assistance to make ends meet. Indeed, as Domestic Workers United ... has put it, care workers live and work in 'the shadow of slavery.'"[21] Similarly, Feder Kittay claims that "neither care ethics nor theories of the just state thus far have seriously grappled with the injustices that result from the gendered assignment of caring labour."[22] She argues that "attention to the care of the clearly inevitable dependencies of a frail, infirm old age and severe mental retardation reveals the ways in which the justice or injustice of the social organization of care has a profound effect on the well-being of the cared-for and the caregiver alike."[23] Although each of the writers that I consider differs in their approach, they draw attention to the ways that contemporary society fails to recognize the caregiver while depending on them. I will use this understanding of the caregiver as a lens for reading relationships of care in Samuel Beckett's plays *Waiting for Godot* and *Endgame*.

Beckett's works are filled with characters who perform caregiving or service roles, including the character Watt who is a servant in the house of Mr. Knott, Murphy who finds employment as an orderly at Magdalen Mental Mercyseat hospital, and Molloy who becomes Lousse's temporary caregiver. Many of these relationships comprise what Beckett has named the "pseudo-couples" in his work, a term that he first used to describe his early protagonists Mercier and Camier but extends to other relationships in his oeuvre including Pim and Pom in *How It Is* and *The Lost Ones*' ghostly figures who roam in search of their missing partners. Most studies of relationality in Beckett's oeuvre concern the cruelty that binds his pseudo-couples, often with reference to Beckett's own interest in Sade. My analysis, on the other hand, examines how Beckett's portrayals of caregiving illuminate the neglect, even cruelty that is afforded to caregivers in modern society. I borrow from Theodor Adorno's now-canonical analysis of *Endgame* in order to situate Beckett's portrayals of caregiving in the context of what Adorno perceives to be the critical message in Beckett's works, which I argue can be read productively alongside the analyses of Federici, Fraser, Garland-Thomson, and Feder Kittay. Rather than taking up Beckett's entire oeuvre, my analysis focuses on *Waiting for Godot* and *Endgame* because these plays portray the problem of care in a more distilled form than Beckett's other works.

Pozzo and Lucky are first introduced in *Waiting for Godot* as a master and his "carrier"[24] respectively: "POZZO *drives* LUCKY *by means of a rope passed around his neck, so that* LUCKY *is the first to enter, followed by the rope which is long enough to let him reach the middle of the stage before* POZZO *appears.* LUCKY *carries a heavy bag, a folding stool, a picnic basket and a greatcoat,* POZZO *a whip.* POZZO: (*off.*) On! (*Crack of whip.* POZZO *appears. They cross the stage*)."[25] Pozzo and Lucky reappear as a blind man and his "menial"[26] in Act Two, thus emphasizing the caregiving aspects of their relationship. The stage directions state, "[*e*]*nter* POZZO *and* LUCKY, POZZO *is blind,* LUCKY *burdened as before. Rope as before, but much shorter, so that* POZZO *may follow more easily.*"[27] Pozzo consistently describes Lucky as something less than human, referring to Lucky variously as "pig," "swine," and one of those "[creatures that] you can't drive…away. The best thing would be to kill them."[28] Pozzo also views Lucky as abject, possessing less dignity than "old dogs"[29] and insisting that Lucky step back because "he stinks,"[30] before finally growing repelled by Lucky's "thinking": "I can't bear it…any longer…the way he goes on…you've no idea…it's terrible…he must go."[31] But Lucky is also a character with impairments, which leads Estragon and Vladimir to speculate that "perhaps he's a half-wit" or "a cretin," with "eyes…Goggling out of his head" who "looks at his last gasp."[32] As I will later analyze via Adorno and theories of care, I claim that the subhuman, abject, and impaired aspects that are associated with Lucky reflect elements of the status that late capitalist society assigns to the caregiver.

The relationships of Beckett's later play *Endgame* are portrayed in more explicitly medical and caregiving terms. The play begins with Hamm performing what appears like a routine medical questionnaire, "HAMM: How are your eyes? CLOV: Bad. HAMM: How are your legs? CLOV: Bad. HAMM: But you can move. CLOV: Yes."[33] This is followed by a string of exchanges lifted from dependency work relationships, such as when Hamm states "I'd like to pee. CLOV: [*With alacrity.*] I'll go and get the catheter. [*He goes towards the door.*] HAMM: Time enough, [CLOV *halts.*] Give me my pain-killer. CLOV: It's too soon. [*Pause.*] It's too soon on top of your tonic, it wouldn't act."[34] Despite Hamm and Clov's rehearsal of the roles of caregiver and dependent, *Endgame* also draws attention to certain tensions that underpin this relationship. For example, although Hamm is Clov's dependent, he is also the failing caregiver for his elderly parents. Unlike Clov, Hamm shirks these responsibilities, crying out to his father "Accursed progenitor! NAGG: Me pap! HAMM: The old folks at home! No decency left! Guzzle, guzzle, that's all they think of,"[35] before summoning Clov with a whistle. Moreover, although Clov is also portrayed as an impaired caregiver, Hamm consistently diminishes the severity of Clov's impairments: "HAMM: Wait! [CLOV *halts.*] How are your eyes? CLOV: Bad. HAMM: But you can see. CLOV: All I want. HAMM: How are your legs? CLOV: Bad. HAMM: But you can walk. CLOV: I come…and go."[36]

In his reading of *Endgame*, Ato Quayson claims that "with Beckett…we find that as he proliferates devices by which to undermine the stability of ontological categories, he ends up also undermining the means by which the many disabilities that he frequently represents in his texts may be interpreted."[37] For Quayson, the promise of interpretation and the legibility of disability carry the same structure of interruption in Beckett's works. This is because Beckett invites allegorical interpretation while ceaselessly frustrating its success, and he fills his works with disabled characters while undermining the representations of their disability by disassociating them from pain. Out of "the abundance of figures with physical and mental impairments and mobility difficulties in works as varied as *Waiting for Godot*, *Molloy*, *Murphy*, *Play*, and *Happy Days*,"[38] Quayson focuses on the "hermeneutical impasse"[39] that surrounds *Endgame*'s portrayal of disability. The dual structure of meaninglessness and painlessness that supports what Quayson identifies as the "aesthetic nervousness" evoked by *Endgame*'s portrayals of disability are facilitated by the ways that "Hamm's disability complements Clov's…He is wheelchair-bound, while Clov cannot sit; Hamm is completely blind, while Clov is partially so. But this apparent inextricable interdependency is also consolidated at other levels: Clov needs Hamm for sustenance (the combination to the larder), while acting in practical terms as Hamm's prosthesis."[40] Michael Davidson expands on this observation, stating,

> Quayson recognizes the foundational importance of disability in Beckett against the critical tendency to see it as a sign of existential alienation in the modern world…We might also see characters' co-dependence as a means of survival, the social contract reduced to its most naked form. Beckett's choice of representing his human comedy by disabled figures

whose bodies have ceased to be 'productive' according to modern imperatives of progress and improvement offers a parable about the limits of agency and community in a post-ableist era.[41]

Davidson advances what he identifies as a "dependency theory"[42] reading of Beckett's pseudo-couples that draws attention to the abjection modernity assigns to dependency: "Beckett's treatment of abject dependence can be stated thus: individuals cannot realize themselves as independent agents without first recognizing their dependent and contingent relations with others and with their own animal bodies. In a world that valorizes independence and able-bodied normalcy, dependent relations are regarded as signs of weakness, usually gendered as 'women's work' or that of ill-paid menials."[43]

Davidson's dependency theory reading of Beckett draws on care theory scholars who have called attention to its gender and class dimensions, notably Feder Kittay and Martha Nussbaum. He states,

> care-givers, as Feder Kittay and Nussbaum demonstrate, are invariably women, responsible both for child-rearing and care for the aged and infirm. Moreover, care-giving is unrewarded, if within the family, and when a component of work, ill remunerated... Clov is not female, but by participating in dependency work, he occupies the subject position often occupied by women as nurses, mothers, midwives, and care-givers.[44]

By drawing attention to the connection between the subjugation of women in caregiving roles and the ideology of ability that reproduces this subjugation, Davidson argues that Beckett's portrayals of dependency resonate with contemporary caregiving debates even if this isn't explicitly articulated in Beckett's works. For Davidson, this is because Beckett's plays reflect and critique the liberal values of Western modernity in ways that parallel Feder Kittay's own dependency critique of equality. Quayson does not discuss caregiving in Beckett's works save for the assertion that "the category of the skeptical interlocutor [in Beckett's works] has multiple articulations along an axis of dialectical oppositions that include those of Invalid/Caregiver, Parent/Child, Master/Slave, and Prospero/Caliban-Ariel."[45] Although Beckett's characters often align with these oppositions, Quayson fails to consider the non-dialectical aspects of his pseudo-couples, which reflect the asymmetry of care distribution in modern caregiving relationships. The master-slave dialectic that Quayson invokes, which is propelled by the pursuit of both subjects to attain recognition from the other, fails to conform with the non-reciprocity that separates Pozzo from Lucky and Hamm from Clov. Similarly, Davidson's assertion that Beckett's works stage a "dialectics of dependency"[46] underplays the core tension in these relationships, that although each character depends on one another, only certain characters have the privilege of meeting that dependency. Davidson is right to point out that Beckett's pseudo-couples reflect the abjection that modern society assigns to dependency, but Davidson's claim ignores how these portrayals of dependency are structured through the abjection of the caregiver. Rather than simply portraying dependency, I argue that Beckett achieves the more critical aim of representing the contradiction within caregiving under conditions of late capitalism.

Indeed, according to Adorno, it is the critical element in Beckett's work that distinguishes him from the "Parisian existentialism"[47] that his work ostensibly resembles. In his 1961 "Trying to Understand *Endgame*," Adorno argues against the claim that Beckett's art is tied to existentialist concerns with spirit, the freedom of the individual, and finding meaning in a meaningless world. Instead, Beckett's poetics deflates all philosophies that champion abstraction, thus revealing the material detritus that makes up modern life. Adorno argues that *Endgame* achieves this effect by privileging a poetics of "unintelligibility, [and] concretely reconstructing the meaning of the fact that [*Endgame*] has no meaning."[48] Here Adorno approximates Quayson's reading by claiming that "interpretation inevitably lags behind Beckett. His dramatic work, precisely by virtue of its restriction to an exploded facticity, surges out beyond facticity and in its enigmatic character calls out for interpretation."[49] Instead of the "meaning" that is central to Heidegger and Sartre's philosophies, Beckett exposes the meaninglessness of life in late capitalism by emptying-out life's "situations" in order to give voice to the "forlorn particulars that mock the conceptual, a layer composed of minimal utensils, refrigerators, lameness, blindness, and the distasteful bodily functions."[50] Adorno thus associates *Endgame*'s portrayals of disability with a critique of philosophy because they draw attention to the "physical reality"[51] that philosophy obscures through its alliance with ideology. Whereas existentialism champions the individual as the absolute determiner of meaning, "*Endgame* destroys such illusions. The individual himself is revealed to be a historical category, both the outcome of the capitalist process of alienation and a defiant process against it, something transient himself."[52] Hamlet, the exemplary individual, is replaced by Hamm, whose "physical suffering…already places the living man among the corpses by reducing him to his body. Beckett stares at such things until the very everyday family life from which they are drawn pales into irrelevance."[53] According to Adorno, the disabled body in Beckett's works represents the materiality that is stubbornly irrecuperable by late capitalist ideology in its existentialist, and implicitly ableist form.

Without explicitly addressing the topic of caregiving, Adorno's analysis of *Endgame* responds to questions that have been taken up in caregiving debates. He points out that "[Hamm] is dependent on Clov because only Clov can still do the things necessary to keep them both alive. That, however, is of questionable value, because like the captain of the ghost ship both must fear that they will not be able to die."[54] For Adorno, Hamm's dependency on Clov contrasts with the individualism that is promoted by both existentialist philosophy and capitalist ideology. Instead, "the outlines of Hamm and Clov are drawn with a single line; the process of individuation into properly autonomous monads is denied them. They cannot live without one another. Hamm's power over Clov seems to rest on the fact that he is the only one who knows how to open the larder, much as only the head of the firm knows the combination of the safe."[55] Despite this dependency, Hamm and Clov fail to achieve the dialectical structure that Quayson and Davidson attribute to them. Adorno states,

> the Hegelian dialectic of master and servant, which Günther Anders discussed in relation to *Godot*, is not 'given form' in accordance with the tenets of traditional aesthetics so much as ridiculed. The servant is no longer capable of taking charge and doing away with domination. The mutilated Clov would scarcely be capable of doing it, and in any case, according to the historico-philosophical sundial of the play it is too late for spontaneous action.[56]

Rather than giving rise to a dialectic, the material reality that is expressed by Hamm and Clov's impairments impede their ability to achieve the confrontation that the master and slave dialectic requires. While Pozzo, Lucky, Hamm, and Clov intimate the roles of master and slave underpinning Hegel's model of the dialectic, Beckett also portrays the flattening of the dialectic beneath the weight of bodies and their needs.

By arguing that "the process of individuation into properly autonomous monads is denied"[57] to Hamm and Clov, the insights that Adorno draws from Beckett's drama resonates with Feder Kittay's dependency critique of equality. For Feder Kittay, liberal ideology promotes ideals of autonomy that conflict with the material reality of our interdependency, a fact that is especially foregrounded in contexts of disability, which results in the formation of subclasses of care workers who satisfy the care needs of some while being deprived of care themselves. Fraser attributes this asymmetry to a contradiction in the very structure of capitalism, whose functioning requires reproducing the ideological veneer of independence. Similarly, Adorno associates the reproduction of the individual as an ideological facet of late capitalism, which is effectively dismissed by Beckett's portrayals of characters who are incapable of independence. Late capitalism thus requires the production of slaves-qua-caregivers in order to keep its myth of individualism afloat. By claiming that Clov fails to attain the dignity of the slave in Hegel's dialectic, Adorno's reading of *Endgame* helps to show how the condition of slavery that Federici associates with housewives and caregivers relates to Beckett's drama. For Federici, housewives and caregivers belong to an underclass of workers whose exceptionality bars them from even the class struggle. Clov, even Lucky, embody this status in more Hegelian terms, since the tension in their portrayals is surrounded by the fact that they are exploited without the exploitation being registered in the worlds of each play. It is this tension in *Waiting for Godot* and *Endgame* that I have analyzed here, one that surrounds the conflict between our shared need for care and the ways that need is denied to those who do the caring. While the needs resulting from the caregivers' impairments in both plays are shown to the audience, those needs are effaced, and the caregivers are rendered abject. By viewing this dynamic from the perspective of Adorno, who interprets *Endgame* as a staging of the tension between late capitalist ideology and brute materiality, we can interpret Beckett's portrayals of caregiving as illustrations of the very contradiction that is at the heart of what Fraser identifies as capitalism's "crisis of care:" the myth of the able-bodied, independent worker depends on an underclass of labour that is exempt from care.

While caregiving is a relatively new topic in scholarly and political discourse, caregiving theorists have drawn attention to its longstanding urgency. *Waiting for Godot* and *Endgame* not only foreground the role of disability and impairment in care work, Beckett's plays also portray caregivers in ways that reflect the abjection and neglect that, according to many care theorists, define the lot of caregivers in late capitalist society. With this in mind, I claim that what underpins Beckett's plays is the same investment as that which has been driving activism in the world of caregiving over the past few decades— a desire for a just society whose basis lies in an awareness of our dependency in common.

Bibliography

Adorno, Theodor. "Trying to Understand *Endgame*." In *Notes To Literature, Volume Two*, translated by Shierry Weber Nicholsen. New York: Columbia University Press, 1992.

Beckett, Samuel. *Endgame and Act Without Words*. New York: Grove Press, 2009.

Beckett, Samuel. *Waiting for Godot* in *The Complete Dramatic Works of Samuel Beckett*. London: Faber & Faber, 2006.

Carlson, Licia and Eva Feder Kittay. "Introduction: Rethinking Philosophical Presumptions in Light of Cognitive Disability." In *Cognitive Disability and Its Challenge to Moral Philosophy*, edited by Licia Carlson and Eva Feder Kittay. Hoboken: Wiley, 2010.

Davidson, Michael. *Invalid Modernism*. Oxford: Oxford University Press, 2019.

Feder, Ellen K. and Eva Feder Kittay. "Introduction." In *The Subject of Care*, edited by Ellen K. Feder and Eva Feder Kittay. Boston Way: Rowman & Littlefield, 2002.

Feder Kittay, Eva. *Love's Labour: Essays on Women, Equality, and Dependency.* New York: Routledge, 1999.

Federici, Silvia. *Revolution at Point Zero: Housework, Reproduction, and Feminist Struggle.* Oakland: PM Press, 2012.

Federici, Silvia. *Wages Against Housework.* Bristol: Power of Women Collective and the Falling Wall Press, 1975.

Fraser, Nancy. "Contradictions of Capital and Care." *New Left Review* 100: pp. 99-117, 2016.

Garland-Thomson, Rosemarie. "The Case for Conserving Disability." *Bioethical Inquiry*, 9, no. 3: pp. 339-355, 2012.

Garland-Thomson, Rosemarie. "Integrating Disability, Transforming Feminist Theory." In *The Disability Studies Reader, Second Edition*, edited by Lennard Davis. New York: Routledge, 2006.

Hobart, Hi'ilei Julia Kawehipuaakahaopulani and Tamara Kneese. "Radical Care: Survival Strategies for Uncertain Times." *Social Text* 38, no. 1: pp. 1-16, 2020.

Quayson, Ato. *Aesthetic Nervousness.* New York: Columbia University Press, 2007.

Siebers, Tobin. *Disability Theory.* Ann Arbor: University of Michigan Press, 2011.

Van Gelder, Sarah. "The Radical Work of Healing: Fania and Angela Davis on a New Kind of Civil Rights Activism." *YES!* February 19, 2016, https://www.yesmagazine.org/issue/life-after-oil/2016/02/19/the-radical-work-of-healing-fania-and-angela-davis-on-a-new-kind-of-civil-rights-activism/.

Notes

[1] Samuel Beckett, *Waiting for Godot* in *The Complete Dramatic Works of Samuel Beckett* (London: Faber & Faber, 2006), 7-88. 30.

[2] Hi'ilei Julia Kawehipuaakahaopulani Hobart and Tamara Kneese, "Radical Care: Survival Strategies for Uncertain Times," *Social Text*, 38, no. 1 (2020): 1-16. 2.

[3] Ibid.

[4] Cited in Sarah Van Gelder, "The Radical Work of Healing: Fania and Angela Davis on a New Kind of Civil Rights Activism," *YES!* February 19, 2016, https://www.yesmagazine.org/issue/life-after-oil/2016/02/19/the-radical-work-of-healing-fania-and-angela-davis-on-a-new-kind-of-civil-rights-activism/.

[5] Silvia Federici, *Wages Against Housework* (Bristol: Power of Women Collective and the Falling Wall Press, 1975), 2.

[6] Ibid., 5.

[7] Ibid., 3-4.

[8] Nancy Fraser, "Contradictions of Capital and Care," *New Left Review* 100 (2016): 99-117. 102.

[9] Ibid., 100.

[10] Ibid., 101.

[11] Tobin Siebers, *Disability Theory* (Ann Arbor: University of Michigan Press, 2011), 4.

[12] Ibid., 8.

[13] Rosemarie Garland-Thomson, "Integrating Disability, Transforming Feminist Theory," in *The Disability Studies Reader, Second Edition*, edited by Lennard Davis (New York: Routledge, 2006), 257-273. 262.
[14] Rosemarie Garland-Thomson, "The Case for Conserving Disability," *Bioethical Inquiry*, 9, no. 3 (2012): 339-355, 342.
[15] "Integrating Disability, Transforming Feminist Theory," 265.
[16] Eva Feder Kittay, *Love's Labour: Essays on Women, Equality, and Dependency* (New York: Routledge, 1999), 65.
[17] Licia Carlson and Eva Feder Kittay, "Introduction: Rethinking Philosophical Presumptions in Light of Cognitive Disability," in *Cognitive Disability and Its Challenge to Moral Philosophy*, edited by Licia Carlson and Eva Feder Kittay (Hoboken: Wiley, 2010), 1-25. 10.
[18] Ellen K. Feder and Eva Feder Kittay, "Introduction," in *The Subject of Care*, edited by Ellen K. Feder and Eva Feder Kittay (Boston Way: Rowman & Littlefield, 2002), 1-12. 2-3.
[19] *Love's Labour*, 50.
[20] Silvia Federici, *Revolution at Point Zero: Housework, Reproduction, and Feminist Struggle* (Oakland: PM Press, 2012), 123.
[21] Ibid., 118.
[22] *The Subject of Care*, 6.
[23] Ibid., 8.
[24] *Waiting for Godot*, 27.
[25] Ibid., 30.
[26] Ibid., 81.
[27] Ibid., 70.
[28] Ibid., 32.
[29] Ibid.
[30] Ibid., 26.
[31] Ibid., 34.
[32] Ibid., 26-7.
[33] Samuel Beckett, *Endgame and Act Without Words* (New York: Grove Press, 2009), 14.
[34] Ibid., 32.
[35] Ibid., 16.
[36] Ibid., 43.
[37] Ato Quayson, *Aesthetic Nervousness* (New York: Columbia University Press, 2007), 28.
[38] Ibid., 55-6.
[39] Ibid., 53.
[40] Ibid., 67.
[41] Michael Davidson, *Invalid Modernism* (Oxford: Oxford University Press, 2019), 86.
[42] Ibid., 90.
[43] Ibid., 88.
[44] Ibid., 98-9.
[45] Quayson, 62.
[46] Davidson, 83.
[47] Theodor Adorno, "Trying to Understand Endgame," in *Notes To Literature, Volume Two*, translated by Shierry Weber Nicholsen (New York: Columbia University Press, 1992), 241-275. 241.
[48] Ibid., 243.

[49] Ibid., 244.
[50] Ibid., 252.
[51] Ibid.
[52] Ibid., 249.
[53] Ibid., 255.
[54] Ibid., 268-9.
[55] Ibid., 268.
[56] Ibid., 269.
[57] Ibid., 268.

Chapter 4

"But of course Rachel's illness is quite different": Reconfiguring the 'Medical' and 'Illness' in Virginia Woolf's *The Voyage Out*

Chloe Leung

University of Edinburgh, UK

Abstract: Scholarship on Woolf and medicine is replete with how illness feeds her genius or how depression perpetuates the melancholic aesthetic of her prose. I am, however, more interested in the very system that generates such a positive-negative dichotomy about illness narratives. Moving away from the popular example of *Mrs Dalloway*, this chapter explores how Woolf's debut novel *The Voyage Out* (1915) reshapes the notion of the "medical" and "illness." Although the novel is often dismissed as pre-modernist and juvenile, canny readers will not overlook how the novel prefigures some of her more "mature" consciousness representations and its complex treatment of illness. This chapter argues that "illness" in the novel outstrips the medical sense of the word. Drawing from disability studies, I argue that *Voyage* interrogates a normative and medical understanding of illness. If medicine cannot fully explain the connotations of "illness," Woolf's novel suggests other possibilities of how "illness" could manifest outside biomedicine. Focusing on the metaphor and language of pain, I explore how "illness" functions as a symptom of our thwarted desire to communicate anti-discursive phenomenon in both social and clinical contexts. I conclude by contending that Woolf's novel adopts a rigorous hermeneutic ambiguity that endorses an epistemic generosity in configuring approaches to therapeutic practice.

Keywords: Critical Medical Humanities, Disability Studies, illness, pain, medicine, narrative, Consciousness, therapy.

* * *

Illness and medicine haunt the work of Virginia Woolf. Ranging from Rachel Vinrace's fatal fever in *The Voyage Out* (1915), the shell-shocked soldier Septimus Smith in *Mrs Dalloway* (1925), Mrs. Rose Partiger's chronic illness in *The Years* (1937), the forlorn invalid in the essay "On Being Ill" (1926), and her own battle with manic depression in her diaries, Woolf implores that attention should be paid to the violence medicine and culture have inflicted upon the ill. In both *Voyage* and *Mrs Dalloway*, the figure of the doctor is condemned as amateurish, insensitive, and unkind. Closely knitted with the historical context in the late nineteenth-century, Woolf's novels depict how scientific advance has dehumanised medical practice: impelled by a Darwinian mission to improve the human race, physicians began to scrutinise patients as unfeeling organisms instead of as people. As *Mrs Dalloway* testifies, a tyrannical prescription of "health" and "proportion" coerces Septimus into the edges of madness and the abyss of death (Woolf 2005, 87). This dehumanisation of the patient is one reason why the narrator in "On Being Ill" demands that interest should be paid to "novel[s] devoted to influenza", novels that represent the patient's side of the medical narrative (Woolf 2009, 101). Woolf's incentive to give voice to the patient anticipates the rise of the medical humanities in the late 1980s. Reacting against the apotheosis of science in therapeutic practice, Arthur Kleinman's *The Illness Narratives* (1988) has galvanised awareness concerning the other side of the medical narrative— the "story the patient tells" (Kleinman 1988, 49). Kleinman and other advocates of medical humanities assert the ethical imperative to reanimate the patient's voice in clinical diagnoses. However, and as Woolf herself was aware, such a narrative approach to medicine is fraught with difficulties. As the narrator in "On Being Ill" laments, there is a "poverty of language" in wording pain.[1] Even when we render weight to the patient's narrative, the patient's experiences remain too ineffable for language to accommodate. As I will show in this chapter, pain's ineffability often yields to its over-representation, which perpetuates painful sensations when patients communicate symptoms to their doctors. While the Medical Humanities has attempted to redress the balance in the doctor-patient relationship, its approach remained passive in alleviating the patient's pain.

Reflecting upon its shortcomings, the Medical Humanities has enforced a more critical framework. In the past decade, the critical Medical Humanities has emerged to ameliorate the theory and praxis of mainstream medical humanities. These critics seek to expand this conversation from the narrow field of medicine by encouraging interactions with political, social, cultural, and ethical contexts. As William Viney et al. sum up succinctly, the critical medical humanities is "a widening of the sites and the scales of 'the medical' beyond the primal scene of the clinical encounter".[2] Rather than configuring its research as "*useful* to biomedicine" (Fitzgerald 2016, 35), Jane

Macnaughton and Havi Carel contend that the critical medical humanities move away from "an exclusively instrumental approach" and seeks to investigate "a clinical culture that itself remains unexamined" (*The Edinburgh Companion*, 296). One way of enforcing this project, Brian Hurwitz and Victoria Bates suggest, is to "deploy narrative contextually in ways attuned to the needs of individuals" (*The Edinburgh Companion*, 8). Involving narrative with medicine is "to recognise that people who are ill or think themselves ill locate concerns and symptoms— often disjointedly— in interpersonal and social networks of meaning that are in different stages of formation" (8). That is, the narrative aspect in the medical humanities does not only concern *what* the patient says, but also *why* they say them. This chapter will follow Hurwitz's and Bates' inquiry in contemplating the role of (modernist) narrative in its weaving together of political, social, interpersonal, and bio-scientific networks in configuring illness.

To carry this conversation beyond "the primal scene of the clinical encounter", this chapter will also engage with how disability studies inform the socio-political and the narrative aspect of "the medical". Contemporary to the medical humanities, disability studies came into fashion around the 1970s to 1980s. In Lennard J. Davis' seminal work *Enforcing Normalcy*, Davis argues that the study of disability is primarily a study of a socially and historically-contrived norm. "[O]ur construction of the normal world", Davis contends, is "based on a radical repression of disability" (Davis 1995, 22) and more broadly, the idea of deviance. The idea of "norm" and "deviance" emerged during 1840 to 1860 from statistics. The norm "pins down that majority of the population that falls under the arch of the standard bell-shaped curve" (29). The discourse of normality thus ensures that "the majority of the population must or should somehow be part of the norm" (29). Such a concept is later migrated from political science to medicine, as physicians utilised the bell curve to "illustrate the natural history of health and disease" (29). Since then, the application of normative statistics has become naturalised in the medical practice. The "medical" has thus been implicitly politicised: "As soon as we use the term 'disabled' we add a political element: suddenly there is a disabler and a disabled" (10). This tenet of disability studies to reassess normative narrative dovetails with that of the Medical Humanities. Medical Humanities shares the same objective to re-evaluate the notions of health and normality: as soon as we use the term "illness", there would be a patient and an authority that deem them ill. In the context of literature, disability critics David Mitchell's and Sharon Synder's *Narrative Prosthesis* have examined how disability "has been used throughout history as a crutch upon which literary narratives lean for their representational power, disruptive potentiality, and analytical insight" (49). Aside from functioning as representational or thematic tropes, Mitchell and Synder draw attention to how literature has been deploying disability as a rhetorical and narrative strategy. With reference to the intertextualities between the critical medical humanities and disability studies, this chapter scaffolds an interdisciplinary theoretical ground, addressing the medical crises that populate Woolf's work.

While scholarship on Woolf and medicine abound, the reciprocity between medical ethics and her modernist literary aesthetics has gathered less attention than it deserves. Criticism on this topic is replete with how Woolf's illness feeds her genius,[3] or how her depression perpetuates the melancholic aesthetic of her prose.[4] I am, however, more interested in the very system that generates the positive-negative dichotomy in narratives about illness. I will move away from the repeatedly deployed example of *Mrs Dalloway* and examine Woolf's debut novel, *The Voyage Out* (1915). *Voyage* is an (anti)bildungsroman tracing the young Rachel Vinrace's expedition to South America and her stymied and fatal voyage of self-discovery. Although the novel is often dismissed as pre-modernist and juvenile, the novel's complex treatment of illness has eluded mainstream criticism. I argue that Woolf's discussion of "illness" in the novel outstrips the medical sense of the word, for Rachel's illness interrogates a normative understanding of illness constructed by the medical narrative. In effect, the novel deploys illness as a rhetorical strategy in deflecting the pathology of our presumptive manner in upholding the status quo of normality in the context of therapy. If medicine cannot fully explain the connotations of "illness", Woolf's novel suggests other possibilities of what "illness" could look like outside the medical purview. Focusing on the metaphor and language of pain, I explore how "illness" functions as a symptom of our thwarted desire to communicate incomprehensible phenomenon in both social and clinical contexts. I conclude by indicating that Woolf's novel adopts a rigorous hermeneutic ambiguity that promulgates an epistemic generosity in configuring approaches to therapeutic practice.

While critics such as Kimberly Coates have explored the productivity of illness in Woolf's work,[5] I suggest that *Voyage* does not so much explore the positive (or negative) connotations of illness as it does to conceptualise illness as a rhetorical strategy. Such a strategy does not invert the hierarchy between health and illness but subverts narrative and ideological assumptions. In other words, it asks us to reflect upon how concepts such as "illness" and "health" acquire their connotations in the first place. In this sense, I propose that Woolf's deployment of illness coordinates with the tenets of disability studies— one that seeks to expose "disabled" or "ill" bodies as "an ideology of thinking about the body" that is naturalised by the society's construction of a "normal" world (*Narrative Prosthesis*, 2). Above all, disability studies aim at "institut[ing] alternative ways of thinking about the abnormal" (*Enforcing Normalcy*, 49). Rather than asking "what is wrong with this patient?" then, disability studies probe the question: "Why do we think that this person is disabled or ill?" If, as "On Being Ill" suggests, Woolf wishes to alleviate the cultural oppression of the ill or disabled/deviant bodies, her deployment of illness in *Voyage* must venture beyond an invasive politics that would only perpetuate such oppression. She must break through and examine the system that reproduces the implicitly political notions of "illness" and "normality". In *Narrative Prosthesis*, Mitchell and Synder ponder on Woolf's cruel portrayal of disabled individuals in *A Room of One's Own*. Quoting the passage in which Woolf "complains that society rates women's abilities even below those of crippled men in the great ladder of existence", Mitchell and Synder wonder: "How might we interpret her squabbles over the invalid pronouncements of men with disabilities on women's writing?" (*Narrative Prosthesis*, 2). In other words, can a self-discriminating representation of the ill function to check the medical profession whom she distrusts?

A study of Woolf's "On Being Ill" will elucidate why Woolf hesitates to endorse narratives of the ill/disabled in the novel. In effect, Woolf refuses to participate in a celebratory but ultimately self-oppressive recovery discourse. Criticism on Woolf and illness favours the positive role of illness on her creativity. However, such a framework remains incarcerated in a narrative of "recovery", a discourse that ostracises ill bodies as "deviant". Janine Utell, for instance, has argued for the restorative function of writing about her illness in managing Woolf's symptoms: "writing can be restorative for a subject grappling with how she has been othered within the context of her most intimate relationships and everyday life" (Utell 2016, 27). Utell adds that for Woolf, "[t]he nature of the everyday is thus changed as illness becomes the everyday" (29). While Woolf has expressed how the therapy of writing "make[s] [her] whole" in "A Sketch of the Past", she is equally hesitant to designate too much positivity in how her illness feeds creativity (Woolf 1985, 72). In endorsing a positive function of illness, Angela Woods posits Woolf as a participant in the discourse of recovery, a discourse that can "silence and exclude, by privileging and valuing certain kinds of reasoning and knowledge" (Woods 2019, 2). Under the recovery discourse, bodies that "fail" to recover are implicitly discriminated against or obviated. Although both "On Being Ill" and *Voyage* have dedicated passages that detail the idiosyncratic vision illness generates, Woolf is simultaneously self-conscious about the danger of an overly-romanticising perspective. The following passage in "On Being Ill" is often compared to a scene in *Voyage*, where Rachel revels in her slanted vision endowed by illness. Like Rachel, the narrator in "On Being Ill" marvels at the new-found scenery her bed rests make available:

> This then has been going on all the time without our knowing it! – this incessant making up of shapes and casting them down, this buffeting of clouds together, and drawing vast trains of ships and wagons from North to South, this incessant ringing up and down of curtains of light and shade [...] – this endless activity, with the waste of Heaven knows how many million horse power of energy, has been left to work its will year in year out. (Woolf *Selected Essays*, 105)

While the narrator appreciates the candid beauty of the vision, she refuses to romanticise it: "Divinely beautiful it is also divinely heartless" (105). Such a "frozen" and "stiff" perspective, Woolf's narrator laments, "has nothing to do with human pleasure or profit" (105). Instead of dwelling on the beauty of the vision, the narrator suggests that we should focus on the "truth" that illness confesses: "There is, let us confess it (and illness is the great confessional) a childish outspokenness in illness; things are blurted out, which the cautious respectability of health conceals" (104). In particular, illness elucidates the "make-believe" of normal people "in health" to sustain a "genial pretence" of everyday life (104). Woolf takes the notion of "sympathy" as an example of this daily pretence. She argues that sympathy is both impossible and undesirable: "That illusion of a world so shaped that it echoes every grown, of human beings so tied together by common needs and fears..." (104). For, each of us possesses an idiosyncratic "virgin forest" that no soul, perhaps including our own, has ever treaded (104). It is thus apt to conclude that: "Always to have sympathy, always to be accompanied, always to be understood would be intolerable. But in health, the genial pretence must be kept up and the effort renewed— to communicate, to civilise, to share, to cultivate the desert, educate the native, to work by day together and by night to sport" (104). For Woolf, illness bespeaks truths that refer not so much to the beauty of the slanted vision as to an ill operation of the "law" of "the normal" (109).

In Lennard J. Davis's *Enforcing Normalcy*, Davis poignantly identifies the pathology of normality as a desire to narrativize and police "strange" behaviour and bodies. The notion of "normal", Davis argues, is "heavily medicalised" (2). As discussed, medicine has borrowed the idea of "norm" from political science to measure the human body. Enthroned as the authoritative taxonomy of health, Davis criticises that the discourse of normality (and by extension, a "normal" recovery narrative arch) "failed to understand dialectically its own position in the economy of power and control, and it failed to historicise its own assumptions and agency" (2). In other words, the very categorisation of "normal bodies" and "disabled/ill bodies" entails a power dynamic that the medical narrative conveniently conceals. It reveals how our culture deems disability/illness as a deviant or a strange phenomenon— in Mitchell's and Synder's words— "an unknown or unnatural device that begs an explanation"

(*Narrative Prosthesis*, 53). Habitually, we single out the bodies that do not comply with the norm and demand a diagnosis/explanation for them. "The very need of a story" for disability, Mitchell and Synder continue, originated from the ways in which our culture seeks to "comprehend that which has stepped out of line" (53). The fact that illness exists as a narrative moment flaunts the imposition of normalcy, which stigmatises bodies that do not satisfy its standards as "strange".

In *Voyage*, Woolf refuses to have this stigma of strangeness reconciled or contained by any recognisable narrative. Even before her diagnosis, Rachel is haunted by a sense of strangeness that, rather than having it explained away by medical symptoms or any specific reason, she knows she must hold on to. An "unspeakable queerness" first strikes Rachel as she is sitting on her armchair in a morning (Woolf 2004, 128). The eccentric sensation is associated with how Rachel is suddenly arrested by an acute "consciousness of her own existence". Her surroundings are estranged, for she does not know how to navigate this new-found consciousness about the "normal" world. This strangeness returns as Rachel observes the people around her:

> For the methods by which she had reached her present position, seemed to her *very strange*, and *the strangest thing* about them was that she had not known where they were leading her. That was *the strange thing*, that one did not know where one was going, or what one wanted, and followed blindly, suffering so much in secret, always unprepared and amazed and knowing nothing… (Italics my emphasis, 335)

Rachel notices how her aunt, the Dalloways, and her father— found "satisfaction and meaning" in the "pattern" of life, and how such meaning is denied to her. Paradoxically, this sense of strangeness offers Rachel a clarity upon life which a complacent mind knows "nothing" about. While this strangeness is unsettling, Woolf suggests that the alternative of "follow[ing] [the norm] blindly" and "suffering so much in secret" are more hazardous options. In clutching to the enigma that this strangeness invokes, Rachel refuses to be narrativized by the discourse of normality. Anticipating Davis' interrogation of normality through "problematic" behaviour and bodies, Woolf quarantines herself from prescribed narratives such as a recovery one. As Davis puts it, "the 'problem'" is not the person with disabilities; the problem is the way that normalcy is constructed to create the 'problem' of the disabled person" (*Enforcing Normalcy*, 24). For, even if disability/illness is "cured", such a narrative could be reconfigured as the new norm. This impetus of seeking cure would only bolster the policing of other bodies that fall outside of the normative recovery narrative. Woolf's resistance to a conventional reading of illness must thus be thorough— it must extirpate narratives that presume non-normative bodies as pathological. Rather than, as Utell contends, arguing that illness has become Woolf's "everyday", it would be more precise to conclude that *illness permeates the discourse of the everyday*— the ways in which it indicates as society's allergic reaction to deviant bodies and thoughts.

With the presence of illness in the everyday, I suggest that illness in Woolf's novel functions as a rhetoric rather than as a representational or thematic device. Specifically, I contend that illness serves as a proxy for the problems of our unreflective faith in cultural discourses, including but not limited to that of the medical and the normal. The notion of normality, as Mitchell and Synder emphasise, implies enforcement of a power discourse that represses deviant bodies and behaviour. They lament that although narratives have been rendering more attention to this problem by using the disabled individual as "a symbolic figure", these narratives "rarely take up disability as an experience of social or political dimension" (*Narrative Prosthesis*, 48). If, however, literary narratives tend to under-develop this politics of disability and illness, Woolf's novel almost over-develops this agenda in its deployment of illness to deflect social problems. For instance, the novel's refusal to fashion a name for Rachel's illness suggests that the implications of illness are not limited to the medical sense of the word. In an earlier draft of *Voyage* titled *Melymbrosia* (1912), it is implied that Terence is more informed with the specificity of Rachel's illness, an information the narrative withholds: "He vaguely expected that it would go as suddenly as it came, and the stories which were told him in abundance of illnesses like hers conveyed little in him. 'But of course Rachel's illness is quite different'" (Woolf 527). The claim that Rachel's illness is "quite different" suggests that Terence may possess extra intelligence about the details of this illness, details that are denied to readers. Tellingly, this excerpt is deleted in *Voyage*. Rachel's illness is only referred to by Terence as "serious illness of this kind" and "illness like this" (Woolf, *The Voyage Out*, 360-361). For Woolf, perhaps this implication of Terence's knowledge still reveals too much underlying certainty about Rachel's diagnosis. The editing of the above passage shows Woolf consciously withholds the surplus meaning of illness in the novel. Although a more specific diagnosis of Rachel's illness emerges after her death, the diagnosis remains a pseudo one. Contemplating their loss, Rachel has, Susan remarks, died of "the fever" she catches in the American jungle (385). Arthur regrets that they should not have gone to the tropical forest, since one "can't expect an Englishwoman to stand roughing it as the natives do who've been acclimatised" (384). Both Susan's and Arthur's "diagnosis" seems to reveal more about their prejudices of the South American primitiveness than about Rachel's condition. Disentangling illness from the medical, Woolf's novel depicts nebulous consciousness surplus meanings for illness that are irreducible to "positive" or "negative" readings. To escape an incarcerating and normative framework in narrativizing illness, Woolf thus deploys "illness" as a rhetoric tool for interrogating the medical system of diagnosis, a rhetoric that resists any narrativizable and discursive explanation about deviant bodies.

Illness Metaphor and the Language of Pain

As Terence teases, the aetiology of "illness" in *Voyage* lies beyond biomedical knowledge. Looking at the manifestation of pain, I will show how the expanded connotation of illness metaphorizes other sufferings that Woolf's protagonists refuse to or are unable to confront. I will refer to the generation of these new meanings of illness as "illness metaphor", a strategy that substitutes illness as symptoms of the discursive failure in describing, understanding, and communicating pain. To clarify what I mean by illness metaphor, I refer to Susan Sontag's use of the word in *Illness as a Metaphor*. With the examples of tuberculosis and cancer, for instance, Sontag suggests that we use metaphors to substitute for explanation about illnesses that we do not understand. In the case of cancer, we metaphorize it as the "obscen[e]" and the "ill-omen[ted]" (Sontag 1977, 9). However, Sontag predicts that "by the time we can identify a cause or cure for cancer, perhaps nobody will want any longer to compare anything awful to cancer. Since the interest of the metaphor is precisely that it refers to a disease so overlaid with mystification, so charged with the fantasy of inescapable fatality" (87). In other words, illness operates as a metaphorical proxy for explaining phenomenon that we are yet to comprehend.

Expanding upon Sontag's deployment of metaphor, I locate "pain" as the cryptic content that resists comprehension in Woolf's novel. As Woolf notes in her diary, her illness is always haunted by a mysterious aura that sensualises pain: "these illnesses are in my case— how shall I express it? —partly mystical. Something happens in my mind. It refuses to go registering impressions. It shuts itself up. It becomes a chrysalis. I lie quite torpid, often with acute physical pain— as last year; only discomfort this. Then something springs" (Woolf 1981, 150). In *Voyage*, Rachel's first symptom of her "painful" headache is similarly measured by an inexplicable "strange[ness]" akin to Woolf's "mystical" pain (Woolf *The Voyage Out*, 348). As Rachel listens to Terence's reading of Milton, she notices how "it was painful to listen" since "[the words] sounded strange" (348). This sense of strangeness pervades: "Owing to the heat and the dancing air the garden too looked strange— the trees were either too near or too far, and her head most certainly ached" (348). It is in failing to account for strangeness that Rachel subsequently ascribes it to and verbalises it as pain: "My head aches…" (348). This metaphorical verbalisation of pain is inextricably bound up with how illness is brought into a state of affair, for it is when we observe that there is pain or discomfort in our bodies that we visit the doctors, who subsequently diagnose us as ill. In referring to illness metaphor then, I do not seek to configure a simple analogy that delineates how illness metaphorically deflects other problems. Rather, I draw on the phenomenon of pain and Sontag's definition of "metaphor" in approaching how illness functions as a narrative substitute for phenomenon, people, or objects that we yearn to explain yet do not comprehend.

In *Illness as Method*, Jayjit Sarkar has mentioned the "metaphorica[l]" association between illness, medicine, and disability: "In modern medical discourse the voice of the sufferer remains unacknowledged and, quite often, the muteness of the sufferer mingles with the deafness of the healer" (Sarkar 2019, 40). My use of metaphor here, however, differs from that of Sarkar's. While Sarkar suggests a literary analogy between the doctor-patient miscommunications and their respective disabilities, I am less interested in this image of disabled participants than in how metaphors clarify the socio-political relations that are bound up with medicine. In this sense, my use of illness metaphor corresponds to Des Fitzgerald's and Felicity Callard's account of "a new metaphor" in the critical medical humanities (Fitzgerald "Entangling", 41). In "Entangling the Medical Humanities", Fitzgerald and Callard contend that metaphors help to delineate the "sets of as yet undermined material-semiotic configurations and alignments (bodily, pathological, cultural, human, and so on)" that correspond to and entwine with medical bioscience (41). Fitzgerald and Callard continue: "Thus the issue is not that illness and healing are multi-faceted phenomena that cannot be understood from a clinical perspective only [...] The issue is that what we get enacted, positioned and understood as moments of suffering, sickness, care, and so on are always in the process of being cut from particular sets of relations" (42). These sets of relations, I suggest, unfold in the metaphorical expression and representation of pain in Woolf's novel. Building upon Sontag's and the medical humanities' metaphorical approach, I thus distinguish "illness metaphor" with the literary kind that Sarkar exemplifies. In critiquing Rachel's and Terence's representation of pain, however, I will draw on the language of literary metaphors in their proliferation of pain in illness.

The ineffable nature of pain illuminates Rachel's compulsive desire to articulate and communicate pain to others, a foiled desire that qualifies the "painful" in pain as failures of communication. As Woolf notes in "On Being Ill", pain resists linguistic descriptions: "English, which can express the thoughts of Hamlet and the tragedy of Lear, has no words for the shiver and the headache" (Woolf *Selected Essays*, 102). This impossibility to word pain, Sara Ahmed argues, engenders a desire to over-represent pain: "I may not be able to describe 'adequately' the feelings of pain, and yet I may evoke my pain, again and again, as something that I have" (Ahmed 2014, 22). Such overcompensating description of pain is particularly attracted to metaphorical language, in which one concept is explained and regenerated through another, *ad infimum*. As Elaine Scarry argues, the language of pain often occupies a metaphorical "as-if" structure where two "problematic" metaphors are at work: "The first specifies an external agent of the pain, a weapon that is pictured as producing the pain; and the second specifies bodily damage that is pictured as accompanying the pain" (Scarry 1985, 15). These two metaphors are deployed in the descriptions of Rachel's headache, a sensation that is imagined to operate firstly by a knife, and secondly, by the bodily damage of being stabbed: "She shut her eyes, and the pulse in her head beat so strongly that each thump seemed to tread upon a nerve, piercing her forehead with a little stab of pain" (Woolf *The Voyage Out*, 349). The metaphorical language pain occupies suggests how pain and illness substitute for indescribable phenomena that thrives on its over-representation. This repetitive obsession to ontologise pain through metaphors, Scarry suggests, is one way in which human beings assert certainty especially when confronted with crises: When a society is confronted with "a crisis of belief", Scarry notes, "the sheer material factualness of the human body will be borrowed to lend that cultural construct the aura of 'realness' and 'certainty'" (Scarry *The Body* 14). Since "pain comes unsharably into our midst as at once that which cannot be denied and that which cannot be confirmed", it stands for an unassailable certainty that anchors our existence especially under upheavals (4). Because of its function as a proxy for other crises, Scarry also refers to the language of pain as an "analogical verification" (14).

It is now apparent that pain, far from being an ontological feeling that is "there" in the first place, is a phenomenon that we repeatedly and metaphorically call into existence for the desire to establish certainty. The "reality" of pain then, is not justified by its often-misunderstood ontology, but in how we relentlessly hail it into an on-going event. In the self-asserting act that is manifested in our metaphorical explanations of pain, we thus proliferate surfaces for physical sensations that are themselves *neutral changes* in the first place. As Ahmed puts it, there is in pain, simply a "sense" that of "intensification and a departure from what is lived as ordinary" (*The Cultural*, 27). To be sure, the sensations of phenomena such as headache exist— but they only exist simply as neutral changes in bodily behaviour. From here, it is not difficult to discern how the discourse of normality actively shapes the experience of pain: Pain becomes "painful" when we unconsciously calibrate certain bodily sensations as "normal" and others as "abnormal". These upheavals in our body only become "painful" when we decide that they are "abnormal" feelings, when we become conscious of them, and when we explain them repeatedly with metaphors, expressions that can never adequately justify our feelings. To put it bluntly, what is "painful" in pain is the unbearable sensation of miscommunication. If "pain", and subsequently illness, metaphorizes the thwarted attempts at asserting certainty and at communication, then what qualifies as "illness" must transcend biomedical knowledge, for it depends upon interpersonal relations and abstracted sensations encrypted and perpetuated by metaphors.

In *Voyage*, Woolf suggests that Rachel's "illness" is a consequence of the interpersonal interactions within the medical experience, an "illness" that a scientific interpretation of pain might not be able to explain. Specifically, Woolf's novel presents pain through language and as a masochistic self-fulfilling prophecy, a prophecy that seeks authorisation from the assumed certainty of medical science. Previously, we have seen how Rachel's headache metaphorizes an unexplainable strangeness. By verbally communicating her pain to Terence, Woolf's novel illustrates how pain occupies a linguistic infection that travels to the doctors, who in turn, reaffirms the patient's initial reading of the signal of pain. Rachel's metaphor of pain "infects" Terence, whose first reaction is to "repea[t]" her language: "Your head aches?" (Woolf 2004, 348). Terence is subsequently overwhelmed by "a sense of dismay" that is "almost physically painful" (348). This pain continues to proliferate through metaphors: "all round him he seemed to hear the shiver of broken glass which, as it fell to earth, left him sitting in the open air" (348-349). Terence's second reaction is to communicate this pain to others as he "fetched Helen" and "asked her to tell them what they had better do" (349). Soon after, the anxiety of pain and illness is spread around the family, who then summon Dr. Rodriguez and later Dr. Lesage. In managing the sensation that Rachel is "not quite certain" of, such an uncertainty becomes contagious through language (348). As Scarry notes, "[b]ecause the person in pain is ordinarily so bereft of the resources of speech, it is not surprising that the language for pain should sometimes be brought into being by those who are not themselves in pain but who speak *on behalf of* those who are" (*The Body* 6). In calling the doctors, Rachel and her family are essentially seeking for an affirmation from the doctor of their own pseudo-diagnosis— that Rachel is "ill".

With Rodriguez, although Terence is "determined that Helen was exaggerating" and "that Rachel was not very ill", implicit in his anxiety is his desire that Rodriguez would affirm his suspicion about Rachel (Woolf *The Voyage Out*, 359). As the narrator puts it, "he wanted a third person to confirm him in his belief" that Rachel is ill (359). When Rodriguez fails the task, claiming that "[t]here is no reason for anxiety", Terence immediately demonised Rodriguez: "His confidence in the man vanished as he looked at him and saw his insignificance, his dirty appearance, his shiftiness, and his unintelligent, hairy face. It was strange that he had never seen this before" (359). James Aho and Kevin Aho explain this conflicting psychology to trust and distrust the doctor through the pun of the word "dis-ease": "Illness can be viewed as a clumsy, often misunderstood, a protolanguage' by which I convey my 'dis-ease' with the world" (*Body Matters* 61). Struck by his "dis-ease" of anxiety, Rodriguez's diagnosis is both *an ease* and *a disease* for Terence. As Aho and Aho put it, "the disease is not so much what I have, but what I do. It is a 'surrogate truth'" (62). For Terence, this "truth" stands for his belief that Rachel is unfortunately ill, a certainty that he is not ready to relinquish despite his hopes for Rachel's recovery. Medical diagnosis thus functions as the self-fulfilling prophecy with which Terence, through the contagion of metaphorical language, seeks to satisfy his self-inflicted "dis-ease" he contracted from Rachel's verbalisation of pain. With Rodriguez, however, this prophecy fails.

When Rodriguez's unprofessional demeanour fails to assure them of Rachel's condition, the family replaces him with a French doctor Dr. Lesage. Yet, like Rodriguez, Lesage's diagnosis and instructions have meant nothing, for the diagnosis has already been made on the part of the family: "Coming downstairs he gave his directions emphatically, but it never occurred to him to give an opinion either because of the presence of Rodriguez who was now obsequious as well as malicious, or because he took it for granted that they knew already what was to be known" (Woolf *The Voyage Out*, 364). In another visit, Lesage, noticing Terence's "certain[n]" belief that Rachel is not dying, compromises his verdict "[t]o Terence's demand" (369). As Rachel's hallucinations heighten, Terence waits for Lesage "with the same certainty at the back of his mind that he would in time force them all to admit that they were in the wrong" (369). As a result, Lesage addresses Terence: "'She seems to be better?' he replied, looking at him in an odd way, 'She has a chance of life'" (369-370). However, such optimism falls short of alleviating Terence's pain. If anything, Lesage's words of reassurance render Terence's pain even more visible: "A fortnight ago she had been perfectly well. What could fourteen days have done to bring her from that state to this? To realise what they meant by saying that he had a chance of life was beyond him" (370). As such, regardless of the doctor's verdict, the diagnosis would be dismissed if it does not match Terence's expectations: On the one hand, Terence wishes the doctors would deny Rachel's illness. On the other, he also wishes them to justify and be complicit in his anxiety. This frustrated encounter between doctor and patients (both Terence and Rachel) qualifies the "pain" in Rachel's illness, a mode of suffering that is disseminated across the family and especially in Terence. In sum, from Rachel's very decision to explain her "pain", she traumatises herself along with Terence by exposing themselves to the infection of metaphors, expressions that are necessarily frustrated and thus "painful". Pain is further proliferated with the doctors' input, who either re-traumatises them by affirming their pain or inflicts further pain by failing to comply with their impossible desire of self-assertion. Reading illness metaphor with the doctor-patient interaction, *Voyage* suggests that pain and illness might not need a scientific explanation even in the medical context. Rather, pain and illness are ontologised by a desire for self-certainty, a certainty that the patient hopes a medical diagnosis would authorise.

In suggesting that Rachel's illness eludes medical knowledge, this chapter neither means to obviate the invaluable technologies medicine has contributed to humanity nor to replace medicine with a "narrative therapy". For such a diagnosis would only repeat the ills of a hubristic and deterministic medicine that Woolf scorns. Rather than following a medical or a textual determinism, *Voyage* confronts readers with unorthodox hermeneutics of the fictional and the socio-cultural narratives in life. With its refusal to stigmatise strangeness, *Voyage* puts forth an anti-narrativized narrative technique that enables— rather than disables — heterogeneous ways of reading and tackling illness. As the novel's illness metaphor suggests, illness lies not so much in the sensation of "pain" itself but in how we react towards it. Even within the medical setting, *Voyage* indicates that pain and illness involve a complex web of (inter)personal relations and judgments that a scientific medical narrative might not accommodate. Woolf's novel exemplifies an anti-discursive stance towards pain and "strange" phenomenon, maintaining a scepticism towards whether unorthodox human behaviour and bodies could be conveniently diagnosed as problematic and "ill".

References

Ahmed, Sara. 2014. *The Cultural Politics of Emotion*. Edinburgh: Edinburgh UP.

Aho, James, and Kevin Aho. 2008. *Body Matters: A Phenomenology of Sickness, Disease, and Illness*. New York: Rowman & Littlefield Publishers, Inc.

Coates, Kimberly Engdahl. 2012. "Phantoms, Fancy (and) Symptoms: Virginia Woolf and the Art of Being Ill". *Woolf Studies Annual*, 18: pp. 1-28. https://search-proquest-com.ezproxy.is.ed.ac.uk/docview/1465247391?accountid=10673&rfr_id=info%3Axri%2Fsid%3Aprimo. Accessed 1 March 2020.

Davis, Lennard J. 1995. *Enforcing Normalcy: Disability, Deafness, and the Body*. London: Verso.

Fitzgerald, Des and Felicity Callard. 2016. "Entangling the Medical Humanities". *The Edinburgh Companion to the Critical Medical Humanities*, edited by Sarah Atkinson, Anne Whitehead, and Angela Woods. Edinburgh: Edinburgh UP.

Hurwitz, Brian, and Victoria Bates. 2016. "The Roots and Ramifications of Narrative in Modern Medicine". *The Edinburgh Companion to the Critical Medical Humanities*, edited by Anne Whitehead, Angela Woods, Sarah Atkinson, Jane Macnaughton, and Jennifer Richards. Edinburgh: Edinburgh UP.

Macnaughton, Jane and Havi Carel. 2016. "Breathing and Breathlessness in Clinic and Culture: Using Critical Medical Humanities to Bridge an Epistemic Gap." In *The Edinburgh Companion to the Critical Medical Humanities*, edited by Anne Whitehead, Angela Woods, Sarah Atkinson, Jane Macnaughton, and Jennifer Richards. Edinburgh: Edinburgh UP.

Mitchell, David, and Sharon L. Synder. 2000. *Narrative Prosthesis: Disability and the Dependencies of Discourse*. Michigan: University of Michigan.

Sarkar, Jayjit. 2019. *Illness as Method: Beckett, Kafka, Mann, Woolf, and Eliot*. Wilmington, DE: Vernon Press.

Scarry, Elaine. 1985. *The Body in Pain: The Making and Unmaking of the World*. Oxford: Oxford UP.

Sontag, Susan. 1977. *Illness as Metaphor*. New York: Farrar Straus Giroux.

Utell, Jane. 2016. "View from the Sickroom: Virginia Woolf, Dorothy Wordsworth, and Writing Women's Lives of Illness." *Life Writing: Body Language: Illness, Disability, and Life Writing* 13, no. 1: pp.27-45. DOI: 0.1080/14484528.2014.895927. Accessed 10 March 2020.

Viney, William., Felicity Callard, and Angela Woods. 2015. "Critical Medical Humanities: Embracing Entanglements, Taking Risks." *BMJ Publishing Group Ltd and Institute of Medical Ethics* 41, no.1: p. 2. DOI:10.1136/ medhum-2015-010692. Accessed 19 March 2020.

Woods, Angela et al. 2019. "The Recovery Narrative: Politics and Possibilities of a Genre". *Culture, Medicine and Psychiatry* 13: pp. 1-27. DOI: 10.1007/s11013-019-09623-y. Accessed 13 December 2019.

Woolf, Virginia. 1998. *A Room of One's Own and Three Guineas*. Oxford: Oxford University.

———. 1981. *A Writer's Diary*. New York: Harcourt Inc.

———. 1985. "A Sketch of the Past". In *Moments of Being: A Collection of Autobiographical Writing*, edited by Jeanne Schulkind. New York: Harcourt Inc.

———. 2002. *Melymbrosia*, edited by Louise A. DeSalvo. New Jersey: Cleis Press Inc.

———. 1985. *Moments of Being*. New York: Harcourt Inc.

———. 2005. *Mrs Dalloway*. London: Vintage.

———. 2009. *Selected Essays*, edited by David Bradshaw. Oxford: Oxford UP.

———. 2004. *The Voyage Out*. London: Vintage.

Notes

[1] "There is nothing ready made for him. He is forced to coin words himself, and, taking his pain in one hand, and a lump of pure sound in the other (as perhaps the inhabitants of Babel did in the beginning) so to crush them together that a brand-new word in the end drops out" (*Selected Essays* 2009, 102).

[2] William Viney et al., "Critical Medical Humanities: Embracing Entanglements, Taking Risks". *BMJ Publishing Group Ltd and Institute of Medical Ethics* 41, no. 1 (2015): p. 2. DOI:10.1136/medhum-2015-010692. Accessed 19 March 2020.

³ See Kimberly Engdahl Coates's "Phantoms, Fancy (and) Symptoms: Virginia Woolf and the Art of Being Ill" and Thomas C. Caramango's *The Flight of the Mind: Virginia Woolf's Art and Manic-Depressive Illness*.

⁴ See Seyedeh Sara Ahou Ghalandari's and Leila Baradaran Jamili's "Mental Illness and Manic-Depressive Illness in Virginia Woolf's Mrs. Dalloway" and Nancy Topping Bazin's "Virginia Woolf's Quest for Equilibrium".

⁵ In "Phantoms, Fancy (and) Symptoms: Virginia Woolf and the Art of Being Ill", Coates ascribes Woolf's creative genius to her illness, which "generates a heightened state of awareness that cannot be learned" (Coates 2012, 9).

Chapter 5

"Between Horror and Hunger": Reflections on the Medical Poems of Miroslav Holub

Anik Sarkar

Salesian College, India

Abstract: A "curious mixture," poet-immunologist Miroslav Holub is unusual in his approach to poetry. As a man of reason, it may seem that Holub resists romantic impulses, while on the contrary, he relishes it with a scientific temperament. His juxtapositions of real and the impossible give way to metaphors that he uses as a "hypothesis, an instrument for testing experience through conjecture and experiment." Because of his belief that there exists in science, a wide body of imagination, away from all-encompassing theories and laboratory work, Holub is able to conjure abstractions that speak of human and non-human conditions, such as war, illness, suffering, pain, childhood and monotony, meanwhile, also alluding to pathological, medical and physical theories.

Starting from Ancient Greece to the Enlightenment, the West has been obsessed with the larger structures: the universe, planets, cosmos and God to understand the mechanics of how the world functions. But with the invention of the microscope, the discovery of atoms and enquiries into genetics, the paradigm shifted from macro to the micro. We were less keen to look for meaning hidden in the folds of the greater cosmic order and instead turned towards the world of quantum particles, atoms, DNA and microorganisms, where understanding the smallest components and their structures would determine how larger societal order and civilisations come into being or operate. Holub's medical poems take on a similar rapport, where through looking into life underneath the microscope, he is able to construct metaphors that comment on society at large. This chapter seeks to analyse the poems of Holub that deal with the "alternating rhythms of cosmological expansion and microscopic contraction", uncovering his pathographical, aesthetic, social and political commentary while closely looking at his "nano-poetics."

Keywords: Pathology, medical, suffering, Microorganisms, poetics.

* * *

A Poet-Scientist

Born in 1923, in Pilsen, Czechoslovakia, Miroslav Holub is unusual in his approach to poetry. He was trained as a pathologist and later worked as an immunologist at Microbiological Institute of the Czechoslovak Academy of Science. During the communist reign in Czech, he was not permitted to publish and hence, he only garnered fame in the Anglophone literary world, after the fall of communism much later in the 1970s. As he had a wide, expansive grip in the intellectual domain of pathology, it occurs as a recurring topic in his poems and essays, but this does not limit his range. Usually, when a man of science indulges in creative writing, he is reckoned to be a person of hard reason and empirical assertion. This cannot hold true and is specially exemplified in the case of Holub. His poetry is sometimes inquisitive and skeptical, sometimes decisively ironic, and because of his belief that there exists in science, a wide body of imagination, away from all-encompassing theories and laboratory work, Holub is able to conjure abstractions that engage both human and non-human conditions, such as war, illness, suffering, pain, childhood and monotony; as well as alluding to pathological, medical and physical theories that govern all existence. The webbing of science and poetry, aesthetics and surgery, history and pathography flourishes in the clinically trained hands of Holub. Even though he insisted that he was primarily a scientist, his poetic genius and versatility confirms otherwise; hardly did we come across a poet in whose oeuvre we find the balance of irony, seriousness, humour and alertness in measured metaphors that inform and attain, delight and shock the unsuspecting readers. As Amy Ling observes, "Holub uses concrete, simple words, yet draws them from such complex areas of study as biology, astronomy, cosmology and cosmogony. With knowledge gained from use of the microscope and the telescope, studying the smallest and the largest units, Holub shows us, concisely and eloquently, the uni in universe" (Ling 1974, 511).

Holub's concern for the life underneath the microscope can be appraised through a large body of poems that he solely dedicates to micro-universes. Being an immunologist, he needed to experiment on several organisms, often dissecting them or subjecting them to harsh chemicals, and all of these professional endeavours are appropriated through an empathetic gesture, as the tiny worlds of microbes and microorganisms find a space and often a homage, in his poetic cosmology. "In the Microscope" begins with a comparison of landscapes that are found in the "large" human spaces contrasted to the "dreaming landscapes" underneath the microscope (Holub 2006, 28). Neglected lands, lands lit by moonlight, the tillers of land and fighters who lay down their life for the lands— instances similar to what can be seen in the everyday life of citizens dwelling in nation-states. The worlds that exist outside our naked visibilities are not very different from our own. As expressed by Holub, the citizens of this world too undergo human desires like fame, human emotions like grief and mourning, climate changes, and political revolutions.

The poem "Wings" by Holub, has an epigraph from William Carlos William's poem "Histology": "We have / a microscopic anatomy / of the whale / this / gives / Man / assurance" (Holub 2006, 60). Carlos Williams posits a relief, a certainty of continuation towards a specific *raison d'être*, or otherwise, objectivity and finality of meaning, the "assurance" that "Man" is on the right track to uncover "truth" and "purpose", their reason of being in the world. If "Man" can perform a detailed anatomical analysis of the largest mammal in the world, he surely can unveil every other mystery. Holub expands on this idea: "We have / a map of the universe / for microbes, / we have a map of a microbe / for the universe", where we begin to think of nano-technology, micro-chips and compression of data as the spaces of information storage gets more and more condensed by the minute, while the anatomy of microbes and microorganisms expand on the screens, the macro lenses zooming in on their organs and "mapping" their, now enlarged existence (60). Technological ascension in the cusp of modernity permits a non-human grandmaster of chess "made of electronic circuits", in a celebratory fashion perhaps, but for Holub, the basic human abilities of reasoning, sorting and physical acts like cupping of water in our hands, "gives us wings": a long-desired, non-human organ that is also an archetype for freedom and imaginative flight (60). Scientific interventions have undoubtedly pushed the limits of possibilities, and as Carlos Williams says, we have been given assurance through the regular feats of science; the assurance in the form of confidence or a promise, both abstract emotions that are exposed to risks. Holub's assertion on "wings", which even though is more metaphorical than literal, warrants an agency— an apparatus, that allows mechanical exercising and action (60). Above all, Holub sees the basic human potentialities (like using hands to perform the most trivial activities)— acts which also separate us from other animals and non-humans, as forerunners of agency and execution, following which comes the benefits of science, and further assurances. Throughout centuries, these characteristic feats— the corollaries of human evolution, cannot be overlooked, as they continue to underlie all complicated procedures and capabilities that have accelerated alongside the rise of the industrial age in Europe.

Jayjit Sarkar, in his *Illness as Method*, makes a distinction between pathography and medical report: "A pathography serves as a counter-narrative to the so-called official medical report; the latter does not take into consideration the lived-experience and the lived-body of the sufferer; the former recovers and puts forth the same. The violence that is often meted out to the patient's body is justified and, sometimes eulogised in medical case histories" (Sarkar 2019, xxxiii). Holub's poetry can then, be read as "pathographies" that document the medical procedures in a different light, sometimes bestowing their subjects with agency, or shedding light on modernity and its unruly effects through the gaze of "suffering" bodies. In "Suffering" Holub refers to the microorganisms as "ugly creatures", perhaps as a conviction to "otherize" them, subject them through torture in the name of science and drive their dissected corpses through fluids (Holub 2006, 105). As a means to de-compassionize, he brackets them as "ugly, grunting creatures", "disgusting", "with foam at the mouth", "who have pink mouths" and "ugly blue eyes" (105). This by no means can be viewed as Holub's standpoint on non-human beings, but only a rhetorical device that generalizes the commonly held perspectives on beings that look different or deviate from "standard" aesthetic benchmarks. With the aid of such pictures, these organisms are "monsterised", made to look filthy, germ-like and undesirable, as a means to vindicate the experimentation on them. The perpetrator though, is aware of a suffering inflicted on them as he watches them like an all-seeing "god".

The fate and destiny of these creatures are in the hands of an immunologist, and no one questions about the rights of such creatures who are otherwise, invisible. Ironically, the cruel satisfaction in the death of others, is suggested through images of flowers in a flower pot, and kittens underneath a pond— all of these are involuntarily chosen for them, and since they have no say in these terrifying actions, they suffer without protest, as though there is a real, crude satisfaction in their (non-existent) "choice". For Holub, the unquestioning plunder meted out through experiments do not have a moral justification, but only a righteousness fuelled by the "Enlightenment thinking" in finding the truth, the "silver bulldozer" that passes through "tumbling darkness". Suffering, pain and injustice are not just confined within the domain of the marginalized and the "otherized", but they are recurring phenomena in the socio-political realities which surround the personal life of Holub, and others like him, as in the end of the poem he states that he keeps finding the same instances of horror, isolation, loss and grief within him. The suffering shared by the tiniest of beings are reverberated and represented in each level, irrespective of the magnitude, as experiments are run in human society, as much as in the animal kingdom. In a poem entitled "Pathology", that is thematically similar (discussed later in the chapter), Holub expresses the involuntary sacrifices made by organisms where the "skins of martyrs" lie underneath the microscope. The fall of rights and values in this pathologic excuse, leads to the death and suffering of a large number of beings, while the scientific knowledge keeps on expanding. As Holub demonstrates, how the very pillars of civilization are under threat, one might begin to consider this as antithetic to the belief in Enlightenment: how far are the recorded convictions of wisdom and progress true, if suffering and bloodshed thrives while the basic problems of sustainability are yet unsolved?

David Graham states in his article, "Thus, for Holub all figurative language, indeed all his various paradoxes, surreal dislocations and fairy tale situations serve as analogues to the endless, serious play of the laboratory" (Graham 1987, 32). Holub with a career in pathology and pathological training had an extensive knowledge of medical sciences, diseases, ailments, medicines, anthropology and human anatomy which enabled him to rationalize and contemplate on the challenges and complexities that arise within these intersecting fields. In addressing these complexities Holub draws out themes of suffering and pain, despair and desolation that is not only physical but psychological. Illness is very much a matter of the mind, as much as it affects the body. As Sarkar states, "The self-conscious modernist work-of-art can roughly be compared to the body which becomes self-conscious during illness. The former calls for attention to the form while, in the latter, the hitherto absent-body (re)appears and seeks attention for itself or its part(s). The body presences itself in illness and disappears in health" (Sarkar 2019, xxii). The suffering patient undergoes many levels of torment and in illness, the vulnerability of his body, as well as the significance of health is fully "realised". Holub as a practitioner himself, is not hesitant to empathize or feel apathetic to the conditions of his patients, as it is popularly connoted that doctors and surgeons should operate without involving in a state of deep empathy, else the tasks with no margins for error as incisions or similar complicated procedures might be affected. Holub's empathy soars beyond the clinic and as a poet-pathologist, he is unafraid to denounce any medical malpractice as he announces his humane verdicts be it on animal rights, scientific experimentation or pathological interventions. "The Festival" is ironically titled, as the poem begins with suffering patients, crutch choirs singing for pacemakers in the wake of a crude festivity (Holub 2006, 314). Similar suffering of vision and internal malfunctions in the body are signified in the lines that follow: "The double astigmatic landscape / gratefully swallows the murmurs / of the mitral valve", and psoriases a skin disease, is anointed with the drug corticosteroid (314). Then, he refers to how a fish with skin disease is given artificial respiration, which could imply malpractices in the medical field adding to the woe of the already suffering patient. The poem ends with a remark that bristles with irony that implies, "we bubble with joy" as "all this torment at least has a name", conclusive of the fact that the modern man celebrates progressions of all sorts, basking in the triumph of civility and advancement, neglecting the trauma, poverty, immense pain and suffering that majority of the population undergo (314). While looking at the holistic picture demonstrated by Holub, the suffering of beings, living and non-living, in all socio-politico-medico levels never cease to exist. In the joy of progress, and will-to-knowledge, people often sideline the traumatic experiences of sufferers, the ill and the deprived, the ones who need immediate attention and substantive care.

From Macro to Micro: The Nano-poetics of Holub

In an article titled, "An Introduction to Nano-poetics", by Gilad Meiri (Translated by Lisa Katz), the term "nano-poetics" is brought into the context of analyzing innovative poetry, that allows the author to further investigate and explore the ideas of "miniaturization" and "duplication" in these new waves, fuelled by technology, compression and reduced spaces. This new wave subverts what is "abstract, divine, sacred, unchanging, collective, serious, familiar, bathetic and ornate" to represent the "concrete, human, mundane, ephemeral, personal, humorous, unusual, ironic and restrained" (Meiri 2010). According to Meiri, the miniaturization is brought in the poetic space in about the same time when the world celebrates nano-technology, a fact that is vital in order to understand and represent ordinary subjects that are often neglected. In the poetry of Holub, we find similar connotations and stylistic approaches that reveal his distinct participation as well as a remodulation of "nano-poetics".

The "everyday" is often rendered trivial, and neglected in a quest for grandeur. Simple pleasures, observations and happenings that constitute the majority of our lived experiences are relayed in the background, omitted from our recollections and pushed deep within the catacombs of memory. Only a careful, persistent observer validates the mundane, the unseen and the neglected, announcing their presence, unveiling the curtain and relocating the spotlight on the centre-stage for a big reveal. For Holub, the simplest of elements that comprises the "everyday", however mundane and insignificant it may appear, holds a key position. His training in immunology taught him to impart close attention to the minute, the seemingly insignificant, the invisible and the neglected. His poetic pieces often consider the "everyday" characters that go on about their daily matters, and are most often overlooked.

That being said, it is vital to note that there is a constant tussle in Holub's works between the human world and the nano-world of microscopic beings, that have been proportioned to a standard size, with their habits, actions and livelihood playing out like how animal life is documented and presented to us. In the vast cosmic order, which for Holub is as mysterious as the thoughts and actions of human beings, we are as microscopic as any other being. For Holub, there is no disparity in the size, which may otherwise lend humanity a self-ordained privilege, because the microscopic beings are as much under suffering, pain, illness as we or any other creature on earth. This eradication of size-based disparity is a central node to understanding the concerns of Holub and his "nano-poetics". When we start to see that beings in the world are undergoing the same circumstances, we find connections across our shared suffering. Holub takes this impulse of connectivity to a broader scale by including non-living substances that surround us. For Holub, comprehending the relations and experiences of all beings, whether living or non-living will enable us to widen our understanding of the strange problems of existence, as both living as well as non-living beings share a complex interconnected relation that affects our experience of the world. The same profundity of Holub can be amassed in a poem called "The Forest". The poem begins in a mystical tone, where the spirits of birds crack open the granite buried inside the earth and an image of trees that stay unmoved like statues "threaten the clouds" (Holub 2006, 49). The natural processes that replenish the earth with resources are given a supernatural touch, but it is not arbitrarily undertaken. In the stanza that follows, there is a rumble capable enough to uproot history, as quakes have been attributed to the act of demolishing civilizations and erasing traces. But this rumble had been an announcement of birth, as mushroom sprouts from underneath the earth: "immense as life itself, filled with billions of cells, immense as life itself, eternal, watery" (49). The seemingly tiny mushroom is as gigantic as life, because it not only represents life, it is life itself— one in many of its manifestations. Mushroom, as it grows out of the earth, is as much a component of the earth's corpus as every other substance. The symbol of the mushroom as embodied on earth, represents the symbiosis of all other seemingly unrelated objects and phenomena that Holub describes in the poem. It is here, that we can begin to see the image of "granite seeds" as fertile that allows for other, bigger objects to grow out of them, like mountains, as tree statues with black arms are mentioned, that "threaten" the clouds (49). Mountain ranges interrupt the clouds to cause rain, which leads to the growth of forests and the cycle continues, as life replenishes life. The metaphors of Holub are carefully planted, as they slowly unfold to become pushy and provocative. Appearing, in the end, is a comment on "difference" as the mushroom comes into being for the first and last time signifying the uniqueness of each birth, and birth itself as a unique event that celebrates the continuity of life in an otherwise dark and decaying universe.

Another instance of his "nano-poetics" can be exemplified in "The Bomb", where a murder occurs on the surface of the Earth, as images of bursting clay and fire leaking suggests mining activities. The quality of pathos is evoked as a naked and tender heart of a frog continues to beat after the detonation. Mining activities often involve many destructive implications, as smaller animals and birds that lodge in those areas are not given substantial considerations. Holub's poem captures the painful image of a tiny beating heart in the wake of an explosion, the spark of life snatched from a heart that continues to pump blood in a desperate attempt for survival. The poem, small in form is also about the strata of categorization, where minor animals are either romanticized or comicalised. It is a resistance to the certain tendencies and trends of high art and literature to exemplify and celebrate animals that are either dear to them, or domesticable or exotic. Frogs are often dissected in laboratory experiments and reading the poem under the light of medical praxis would ascertain his concern. Holub writes about the ordinary, the neglected, the sidelined, the minor, the minuscule, the invisible and the "nanoscopic", in a different vein. His poems illuminate the life under a microscope, as he places a rhetorical as well as a scientific microscope under the eye of the readers so that they can witness life with a microscopic gaze. This shift from the ordinary to infra-ordinary imparts a distinguished quality to his praxis.

In "Heart Failure", one among his ambiguous poems, a pattern begins to surface. Divided in segments, it has repetitive lines that section out what seems to be a particular observation. For instance:

> The airport is closed.
> The plane circles round like
> a fixed idea
> over the closed city,
> over porters, over dogs,
> over troughs, over not-for-sale window-dressing, over postmen, roosters, and hens,
> over brewers and tiny springs.
> The airport is closed. (Holub 2006, 94)

The closure of the airport suspends many activities, as the city shuts down, plane circles without much of an option. Reminiscent of Yeats' "The Second Coming", the plane turns and turns around over the heads of city dwellers, animals and objects that the poem will turn to, as it proceeds. As things shut down, the rooster does not get water, and the speaker remarks that it is slowly dying. But in the very next line, the dripping of water from taps in the city suggests availability and carelessness. Human's ample resources are put to waste while there is a larger section that is deprived. Next, commenting on the image of the ferryman Charon and the river Styx, the speaker remarks on the impending judgement that gets postponed time and again because humanity has not yet faced a dire crisis. The poem further builds on the system of interdependency, almost Kafkaesque in style, where one favour leads to another and the finality of purpose is out of bounds. The dying rooster does not get the share of a basic resource like water, because a line of favours like a scarf for the spring, shoe for the seamstress, bristles for the shoemaker and draff for the swine are needed as requirements. Modern life and complicated systems of market economics often push individuals through such negotiations. Commenting on the decay and decadence that characterises modern anxieties, Holub necessitates a return to our roots, to harness the basic feeling of compassion.

Interferon and the Puppet Theatre

In the essay "Real Deep Surprises", Bloyd relates to the dramatic action unfolding in the poems of Holub, where he often alludes to Greek and Roman epics "with well-chosen images that allowed contemporary commentary on human triumphs, foibles, even stupidity, under Communism and in the years post-89" (Bloyd 1970, 14), and this dramatic action often appears as short independent instances, perhaps a reflection or an event that may or may not play a role in the core narrative of his poem. They also appear as companion images, which may be a surprise, a shock or a surreal burst of expression and in his words, Holub explains, "There are lines which are just intended as a sort of graphic image of something, and which are not obscure by nature or because I couldn't find a better solution, but because I wanted to make them less comprehensible in order to describe a certain difficulty" (McClatchy 1996, 181).

Drama and theatre were always integral to Holub and his poetic thought. Bloyd recalls her days with Holub at Death Valley, who was on his tour to America as a visiting professor, amazed to see Martha Becket, a 61-year-old ballerina artist perform in the desert space for about twenty years. Bloyd relates to this as: "The marvelous moments of daily life appealed to Holub: the aging dancer who suddenly enlivened the stage, the pinfeathered, stinky angel who graced a town" (Bloyd 1970, 10). As mentioned by Bloyd, Holub admired the performance artist Laurie Anderson for reasons such as: "weird audio effects", "bold paint", "energized juxtaposition", "sequencing of word and image", the "inventiveness" that he connected with the Czech Black Box Image theatre and "Laterna Magika". Bloyd explains: "In the first, brilliantly-colored objects and figures assume a magical agency against a pitch-black backdrop; in the second, film and live actors come together in unusual ways" (Bloyd 1970, 16). Hence closely associated to theatre, "puppets" are a recurring metaphor for Holub, as he is a harsh critic of control and power-politics. The puppets tied to invisible threads are bound to orders, which they undeniably entertain, even though sometimes it may seem that they have free-will. Puppets and puppet-theatre symbolize the close-knitted playhouse where living and non-living beings function according to set directions, but it is also theatre that acts as a resistance to control politics, subverting forms of maginalization, through parody and counter-representation.

Holub's idea of theatre is most profound in the poem "Interferon", a surprisingly long poem that narrates many different instances of interference: the power of the theatre in a time of crisis, the potential of human will and freedom, the will to survive in a catastrophe and the continuous interference of life-forces that block the "malignant growth" of all that are threatening. In medical terminology, "Interferon" stands for proteins that are produced by cells infected with a virus that interferes with further viral infections and sends out signals to all other non-infected cells, helping them produce anti-viral protein, hindering any other possibility of viral infection and spread. Holub addresses this concept first, by comparing it to the phenomena of life and death: the void of death in a village is counteracted with the arrival of a newborn child. If demon in an attic symbolizes the death bringer looming in the dark, shady, isolated corners of residences as popularised in films— its roots engraved in mythology such as the character of grim reaper, this is the entry of the virus into the body and the eventual death of infected cells. The howling of dog's act as a force of mobilization, a signal that goes on to act in accordance with the natural forces, to bring forth a newborn child as a replacement for the dead: "the only one to fill the empty space in the wide air" (Holub 2006, 209). This process of "interference" can be broken down into three segments, as in the second stanza, where the actual medical jargon has been relayed open by Holub: the first is the infected virus sending out signals, the second phase is the mobilization of the defenses, the third is the birthing of new cells to replace the dead ones. These phases continuously appear in different instances, throughout the poem, such as the death of a poet is symbolic to the death of a person in a village, but instead of a dog, a bird sings to mobilize the defenses. The bird, often recurring as a symbol of an artist, or the process of creation "sings for all it's worth", as the creative process brings in the fertilizing rain: "black rain trickles down like sperm or something" (209). As the soil is fertilized for the birth of probable vegetation, it counterbalances the loss brought about by the death of a poet and also symbolizes a "pure" natural replacement, the roots connected to the earth— fulfilled only by plants and trees.

For Holub, interferon and theatre are similar in their functions, as they both interfere during an attack or in a state of crisis. Art is therapeutic and he returns to this through the characters of a Jewish shopkeeper and his wife who sold quilted bedcovers in Pilsen. They continue their pantomime outside time and action, as theatre or any performing art is always beyond the concurrent time and action: it is a portal to a different time and a different space, as their act becomes an "interference" to the Holocaust. In staging a performance, they go out of character and defy their normalised roles, folly the prevalent act of the time: genocide. The pantomime allows them to move beyond despair, anxiety and atrocities, interfering with routine, custom, pain and the horrors of war. It unleashes the power of theatre at a time of desolation, where "music of fifes and drums did not reach them" and thus art transgresses from a mode of escape to a form of resistance (211).

Holub proceeds to comment on the state of war and the dire effects on children. Just as puppets, humans under the communist rule in Czech did not have free will; they constantly repeated "we don't need prompters". This politically charged metaphor goes on to ascertain the illusion of free-will and how a large segment of society is under propaganda, influence and control. Just like the non-Euclidean curved space and entropy eludes our understanding, the interference of the theatre too is a grey area and is not easily comprehensible. Holub has no answers to the cruelty that is thrust upon children, born out of the "puppet tragedies", children who do not understand why they suffer in spite of having done all their tasks: "But we've washed behind our ears,/ we've stopped pulling the cat's tail,/ we've stopped shoving our fingers /into electric sockets" (214). He compares this idea of human brutality, to the thought that the high priests do not offer sacrifice in the skin of fleshly flayed prisoners. The brutal mutilation of innumerable children meant the act of destabilizing a species' own continuity which goes against the hominization, an act as slow as the "decay of tritium". In the end of the poem, the tradition of St. Nicholas's Day is mentioned where typically in the Czech and other European nations, people dress up as three figures— St. Nicholas, Devil and Angel. When they are confronted, children are supposed to sing or recite a poem and when unable to do so, they are believed to be punished by the Devil while those who comply are rewarded with gifts. On one such occasion, the actor dressed up as the Devil fell down the stairs while a child, at the moment of his confrontation, excitedly points out at this embarrassing scene. The sequence of interference had started to begin, as the dogs howled in a "black mistake" while the bird was about to sing, but soon the actor got up, cancelling the process. The child, one who was being terrorized by the devil, had been "prompted poetically" about the death of the Devil: that the flowers are restored in the world, and the paradise is closer which signifies the eradication of loss and terror from the face of earth. As is, with the preservation of innocence and the importance of instilling positivity in children, he too was being persuaded by the end of evil. But this was a façade, which the child already knew: "He believed and yet he didn't" (215).

For Holub, genocide is an idea that eludes understanding. All the things in the universe preserve their kind. The felled trees preach about their saplings, and as he observes, even the stars of the main sequence keep burning to continue the process and progression of existence. Yet, certain sections of humans slaughter one another to replenish their hunger for greed or power, and this for Holub is a baffling circumstance that he explores in many of his poems.

"Horror and Hunger": The Human and Non-human condition

In the poetry of Holub, there is very little distinction between "human" and "non-human" condition, as subjects that are part of either of these categories undergo constant "horror" and "hunger". These two primary phenomena underlie all other experiences as, to exist means to continually face and escape the visitation of "horror" and "hunger" in their several manifestations. The "hunger" is the literal hunger for food, while it also stands for bodily hungers, desire, greed, power and material wants while "horror" could be in the form of constant fear of death, experiencing illness and the loss of health, the fear of the inevitable, the loss of loved ones and the existential dread. "Distant howling" narrates the story of Joseph Meister, who was the first person to have been inoculated with the rabies vaccine, by Louis Pasteur. It marks the saving of Meister with the weaker doses of the virus, followed by the death of Pasteur by ictus, and the eventual suicide of Meister, who worked as a caretaker in Pasteur institute:

> Meister was the first patient
> saved by Pasteur
> with his vaccine, in thirteen
> progressive doses
> of the attenuated virus. (203)

The poem ends with a strange remark, which in the instant will intrigue the reader, nudging him/her to look for a deeper revelation. It seems on the first instance that Holub insists on the intransience of the virus, as an entity that carries on living, after the death of two individuals who have a shared history on an apparent "defeat" of the virus. Tom Paulin remarks in his introduction to *Minotaur: Poetry and the Nation State*, that the last lines are "aimed against the idea of critical disinterestedness" and "denies us the consolation of a final transcending image" (Paulin 1992, 5).

"Pompeii" is Holub's take on the historic catastrophe that occurred at Mount Vesuvius, in modern-day Italy, after an active volcano turned a city into ashes.

Little Red Riding hood features in the opening lines, where she drags her gift basket that contains a pie infected with Cholera, while her grandmother suffers from "genital herpes". These pathological references, which indicate a Roman disbelief in infections, followed by the reference to the death of Empedocles, where Holub states that geology had ended, chronicles the fate of many thinkers and scientists throughout human civilization, who tried to warn populations about an impending doom. The warning signs of Pompeii were not paid heed to as citizens were "baked in the stony mud", while the future excavations led to the resounding of "wolf chorals, Hamlet chorals, concubine chorals" that are a grave reminder of potential geological disasters. Holub blends history, science and fairy tale, basking in sarcasm as the devastating plight of Pompeii and the death of Empedocles is followed by: "Such a perfect epoch" (Holub 2006, 392-93).

The poem "Injection" is a pitiful, empathetic concern for lab rabbits, and all other animals that are meant to be caged for scientific experimentation. The poem states how orders arrive from higher officials, "with three-inch boots / judgment arrives", to begin the experimentation while the blood oozes from poor rabbits like voices crying from deep within. He reflects on the act of oath-taking that permits him to take the life of animals or cause pain to them: "How else could the heart / swear an oath?", lines that reflect his empathetic plight, as a rupture occurs between his moral self and his professional obligation (104). The pathologist has the weight of lives on his hands and unlike other non-humans, a freedom that is guaranteed, and this privilege allows him to choose certain actions without having to sway in the bridge that oscillates between life and death. On the other hand, his poetic persona also allows him to question actions even though the answers seem strange and mystical, or like in many of his poems, there might not be any validity in the answers, that leaves him in a position of uncertainty and aporia which is not commonly associated with professional scientists.

The poem "Pathology" is yet another contemplation on bacterial life and human conflicts, where "tongues of beggars", "lungs of generals", "eyes of informers" and "skins of martyrs" rest in a decaying wasteland (29). These images, as much as they apply to "martyred" microorganisms, they also refer to the abundant human lives laid on a waste during wars, or conflict such as the movement and uprising connected to communism in Europe, a segment of which had censored Holub's poems. The anatomical part as chosen for each category determines the most important organ, related to the specific category. Holub comments on the failure of equality, fraternity, patriotism and history to thrust mankind towards a state of peace. Like how lab animals and microbes are tortured and sacrificed to attain wisdom, similarly, the death and loss of many individuals secure profit or power to the ones in control of the system. Holub finds similarities in the fate of microorganisms and common men who are trapped in the agendas of control politics, and in the greater picture, how the system is designed to operate by surveilling, dominating and exploiting. Many pathological poems by him circle around the idea of death, through a variety of approaches. He explores death of the physical body, of a wish, of non-living beings and aspects that surround the event of death, like suffering, illness, pain, as well as literal and philosophical ideas that re-conceptualize existing notions. For instance, "Brief reflection on the word Pain", is a musing on the harrowing void that the word can bridge in, between feeling the actual "pain" and expressing it (147). Holub refers to Wittgenstein's idea that "it hurts", conceals the emotional and demonstrational qualities of crying (147). The word attaches itself to the actuality of pain which can otherwise foster empathic feeling in others, thus reducing the raw experiential impact. The word pain becomes an act of "silencing" the severe feeling of pain, and creates a "new behavior pattern" detaching the person from the feeling and expression in the presence of others, as everyone else is alienated, unable to reciprocate or understand the magnitude (147). Holub draws into focus the sharp disparity between an emotion and the word, experience and expression, signifier and signified, that further separates one human from another. Because there are no words sufficient to transfer the actual suffering attached to the bearer of pain, it becomes a gruesome, individual experience. "The Earth is Shrinking" is one of his poems that has an eco-critical undertone blended with his recurring pathological symbols, that manages to conjure some surreal images, where nature blends with physical ailments. In the beginning, there is a comment on the shortage of space for flowerpots as the earth is shrinking- which is more symbolic than literal. The cramping of spaces led by urbanization and clearing of forests do not allow vegetation to flourish in cities. Hence, the next image is of confused rain-worms that do not have a space on the natural earth, so they begin to grow inside the brain of a temple dancer. This view of illness as a result of modernity, and the modern condition, both from industrial expansion and anxiety is radical in his time.

The next ironic statements like: "The earth is shrinking may be due to the evaporation of good intentions" and "certainly due to the dead devouring the earth" follow up with a closure that parodies the administration and function of the system. The real problems such as exploitation, marginalization, warfare, pollution have been masked in images like "baldachin" over a marsupial's head (387).

"Intensive Care Unit" is truly pathological in the proper sense of the word (421). Among the many other poems that otherwise are a combination of several pressing themes, this poem exemplifies the vitality of medical science in fostering human health— over great wars, gods, prophets and writers. The poem begins with a scene from an ICU where a patient lies with pins all over. He refers to the patient as "whining puppet", one who is rendered immovable and is solely dependent on treatment as the soul is "dripping from plastic tubes" (421). There on, Holub unleashes a series of instances that evoke the idea of change and transformation but unlike everything else, the medicine "amikacin" remains constant. The progress of medical science has soared during the modern period, but the advancement of scientific temperament and technological innovation also fosters the rise of unaccustomed, modern ailments.

For Holub, poetry is much more than an escape, a source of pleasure or a mode of fanciful expression. Poetry is a serious pursuit and has the potential to unlock strange and sometimes, incomprehensible experiences of existence. Holub imparts his worldview coupled with philosophy of science in many of his poems, and he often does that in a non-ambivalent yet thought-provoking expression. An entire domain of narratives that include diagnosis, tragedy, myth, history, suffering and pathography lurk in the depths of scientific academia, out of reach for many, who presumably, never contemplated the possibility of a cross-disciplinary approach before poets like Holub emerged and incorporated medical thought, scientific wisdom and acute clinical life in their measured analysis of the quotidian.

References

Bloyd, Rebekah. 2010. "Real Deep Surprises". *Brno studies in English* 36, no, 2: pp. [9]-20 http://hdl.handle.net/11222.digilib/105071.

Graham, David. 1987. "'The Frightened Fawn of Sense:' Mind and Nature in the Poetry of Miroslav Holub." *The American Poetry Review* 16, no. 4: pp. 31-33. Accessed July 1, 2020. www.jstor.org/stable/27778294.

Holub, Miroslav and Ian Milner. 2006. *Poems Before & After: Collected English Translations*. UK: Bloodaxe Books.

Ling, Amy. 1974. "The Uni(que)verse of Miroslav Holub." *Books Abroad* 48, no. 3: pp. 506-511. Accessed June 18, 2020. doi:10.2307/40128700.

McClatchy, J. D. 1996. *The Vintage Book of Contemporary World Poetry*. New York: Vintage Books.

Meiri, Gilad. 2010. "An Introduction to Nano-Poetics." *An Introduction to Nano-poetics* - Israel - Poetry International. Poetry International Archives. https://www.poetryinternational.org/pi/cou_article/15836/An-Introduction-to-Nano-poetics/en/nocache.

Paulin, Tom. 1992. *Minotaur: Poetry and the Nation State*. Cambridge, Massachusetts: Harvard University Press.

Sarkar, Jayjit. 2019. *Illness as Method: Beckett, Kafka, Mann, Woolf and Eliot*. Wilmington, DE: Vernon Press.

Chapter 6

"I am God in a body": *The Diary of Vaslav Nijinsky* as Initiation into Psychosis

Jamil Ahmed

Middlesex University, UK

Abstract: Written before his hospitalisation, *The Diary of Vaslav Nijinsky* represents an account of a diary that reads like dance notation with its swishes, swirls and rigid stances. For Nijinsky, words were lacklustre in comparison to dancing as a form of expression. Although the diary mentions very little about dance, his rhythmic style of writing suggests that it is to be read in the embodied way that Nijinsky expressed himself– like a dance. If this is the case, then perhaps there has been an injustice by previous interpretations of his writing, focusing on the tautologies and non-sequiturs. Eschewing this popular form of exploration, this chapter seeks to demonstrate how Nijinsky gives us insight into his alienation from the world through his embodied autopathography, documenting his slow retreat from the storehouse of everyday meaning.

Keywords: Nijinsky, psychotherapy, illness narratives, phenomenology, schizophrenia, psychosis, madness.

* * *

A Short History of Vaslav Nijinsky

Vaslav Nijinsky was born in Ukraine in 1889 to Eleanora and Thomas, both of whom were of Polish origin and ballet dancers themselves. A family of five, he was the middle sibling, with Stanislaw his older brother and Bronislava, his younger sister. Misfortune seemed to loom over Nijinsky's family; his older brother Stanislaw suffered a severe brain injury at a young age after falling from a window and spent most of his life in institutions.

Described as energetic and drawn to physical modes of expression, he gained entry into The Imperial Russian Ballet School based in St Petersburg. His dancing was so impressive that he was allowed by the Imperial Ballet School to participate in solo performances before the age of 18— a rare occurrence. As his local fame grew in St. Petersburg, it was not until he became part of the company Ballets Russes that his stature as a dancer grew. It was in part due to Sergei Pavlovich Diaghilev— a prominent figure in facilitating the Russian art scene. For ten years, Nijinsky was the leading principal dancer who composed a series of sophisticated and innovative ballets: Jeux, Afternoon of a Faun and The Rite of Spring.

Nijinsky's relationship with Diaghilev was complex as he was not only the manager of Ballets Russes, but he was also Nijinsky's lover. It was commonplace for ballet performers to come under the patronage of wealthy art enthusiasts. Nijinsky's mother, hoping that he does not inherit his father's womanising traits ending in a loveless marriage, also encouraged it. During this period, Nijinsky was able to have creative freedom, under Diaghilev's management despite his interpersonal and interrelational difficulties. Since his childhood he was aloof, introspective and socially awkward and was no different at the Ballets Russes. Over time, Nijinsky's behaviour towards Diaghilev became resentful, and he started to exercise his own independence. It was during this time that Nijinsky encountered a Hungarian socialite, which was to have a profound impact on his life.

On a South American tour, without the presence of Diaghilev, he met Romola and in an impulsive act— married her. This led to an angry Diaghilev replacing Nijinsky and eventually dismissing him from Ballets Russes. He later rehired him, leading to tours in the United States and South America. However, Nijinsky's behaviour started to become more erratic. Eventually, Romola and Nijinsky decided to return to Europe and settled in Switzerland.

It was during this time that Nijinsky started to write in his notebooks, documenting his stream of consciousness. *The Diary of Vaslav Nijinsky* is a monumental work written over a period of 45 days. He started on 19 January 1919, the day when he performed his last dance recital at St. Moritz. He continued to write feverishly until 4 March 1919— when he was taken to Zurich and hospitalised at Burgholzi Hospital. The significance of his diary cannot be overstated historically prior to any counts of hospitalisation, making it virtually free from common psychological ideas, often making their way into explorations of madness. The manuscripts were accumulated and published in 1936. Whatever approaches we take in his work, in Nijinsky's words— "it remains true that: Scholars will ponder over me, and they will rack their brains needlessly…" (*The Diary*, 24).

Prenarrative space and subpersonalities

Reading Nijinsky's diary, one is immediately taken by the motion of the text, such as the circularity, dead ends and non-sequiturs. This often presented as evidence of a disorientated mind, which cannot easily fall into a conventional narrative framework. It is an unfair association, since anything unusual will seemingly reinforce his disordered mind. In other words, his madness, to others, explains his creativity and his flight from normalcy. We ought to consider the diary as representing a pre-narrative space, something in and of itself apart from narrative proper. This pre-narrative space is not a mass of text, waiting for someone to punctuate it. Rather, according to Paul Ricoeur (1984), it is already imbued with meaning, symbols and temporal structure. However, where we divert from Ricoeur is that Nijinsky is not independent from the meaning. The pre-narrative space that Nijinsky's diary occupies is of possibilities.

Pre-narrative objects do not often make their way into texts, usually edited or shaped before the pen hits the page. For Nijinsky, he does not censor what he writes and it beautifully captures the subject, predicate and his transgressions: "I will write what comes to mind." Following the line of motion, along the pre-narrative objects what we find are the closest one can get to recording one's unadulterated experience of fluctuating psychosis and possibilities. I am not interested in the formal diagnoses of his psychosis, whether it was Schizophrenia, Bipolar Disorder or a form Schizoaffective Disorder (suggested by a range of authors and clinicians). What concerns me rather is the concrete lived experience of psychosis for Nijinsky. It is through allowing ourselves to follow those possibilities that we can discern pre-narrative themes. One of those themes is the subpersonalities that arise from pre-narratives. John Rowan (1993), the transpersonal psychotherapist conceptualises subpersonalities as the varied constituent parts of our personality, which emerge in the social space as different roles. Often, tension can arise in these subpersonalities manifesting in inner conflict. If we are to explore what the diary makes possible, it is that his psychosis is often represented through these subpersonalities and their conflicts between a dancer, a pilgrim and a patient, which will be the focus of this chapter.

Firstly, Nijinsky's name is still associated with dance even, as Joan Acocella (2006) mentions, with the limited evidence of his dancing creativity in the form of a few photographs and his eleven-minute ballet titled *The Afternoon of a Faun*. Secondly, Nijinsky was frequently going on long walks by himself and often his anomalous experiences were framed by his religious and spiritual beliefs. He writes of an account where he walks literally to an abyss and he contemplates whether to jump— the start of a transformational journey. Thirdly, Nijinsky refers to the events occurring under the regulatory gaze of Dr. Frenkel (a local medical practitioner) and Romola (his wife); thus, analysing how his behaviour can be reframed into a patient. All three phases represent subpersonalities, an ontology of psychosis that Nijinsky inhabited time and again. He was seen as the dancer extraordinaire, but became alienated from it resulting in an inner retreat— the pilgrim stage, and emerged only to be later identified as a patient.

What follows next is further exploration into the roles of the dancer, the pilgrim and the patient:

a. The Dancer

The first few pages of the diary provide a nebulous account of the last dance that Nijinsky will ever perform. Two hundred people were in attendance at Suvretta House hotel, a private resort in St Moritz, Switzerland. The role of the dancer is perhaps the first that he was socialised into at an early age. His parents who were both dancers, trained Nijinsky and his siblings in dance. Although he demonstrated physical mastery within dance, nonetheless it remains a role that others had vested interest in, including the audience. Just as much as he embraced dancing as a creative endeavour for himself, it is also true that he danced for others. The difficulty in separating the two was at the heart of his anxiety, especially during the performance at St Moritz. He wanted to demonstrate his art form and at the same time was aware that the audience expected something from him. Nijinsky made reference to his affective state before the dance: "I played nervously on purpose, because the audience will understand me better if I am nervous" (*The Diary*, 6).

Nijinsky uses the word "played" to mean danced. The level of stress and anxiety from the public performance was preying on him, suggesting his level of reality orientation was somewhat intact. He had many reasons to be nervous, it was his first recital after many years, he possessed a near-mythical status within the dance world, and there were growing reports about his anxious mental state. But so far, there was nothing in his diary that could suggest he was experiencing a unique phenomenon, for many experienced performers would be undergoing similar emotional experiences. However, he also writes: "I was nervous because God wanted to arouse the audience" (*The Diary*, 6). Nijinsky is delegating causality to God and divine intentions, for his nervousness. So, his anxiety is not attributed to the level of exposure that a public performance may bring but rather God's desire for the audience to be aroused by his emotive state. Here we begin to see signs of a psychological split within Nijinsky when he experiences an inner conflict— attributing his difficult actions and intentions to others. This process of splitting is also apparent within his role as a dancer, something that is both private and public. The individual experience of dancing as well the public demonstration and reception co-exist. The implication of this dual process is that one can never wholly own the role of the dancer. Despite what one does, the audience validates the dancer: "The audience did not like me, because they wanted to leave. Then I began to lay cheerful things. The audience cheered up. They thought that I was a boring artist, but I showed that I could play cheerful things" (*The Diary*, 6).

Nijinsky here experiences what he perceives to be dissatisfaction in his dancing and so by responding to the social cues, he changes himself to suit their tastes. There is a sense that he feels compelled to dance to their tastes rather than his own, primarily because the dancer and his audience are intimately linked.

Insight into the act of creation, as Romola mentions, was Nijinsky's intention for holding the St. Moritz dance performance. As Oswald describes, there were moments of frenzied action, to stillness of staring at the audience and then outbursts of sermon admonishing those responsible for the war. The audience often see the finished product without understanding the conceptual space in which the artist is attempting to make the intangible tangible. One must appreciate the ephemeral nature of a dance, once performed, it is no longer there. The dance then is a disappearing act, a living, breathing text in motion. The dance text leaves an impression in the mind of the audience that continues to generate movement anytime one accesses those memories. However, as an audience we may not always appreciate the pre-conditions in which the very act of dance emerges. Nijinsky, through his role as a dancer, wanted to provide insights into the possibilities of creativity.

The themes, according to Romola— his wife, that Nijinsky wanted to embody in this dance were lunacy and the horror of war: "They thought that I was dancing to amuse them. I danced frightening things. They were frightened of me and therefore thought I wanted to kill them" (*The Diary*, 6).

There are two historical events that throw light on Nijinsky's themes. A few months prior, he had received a telegram notifying him of his brother's death. Also, at approximately the same time of hearing the news of his brother, the armistice was signed in November 1918 ending the fighting in World War I. It was during this period that Romola became aware of his creative work taking a turn towards a darker tone. How does one, process the trauma – one personal and the other collective? For Nijinsky, perhaps it is his role of a dancer and performer, which was used as a vehicle to transmit his grief. It is also possible that Nijinsky saw this, in this instance, as a religious act. In an improvisional performance, the act and creation are intertwined. There is something about the movement, space and time exploding into being— through the intention of the dancer. Obvious parallels can be drawn with God's willing into existence in the world. Both require the intention, desire and the will. With the death that surrounded him, Nijinsky offered back his creation of dance.

Just as much as it was an entrenched role, there were signs that the dancer was disappearing from his behavioural repertoire: "I danced badly because I kept falling when I did not have to" (*The Diary*, 7). Focusing on this statement, one may be drawn to the last segment "when I did not have to". Why would one intentionally fall in the dance, unless it was part of the performance? Presumably, he means that he was unable to control his movements wilfully resulting in falling. Peter Ostwald (2002), the late professor of psychiatry, follows this tract and attributes the lack of coordination to the reduced space, hindering Nijinsky's usual leaps. We assume that in order to dance, the prerequisites are coordination, dexterity and motor control. So, Nijinsky required a sense of those fundamental elements prior to improvisation and performance. An exceptional dancer such as Nijinsky would perhaps have made adjustments in line with the environment. Eugen Bleuler, the 19th-century psychiatrist who initially coined the term Schizophrenia and would later diagnose Nijinsky, believed that a reduction in psychomotor processes were signs of schizophrenia (Bleuler and White 1970). There is a possibility that Nijinsky's movements and accidental falls were indicative of something more, perhaps: "I wanted to dance more, but God said to me 'Enough'. I stopped" (*The Diary*, 7).

And with that, he danced no more.

b. The Pilgrim

After their move to Switzerland, Romola noticed that Nijinsky would often go for long walks in the evening, along the snowy trails. On one particular occasion noted in the diary, Nijinsky says: "I went for a walk once. And it seemed to me that there was blood on the snow, and so I ran, following the trail" (*The Diary*, 13).

Noticing tracks in the snow, suggesting the malice presence of another, he surmises there has been a murder. The arousal of fear makes him flee the scene, but he returns after a few moments: "I am not afraid therefore I came back. I then felt that it was God who was checking to see whether I was afraid of him or not" (*The Diary*, 13).

He is able to walk past what he perceives to be bloodstains in the snow to a cliff. As he looks out into the abyss, he then hears: "'Jump down and I will believe in you'. I was scared, but after standing for a while, I felt a force that was drawing me in the direction of the abyss" (*The Diary*, 13). As Nijinsky stands looking into the abyss, he interprets this as a possible sign from God:

"Then God forced me to go in the direction of the abyss, saying that a man was hanging there and had to be saved. I was afraid" (*The Diary*, 13).

He seems to be locked into a conflict. If he does not walk over to the edge of the abyss, he cannot save the person and if he cannot save the person because of fear— he would disobey God's command. He thus enters into a double bind with God. Gregory Bateson (1956), the anthropologist, saw this double bind to be an inherent feature in the communicative acts of someone with Schizophrenia. They are seen as "unresolvable sequences of experiences" (Lipset 1982, 210) not readily dismissed due to the misalignment of contextual cues. Following Bateson's original formulation for a double bind, it can be split into a primary, secondary and tertiary injunction:

i) If do not go to the cliff, I will save the man.

ii) If I do not save the man, I disobey God.

iii) I am scared, therefore I disobey God.

The series of injunctions all work together, with each one building tension from the previous one, ensuring Nijinsky is experientially locked into a conflict. Without critically being able to process environmental and social cues, he takes the perceptual experiences of God speaking to him as literal. There is doubt regarding the voices, however, not over the veracity of the voices but the actual communicator: "I thought the devil was tempting me, as he did to Christ on the mountain" (*The Diary*, 13).

So, Nijinsky takes it as given that a supernatural being is communicating with him. The polarity between God and the devil could provide insight into his fractured experience. In a world that is ambivalent and harsh, binary thinking may provide a tolerable way forward. It could be indicative of an inability to integrate diverse experiences in order to gain insight. His anxiety can only be alleviated through splitting, or in other words, "hearing God": "I went to the abyss and fell down, but was caught in the branches of a tree, which I had not noticed. That amazed me, and I thought it was a miracle. God wanted to test me" (*The Diary*, 14).

He interprets this as a divine intervention for his love towards God.

Now, the question remains, how does Nijinsky distinguish God's speech, from the devil and his own inner speech? Typically, ownership over one's own thoughts is conferred by virtue of having them. The quality of *mineness* is intuitive. However, Nijinsky hears God, which means, although it is an inherently subjective experience, he attributes the cause to another and in turn, disowns his thoughts. So, if Nijinsky does experience temporary disownership of his thoughts, what is the function? Staying with the idea of psychological-splitting due to an internal conflict, disownership allows Nijinsky to transfer agency and responsibility to another, freeing him to experience thoughts without the accompanying difficulties of affective states. This allows him to move towards the abyss: "'Go home to your wife and tell her you are mad'. I realised that God wished me well, and therefore I went home with the intention of breaking this news to her" (*The Diary*, 14).

With the endorsement of God, he can now disclose to his wife that he is mad. The underlying motivations for the pilgrim's journey are beginning to emerge. He now has agency, from God, to declare it rather than get labelled by others. As he prepares to leave, he sees the same bloodstains: "I realized that the trail was partly obliterated with a stick so that people would think it was piss. I looked closer and realized that it was piss" (*The Diary*, 15).

Although, the strong affective state is indicating it is blood, he is also able to hold a conflicting view that it is urine. Seeing cognitive dissonant views as only a cognitive process, excludes the bodily distress one also presumably experiences. So, Nijinsky's underlying difficulty is not only holding conflicting experiences, but also the corresponding bodily tension. Exploring this tract further, it could be more fundamental, in that his bodily pragmatic context of meaning is no longer an accessible storehouse. To explore this further, an appeal to corporeal categories will be made.

Merleau-Ponty (1974), the phenomenological philosopher, notes that the body is always embedded in the process of cognition, perception and narrative ordering. Every time we talk about x, we also implicate the body from which the experience of x arises from. That is to say, when one says I think, or feel x, it corresponds with an embodied category in the background, which is part of the truth function of the proposition. These bodily felt senses provide a grounded shape to our experiences like emotions, time, language, self, other and the world. It is from these corporeal categories from which narrativisation is made possible. A bodily sense of time, self, others, world, language must operate in the background in order for us to draw meaning which forms the basis of narrative. This demonstrates that rather than an abstract act, arriving at narrative categorisation is an embodied act.

For Nijinsky, it is the disruption of those corporeal categories, which impacts his ability to make sense from what is happening. The primacy is given to the immediate contemporary at the expense of the past and future. As he is returning home, he immediately becomes suspicious of an old man:

> I ran home, glad that these trials were over, but God commanded me to direct my attention to a man who was coming toward me. God commanded me to turn back, saying that the man had killed another man.

I knew I was wrong, but I felt it. (*The Diary*, 15)

Once again, we see a split in Nijinsky's processing of the situation, holding both the cognitive and the emotional aspect. Nijinsky cannot rely on his corporeal categories to provide any epistemic security. Seeing this old man, who is later to be found tending to the grave of his wife, gets us to the crux of his retreat into the pilgrim role. The journey of the pilgrim allows Nijinsky to come to terms with his difficult feelings towards his own wife: "I was frightened and ran thinking that my wife had fallen ill. I am afraid of death and therefore do not want it" (*The Diary*, 16). The conflicting feelings he holds about his wife, who may or may not be attempting to hospitalise him, is being addressed. The pilgrim's journey allows Nijinsky to comply with his wife's demands. It absolves her and in turn his need to resent her for what will eventually follow.

c. The Patient

Nijinsky's last subpersonality was that of the identified patient, typically attributed to individuals, through the consensus of others. In the diary, there is a suggestion that Dr Frenkel had already begun to "analyse" Nijinsky. He was a local general practitioner in the area that Nijinsky and Romola had settled. Frenkel eventually became a regular visitor to their household: "I do not like a wife and a husband who do depraved things while they look at depraved Japanese books and other books and go through all the motions of bodily love" (*The Diary*, 46).

Ostwald suggests that the reference to the books was in fact pornographic Japanese engravings that Frenkel had shown Nijinsky with the view of inducing his sexual fantasies. Regardless of the situation, Nijinsky understood the functions of Frenkel: "He wants to examine my mind. I want to examine his mind. I have already examined his mind. He cannot examine my brain, because he has not seen it. I have written some poetry for him. This poetry I have written on purpose so that he could see my brain" (*The Diary*, 61).

The poetry that he refers to is possibly word association tests that Frenkel was applying on Nijinsky. In his care package, at home, there was also an addition of a male nurse, with whom Nijinsky had good rapport. However, he was under the assumption that the nurse was a masseur. Adding further to the subterfuge, Frenkel was also having an affair with Romola. It has been suggested Nijinsky was aware but, based on what he wrote perhaps this was not the case: "I told Dr Frenkel that he was a good man. He was touched. I shook him by the hand" (*The Diary*, 49).

Nijinsky often refers to key figures such as Diaghilev, Romola, and Dr. Frenkel. It may be tempting to see them as figures, which play specific roles in

Nijinsky's life, but as he is often writing (sometimes indirectly) about what is occurring, Nijinsky is also implicated in these relationships. The focus on relationships is warranted as it was often the case through which others defined Nijinsky, especially the role of the patient.

The particularity of the relationships took on a triadic structure: a) Diaghilev-Nijinsky-Romola; b) Dr Frenkel-Nijinsky-Romola. If we see the triangle in light of Karpman's drama triangle (2014), we could position the key players as the persecutor (Diaghilev), victim (Nijinsky) and rescuer (Romola). A drama triangle emerges within conflict, when an individual in the role of a victim or persecutor identifies other players into the conflict. The triangle helps us to understand how Nijinsky may have internalised what was happening. From the diary, he does not explicitly state his role as a victim but it can be inferred from this section: "I have come to conclusion that it is better to be silent than to talk nonsense. Diaghilev realised that I was stupid and told me not to speak" (*The Diary*, 52).

If we explore what is happening, the early formation of the triangle is always a two-person dyadic system where the distress caused between them leads one to enlist the third member to alleviate stress. For instance, due to Diaghilev's difficult presentation in the relationship with Nijinsky, he then leaves and meets Romola alleviating some of the stress contained in the previous dyad. Likewise, in the second triangle mentioned above, when the Nijinsky-Romola dyad becomes difficult, Dr. Frenkel as the third is enlisted to alleviate the stress. Murray Bowen, the American psychiatrist, found that the appeal of the triangle is not just the alleviation of stress but also a confirmation of worldview (Kerr 2019). As long as Nijinsky sees others as hostile members, he will have a sense of his role in the triad— the patient: "I do not know what to write, because I was thinking of Frenkel and my wife, who are talking in another room. I know they do not like the things I am up to, but I will continue to them as long as God wants it" (*The Diary*, 54).

The presence of Frenkel and his wife have clearly impacted Nijinsky to the point where his attention has been derailed. There looming regulatory presence, over time becomes a well-entrenched script providing consistency in a world that is constantly changing. Whether or not Nijinsky is aware of what is happening, he has found his role in the triad, that of the identified patient.

As mentioned before, Frenkel had already begun his treatment of Nijinsky, psychoanalytically and medically. Ostwalt states that Frenkel prescribed Choral Hydrate to subdue Nijinsky, which may have worsened his condition over time: "I knew he was upstairs. You are mistaken, for you felt me. I wanted you to feel that Dr Frenkel was here" (*The Diary*, 57).

This particular section demonstrates how pervasive Frenkel's presence had become in his life. As Nijinsky writes, he thinks that Frenkel has entered his room but then realises otherwise. Instead of acknowledging the mistake, he shifts his perspective to the voice of God, and it becomes God's intention to let him think Frenkel had entered the room. It could demonstrate another example where he is unable to utilise his corporeal categories to represent the environmental cues coherently. Often when we get into a situation that we may not understand or fully comprehend, we may ask for clarification such as *what does that mean?* or *I'm just not following?* To fully understand this, we may have to uncover the key element(s) that frame this situation. However, for Nijinsky this did not always seem possible.

The role of the identified patient, including the dancer and the pilgrim— demonstrate the constant objectification of Nijinsky throughout his life. For instance, Frenkel's visits were to ascertain the level of his psychosis as his madness was already accepted. Romola, a constant force in encouraging him to continue dancing, now saw that her husband could not inhabit this role. Even Nijinsky had internalised aspects of this role: "I know your mistakes, because I committed them. I put on the cross deliberately because she felt you. Dr Frenkel feels you. He came on purpose to study your intentions and does not understand anything" (*The Diary*, 56).

Nijinsky writes once again, from God's perspective, both acknowledging his mistakes and understanding that Dr Frenkel is here to identify whether those mistakes amount to hospitalisation. The presence of Frenkel and Romola's increasing concern over his behaviour, lead Nijinsky to a schism— an experiential disjuncture. R.D Laing (1969), the existential psychotherapist, believes there's a dualism at the core of our existence a) being-for-myself and b) being-for-others. That is, whether we agree or not, part of a tension we hold in our attempt at balancing our private existence with our social one. A sense-of-self is predicated on a sense-of-self-for-others and vice-versa. We understand ourselves more when encountering the other and in turn the other understands their stance when encountering us: "People like eccentrics and they will therefore leave me alone, saying that I am a mad clown" (*The Diary*, 11).

So here, Nijinsky is disclosing that although he may see himself as eccentric, others see him as "a mad clown". Given the opportunity, as the diary affords him— his sense of being was radically different to that of the "mad clown". Laing explores this further and suggests that an identity that is a radical departure from the consensus of others provides a sense of distress. The continued tension, leading to a rupture— could be an essential etiological feature of psychosis: "I like lunatics because I know how to talk to them. When my brother was in a lunatic asylum, I loved him and he felt me. His friends liked me. I was eighteen years old. I understood the life of a lunatic. I know the psychology of the lunatic. I do not contradict a lunatic, and therefore lunatics like me" (*The Diary*, 11).

From this extract, it seems that there is a genuine relational bond with the "lunatic" because they do not define or objectify others. It is those who contradict the "psychology of the lunatic", the others who objectify that leads to an internal conflict. Nijinsky's radical departure also has a corresponding private language, as he knows "how to talk to them". However, a private language, something beyond the borders of consensus, cannot always be understood. This may throw light on some features within Nijinsky's writing that were difficult to discern such as attentional shifts and multiple subpersonalities. It is possible that the thread that integrates all those aspects was no longer as effective. The continued stress of being defined by others, contrary to their experience, only lead to further alienation until there is a complete retreat.

At the age of 29, Nijinsky would never dance or write in his journal again. He would live most of his life within mental institutions occasionally returning home for visits.

An Initiation into Psychosis

At the end, what does Nijinsky reveal in his diary about himself and, in turn, his illness? *The Diary of Vaslav Nijinsky* is a personal and situated journey that documents his fluctuations between being orientated to the world and his retreat to the inner private world. His role of a dancer served two functions. Others projected onto Nijinsky how they wanted to see him. In turn, Nijinsky reluctantly internalised that image, and the resulting tension enabled spaces of creativity to emerge. As a pilgrim, he continued the tension between the public and private self through an inwardly outward journey enabling him to process difficult emotional states. And lastly, the role of the patient was an inevitable formal acceptance of his alienation and final retreat from the public sphere to his private realm.

In many ways, it is through his diary that he is able to provide an anchor to the ephemeral nature of his pre-narrative, the content and process of his mind. It is not like the dance, the act that disappears into the background of our memories once the pirouette has been performed. The diary may have fulfilled a function of integrating his psychological experiences. How else can one make sense of the world if he is not constrained through the corporeal categories? In the end, the psychosis or madness that Nijinsky entered into only intensified the internal conflict he experienced. However, that which Nijinsky found difficulty in doing was made possible through the binding of the notebooks. By explicitly writing his pre-narrative, it provided him with the possibility of *being*.

References

Acocella, Joan Ross. 2006. "Introduction." In *The Diary of Vaslav Nijinsky*, vii–xlvi. Urbana: University of Illinois Press.

Bateson, Gregory., Don D Jackson., Jay Haley, and John Weakland. 1956. "Toward a theory of schizophrenia." *Behavioral Science* 1, no.4: pp. 251-264.

Bleuler, Eugen and William A White. 1970. *The Theory of Schizophrenic Negativism*. New York: Johnson, Reprint.

Jackson, Murray and Jeanne Magagna. 2015. *Creativity and Psychotic States in Exceptional People: The Work of Murray Jackson*. UK: Routledge.

Karpman, Stephen B. 2014. *A Game Free Life: The Definitive Book on the Drama Triangle and the Compassion Triangle by the Originator and Author*. USA: Drama Triangle Publications.

Kerr, Michael E. 2019. *Bowen Theory's Secrets: Revealing the Hidden Life of Families*. New York: W. W. Norton & Company.

Laing, R. D. 1969. *The Divided Self*. New York: Pantheon Books.

Lipset, David. 1982. *Gregory Bateson: The Legacy of a Scientist*. Boston: Beacon Press.

Merleau-Ponty, Maurice. 1974. *Phenomenology of Perception*. London: Routledge & Kegan Paul.

Moore, Lucy. 2014. *Nijinsky*. London: Profile Books.

Nijinsky, Romola. 1980. *Nijinsky*. London: Sphere Books.

Nijinsky, Vaslaw, and Joan Ross Acocella. 2006. *The Diary of Vaslav Nijinsky*. Urbana: University of Illinois Press.

Ostwald, Peter F. 2002. *Vaslav Nijinsky: A Leap into Madness*. London: Robson Books.

Rowan, John. 1993. *Discover your Subpersonalities: Our Inner World and the People in it*. London: Routledge.

Chapter 7

Doctor, Soldier, Writer: António Lobo Antunes as Portugal's Pathographer

Ricardo Rato Rodrigues

Uniwersytet Marii Curie-Skłodowskiej w Lublinie, Poland

Abstract: António Lobo Antunes is one of the major voices in Portuguese literature of the second half of the 20th century. His unique biographical trajectory crucially imbues his novels and chronicles in a mapping of the mental and physical suffering of human beings. A psychiatrist by training, Lobo Antunes, also participated in the Colonial War that opposed Portugal and its African colonies. Both experiences (doctor and soldier) are central to his literature and its articulation of the diversity of illnesses affecting Portuguese society post-1974. Ranging from an initial trilogy in which post-traumatic stress disorder and other mental afflictions are explored in a compassionate and encompassing way to his own autobiographical experiences (with PTSD, etc.), the author's oeuvre is particularly attuned to the pathological suffering of human beings. Moreover, it is not only an ethical preoccupation with illness that feeds Lobo Antunes' writing momentum, but a deep engagement with the universal questions about what it means to be human, with death and with the body and the mind. Even in terms of language, his writing shows an attention to the medical dimension of the world at large, sometimes as an ironic attack towards an ill society, sometimes in a compassionate understanding of human misfortunes. This chapter aims to bring forth the way in which the intersection between different dimensions (doctor, soldier, writer) is at the core of the author's artistic ethos, paying attention to the constant dialogue between the doctor, the patient and illness.

Keywords: Illness, psychiatrist, Pathography, Portuguese literature, doctor, soldier.

* * *

The intersection between literature and the natural sciences is not new, however, it appears to seemingly be so, given the flourishing of interdisciplinary contact between the two fields. Nevertheless, this development has not been an easy one and it has been marred by constant tensions. Indeed,

> (…) relations between literature and the sciences (…) have been a complex and fraught process. These exchanges have proved to be multiple, contradictory, and notoriously marked by enthusiasm, scepticism, gradual or forceful separations, and attempted convergences, in an understandable manifestation of discomfort at the perceived rift between competing claims for representing reality.[1]

This is not to say that such a complex process has stifled literary endeavours attempting a foray into the interconnecting space between science and literary artistry. In the particular case of medicine, these forays seem to have been more successful than in other scientific fields, perhaps due to a closer affinity of the medical realm with literature or simply because its sharing of the same central concern – the human. In fact, the number of doctors who also dwelled in the art of literary craftsmanship is abundant, crossing different epochs and different literary traditions. From fifteenth-century Rabelais to nineteenth-century Chekov, from Soviet Russia's Bulgakov to France's Louis-Ferdinand Céline, the examples are many and span across the whole political spectrum and can be found in probably every single literary tradition, no matter the language. As Iain Bamforth has pointed out in his illuminating historical analysis of the relationship between literature and medicine: "Clinical skills might have been learned at the bedside, but doctors wrote and wrote: medicine was moving back to the library."[2] Yet, parallel to this "moving back to the library", medicine had also moved towards a greater crystallisation as a proper scientific discipline and naturally has become more objective and evidence-based. A consequence of its development as a scientific discipline has been its moving away from its human source, its central point of contact with literature: "Doctors were encouraged to be as objective as scientists. Indeed, they had absorbed enough of the scientific spirit (through Popper) to know that they could only be right if they tried hard enough to show why they might be wrong: such was the mark of a sceptical and honourable intelligence."[3]

Evidently, medicine's advance is something that has brought about more benefits than damage and thanks to its developments that human society has achieved so much in terms of health and well-being in the past decades. But like in any other field, achievements and advances have not been without its counterparts and it is here that literature has been of importance. It has been this tension, this dialogue (peaceful at times, sometimes belligerent) that has permitted the creation of literary works that have excelled in their relevance for the bridging together of the two dimensions, of reminding medicine of its humanity and humanity of its material bounds (whether in terms of the body or the mind).

Perhaps one of the most important examples in contemporary literature can be found in the works of Portuguese writer António Lobo Antunes, whose oeuvre embodies precisely these aspects, particularly elevated in its anchoring in the gap that exists in the friction between the scientific and the human. In truth, it would be unfair to postulate that the author is in any sense a neutral observer, or a disinvested chronicler of such friction. His work is undoubtedly charged with an all-encompassing humanism, at times sharply critical of medicine and its institutions, but never dismissive of the necessity of the ethical commitment and urgency of care which are synonymous of the medical profession. Before focusing on Lobo Antunes and his work, it is worth noting that the conflict here illustrated has been a preoccupation not only for literature and medicine, but also for philosophy, thus illuminating the ethical, epistemological and sociological issues in which the author is imbued. This is fundamental to the understanding of why his importance has transcended geographical limits, establishing him as one of the most important writers of the second half of the twentieth century.

In his essay "Is Science Superstitious?" Bertrand Russell highlights the tendency of the scientific outlook to go overboard in its pursuits and manifesting a nefarious hubris:

> Science as it exists at present is partly agreeable, partly disagreeable. It is agreeable through the power which it gives us of manipulating our environment, and to a small but important minority it is agreeable because it affords intellectual satisfaction. It is disagreeable because, however we may seek to disguise the fact, it assumes a determinism which involves, theoretically, the power of predicting human actions; in this respect it seems to lessen human power.[4]

Although Bertrand Russell's words are directed at the larger field of natural sciences, a not so farfetched leap could be made, and the words would be no less valid if applied exclusively to medicine. And as we will see (through Lobo Antunes) this seems to be even more true of a particular discipline within the medical sciences, that is, specifically, psychiatry.

In fact, the Portuguese writer inherits this very sceptical approach from Russell and his literary approach is permeated by the same suspicions towards an unchecked and uncritical positivistic outlook. Even though Russell's words precede the works of Lobo Antunes by decades,[5] the preoccupations are the same and in the case of the novelist, will prove to be essential for his writing ethos. In the postmodern literary world, it is of note that the author manifests a commitment to a type of writing anchored in humanism (and indeed there is some difficulty in applying postmodernism as a literary category to the author's works), revealing a philosophical self-positioning which is clearly grounded. If for Russell, "(...) science and philosophy can no longer preserve an armed neutrality, but must be either friends or foes",[6] for Lobo Antunes, the same could be applied between medicine and literature. The writer seems to share Russell's scepticism towards giving science (or medicine) complete unaccountability, imbuing his writing with the same spirit advocated by Russell: "They cannot be friends unless science can pass the examination which philosophy must set as to its premises."[7] And it is this same sceptical scrutiny that Lobo Antunes uses when establishing his place as a great *pathographer* of human suffering.

Doctor/Soldier/Writer

Although the biography of writers is something that most contemporary literary theory has minimised or even dismissed altogether, in the case of Lobo Antunes it would be difficult not to take into consideration and give it proper critical attention given its uniqueness and relevance for his writing. António Lobo Antunes was born in Lisbon in 1942, the eldest son of a prominent neurologist and close collaborator of Egas Moniz, the inventor of the controversial procedure of leucotomy (or, as it is known today, lobotomy).[8] Following the family tradition, António also became a doctor, albeit reluctantly, later specialising in psychiatry. Upon finishing his medical education, Lobo Antunes was drafted, like many other men of his generation, to the Portuguese Colonial War (1961-1974), where he served as a medic for two years (1971-1973). Both biographical "details", his medical profession and his war experiences, would prove to be essential for his writing as they would feature heavily in his first novels and he would return to them several times, directly or indirectly, throughout his writing career, never really abandoning them but rather articulating them in increased complexity.

But before delving into the works themselves, it is necessary to engage in a theoretical preamble regarding the presence of these biographical elements in the fabric and ethos of the author's writing. Several questions are posed: has the fact that he was doctor shaped his writing? How does his writing relate to those produced by other writers who were also doctors? When and how, if at all, does he stop being a doctor and starts being a *pathographer*? What about his experiences as a soldier, are they articulated in his writing and taken into consideration by his medical outlook? All these questions are of course relevant and by attempting to answer them, one should achieve a higher degree of clarity about the type of writer Lobo Antunes is. If these qualms seem irrelevant for now, it is perhaps important to note that the writer's approach, even though departing from a medical background, far surpasses this, entering the spheres of inner suffering only known to patients and even the collective traumas of a generation of men. So it is indeed important to explore the different facets of the writer, thus avoiding the mistake of considering his writing as a simple product of a doctor looking at suffering, when in reality Lobo Antunes happens to be a writer who brings a wealth of perspectives, including his medical experience, into his writing. That is to say that the point here is not to bring forth the literature of a doctor but the literature of a *pathographer* who also happens to be a doctor. The distinction may seem pernickety but is in fact crucial to understanding the extent to which his writing embodies but simultaneously rejects the totalizing effect of the medical outlook. It is by successfully existing as a writer in the space of this tension that Lobo Antunes avoids falling into the trap that has limited the range of other doctor-writers— the medical gaze. He managed, through his writing, to free himself of the reductivity of such gaze, thus avoiding an epistemic disappearance, or rather, displacement, which Foucault has identified in *The Birth of the Clinic*:

> Not all the powers of a visionary space through which doctors and patients, physiologists and practitioners communicated (…) have disappeared; it is, rather, as if they had been displaced, enclosed within the singularity of the patient, in that region of "subjective symptoms" that — for the doctor — defines not the mode of knowledge, but the world of objects to be known.[9]

Lobo Antunes writes against the grain of the medical outlook, an outlook, a gaze, that reduces the multiplicity of human experience (especially the multiplicity of suffering and pain), a gaze in which "(…) the silent world of the entrails, the whole dark underside (…) lined with endless unseeing dreams, are challenged as to their objectivity by the reductive discourse of the doctor, as well as established as multiple objects meeting his positive gaze."[10] In this respect, Lobo Antunes has rebelled against his own literary tradition, a tradition full of doctor-writers who have made the coexistence between the two dimensions of their life (writer and doctor) peaceful. For Lobo Antunes, however, this coexistence is not peaceful but belligerent. And it needs to be so, for it is due to the conflict that the "(…) residence of truth in the dark centre of things is linked, paradoxically, to this sovereign power of the empirical gaze that turns their darkness into light."[11]

From the point of view of literary criticism, this is extremely important. In an era where the figure of the author has been proclaimed dead, the text trusted solely into the reader's care, here is a writer who seems to bring back the idea of author. An author not from a place of author*ity*, but from a place of human exchange, reminding the reader that the text he/she is reading has been produced not by a non-existent entity but by a real, mortal, flesh and bone human being. And if one extends the metaphor, isn't that we also want from our doctors? Not a clinical, cold abstract concept who is interested not in the patient but in the illness, but a doctor who is able to empathise, who is fundamentally *human*.

Lobo Antunes' writing ethos is, then, very close to this humanist perspective and it is precisely because of this positioning that he does not seem to sit comfortably in the realm of post-modernism and its claims to both the death of the author and the (sometimes extreme) relativisation of human experience. For him, the direct human experience is never far from the text itself and it is not surprising that the boundaries between "life" and "text" are so thin in his writing. It is that lack of definitive boundaries, that porosity of his writing that configures Lobo Antunes as a great *pathographer*, that gives his works a great sense of humanity and that makes him such a unique voice in literature. It is by transcending the constraints of these literary theoretical presuppositions that he transcends what Seán Burke has identified, in his book *The Death and Return of the Author*:

> For the best part of the twentieth century, criticism has been separated into two domains. On the one side, intrinsic and textualist readings are pursued with indifference to the author, on the other, biographical and source studies are undertaken as peripheral (…) exercises for those who are interested in narrative reconstruction of an author's life or the empirical genealogy of his work. The proximity of work and life, the principles of their separation and interaction are neglected by the representatives of "work" and "life" alike. Work and life are maintained in a strange and supposedly impermeable opposition, particularly by textualist critics who proceed as though life somehow pollutes the work, as though the bad biographicist practices of the past have somehow erased the connection between *bios* and *graphé*, as though the possibility of work and life interpenetrating simply *disappears* on that account.[12]

As we will see, in Lobo Antunes' literature, this proximity between life and work is a carefully crafted balancing act. It would be one thing to bring into his writing his experiences as a doctor, engaging with the texts using his clinical eye and detaching himself from the writing, but given the fact his biography has been marked by another significant experience — the war — the balancing act becomes even more of a necessity. The combination of both biographical experiences would leave a heavy mark on any biography and it is easy to comprehend that for a writer that knows both sides of suffering and pain, it would be very hard not to bring both into the act of writing. And by perceiving it as a balancing act, we can own the key to unlock the author's oeuvre. The light that illuminates his books can be found in the space between the subjectivity of writing and the objectivity of the biographical facts.

As for the topic of the war, some contextualisation is needed in order to enlighten how traumatically significant it has been for the Portuguese collective psyche and for Lobo Antunes' individual experience in dealing with the conflict, both as a medic and as a person. War and psychiatry are the two major motifs of the author's first three novels, also featuring in some of his chronicles. They will also be recurrent topics in later writing, appearing intermittently and under different guises, but nevertheless always there.

Exacerbating the suffering, pain and illness found in these two areas, is Portugal's history. The war cannot be understood without placing it within the colonial, imperialistic fascism of the Estado Novo Dictatorship, started in 1933 and ending only in 1974. Naturally, the dictatorship and its nefarious influence on Portuguese society is a background that the writer confronts by articulating this traumatic past with the traumatic present that resulted from it. A quick look at the numbers is all it takes to understand the size of the conflict for a country consisting of a mere 10 million inhabitants.[13]

Between 1961 and 1974, the Portuguese military was involved in what is commonly known as the Portuguese Colonial War (or War of Liberation, for the African nations involved). This conflict took place in Angola, Mozambique and Guinea, three countries that at the time were Portuguese colonies. A total of 1,000,000 Portuguese soldiers involved (about 10% of the country's population), 10,000 were killed, and 40,000 wounded.[14] To these, we have to add the number of soldiers who have later developed traumatic mental conditions (PTSD and others), which is estimated at around 120-140 thousand men.[15]

Amongst the participants was Lobo Antunes and although it is not possible to take any conclusions regarding the author's own traumas, it is fair to say that such a contact with this violent reality has sharpened his necessity to put into writing all the pain and suffering he had witnessed. In fact, and as we will see, the war and its horrors is a topic to which he returns consistently throughout his entire oeuvre. The narrative that emerges is one in which a doctor and soldier has filtered the *pathos* of a violent reality into the performative summoning of the writer. Lobo Antunes is undoubtedly aware that his role as a writer is not merely the role of an individual who creates a narrative, but rather that "[...] the responsibility for a narrative is never assumed by a person but by a mediator, shaman or relator whose 'performance'— the mastery of the narrative code— may possibly be admired but never his 'genius'."[16] His particular performance is one in which he has decided to use his own biography as the object and subject of his writing.

The argument here presented may look, at the surface, confusing or contradictory. In an effort to disentangle what is here proposed, it has to be said that this is not an attempt to affirm Lobo Antunes' genius *as a person*, or a form of glorifying a biography. What is being affirmed, rather, is that Lobo Antunes did not ignore his own biography in his writing, did not eschew from using his own life (or experiences derived from his own life) as material for his literature. When he took on the role of the Barthesian mediator, he turned inwards, thus inserting himself and his voice in the collective experience of his writing. When the biographical facts that surround your existence are as important as the ones surrounding Lobo Antunes, why shy away from them and hide in authorial invisibility? Why not make yourself an active, dialoguing part of the collective? Why lock yourself in a prescriptive role assigned by the literary school of postmodernism when by doing so, you would be limiting your voice, your reach?

Terry Eagleton has presented a similar argument, one that seems perfectly suited to describe the writing of Lobo Antunes:

> We tend to think of the subjective as pertaining to the self, and the objective to the world. The subjective is a matter of value, while the world is a matter of fact. And how these two come together is often something of a mystery. Yet one way in which they converge is in the act of self-reflection. (…) Objectivity is not just a condition outside the self. In the form of self-knowledge, it is the pre-condition of all successful living.[17]

At this point, the reader is perhaps wondering what the relevance of these theoretical musings is and what they have to do with the topic of the writer as a *pathographer*. However, such theoretical considerations are indeed necessary to establish why Lobo Antunes is one of the most interesting and relevant names in contemporary literature, achieving his stature by having carefully created a work that is all-encompassing, empathetic and multidimensional. Antunes is not simply a doctor who decided to write, or a soldier who decided to purge himself via writing, but rather a writer who transcends that, creating an original space for his literary voice. By keeping the objective and the subjective in constant articulation and dialogue in his inwardly narrative voice, the author is simultaneously expanding the inner emotional lives of his characters, permitting access to their intimate nature (fears, obsessions, traumas, etc.) and replicating the process of therapy such as it would exist in a psychiatric consultation, that is, a sort of back and forth between the narrators' voices (as when the patient is describing his or hers personal history) and the silent listening of the doctor (reader). The difference is that Lobo Antunes' own voice emerges amongst the multitude of other voices, linking us to both what is intimately being said and the world at large (with its very concrete objectivity), be it in the particularities of Portuguese society and culture or more universally, when tackling issues such as death, trauma, madness, old age, the decay of the body and the mind. And it is precisely the multiplicity of what emerges from his books that makes him one of the great *pathographers* of our time.

Lobo Antunes, the pathographer

The common definition of pathography is that of a narrative or study of the life of an individual or the history of a community in relation to a particular disease, psychological disorder or other medical experience. It is normally authored by a patient, a doctor or someone who has been in close contact with these illnesses and ailments. Literary examples are abundant, from XVIIth-XVIIIth century Jonathan Swift to XXth century Oliver Sacks, and many others. Anne Hawkins, in her article "Pathography: Patients narratives of illness," has observed that not only are they abundant, they have also become popular:

> In ever greater numbers, people are writing autobiographical accounts of their experience of illness and treatment, narratives that are often called pathographies or autopathographies. Increasingly patients are turning to these narratives for anecdotal information about particular illnesses and their treatments, conventional and alternative. Hence the remarkable popularity of such books, many of them bestsellers.[18]

There is nothing inherently wrong about this increase in number and the genre might have now established itself as a legitimate literary expression, with the added benefit of serving patients, doctors and the community alike. Pathographies not only articulate the hopes, fears, and anxieties so common to sickness, they also serve as guidebooks to the medical experience itself, shaping a reader's expectations about the course of an illness and its treatment. Pathographies are a veritable gold mine of patient attitudes and assumptions regarding all aspects of illness. These narratives can be especially useful to physicians at a time when they are given less and less time to know their patients but are still expected to be aware of their patients' wishes, needs, and fears.[19]

However, it would be limiting to place Lobo Antunes as another representative of this genre. To perceive him as a *pathographer*, the impact and depth of his oeuvre has to be taken into account. He is another type of *pathographer*, not one that limits himself to the precepts of a genre or one that has a specific writing subject (an illness) as his main focus. In order to understand what is here meant by *pathographer*, we must return to Seán Burke's etymological note on the separation of *bios* from *graphé*. This separation of the basic elements of the word is the key. To a "pathographer", the same logic must be applied: *pathos* and *graphé*. The separation allows the two elements to become two separate units (albeit communicating ones), existing independently but coming together to form a concept. In other words, Lobo Antunes is not *writing illnesses*, but rather summoning the *pathos* to his writing. The return to the etymological source of the word *pathos* is perhaps a basic, yet necessary, turn: "*Pathos* (Greek, 'suffering, feeling'), that quality in a work of art which evokes feelings of tenderness, pity or sorrow."[20] Simply put, Lobo Antunes' writing recuperates that quality, of suffering, of feeling, weaved in the very fabric of human experience.

A pathographer and his pathographies

António Lobo Antunes' work is vast, sprawling between twenty-nine novels, five volumes of chronicles and one book of letters (edited by his daughters).[21] In the scope of this chapter, it would be impossible to address his work in its totality and detail how in all of them, the author has articulated the medical and the literary aspects. Nevertheless, some of the most representative works, from different periods of his writing, have been selected and will be analysed here. As a starting point, it is indispensable to consider the author's first three novels, a loose trilogy that has been called the "trilogy of learning".[22] It consists of the novels *Memória de Elefante* (1979), *Os Cus de Judas* (1979) and *Conhecimento do Inferno* (1980).[23] These three novels are fundamental in assessing the presence of those biographical elements in his writing, for they are, by far, the most autobiographical and more intensely populated by those dimensions highlighted before (medicine and war).

The first novel, *Memória de Elefante*, introduces the reader to a young, divorced psychiatrist, working at the biggest mental hospital in Lisbon, Hospital Miguel Bombarda. The novel follows a day in the life of the said psychiatrist and nothing out of the ordinary happens. He sets out to pick up his daughter from school but ends up spying on her from a distance, never bringing himself to follow through. He follows her home, to the flat where he also used to live in, but ends up staying outside, reliving his previous life in his mind. Other insignificant and inconsequential daily episodes are also presented, but nothing that represents a proper plot. However, the main preoccupation of the novel is to follow the psychiatrists' thoughts and emotional ennui. He is extremely pessimistic and delves into despair, so his worldview is exaggeratedly sarcastic and corrosive. He is unhappy and confesses this unhappiness in anger: "Puta que pariu os psiquiatras [...] puta que me pariu a mim."²⁴ ("Fuck psychiatrists [...] fuck me").²⁵

The readers witness his inner turmoil and suffering, his revisiting of pleasant and unpleasant memories, discovering that the psychiatrist also goes to therapy, more specifically, group therapy. The novel, via its narrator, presents several of these fellow patients and their stories. However, since the narrator's voice is of an exaggerated sarcasm and pessimism, the other patients' narratives are mocked and ridiculed, thus augmenting the sense of alienation and despair in which the narrator is immersed. This does not mean, though, that the writing only dwells on the inner suffering of the narrator, for the recollections of the doctor are presented alongside the suffering of others, patients in the mental institution, and others with whom he shares the group therapy, his ex-wife, etc. allowing individual inner suffering to be transferred to a shared collective sphere, which would include the readers.

In terms of pathography, the novel can not only be read as both a scream of rebellion against the oppressiveness and dehumanisation of medical institutions but also a detailed account of the mental suffering of a post-dictatorial Portuguese society. No wonder, then, such an emphasis on memory, a memory that is obviously traumatic, for both the individual and the collective, wouldn't be a stretch to understand the novel as a literary re-enacting of PTSD. As Ruth Leys has pointed out: "Post-traumatic stress disorder is fundamentally a disorder of memory [...] The experience of the trauma, fixed and frozen in time, refuses to be represented as past, but is perpetually reexperienced."[26]

The second novel, *Os Cus de Judas* (*The Land at the End of World*), presents us with a narrator— a man, divorced— who recounts his war experiences to an unnamed and silent woman, while trying to seduce her in a bar. Ironically, the conversation also resembles a psychotherapeutic session, where the patient retells his traumatic experiences to a silent listener. In each chapter of the novel, the narrator asks for an increasingly stronger alcoholic beverage, his narration becoming more and more candid. The mental digressions take the reader to the narrator's memories of the war and of its traumatic episodes— death of fellow soldiers, mutilations due to landmines and other violent realities. As it is easy to understand, the writing is focused precisely on that darker dimension, the night-side of life (Sontag)— illness.[27] Indeed, the narrator is retelling his experiences in the war in Africa, throughout the night, as he suffers from insomnia: "Há quanto tempo não consigo dormir? Entro na noite como um vagabundo furtivo com bilhete de segunda classe numa carruagem de primeira." ("How long have I not slept? I enter the night like a furtive vagabond with a second-class ticket in a first-class carriage").[28]

Relevantly, it is interesting to note that insomnia is a common complaint amongst PTSD sufferers.

The third novel, *Conhecimento do Inferno* (*Knowledge of Hell*), gives us more of the same, but this time combining both narrative spaces— war and medicine. By concatenating both the war and his psychiatric practice, the narrator creates a poignant portrayal of a psychiatrist afflicted with his traumatic memories of the war and of the suffering patients he encounters in his work at Miguel Bombarda. The tone is somewhat less sarcastic and negative than that of *Memória de Elefante*, but no less aware of the horror of the reality it is describing: "No andar de baixo (…) um homem invisível gritava a aflição dos porcos em matança, de pescoço golpeado pela grossa lâmina das facas." ("Downstairs […] an invisible man screamed with the agony of pigs in slaughter, neck wounded by the thick blade of knives").[29] The antipsychiatry *spirit* that animates the novel is one that strives for a more humane medicine, a psychiatry that is more attentive to human suffering, but also a cry of despair for all humanity, a cry that culminates with the call for the destruction of the hospital, the embodiment of suffering and oppressiveness:

> a única coisa a fazer era destruir o hospital, destruir fisicamente o hospital, os muros leprosos, os claustros, (…) a sinistra organização concentracionária da loucura, a pesada e hedionda burocratização da angústia, e começar do princípio, noutro local, de uma outra forma, a combater o sofrimento, a ansiedade, a depressão, a mania.
>
> (the only thing to do was to destroy the hospital, physically destroy the hospital, the leper walls, the cloisters, (…) the sinister concentration organization of madness, the heavy and hideous bureaucratization of anguish, and start from the beginning, elsewhere, from a otherwise, to fight suffering, anxiety, depression, mania.) [30]

This last cry of despair also amounts to the final purge that the author goes through before embarking on an expansion of the universe of his writing. Even if these three novels are the most condensed and closest to their biographical origin, it does mean that the author gets rid of his *pathographical* preoccupations. Characters who suffer from some kind of physical or mental afflictions are common in the author's work, such as the autistic narrator of *O Arquipélago da Insónia* (*The Archipelago of Insomnia*),[31] chancing a description of the world through the lens of an affected inner world; or the heroin-dependent young man in *Que farei quando tudo arde?* (*What Can I Do When Everything's on Fire?*): "(…) eis-me a empurrar o êmbolo da seringa para o interior da pele (…) transformo-me bum balão de gás encostado ao tecto," ("here I am pushing the plunger of the syringe into the skin (...) I become a gas balloon leaning against the ceiling");[32] or the old actress with dementia in *Para Aquela que Está Sentada no Escuro à Minha Espera* (*For the One Who Is Sitting in the Dark Waiting for Me*): "(...) há dois meses, minto, quase três que deixei de conseguir falar, o médico / - A demência é assim" ("two months ago, I lie, almost three that I stopped being able to speak, the doctor / - Dementia is like that").[33]

In another novel, the medical dimension is even more immediate. *Eu Hei-de Amar uma Pedra* (*I Shall Love a Stone*) is a novel where a young couple is broken apart because of the diagnosis of tuberculosis of the female half of the couple, meeting again only in old age. Despite the obvious pathographic interference of a major illness (TB), the novel also displays another curious aspect. Its second part, named "as consultas" ("the consultations"), consists of several chapters depicting the woman's consultations with a doctor, thus permeating the writing with medical language: "Doente de 82 anos, sexo feminino, idade aparente coincidindo com a real, Orientada no tempo e no espaço, alo e heteropsiquicamente, memória conservada de acordo com os parâmetros etários, contacto adequado, sintónico embora retraído, com dificuldade em verbalizar o motivo da consulta (...)." (82-year-old patient, sex ♀, apparent age coinciding with the real one, oriented in time and space, all and heteropsychically, memory preserved according to age parameters, adequate, syntonic although withdrawn contact, with difficulty in verbalizing the reason for the consultation).[34] This is an interesting shift, for it permits a change in perspective, again finding balance between the inner and the outer realities, but never losing the human sensitivity and ethical commitment that characterise the author's writing.

Therefore, as we can see, the presence of illness and suffering is indeed abundant and displayed in a plethora of perspectives, enriching the various *pathographies* of this particular *pathographer*. It is only by crafting his art the way he did, that Lobo Antunes avoids falling into the trap identified by Susan Sontag when criticising a certain tendency to romanticise illness in its depiction: "That illness can be not only an epic of suffering but the occasion of some kind of self-transcendence is affirmed by sentimental literature and, more convincingly, by case histories offered by doctor-writers."[35] Lobo Antunes' literature successfully manages to illuminate the *pathographies* of his self, of his country's history and culture and ultimately, of society at large. His works present not a romanticising of illness and its sufferers but a deep ethical commitment to *pathos*, thus establishing him not only as a great writer, but also as a great *pathographer*.

Bibliography

Bamforth, Iain, ed. *The Body In the Library: A Literary Anthology of Modern Medicine.* London and New York: Verso Books, 2003.

Barthes, Roland. *Image, Music, Text.* London: Fontana Press, 1977.

Burke, Seán. *The Death and Return of the Author: Criticism and Subjectivity in Barthes, Foucault, and Derrida.* Edinburgh: Edinburgh University Press, 2008.

Carlos, João; "25 de abril: Traumas da guerra colonial aindapersistem" DW.com, (accessed 10/07/2020) https://www.dw.com/pt-002/25-de-abril-traumas-da-guerra-colonial-ainda-persistem/a-48474955.

Cuddon, J. A. and M. A. R. Habib. *The Penguin Dictionary of Literary Terms and Literary Theory: Fifth Edition.* London: Penguin, 2015.

Eagleton, Terry. *After Theory.* London: Penguin, 2004.

Foucault, Michel. *The Birth of the Clinic.* London and New York: Routledge, 2003.

Hawkins, Anne H. "Pathography: patient narratives of illness." *The Western Journal of Medicine* 171, no. 2 (August 1999): pp. 127-129.

Lemos, Márcia and Miguel Ramalhete Gomes. "Introduction." In *Converging Realms: Exchanges between Literature and Science from the 1800s to the 2000s,'* edited by Márcia Lemos and Miguel Ramalhete Gomes. Newcastle: Cambridge Scholars Publishing, 2017.

Lobo Antunes, António.*Conhecimento do Inferno.* Lisboa: Dom Quixote, 2010.

———. *Eu Hei-de Amar um Pedra.* Lisboa: Dom Quixote, 2004.

———. *Memória de Elefante.* Lisboa: Dom Quixote, 2004.

———. *OsCus de Judas.* Lisboa: Dom Quixote, 2010.

———. *O Arquipélago da Insónia.* Lisboa: Dom Quixote, 2008.

———. *O que farei quando tudo arde?* Lisboa: Dom Quixote, 2001.

———. *Para Aquela que Está Sentada no Escuro à minha Espera.* Lisboa: Dom Quixote, 2016.

Leys, Ruth. *Trauma: A Genealogy.* Chicago: The University of Chicago Press, 2000.

Portugal. *Resenha Histórico-militar das campanhas de África: 1961-1974.* Lisboa: EME, CECA, 1988.

Russell, Bertrand. *Sceptical Essays.* London and New York: Routledge, 1970.

Sontag, Susan. *Illness as Metaphor & Aids and its Metaphors.* London: Penguin Books, 1991.

Notes

[1] Márcia Lemos and Miguel Ramalhete, "Introduction" in *Converging Realms: Exchanges between Literature and Science from the 1800s to the 2000s'*, ed. Márcia Lemos and Miguel Ramalhete Gomes (Newcastle: Cambridge Scholars Publishing, 2017), p. *x*.

[2] Iain Bamforth, "Introduction", in *The Body in the Library: A Literary Anthology of Modern Medicine* (London and New York: Verso Books, 2003), p. xiv.

[3] Bamforth, "Introduction", p. xxii.

[4] Bertrand Russell, *Sceptical Essays* (London and New York: Routledge, 1970), p.35.

[5] The philosopher's essay appeared as early as 1928 whilst the novelist first work dates from 1979.
[6] Russell, *Sceptical Essays,* p.33.
[7] Ibid., 33.
[8] Given the nature of the writer's work, this association is very ironic. However, it would be farfetched to create any type of deeper connection. An ironic fact, no more than that.
[9] Michel Foucault, *The Birth of the Clinic* (London and New York: Routledge, 2003) p. xi.
[10] Ibid., xi.
[11] Foucault, *The Birth of the Clinic*, p. xv.
[12] Seán Burke, *The Death and Return of the Author: Criticism and Subjectivity in Barthes, Foucault, and Derrida* (Edinburgh: Edinburgh University Press, 2008) p.180.
[13] Here is only presented the Portuguese perspective. If one was to engage with the African side of the conflict, not only the numbers will be higher, there would also be a lot more to be said, certainly exceeding the scope of this chapter.
[14] These figures were obtained from consulting the findings of the Comissão para o Estudo das Campanhas de África (1988), in Portugal. 1988. *Resenha Histórico-militar das campanhas de África: 1961-1974.* (Lisboa: EME, CECA. 1988).
[15] João Carlos, "25 de abril: Traumas da guerra colonial aindapersistem" DW.com (accessed 10/07/2020) https://www.dw.com/pt-002/25-de-abril-traumas-da-guerra-colonial-ainda-persistem/a-48474955
[16] Roland Barthes, *Image, Music, Text* (London: Fontana Press, 1977) p.142.
[17] Terry Eagleton, *After Theory* (London: Penguin, 2004) p.137.
[18] Anne H. Hawkins "Pathography: patient narratives of illness." in *The Western journal of medicine,* 171 (2), (California, 1999), pp. 127–129.
[19] Ibid., pp. 127-129.
[20] J. A. Cuddon, M. A. R. Habib, *The Penguin Dictionary of Literary Terms and Literary Theory: Fifth Edition 5th Revised ed.* (London: Penguin, 2014) p. 520.
[21] At the time this text was written, this was the number of published books. However, the reader might find that by the time he/she is visiting these words, this number has increased.
[22] There is no actual name for this trilogy, and in fact, it can be argued if it is even a trilogy given that the author revisits the same environment in later books. The classification was made by the author himself when explaining that these three books were written when he was still learning how to be an author.
[23] *Memória de Elefante* (Elephant's Memory) is not translated into English. Both *Os Cus de Judas* (The Land at the End of the World) and *Conhecimento do Inferno* (Knowledge of Hell) are translated in English.
[24] António Lobo Antunes, *Memória de Elefante* (Lisboa: Dom Quixote, 2004) p. 20.
[25] All translations are mine.
[26] Ruth Leys; *Trauma: A Genealogy* (Chicago: The University of Chicago Press, 2000) p. 2.
[27] "Illness is the nigh-side of life, a more onerous citizenship." Susan Sontag; *Illness as Metaphor & Aids and its Metaphors* (London: Penguin Books, 1991) p. 3.
[28] António Lobo Antunes; *OsCus de Judas* (Lisboa: Dom Quixote, 2010) p. 69.
[29] António Lobo Antunes; *Conhecimento do Inferno* (Lisboa: Dom Quixote, 2010) p. 40.
[30] Ibid.,185.
[31] António Lobo Antunes; *O Arquipélago da Insónia* (Lisboa: Dom Quixote, 2008).

[32] António Lobo Antunes; *O que farei quando tudo arde?* (Lisboa: Dom Quixote, 2001) p. 198.
[33] António Lobo Antunes; *Para Aquela que Está Sentada no Escuro à minha Espera* (Lisboa: Dom Quixote, 2016) p. 255.
[34] António Lobo Antunes; *Eu Hei-de Amar um Pedra* (Lisboa: Dom Quixote, 2004) p. 251.
[35] Sontag; *Illness as Metaphor & Aids and its Metaphors,* p. 123.

II.
American Literary Pathographies

Chapter 8

"To Him Who Wants It!": Understanding William Carlos Williams' Pathography

Seunghyun Shin

University of Vermont, USA

Abstract: This chapter explores short stories, poetry and prose of William Carlos Williams that engage with the interplay between medicine and literature. The central aim of the chapter is to demonstrate Williams' anti-modernist impulse in poetic projects, which were inspired by his own medical practice, while attempting to provoke a meaningful dialogue with townspeople both as a modernist poet and a physician. In illuminating how medical practice has driven the anti-modernist impulse in his experimental poetics, this chapter ultimately discusses how Williams' empathy clashed with his professionalism and, therefore, portrays his work as pathography. The interplay of medicine and poetry in his writing supplements the reshaping of pathography in literary studies by portraying him as a pathographer of the local streets in New Jersey. He was always prepared to ask his patients and readers to maintain the hope of effective communication and productive human relationships in modern America. Taking his poetry as an exemplary synthesis of poetry and medicine, I wish to show that Williams presented a vision of poetry as a uniquely positioned medium for communicating with his patients who had physical, mental, and psychological pain. To make this argument, I first discuss how pathography is defined in literary studies. After reshaping pathography in literary studies as "the language of pain," I will refer to Williams' short stories that reveal Williams' empathy clashing with the professionalism as a physician. In the end, the chapter will contend that the writing of poetry was cathartic to Williams as a pathographer, along with the fact that his medical practices shaped his poetry to satisfy the pathographic fever of understanding the language of pain.

Keywords: Williams, Pathography, pain, Physician-writer, empathy, Modernist, Objectivist.

* * *

When I worked at the local hospital before coming to America, my first mission as the youngest doctor was to study a patient's personal history. I remember that I had not realised how vital the fundamental study of a patient's biography was until one of my colleagues prescribed inappropriate analgesics to his first patient and he had frequent paroxysms. In medicine, *pathography* stands for such individual biographies that explore the effect of a disease or drug on a patient's life. Most young doctors, at least when I was a resident physician of that hospital, learn how to read and analyze a patient's biography. It is sometimes written by each specialist in a medical field or psychologists who observe and interact with patients carefully.

The term's definition is extended to indicate a contemporary subgenre in literary studies. My topic in this essay is to critique on and supplement its definition by illuminating the attempt of William Carlos Williams' to converge his physical experience as the local doctor with literary composition as a writer. Considering his work as pathography has two stakes: (i) it provides an exemplary model of pathography that has been written by a physician-writer; and (ii) it shifts the critical attention from Williams' achievements as a modernist poet on which many scholars focus—the Pulitzer Prize and National Book Award that won him national acclaim—to his complex identity as a physician-writer and how the medical practice influenced the shaping of his work. To do so, I will discuss the problems that I noticed about the definition of pathography in literary studies and then distinguish its characteristics in Williams' fusion of medical practice and literary composition by examining four of his works that range from short stories to poetry and hybrid-prose: "Jean Beicke," "A Night in June," *Al Que Quiere!,* and *Spring and All.* This selection does not, of course, imply that I am ignoring the significance of his experimental poetics or the Objectivist language that marks him as a major modernist poet on the literary map; it suggests that such modernist milestones—later succeeded by the Black Mountain and the Beat poets—were not only socio-political methodology for him as a leftist of the 1930s but also derived from a pathographic fever of the local physician in New Jersey who sought productive human relationships with the local townspeople as well as his patients in modern America, managing to write more than thirty books while delivering over 3,000 babies in Rutherford over forty years.

Re-shaping Pathography in Literary Studies

For a start, in literary studies, pathography is considered a subgenre of autobiography that explores the effects of a certain disease or psychological disorder on a patient's life—whereas it stands for a biography that is solely studied by a physician in medicine. As it links illness and treatment with the author's personal history, it provides an opportunity for writers to share the story of illness from the perspective of the individual. There are two major problems that I notice in this general definition. First, Anne Hawkins begins to unravel the intricacies of pathography's definition in her essay "Pathography: Patient Narratives of Illness," defining pathography as a new literary practice that belongs "exclusively to the second half of the 20th century."[1] Similar to her discourse, it is not difficult to find contemporary critics that highlight it as a new practice emerged in the late twentieth century: in his 2000 essay, John Wiltshire defines pathography upon the premise that it "has emerged in the last forty or so years;" and Arthur Frank also argues that pathography is a post-modern conception that has been developed to declare a sick person's reclamation of the agency when he hands over his body to biomedical expertise.[2] But what such treatments of pathography do not consider is that disease has spread its tentacles into history as it has been part of writers' personal histories, and therefore, appeared in different forms, nestled into poetry, disguised as essay, and transformed into a novel. For example, John Keats' "Ode to a Nightingale" manifests his pain after the death of his brother due to the family disease tuberculosis and Virginia Woolf also suffered from a mental disorder so much so that she reflected on this in her 1925 essay, "On Being Ill." This linear view of critics on pathography that overlooks it as contemporary illness narratives denies developing its literary boundaries beyond the feature of biographical landscapes.

Simultaneously, it is important to note that the epistemological aspects of medicine in pathography have it focus on a single diseased patient to ultimately understand the medical issue. The functionalities of illness and the narrators are poorly defined in this discourse as pathography is simplified to the memoir of the illness experience and such illness narratives commonly give more attention to individual remarks of a sick person, his relatives or caregivers. Such simplified treatments of pathography implies that illness has been considered plausibly presented in individual perspectives rather than as socio-political processes. It is necessary to develop them in more diversified terms since the so-called illness narratives do not always conform to the tradition of being written exclusively in the patient's perspective and elaborates self-consciously about the illness. As the so-called pathography appears in different forms, it can either transform into philosophical meditation or convey socio-political questions not only in a patient's perspective but also through other biographical accounts. To provide an exemplary model, I refer to Daniel Defoe's novel *A Journal of the Plague Year*. At the beginning, the novel begins with an introduction under the title that explains its context:

> being Observations or Memorials
> of the most remarkable occurrences,
> as well public *as* private, which happened in
> London during the last great visitation in 1665.
> Written by a CITIZEN who continued
> all the while in *London*.[3]

Regardless of the past disputes in literary studies whether the journal is historiography or novel, Defoe elaborates the account of the Great Plague of 1665 in a citizen's perspective; the narrator explains what happens in London and how the community is influenced by the bubonic plague. As *Journal* is considered as one of the first novels by many literary critics and they theoretically treat the plague's impact on the community described in the narrative as a socio-political phenomenon, the novel has been scrutinised by many scholars while there has been lack of critical attention to the role of illness itself in such contexts.[4] This illness narrative of Defoe, therefore, traces the history of pathography at least back to the eighteenth century and socio-political narratives of the unidentified narrator "HF" in the novel exemplifies that the illness experience could be depicted by other perspectives than that of the patient.[5]

As exemplified by the *Journal*, we can suggest that illness in illness narratives is "public *as* private" so that it implies an informal literary framework based on the relationship between individuals—patients, relatives, caregivers, doctors—and the literary world. Here, we can suggest that illness produces the language of pain— pain can be a private pain of a patient and the empathy of a doctor as well as the public frustration of citizens in London as observed in the *Journal*. This language of pain simultaneously positions the world as their context, something they change on their own, either individually or culturally; medicine, as a feature of the experience of illness, is an exemplary form of such changes. This interdisciplinary approach to the practice of medicine in this conversation implies a degree of critical distance from reductionist viewpoints of medical education and practice that limit the boundaries of pathography to medical, psychological, and psychiatric sub-disciplines. In this sense, pathography in literary studies documents the language of pain. Accepting this, I will treat pathography as literature of pain that extends the epistemological aspects of medicine by diversifying its literary characteristics: (i) it refers to a specific study of either individual personae or community based on the effects of a certain illness or medical practice; (ii) it describes an author's account in the perspective of a patient or anyone related to the medical issue; and (iii) it does not necessarily have to be exclusively about illness and has flexibility as a literary genre. In light of this, we can suggest that its literary characteristics are more eclectic than how Hawkins metaphorically represented—our modern adventure story.[6] Regardless of whoever the narrator of the adventurous illness narrative is and whatever literary genre that it disguises into, pathography is an experimental fusion of medicine and literature that assembles its tradition of biographical accounts and the language of pain.

Language of Pain in "Jean Beicke" and "A Night in June"

William Carlos Williams' short stories participate in this realm in which medicine and literature come together as pathography. As we take a closer look at his short stories, Williams' account reveals the discrepancy between the verisimilitude of the doctor and the self-consciousness as a modernist writer to dramatize the language of pain he had during his life along the Passaic river.[7] Two of the short stories I have in mind—"Jean Beicke" and "A Night in June"—narrate a survey of struggles between professionalism and empathy that he inevitably had to endure as a doctor: the pediatrician who starts to realize the horror of treating human bodies as medical specimens in the former realises that he does not fully understand a patient's pain in the latter. On the one hand, Williams' narrator in "Jean Beicke" is the local physician whose mission is to save impoverished infants from pneumonia:

> The poor brats are almost dead sometimes, just living skeletons, almost wrapped in rags, their heads caked with dirt, their eyes stuck together with pus and their legs all excoriated from the dirty diapers no one has had the interest to take off them regularly…The mother gave a story of having had it in some sort of home in Paterson. We couldn't get it straight…We take'em and try to make something out of them.[8]

The physician seemingly presents an inherently cold outlook that emotionally detaches himself from the poor kids and one of their mothers. The emotional detachment and his conversation with the mother call into question a consensus among doctors, nurses and other medical specialists who "try to make something out of them" instead of attempting to save—it is important to note here that Williams was a physician during the Great Depression and many of the local patients in New Jersey could not financially afford medical treatments. For this reason, when the physician has to conduct postmortem examination on dead bodies of those kids, he refuses to empathize with them: "And sometimes the kids are not only dirty and neglected but sick, ready to die…when I, for one, wish they'd never get well."[9]

Here, we can reflect that the refusal is not equivalent to the refusal to lament the death of the young kids but implies his refusal to implicate himself in the horror and the complexity of the world in which the kids are treated as mere clinical specimens. For this reason, he positions himself in that world in a brash manner as he orders nurses: "give it an enema, maybe it will get well and grow into a cheap prostitute or something."[10]

When a little girl "Jean Beicke" arrives at the hospital, however, we can observe significant changes in the narrator's disguised emotional distancing. It is surprising to see how Jean must have somehow awakened his sympathy as he says: "I had to laugh every time I looked at the brat after that, she was such a funny looking one but one thing that kept her from being a total loss was that she did eat…As sick as she was, she took her grub right on time every three hours, a big eight-ounce bottle of whole milk and digested it perfectly…she began to gain in weight. Can you imagine that?"[11]

To the physician narrator and other nurses, looking at Jean as being able to eat and gaining weight is miraculous to them since they could not expect it. This growing sympathy clashes with his professional determination to detach himself from the patients. Although Jean ends up dying in the narrative, the sympathy makes the narrator recognise what his professionalism should aim at and confess the refusal to implicate himself in the world:

> Poor kids! […] They come in with pneumonia, a temperature of a hundred and six, maybe, and before you can do a thing, they're dead.
>
> This little Jean Beicke was like that. She was about the worst you'd expect to find anywhere…I couldn't get used to it.[12]

It is remarkable to see a change in the narrator's tone as he says that he can never be accustomed to treating poor kids as mere objects to be examined on the autopsy table. It is not clear how Jean specifically awakened the determination and sympathy of the physician narrator who briefly implicates the horrendous medical world in which he has to see patients die. Here, we can suggest that death was no tragedy but a biological process for Dr. Williams and the brash pediatrician's sympathy to the death of Jean's—and the other poor kids—reveals the façade. As he makes the last assessment, his confessional tone of language indicates that he is more emotionally attached to Jean:

> She was such a scrawny, misshapen, worthless piece of humanity that I had said…but after a month watching her suck up her milk and thrive on it—and to see those alert blue eyes in that face—well, it wasn't pleasant…There was an older woman there looking in at that baby

also—no better off than Jean, surely. I spoke to her, thinking she was the mother of this one, but she wasn't.[13]

As Jean's death slowly shifts his manner, we can reflect that it reshapes his language into the language of pain. He also realises how incomprehensible he is as he does not know her mother until then. This shift is crucial for the narrator as he tries his best to save Jean, and his persona is, therefore, transformed into the narrative as, for him, Jean's existence is changed from a medical specimen to her blue eyes. Beginning with the development of this language of pain, we can observe that the influences of Jean's death on the physician were manifold. As he mourns Jean's death, he starts to empathize with her mother who tries to move on from her death as she could not afford medical treatments after her husband abandoned her. As a result of this empathy, the physician ends the narrative by his conversation with the ear man who says the autopsy proved that they could have saved her if she could have come to the hospital earlier.

Here, we can suggest that the language of pain that Williams develops in this narrative consists of a physician's empathy and the emotional attachment to his patients. As Williams manifests the closer relationship between a physician and his patients, it produces the language of pain that turns him into a pathographer. But this statement has a problem though: if the physician narrator in "Jean Beicke" apparently becomes emotionally more attached to Jean, how could he claim the closer relationship between a physician and his patient if he does not understand her language of pain? In the narrative, the physician does not know who her mother is and what she and her family have been through. More importantly, he mourns Jean's death but this sympathy is exclusive to his position as a physician of an infant who cannot speak. In other words, his language of pain is accessible to readers but he does not fully understand that of his patient's. The narrator in "Jean Beicke" does not recognize this until the end whereas the one in "A Night in June" doubts whether he understands his patient's pain. In contrast to Jean's physician, the physician narrator in "A Night in June" traces his history back to eighteen years before—as he briefly mentions that this baby is eighteen when he delivers the ninth baby from her later in the narrative—when the young man delivered the first baby for a peasant woman who did not speak English fluently:

> Sometimes she'd cry out at her husband, as I got to know her later, with some high pitched animalistic sound when he would say something to her in Italian that I couldn't understand and I knew that she was holding out for me. Usually though, she said very little, looking at me straight in the eye with a smile, her voice pleasant and candid through I could scarcely understand her few broken words. Her sentences were

seldom more than three or four words long. She always acted as though I must naturally know what was in her mind and her smile with a shrug always won me.[14]

It is rare to see home delivery in the twenty-first century and the young physician seemingly fails to deliver the baby as he has no nurse, anesthetist, and even hot water. He comprehends the pain in the "animalistic" sound though he cannot fully understand her spoken words. Her smile, pleasant and candid voice, is more comprehensible than the verbal language as the narrator seems to empathize with her pain. Here, it is paradoxical that the candidness of incomprehensible sound is more comprehensible to the narrator than verbal language that he has to comprehend. This sense of candidness is not directly given in sensuous intuition but derived from empathizing with the patient's experience of physical pain. The "animalistic sound", therefore, conveys the physical pain so that less sound could be misinterpreted as it is equivalent to less pain. On a beautiful night in June after eighteen years, the narrator seems to be accustomed to deliver her ninth baby for the peasant woman. While delivering the baby, he finds out that he starts to recognise that the "animalistic sound" does not fully represent the language of pain:

> She doesn't seem to be having many strong pains, I said to my companion in the kitchen, for there wasn't a sound from the labor room and hadn't been for the past half hour.
>
> She don't want to make no noise and wake the kids.
>
> How old is the oldest now? I asked.
>
> He's sixteen. The girl would have been eighteen this year. You know the first one you took from her.[15]

As the physician realises that quietness does not refer to less pain, he also empathises with the woman over the boundary of physical pain. Thus, we can reflect that Williams diversifies a patient's language of pain simultaneously to mental and emotional dimensions as they constitute another core when the physician or relatives empathises with. This signifies the exchange of language between the physician and his patient:

> Go ahead, I said. Pull hard. I welcomed the feel of her hands and the strong pull. It quieted me in the way the whole house had quieted me all night.

> This woman in her present condition would have seemed repulsive to me ten years ago—now, poor soul, I see her to be as clean as a cow that calves. The flesh of my arm lay against the flesh of her knee gratefully. It was I who was being comforted and soothed.[16]

As the narrator exchanges the language of pain with the woman in this scene, we can suggest that Williams instances the different forms of pain in language, analogous to influences of illness on the individual personae. In this process, the comprehensibility and candidness of language are vital for satisfying his pathographic fever as the narrator is more emotionally attached to his patient. This exchange is ultimately productive of the physician narrator as an inner theatre of Williams himself, manifested in humane relationship between a doctor and his patient, beyond a certain point of emotional intimacy, resulting in Williams' pursuit of effective communication between him as a pathographer and his patients as the local townspeople in Rutherford.

Pathographer Williams in *Al Que Quiere!* and *Spring and All*

For this reason, both physician narrators in the two short stories portray Williams as a pathographer who documents the language of pain. As the narrator of "A Night in June" reveals the candidness of the animalistic sound and realizes that the language of pain has more capacity for referring to pain beyond the physical dimension, we can suggest that Williams, as the local physician, oscillated between being a physician and a modernist writer. This oscillation between medical practices and the emotional attachment to patients as a physician-writer is a key to understanding how his poetry is differentiated from the work of other modernists. As Yvor Winters once infamously underappreciated his career by calling him "a foolish and ignorant man," a handful of Williams' colleagues mark his work as local and regional compared to the high modernist contemporaries—such as James Joyce, Ezra Pound, and T.S. Eliot.[17] As a reaction to this, and central to discussions about Williams' literary career, Williams as a writer had a poetic goal of his locally-based writing to be understood by his patients and it meets an international standard of his expatriate contemporaries. As exemplified by the two short stories, Williams encountered patients who were poor and often illiterate— the peasant woman who had the ninth baby could not speak English fluently and she was as poor as the impoverished kids like Jean Beicke—while working as a physician in the suburb of Rutherford, which had socioeconomically diverse demographics in the Depression-era. The goal has driven Williams to exploit the resonances of small words that depict quotidian experience in modern America. Among major twentieth-century Objectivist poets—such as Louis Zukofsky, George Oppen, and Charles Reznikoff— Williams' quotidian experience in poetry as a physician-writer predates many of the later Objectivist poems that emerged in the 1930s. What separates Williams' work from the other major figures is such influences of the medical practice that gave him the pathographic fever to pursue an effective understanding of language between a doctor and his patients. In his 1917 collection of poems, *Al Que Quiere!* for example, he describes the daily life of a local doctor of New Jersey in a poem entitled "January Morning: Suite." The poem begins by describing local America in the early twentieth century: even if his "operation was postponed," he sees "the tall probationers / in their tan uniforms / hurrying to breakfast!"[18] At the end, he articulates the purpose of writing poetry in his quotidian experience as the local physician:

> All this —
> was for you, old woman.
> I wanted to write a poem
> that you would understand.
> For what good is it to me
> if you can't understand it?[19]

The physician's desire for the old woman to understand his poem not only demonstrates Williams' commitment to writing in comprehensible language to every reader but also implies his attempt to fuse the act of writing poetry with the quotidian experience of the local doctor. By asking "For what good is it to me if you can't understand it?" Williams declares an intimacy with readers and simultaneously attempts to provoke meaningful dialogue. For Williams, this intimacy is equivalent to the language of pain that he exchanges with his patients. About this literary pursuit of human relationship and effective communication in a physician's perspective, George Monteiro states: "The point in calling them a doctor's stories is that at their best they draw essentially both from the doctor's quotidian experiences upon his embodied conflicts between his learned professionalism and his affective impulses. His practice was his avenue to particular kinds of sociological experience that would otherwise have been unknown to him."[20]

What Monteiro states in this paragraph reverts us back to the idea that the exchange of language of pain as a physician with his patients made him vacillate between the professionalism and the contradictory impulses as a writer. As Williams writes in *The Autobiography*, "All that I have wanted to do was to tell of my life as I went along practicing medicine and at the same time recording my daily search for…what? As a writer, I have been a physician, and as a physician a writer," this oscillation shapes his work as pathography based on the relationship between him, his patients, and the local townspeople.[21] It also explains his translation of the title *Al Que Quiere!*, "To Him Who Wants It!"

that he explains in the conversation with Edith Heal: "I was convinced nobody in the world of poetry wanted me but I was there willing to pass the ball if anyone did want it."[22]

Here, we can also reflect that, for Williams, the oscillation between the professionalism in the medical practice and the affective impulses as a poet has driven the rejection to the high modernist poetry—which we would now label anti-modernist—of Eliot, Pound, Stevens, Moore, and others. In 1923, after six years of throwing the ball to patients and the townspeople who wanted his, he stands against those he calls "moderns" in the hybrid-prose work, *Spring and All*:

> Poetry that used to go hand in hand with life, poetry that interpreted our deepest promptings, poetry that inspired, that led us forward to new discoveries, new depths of tolerance, new heights of exaltation. You moderns! it is the death of poetry that you are accomplishing. No. I cannot understand this work. You have not yet suffered a cruel blow from life. When you have suffered you will write differently?[23]

As hinted previously, the pursuit of comprehensible language for his patients and the local townspeople suggests that his literary colleagues do not satisfy his pathographic fever. Hence, Williams debunks the high modernist poetry by identifying its detachment from history, society, and politics while claiming that the formal innovation in aesthetics makes the high modernist literature too high for readers and it does not, therefore, bear any relevant difference from the work of precursors who placed a barrier between the reader and the world. For example, symbolism is too obscure for Williams:

> Crude symbolism is to associate emotions with natural phenomena such as anger with lightning, flowers with love it goes further and associates certain textures with. Such work is empty. It is very typical of almost all that is done by the writers who fill the pages every month of such a paper as … It is typified by use of the word "like" or that "evocation" of the "image" which served us for a time. Its abuse is apparent. The insignificant "image" may be "evoked" never so ably and still mean nothing.[24]

Just as this reinforces the sense that the formal innovation in aesthetics still made the high modernist poetry obscure, so it also implies that, Williams as a pathographer provoked himself to escape the incomprehensibility of the high modernist language that detached poetry from the real world: "crude symbolism, the annihilation of strained associations, complicated ritualistic forms designated to separate the work from 'reality'".[25] Here, we can add that comprehensibility of language and the poet's literary intimacy with readers constitute the correspondence of the literary world to the real world, and readers' cognitive processes involved in reading poetry—which Williams conceptualizes as imagination.[26] It is this very immersion to the comprehensible language that readers imagine through their consciousness, awareness, and the hyperreal experience of identifying the real world with the literary world.

In this sense, therefore, Williams considered language as another interface for readers to identify reality with the literary world. This anti-modernist hallmark derived from the patient-physician exchanges marks a significant change in Williams' literary career as he is also one of the major figures in establishing the Imagist poetry during the 1910s with Pound. At this point in his literary career, the pathographic fever he had as a physician forced him to innovate not only the aesthetics but the ways to think about the purpose of literary composition. For Williams, medicine and poetry come together as pathography that has provoked the anti-modernist impulse: we can reflect that the poet's literary intimacy with readers is equivalent to the local physician empathising with his patients and the anti-modernist impulse to find comprehensible language is derived from attempts to understand the language of pain. He was able to turn medical jargon into more comprehensible narratives to patients as medicine differentiated him from the high modernist innovation in the aesthetics. In the light of all this, his experimental pursuit, which is later succeeded by the Objectivists, the school of Black Mountain, the Beat generation, and even other poets of the mid-twentieth century—such as Charles Olson and Allen Ginsberg—was part of Williams' journey as a poet of the street, a physician of people who was determined to call him doctor, and an ordinary man who wanted to compose poetry for the people in Rutherford; thus, separating his work from the high modernist expulsion of socio-political contexts. In this sense, Coles' title of the anthology *The Doctor Stories* does not somewhat fully represent Williams' work. Williams' idiosyncratic journey as a pathographer proves that his work is not an exclusive story of the local physician in New Jersey but the language of pain archived by a documentarian of the street who wanted his language to be an interface for people to exchange their pain.

Acknowledgement

To my mentor, James H. Searle—the most inspirational activist, writer, and Marxist whom I met in the United States of America.

To my current mentor, Dr. Todd McGowan—the only pedagogue in the world who has been capable of making me enjoy reading critical theories.

And to my mom—the only woman who has shown me what feminism truly means throughout her life.

Bibliography

Coles, Robert. "Introduction." In *The Doctor Stories. Introduction to the Compiled Work of William Carlos Williams*, New York: New Directions, 1984.

Defoe, Daniel. *A Journal of the Plague Year*, edited by Louis Landa. Oxford: Oxford University Press, 1969.

Foucault, Michel. *Discipline and Punish*. New York: Random House, 1978.

Grube, C. M. A. "Greek Medicine and the Greek Genius." *Phoenix* 8, no. 4 (1954): pp. 123-35, https://www.jstor.org/stable/1086122.

Hawkins, A. H. "Pathography: Patient narratives of Illness." *Western Journal of Medicine* 171, no. 2 (1999): pp. 127-9, https://www.ncbi.nlm.nih.gov/pmc/articles/PMC1305776/.

———. *Reconstructing Illness: Studies in Pathography*. 2nd edition. West Lafayette: Purdue University Press, 1999.

Monteiro, George. "The Doctor's Black Bag: William Carlos Williams' Passaic River Stories." *Modern Language Studies* 13, no. 1 (1983): pp. 77-84, https://www.jstor.org/stable/3194321.

Watt, Ian. *The Rise of the Novel: Studies in Defoe, Richardson and Fielding*. Berkeley and Los Angeles: University of California Press, 1957.

Williams, William Carlos. *Al Que Quiere!*. Boston: The Four Seas Company, 1917.

———. "A Night in June." *The Farmers' Daughters: The Collected Stories of William Carlos Williams*, 136-43. Introduction by Van Wyck Brooks, New York: New Directions, 1961.

———. *I Wanted to Write a Poem: The Autobiography of the Works of a Poet*. New York: New Directions, 1967.

———. "Jean Beicke." *The Doctor Stories*, 69-77. Introduction by Robert Coles, New York: New Directions, 1984.

———. *Spring and All*. New York: New Directions, 2011.

———. *The Autobiography of William Carlos Williams*. New York: Random House, 1951.

Wiltshire, J. "Biography, Pathography, and the Recovery of Meaning." *The Cambridge Quarterly* 29, no. 4, (2000): pp. 409-22, https://www.jstor.org/stable/42968081

Winters, Yvor. "Poetry of Feeling." Reprinted in *William Carlos Williams: A Collection of Critical Essays*, edited by J. Hillis Miller. Upper Saddle River, NJ: Prentice-Hall, 1966.

Notes

[1] Hawkins, "Pathography: Patient narratives of Illness." *Western Journal of Medicine* 171, no. 2 (1999): 127, https://www.ncbi.nlm.nih.gov/pmc/articles/PMC1305776/.

[2] Wiltshire, "Biography, Pathography, and the Recovery of Meaning." *The Cambridge Quarterly* 29, no. 4, (2000): 409, https://www.jstor.org/stable/42968081; for a full discussion of Frank's definition of pathography, look at *The Wounded Storyteller* (Chicago: University of Chicago Press, 2013).

[3] Defoe, *A Journal of the Plague Year*, the cover page.

4 For example, there are scholarships about the connection between Michel Foucault's discourse on discipline and Defoe's plague narrative. The novel itself is also studied by literary critics who consider Defoe as one of the first novelists. For an exemplary model, I recommend Foucault, *Discipline and Punish* (New York: Random House, 1978) and Watt, *The Rise of the Novel: Studies in Defoe, Richardson and Fielding* (Berkeley and Los Angeles: University of California Press, 1957).

5 History of pathography could be traced back even to ancient times. For a full discussion about history of pathography that is derived from Hippocrates, look at Grube, "Greek Medicine and the Greek Genius." Phoenix 8, no. 4 (1954): pp. 123-35, https://www.jstor.org/stable/1086122.

6 Hawkins, *Recontructing Illness* (West Lafayette: Purdue UP, 1999), 1.

7 Williams originally published the short stories in 1938 and the collection of them is entitled *Life Along the Passaic River*. The collection has been later anthologized in *The Farmers' Daughters* (New York: New Directions, 1961) and some of the stories were selected and compiled by Robert Coles in *The Doctor Stories* (New York: New Directions, 1984).

8 Williams, "Jean Beicke," 70.

9 Ibid., 71.

10 Ibid., 76.

11 Ibid., 73.

12 Ibid., 71.

13 Ibid., 74.

14 Williams, "A Night in June," 136.

15 Ibid., 139.

16 Ibid., 142.

17 Winters, "Poetry of Feeling," 69.

18 Williams, *Al Que Quiere!*, 66.

19 Ibid., 67.

20 Monteiro, "The Doctor's Black Bag," 77.

21 Williams, *The Autobiography*, xii.

22 Williams, *I Wanted to Write a Poem*, 19.

23 Williams, *Spring and All*, 2.

24 Ibid., 20.

25 Ibid., 22.

26 For a full discussion about imagination, see Williams, *Spring and All* (New York: New Directions, 2011).

Chapter 9

Lesbianism, Disability, and Pain: Shirley Jackson's *We Have Always Lived in the Castle* as a Pathography

Tatiana Prorokova-Konrad

University of Vienna, Austria

Abstract: This chapter focuses on Shirley Jackson's novel *We Have Always Lived in the Castle*, written in 1962. Examining two female characters, the sisters Merricat and Constance, from the perspective of disability studies and queer studies, I wish to demonstrate how the novel reflects the discriminating nature of patriarchy on women, particularly women with disabilities and lesbianism. I argue that the sisters' gender, sexual orientation, and disability intersect in the novel, showcasing oppression on females during the times of patriarchy in the mid-twentieth-century United States from a very specific perspective, helping reinforce the perverse nature of patriarchy. Love plays an important role in the novel, as it is with the help of love that the women withstand homophobia and ableism. At the same time, their love, as this essay will claim, is viewed as "perverse" and "abnormal" by the villagers, which results in the two characters' complete isolation from society. They choose to never leave their house again. This, I argue, is a response to the hatred toward queer individuals and people with disabilities. It is through the issues of love, disability, and queerness that I explore Jackson's novel as a powerful illustration of how society discriminated against and publicly humiliated lesbian and/or disabled women.

Keywords: Patriarchy, disability, lesbian, gender, homophobia, ableism, isolation, love.

* * *

The themes of domesticity and female oppression can frequently be found in the works of American female writers of the mid-twentieth century. These themes arguably unite the female writings of the twentieth century with the writings of the nineteenth century. Just as "the female characters created by Victorian women writers appear continually conscious of their own vulnerability in the face of male potency and privilege,"[1] so the female characters of the 1950s were deeply aware of still firmly existing patriarchy. Patriarchy that continued to reign in society in the middle of the twentieth century, cutting off any chance for a female equality, formulated a certain "postwar feminine ideal that limited their [women's] lives to the domestic sphere."[2] Patriarchy, as I have argued elsewhere, "vehemently diminished the role of a woman to a biological and sexual object only."[3] Women were expected to "seek fulfillment as wives and mothers."[4] An understanding of a woman as a purely domestic object was often reflected, discussed, and criticized in American writings of that time. Female writers' protest against such a social "norm" in the twentieth century is somewhat reminiscent of "a common, female impulse to struggle free from social and literary confinement"[5] that took place a century earlier. Shirley Jackson is one of those twentieth-century female authors who widely reflected the issues of patriarchy and female struggle in her short stories and novels. Such is her last novel published in 1962 *We Have Always Lived in the Castle*: the narrative articulates the author's protest against patriarchy through two powerful female characters — the Blackwood sisters, Constance and Mary Katherine (usually referred to as Merricat) — who demonstrate a strong wish to be able to control their lives in spite of the pressures from society.

The life of Shirley Jackson, and specifically her worsening psychological condition, along with the fact that she was a woman in a patriarchal society, both influenced her writing and were implicitly reflected in her last novel. There are also other interpretations of both Jackson's oppression based on her gender and of her mental health. For example, there is an opinion that Jackson's claim about she being treated as unequal to men was nothing more than the author's sanctimony: in other words, she thought of herself as a housewife while, in fact, she had a profession, i.e., she was writing for the public.[6] As for the reference to Jackson's psychological illness, her husband Stanley Edgar Hyman underlined the fallacy of construing Jackson's "fierce visions of dissociation and madness, of alienation and withdrawal, of cruelty and terror" as "personal, even neurotic, fantasies" because in reality, those were "a sensitive and faithful anatomy of our times, fitting symbols for our distressing world of the concentration camp and the Bomb."[7] It is, of course, difficult to completely refute this standpoint— after all, the complex political and social events that took place during World War II and the Cold War were largely influencing individuals worldwide; yet I contend that, first, Jackson's deteriorating mental health and, second, her living in a society where women were considered inferior to and dependent on men, patently left an indelible stamp on the author's way of thinking and, hence, became an integral part of her novels, including *We Have Always Lived in the Castle*.

In this chapter, I explore the debilitating influence of patriarchy on women through Jackson's novel *We Have Always Lived in the Castle*. I argue that the novel dramatically expands the problem of gender inequality through lesbianism and disability. I examine the sisters Merricat and Constance from the perspective of queer studies and disability studies, and demonstrate how the novel reflects the discriminating nature of patriarchy on lesbians and women with disabilities. I argue that the sisters' gender, sexual orientation, and disability intersect in the novel. The society's inability to accept the two women and the sisters' ultimate social alienation are the results of a complex nature of women's oppression during the times of patriarchy in the mid-twentieth century U.S.

We Have Always Lived in the Castle is a novel about two sisters, Constance and Merricat. They live isolated from the other villagers. Six years ago, the sisters' parents, brother, and aunt were mercilessly murdered in the house. The main suspect was Constance but she was discharged due to lack of evidence. Since then, the sisters have been living together with the only survived yet physically and mentally ill Uncle Julian. Merricat's pet, Jonas, is described as an important member of their family. The villagers hate the family and therefore the Blackwoods mostly stay at home, excluding these rare times when Merricat has to go shopping. The villagers use these times as an opportunity to spite the girl, trying to make it clear that they do not want the family to be part of their community. For example, when one of the villagers joins Merricat for coffee, he intentionally tells her about a "gossip" he heard from somebody: "I'm just asking Miss Mary Katherine Blackwood here how it happens everyone in town is saying she and her big sister are going to be leaving us soon. Moving away. Going somewhere else to live. . . Here I was all upset . . . thinking the town would be losing one of its fine old families."[8] What the man really tries to say, however, is that the whole village, including him, hates the sisters and will be happy when they finally leave. Thus, the impression that the reader gets from the beginning of the novel is that the Blackwoods are outsiders who have to live in seclusion because the villagers do not accept them. The village, therefore, represents a dominating power — a form of a patriarchal institution — that subdues the weak, unprotected members of the family.

The novel's focus on inequality is overt. The village, that essentially is an embodiment of patriarchy, rejects the two women; moreover, it rejects people with disabilities (consider Uncle Julian who is largely de-masculinized in the novel and Merricat who can be viewed as a mentally disabled individual and who is not welcome in the village) and lesbians (as I will further argue, one way to interpret the relationship between the two sisters is as a form of lesbian love). Jackson's novel unveils the perverse and discriminating nature of patriarchy. While displaying inequality that women face, however, *We Have Always Lived in the Castle* does not portray the sisters as inferior members of society but instead focuses on how they rebel against the existing patriarchal rules and choose to be isolated because they do not want to conform to certain norms that are imposed on them. While the sisters' isolation is an inevitable result of societal rejection, it is also empowering because it symbolises the sisters' ability to withstand patriarchy (even though not entirely destroy it) and confute men's power as the sociopolitical superior. Moreover, through the absence of patriarchs (the family includes the two sisters as well as Uncle Julian, whose disability is portrayed as largely demasculinizing), the author celebrates female power and promotes feminism.

The murder of the family members, precisely their poisoning by adding arsenic into sugar, is crucial in the novel. Albeit the reader finds out that Merricat is the real murderer relatively late, one suspects that it was one of the sisters who killed the family. The motive of the killing was not personal hatred (although this factor should not be completely excluded); rather, these were inability and unwillingness to bear through conservative canons of patriarchy that the family so strictly followed before the murder of her relatives. The head of this overtly patriarchal family was, naturally, the sisters' father who is described as a very strict and severe man — a true patriarch: "John Blackwood took pride in his table, his family, his position in the world."[9] Additionally, the reader is informed about material wealth that the sisters have now inherited and that had obviously belonged to their father before his death:

> The people of the village disliked the fact that we always had plenty of money to pay for whatever we wanted; . . . I knew they talked about the money hidden in our house, as though it were great heaps of golden coins and Constance and Uncle Julian and I sat in the evenings, our library books forgotten, and played with it, running our hands through it and counting and stacking and tumbling it, jeering and mocking behind locked doors.[10]

Thus, in addition to the father's power in the family, automatically guaranteed by his gender, he was also a man of high social status, secured by his money.[11] Together with the economic power, the sisters, however, have also inherited "hostility" that the villagers at first felt toward their father, but now, accordingly, feel toward them.[12]

Their brother Thomas was rather similar to their father: "He was ten years old and possessed many of his father's more forceful traits of character."[13] It, therefore, comes as no surprise that the only male descendant that was to take the place of his father one day "used the most sugar" on the fatal day.[14] The murder of their mother that might seem a tragic surprise at first sight can, nevertheless, be easily explained by the woman's traits of character and the role she played in the family. Lenemaja Friedman characterizes her as a "selfish, domineering woman."[15] Additionally, Mrs. Blackwood was not a proper housewife as she could neither cook good nor take care of the garden, which, as Lynette Carpenter claims, "not only sets her apart from her daughters but violates the creative tradition of the Blackwood women."[16] Thus, the inability to be a woman in its traditional sense equates Mrs. Blackwood to the male members of the family. Finally, I argue that the murder of their aunt Dorothy was not "unavoidable," as Carpenter states,[17] but rather it was committed on purpose — for the woman's "civil"[18] attitude towards Mrs. Blackwood, which turned her into the sisters' enemy too. The survival of the only family member, Uncle Julian, is not to be treated as a threat to the sisters' existence since he is depicted as the "most feminized male" in the novel.[19] These are, however, not only his physical and mental disabilities as well as full dependence on Constance that deprive him of his manliness. Before the incident, he was financially dependent on his brother, being unable to provide for his own family as a real man: "[W]e lived in my brother's house and ate his food."[20] Having got rid of all the representatives of and advocates for patriarchy, the sisters therefore, have managed to free themselves and their house from the burden of subordination, humiliation, and inferiority — from the burden of patriarchy.

After the murder of the father (and the brother), the position of the family's patriarch is vacant. Crucially, none of the sisters inherits this position: not because they are women but because they build a family where every member is considered equal. The first impression of Constance and Merricat that the reader might get is that the elder one— the murderer, as it is largely foregrounded at the beginning of the narrative — is a very balanced, neat, and careful person, as one might grasp from her taking care of Uncle Julian. While her grown-up sister plays and just loiters around (it is not surprising that Constance calls her once "Miss Idleness"[21]), Constance is responsible for the household, including cleaning the house, cooking, and taking care of the garden. The elder sister remains figuratively locked in the house. However, it happens not only because she is an exemplary housewife but also because she is afraid of leaving the house. The reader assumes that Constance is scared of people's judgment, since everybody thinks that she killed her family. Merricat, on the contrary, is represented as the direct opposite of her sister: she is careless but also sinister as the only thing she constantly talks of is that she "wished all the village people dead."[22] She always digs something in the garden or nails objects to a tree. The only friend Merricat has is her cat, whose stories she likes listening to, running away from home and lying in the grass. Therefore, as Darryl Hattenhauer argues, there is a clear difference between Constance who is portrayed as a traditional woman and Merricat who is "generally more male-identified," as she is responsible for such "duties" as "carpentry, trading downtown, and killing people."[23] I would like to add to this list another very important fact: Merricat's persistent references to a poisonous mushroom that is to be understood as a phallic symbol as well as her detailed knowledge of how the mushroom "works" as it helps her acquire a figurative role of a man in the family. This ambiguity in how the two sisters are portrayed — that is, while never establishing patriarchy in their family, they seem to embody a traditional heterosexual family (except for they both are women) — makes me question the relationship between the sisters.

Roberta Rubenstein contends: "If Merricat embodies the principles of infantile impulsive anger and selfish action, Constance is her complementary double, representing a selfless, idealized maternal love whose virtue is its own reward."[24] One way to interpret the relationship between Constance and Merricat is through the parent-child perspective: Constance performs the role of a mother, whereas Merricat appears as her daughter. Constance is the mother in the novel: a housewife who takes care of the house and everyone who lives under its roof. Yet the reader finds out that it was Constance who bought the arsenic, which, she comments on with a smile, which was meant "to kill rats."[25] Then, "it was Constance who saw them dying around her like flies . . . and never called a doctor until it was too late."[26] Hence, Constance planned the murder, she taught her younger infantile sister (who has always admired Constance) how to use the poison so that it would work for sure, and was just waiting for the child (Merricat was only twelve when she poisoned her family) to do all the dirty work. Moreover, Constance persuaded Merricat that she did it. The elder sister forgave Merricat and generally approved of her deed, while, at the same time, putting the blame on Merricat. Thus, when Merricat, being upset and outraged by what the villagers did to their house, in a fit of temper says, "I am going to put death in all their food and watch them die," Constance reminds her: "The way you did before?"[27] Hence, Merricat becomes trapped in the web of her sister's cunning plan. This "pretty young girl" or "such a charming girl," as people call Constance, turns out to be "a homicidal maniac" — the image that the villagers would never think to associate her with.[28] It is no surprise that the only thing that quiet and careful Constance is known for being afraid of is a spider: because she herself is portrayed acting as a spider, who, acting silently and imperceptibly, has sucked out the lives of her relatives. In turn, eccentric Merricat is always easily and erroneously associated with a murderer due to her nature.

The relationship between Constance and Merricat is portrayed rather equivocally in the novel. On the one hand, they are sisters who live under the same roof and try to get back to some sort of normality after the incident, supporting each other as much as they can. They are obviously friends, as they share everything with each other, and when one of them needs help or moral support, the other sister is always there. On the other hand, their relationship can be interpreted as one of mother and daughter. Yet, the relationship between Constance and Merricat can be understood as indeed deeper and more intimate. Were the sisters also lovers? The answer is not given explicitly in the novel. Nonetheless, the way they communicate with each other overtly hints at it, as the phrase "I love you" sounds insistently often in the novel.[29] The feeling of possession that each sister has over the other one is transferred by their references to each other as "my Merricat" and "my Constance."[30] They can hardly imagine being without each other for a long time. For instance, Constance does not like it when Merricat goes shopping and further explains it as simple as: "I miss you."[31] Their sensual, intimate, and very tactile relationship can be perceived in multiple scenes. For example, Merricat describes very special moments that the sisters have during their talks: "She touched my cheek quickly with one finger."[32] There are more instances like Merricat desires to "brush Constance's hair until she fell asleep", Merricat "went over and kissed Constance" after a tea party, Merricat "went to her [Constance] and put my [Merricat's] arms around her"; after the attack on their house, in order to calm down Constance, Merricat "held her tight."[33] Merricat's description of Constance reveals the emergence of pure affection already at Merricat's early age that might have later developed into lesbian love:

> When I was small I thought Constance was a fairy princess. I used to try to draw her picture, with long golden hair and eyes as blue as the crayon could make them, and a bright pin spot on either cheek; the pictures always surprised me, because she did look like that; even at the worst time she was pink and white and golden, and nothing had ever seemed to dim the brightness of her. She was the most precious person in my world, always.[34]

Their mutual understanding that only being together they are "happy," along with Merricat's claims that everything about Constance matters to her, like, for example, "I would care, if you looked more beautiful," only emphasizes the bond that exists between the sisters.[35] Finally, a rather ambiguous talk about necessary changes in their lives hints at their relationship to be more — or essentially something different — than that between sisters. When Constance says to Merricat that the latter "should have boy friends," Constance immediately "began to laugh because she sounded funny even to herself."[36] Indeed, one way to view the sisters is as lesbian lovers.

The emergence of the sisters' cousin Charles, shortly after the murder, dramatically challenges their ideal world. First of all, he becomes a male "intruder,"[37] a person who can and wants to, once again, impose the laws of patriarchy that the sisters dealt rather radically with earlier. And while Constance is easily persuaded by Charles that their life is abnormal, Merricat recognizes in him as someone really scary for their new family — someone reminding them of their dead father. "Charles is a ghost," endlessly repeats Merricat, trying to make Constance listen to her and recognize the danger.[38] Charles slowly starts taking the position of their father, essentially by using the objects that belonged to Mr. Blackwood: at dinner, he takes their father's chair because, as Constance notes, "[h]e's a guest, and he even looks like Father," he likes the scarf that "belonged to Father," and very soon Merricat notices that "he already had our father's bedroom, . . . and our father's watch and his gold chain and his signet ring."[39] Even Uncle Julian warns: "He is a dreadful young man . . . . He is dishonest."[40] Yet every attempt of Merricat to draw Constance's attention to the fact that Charles is here to substitute their father is in vain.

Charles soon invades the sisters' private territory — the territory that Merricat so vehemently was trying to protect, regularly checking the fence. Rubenstein calls Charles' intrusion "male sexual penetration of female space,"[41] as "he was the first one who had ever gotten inside and Constance had let him in."[42] Yet I argue that the "penetration" was not only that of the "space" itself but rather, and perhaps even more importantly, of Constance. Thus "a key to the gates"[43] that Charles gets from Constance is not only the key to their property but also the key to Constance herself. She figuratively becomes his sexual capture. This reinforces the idea that heterosexuality is a norm in a patriarchal society and destroys the possibility of lesbian relations between the two women, essentially foregrounding them as illegitimate. It is no surprise then that Merricat dislikes Charles not only because he is a manifestation of patriarchy in flesh but also because he is taking away her Constance. There are several moments in the novel when Merricat is overtly jealous. For example, earlier, when Charles first intrudes the family, Merricat feels betrayed: "Constance stood up; she knew better than to touch me but she said 'Merricat, Merricat' gently and held out her arms to me. I was held tight, wound round with wire, I couldn't breathe, and I had to run."[44] Next day, when Merricat wakes up and realizes that Charles is still there, she describes her state as follows: "I could not breathe, I was tied around tight, everything was cold."[45] Later, Merricat comments on Constance's behaviour as follows: "Constance laughed. 'We don't see many strangers,' she said. She was not at all awkward or uncomfortable; it was as though she had been expecting all her life that Cousin Charles would come, as though she had planned exactly what to do and say, almost as though in the house of her life there had always been a room kept for Cousin Charles."[46] More than that, Merricat's place is now literally taken by Charles, for he is now responsible for buying products that the family needs and thus Merricat has "nothing to do."[47] He brings chaos into the sisters' life, and Constance now starts reacting "unpleasantly"[48] towards Merricat's ideas.

In order to get rid of Charles or literally to expel the "demon-ghost"[49] of their father from the house, Merricat considers the best possible method:

> I could turn him into a fly and drop him into a spider's web and watch him tangled and helpless and struggling, shut into the body of a dying buzzing fly; I could wish him dead until he died. I could fasten him to a tree and keep him there until he grew into the trunk and bark grew over his mouth. I could bury him in the hole where my box of silver dollars had been so safe until he came; if he was under the ground I could walk over him stamping my feet.[50]

The sinister images that the girl has in her mind strike with their sophistication and brutality. They are portrayed as part of Merricat's magical abilities that she believes she has. Indeed, she constantly buries different objects, for instance, her "baby teeth," believing that "someday they would grow as dragons"; she thinks that "Thursday . . . [is her] most powerful day"; she tells her sister that they can build their happiness "on the moon" where "a winged horse" could take them to.[51] Merricat invents her three "magic word[s],"[52] which might be considered as a spell. Additionally, black cat Jonas always accompanies her. Magic elements that are vividly present in the novel stand for Merricat's power. Carpenter comments on the emergence of these elements as follows: "Her magic words and charms constitute attempts to gain power over a world in which, first as the second girl child in a patriarchal family and then as a grown woman in a patriarchal society, she is essentially powerless."[53] Only with the help of magic, she can make Charles go. And she succeeds when she commits the final ritual, i.e., burning the house, which innocently starts from Charles' pipe left in the father's room. Alexis Shotwell argues that for Merricat, this was the only solution "to be safe from surveillance and 'normal' heterosexual pair-bonds in intact country houses."[54] Having burnt the house, she did not only get rid of Charles but she also made other villagers fear her, as she and her sister barricaded themselves in a practically destroyed (not only by the fire but also by the villagers' marauding) house. "The world has obliged, and placed a crown on Merricat's head. Her empire is stasis," writes Jonathan Lethem.[55] Stoning of the house that the villagers performed, however, can also be interpreted as a stoning of witches widely performed in the Middle Ages. This interpretation foregrounds the magic abilities of the Blackwood sisters: "The sisters' perceived power has grown since the fire: after all, they are two witches who have survived a burning and a stoning," claims Carpenter.[56] After some time, there are even rumors circulated about the sisters, for example, that they eat children. Interestingly, the sisters do not completely reject this idea, when Merricat says to Constance, "I wonder if I could eat a child if I had the chance," and Constance replies, "I doubt if I could cook one;" Merricat, in turn, says, "Poor strangers. ... They have so much to be afraid of."[57] Notably, having once referred to Constance as "Old witch, ... you have a gingerbread house,"[58] which, of course, was meant as a joke, Merricat prophesied the future of the house and its inhabitants. But portraying the sisters as witches also largely emphasizes their Otherness: powerful women, lesbian women, and disabled women — all of these characteristics can to various degrees be applied to the two sisters— are considered outcasts in a patriarchal society. Power, lesbianism, and disability are forms of abnormality in a heterosexual, male-dominated society, which lead to a dramatic reimagining of the two sisters as witches.

Just as is the case with the sisters' sexuality, their ability is portrayed rather ambiguously. It is plausible to argue that Merricat and Constance are both mentally disabled and not. If they are mentally disabled, their isolation is the result of the society's rejection of disabled people. But one can also claim that what might falsely be perceived as the sisters' mental disability is, in fact, a manifestation of their power (their ability to withstand patriarchy, reject various imposed norms, and celebrate their lesbianism). Certainly, in such a case, disability is abused to emphasize another issue. It is crucial, however, that portraying their power through disability, the novel reinforces the fact that women's power in a patriarchal society is itself a form of disability — disability, in this context, being perceived as something negative, a lack of something, an impossibility of doing or achieving something. Such an overtly problematic, ableist perspective is used to reinforce the unequal and unfair position of women in a patriarchal society.

Scholars have made attempts to interpret the sisters' behavior and societal reactions to the two women. Carpenter notices that the events and attitudes described in the novel are real, except for Merricat's fantasies about trips to the moon and similar stories that only reinforce her childishness: "but immaturity is not madness."[59] Hattenhauer, however, claims that the end of the novel reveals how "the sisters become part of the social text of the madwomen in the attic."[60] The sisters, indeed, prefer solitude and live in, as it seems, a world of their own, but if their understanding of happiness differed from the one that is imposed by patriarchy, it does not make them mentally disabled. The villagers' perception of the sisters as witches or mentally disabled women, however, derives from a solidly routed dogma that still existed in the society even in the second half of the twentieth century, namely "that survival without a man is next to impossible."[61]

Lesbianism and disability intersect in the novel, foregrounding inequality and discrimination generated by patriarchy. Rejection that the sisters face and their inevitable social isolation are vivid illustrations of not only gender inequality but also of discrimination against queer individuals and people with disabilities. Carrie Sandahl emphasizes that "sexual minorities and people with disabilities share a history of injustice."[62] Discrimination against mentally disabled people and queer individuals in the mid-twentieth century was essentially based on false medical assumptions. Thus, homosexuality was perceived as a "sexual deviation" and "a classifiable mental illness."[63] Moreover, "[q]ueerness was viewed as a contagious disease, for gays and lesbians could spoil the body and the mind of a 'decent' person, turning him/her into a mentally impaired one, too."[64] Lesbianism as such was "repressed, rendered invisible and impotent by society."[65] The disease-like nature of both lesbianism and mental disability— as they were interpreted in the mid-twentieth century— largely reflects sociopolitical and cultural atmosphere of that time. Mental disability was used as a metaphor for women's inferior position in a patriarchal society, and a double oppression that lesbians faced (being women and homosexual). Mental disability as such was "the inside of a culture."[66] In turn, the condition of being disabled was essentially a reflection of specific norms; or, to borrow from a disability activist Mary Johnson, "'disabled' is in the final analysis a political or a moral judgment, based not on anything about the individual in question so much as the viewer's own perception and attitudes about the way society should function."[67] *We Have Always Lived in the Castle* is a novel that envisions gender, lesbianism, and disability, by unveiling the problematic nature of patriarchy. I have argued elsewhere that fictional stories "explore the cultural and social factors that provoke madness."[68] Mental disability and isolation in Jackson's novel are largely the results of societal rejection, gender inequality, homophobia, and ableism. The novel, thus, effectively foregrounds patriarchy as a system that is against lesbians and people with disabilities, and that does not accept any deviation from patriarchal norms.

Constance and Merricat's power is their will (and actions) to prove that men are not the main, or even necessary part of women's happiness, that there is life beyond the laws of patriarchy, and that patriarchy is a mechanism or a system aimed at suppressing women who turn into men's servants or silent followers. It is through the intersection of women's power, lesbianism, and disability that the novel explores the problem of gender inequality in the mid-twentieth century and the dangerous, criminal nature of patriarchy. We Have Always Lived in the

Castle, of course, could not break the firm social norms, but it manages to figuratively smash the ideology of patriarchy to smithereens.

Bibliography

Anderson, Joel, and Elise Holland. "The Legacy of Medicalising 'Homosexuality': A Discussion on the Historical Effects of Non-heterosexual Diagnostic Classifications." *Sensoria: A Journal of Mind, Brain & Culture* 11, no. 1 (2015): pp. 4-15.

Arnup, Katherine. "'Does the Word Lesbian Mean Anything to You?' Lesbians Raising Daughters." In *Redefining Motherhood: Changing Identities and Patterns*, edited by Sharon Abbey and Andrea Reilly, 59-68. Toronto: Second Story Press, 1998.

Carpenter, Lynette. "The Establishment and Preservation of Female Power in Shirley Jackson's 'We Have Always Lived in the Castle.'" *Frontiers: A Journal of Women Studies* 8, no. 1 (1984): pp. 32-38. Accessed May 20, 2020. https://www.jstor.org/stable/3346088.

Felman, Shoshanna. *Writing and Madness*. Trans. Martha Noel Evans, Brian Massumi, and Barbara Johnson. Palo Alto: Stanford University Press, 2003.

Friedan, Betty. *The Feminine Mystique*, 20th ed. New York: W. W. Norton & Company, 1983.

Friedman, Lenemaja. *Shirley Jackson*. Boston: Twayne Publishers, 1975.

Gilbert, Sandra M., and Susan Gubar. *No Man's Land: The Place of the Woman Writer in the Twentieth Century*, Vol. 1. *The War of the Words*. New Haven: Yale University Press, 1988.

Gilbert, Sandra M., and Susan Gubar. "Preface." In *The Madwoman in the Attic: The Woman Writer and the Nineteenth-Century Literary Imagination*, xi-xiv. New Haven: Yale University Press, 1979.

Hague, Angela. "'A Faithful Anatomy of Our Times': Reassessing Shirley Jackson." *Frontiers: A Journal of Woman Studies* 26, no. 2 (2005): pp. 73-96. Accessed May 20, 2020. https://doi.org/10.1353/fro.2005.0025.

Hattenhauer, Darryl. *Shirley Jackson's American Gothic*. New York: State University of New York Press, 2003.

Jackson, Shirley. *We Have Always Lived in the Castle*. New York: Penguin Books, 2006.

Kudlick, Catherine J. "Disability History: Why We Need Another 'Other.'" *The American Historical Review* 108, no. 3 (2003): pp. 763-793.

Lethem, Jonathan. "Introduction: Life in Shirley Jackson's (Out) Castle." In *We Have Always Lived in the Castle*, written by Shirley Jackson, vii-xii. New York: Penguin Books, 2006.

Neuhaus, Jessamyn. "'Is It Ridiculous for Me to Say I Want to Write?': Domestic Humor and Redefining the 1950s Housewife Writer in Fan Mail to Shirley Jackson.". *Journal of Women's History* 21, no. 2 (2009): pp. 115-137. Accessed May 20, 2020. https://doi.org/10.1353/jowh.0.0071.

Prorokova, Tatiana. "Alcoholic, Mad, Disabled: Constructing Lesbian Identity in Ann Bannon's 'The Beebo Brinker Chronicles.'" In *Literatures of Madness:*

Disability Studies and Mental Health, edited by Elizabeth J. Donaldson, pp. 127-143. New York: Palgrave Macmillan, 2018.

Prorokova, Tatiana. "Gender, Psychology, and Breastfeeding as 'Perverse': From *A Clockwork Orange* to *Game of Thrones*." In *Breastfeeding and Culture: Discourses and Representation*, edited by. Ann Marie A. Short, Abigail L. Palko, and Dionne Irving, pp. 134-148. Bradford: Demeter Press, 2018.

Prorokova, Tatiana. "Madness and Imagination in Washington Irving's 'The Adventure of the German Student.'" In Hermeneutics of Textual Madness: Re-Readings/Herméneutique de la folie textuelle: re-lectures, vol. 2, edited by. M. J. Muratore, 609-621. Fasano: Schena Editore, Paris: Alain Baudry, 2016.

Rubenstein, Roberta. "House Mothers and Haunted Daughters: Shirley Jackson and Female Gothic." *Tulsa Studies in Women's Literature* 15, no. 2 (1996): 309-331. Accessed May 20, 2020. https://www.jstor.org/stable/464139.

Sandahl, Carrie. "Queering the Crip or Cripping the Queer?: Intersections of Queer and Crip Identities in Solo Autobiographical Performance." *GLQ: A Journal of Lesbian and Gay Studies* 9, no. 1-2 (2003): pp. 25-56.

Shotwell, Alexis. "'No Proper Feeling for Her House': The Relational Formation of White Womanliness in Shirley Jackson's Fiction." *Tulsa Studies in Women's Literature* 32, no. 1 (2013): pp. 119-141. Accessed May 20, 2020. https://muse.jhu.edu/article/536387.

Smyth, Cherry. "The Pleasure Threshold: Looking at Lesbian Pornography on Film." *Feminist Review* 34, "Perverse Politics: Lesbian Issues" (1990): pp. 152-159.

Wallace, Honor McKitrick. "'The Hero Is Married and Ascends the Throne': The Economics of Narrative End in Shirley Jackson's 'We Have Always Lived in the Castle.'" *Tulsa Studies in Women's Literature* 22, no. 1 (2003): pp. 173-191. Accessed May 20, 2020. https://www.jstor.org/stable/20059137.

Notes

[1] Sandra M. Gilbert and Susan Gubar, *No Man's Land: The Place of the Woman Writer in the Twentieth Century*, vol. 1. *The War of the Words* (New Haven: Yale University Press, 1988), 74.

[2] Jessamyn Neuhaus, "'Is It Ridiculous for Me to Say I Want to Write?': Domestic Humor and Redefining the 1950s Housewife Writer in Fan Mail to Shirley Jackson," *Journal of Women's History* 21, no. 2 (2009): 115, accessed May 20, 2020. https://doi.org/10.1353/jowh.0.0071.

[3] Tatiana Prorokova, "Gender, Psychology, and Breastfeeding as 'Perverse': From *A Clockwork Orange* to *Game of Thrones*," in *Breastfeeding and Culture: Discourses and Representation*, ed. Ann Marie A. Short, Abigail L. Palko, and Dionne Irving (Bradford: Demeter Press, 2018), 136-37.

[4] Betty Friedan, *The Feminine Mystique*, 20th ed. (New York: W. W. Norton & Company, 1983), 15.

[5] Sandra M. Gilbert and Susan Gubar, "Preface," in *The Madwoman in the Attic: The Woman Writer and the Nineteenth-Century Literary Imagination* (New Haven: Yale University Press, 1979), xii.

[6] Neuhaus, "'Is It Ridiculous for Me to Say I Want to Write?,'" 116.

[7] Stanley Edgar Hyman qtd. in Angela Hague, "'A Faithful Anatomy of Our Times': Reassessing Shirley Jackson," *Frontiers: A Journal of Woman Studies* 26, no. 2 (2005): 74, accessed May 20, 2020, https://doi.org/10.1353/fro.2005.0025.

[8] Shirley Jackson, *We Have Always Lived in the Castle* (New York: Penguin Books, 2006), 12, 13.

[9] Ibid., 33.

[10] Ibid., 7.

[11] Lynette Carpenter, "The Establishment and Preservation of Female Power in Shirley Jackson's 'We Have Always Lived in the Castle,'" *Frontiers: A Journal of Women Studies* 8, no. 1 (1984): 32, accessed May 20, 2020, https://www.jstor.org/stable/3346088.

[12] Honor McKitrick Wallace, "'The Hero Is Married and Ascends the Throne': The Economics of Narrative End in Shirley Jackson's 'We Have Always Lived in the Castle,'" *Tulsa Studies in Women's Literature* 22, no. 1 (2003): 179, accessed May 20, 2020, https://www.jstor.org/stable/20059137.

[13] Jackson, *We Have Always Lived in the Castle*, 34.

[14] Ibid., 34.

[15] Lenemaja Friedman, Shirley Jackson (Boston: Twayne Publishers, 1975), 142.

[16] Carpenter, "The Establishment and Preservation of Female Power," 33.

[17] Ibid., 33.

[18] Jackson, *We Have Always Lived in the Castle*, 49.

[19] Darryl Hattenhauer, *Shirley Jackson's American Gothic* (New York: State University of New York Press, 2003), 175.

[20] Jackson, *We Have Always Lived in the Castle*, 49.

[21] Ibid., 22.

[22] Ibid., 11.

[23] Hattenhauer, *Shirley Jackson's American Gothic*, 177.

[24] Roberta Rubenstein, "House Mothers and Haunted Daughters: Shirley Jackson and Female Gothic," *Tulsa Studies in Women's Literature* 15, no. 2 (1996): 324, accessed May 20, 2020, https://www.jstor.org/stable/464139.

[25] Jackson, *We Have Always Lived in the Castle*, 37.

[26] Ibid., 37.

[27] Ibid., 110, my italics.

[28] Ibid., 38.

[29] Ibid., 59.

[30] Ibid., my italics.

[31] Ibid., 21.

[32] Ibid., 21.

[33] Ibid., 30, 39, 79, 110.

[34] Ibid., 19-20, italics in original.

[35] Ibid., 61, 68, italics in original.

[36] Ibid., 82, my italics.

[37] Ibid., 58.

[38] Ibid., 69.

[39] Ibid., 70, italics in original, 82, 83.

[40] Ibid., 83, italics in original.

[41] Rubenstein, "House Mothers and Haunted Daughters," 321.

[42] Jackson, *We Have Always Lived in the Castle*, 57.
[43] Ibid., 74.
[44] Ibid., 57.
[45] Ibid., 61.
[46] Ibid., 64.
[47] Ibid., 75.
[48] Ibid., 79.
[49] Ibid., 87.
[50] Ibid., 89.
[51] Ibid., 41, 44.
[52] Ibid., 44.
[53] Ibid., 34.
[54] Alexis Shotwell, "'No Proper Feeling for Her House': The Relational Formation of White Womanliness in Shirley Jackson's Fiction," *Tulsa Studies in Women's Literature* 32, no. 1 (2013): 132, accessed May 20, 2020, https://muse.jhu.edu/article/536387.
[55] Jonathan Lethem, "Introduction: Life in Shirley Jackson's (Out) Castle," in *We Have Always Lived in the Castle*, written by Shirley Jackson (New York: Penguin Books, 2006), xii.
[56] Carpenter, "The Establishment and Preservation of Female Power," 36.
[57] Jackson, *We Have Always Lived in the Castle*, 146.
[58] Ibid., 75.
[59] Carpenter, "The Establishment and Preservation of Female Power," 36.
[60] Hattenhauer, *Shirley Jackson's American Gothic*, 182.
[61] Katherine Arnup, "'Does the Word Lesbian Mean Anything to You?' Lesbians Raising Daughters," in *Redefining Motherhood: Changing Identities and Patterns*, ed. Sharon Abbey and Andrea O'Reilly (Toronto: Second Story Press, 1998), 63.
[62] Carrie Sandahl, "Queering the Crip or Cripping the Queer?: Intersections of Queer and Crip Identities in Solo Autobiographical Performance," *GLQ: A Journal of Lesbian and Gay Studies* 9, no. 1-2 (2003): 26.
[63] Joel Anderson and Elise Holland, "The Legacy of Medicalising 'Homosexuality': A Discussion on the Historical Effects of Non-heterosexual Diagnostic Classifications," *Sensoria: A Journal of Mind, Brain & Culture* 11, no. 1 (2015): 4, 6.
[64] Tatiana Prorokova, "Alcoholic, Mad, Disabled: Constructing Lesbian Identity in Ann Bannon's 'The Beebo Brinker Chronicles,'" in *Literatures of Madness: Disability Studies and Mental Health*, ed. Elizabeth J. Donaldson (New York: Palgrave Macmillan, 2018), 127.
[65] Cherry Smyth, "The Pleasure Threshold: Looking at Lesbian Pornography on Film," *Feminist Review* 34, "Perverse Politics: Lesbian Issues" (1990): 154.
[66] Shoshana Felman, Writing and Madness, trans. Martha Noel Evans, Brian Massumi, and Barbara Johnson (Palo Alto: Stanford University Press, 2003), 13, italics in original.
[67] Mary Johnson qtd. in Catherine J. Kudlick, "Disability History: Why We Need Another 'Other,'" *The American Historical Review* 108, no. 3 (2003): 767.
[68] Tatiana Prorokova, "Madness and Imagination in Washington Irving's 'The Adventure of the German Student,'" in *Hermeneutics of Textual Madness: Re-Readings/Herméneutique de la folie textuelle: re-lectures*, vol. 2, ed. M. J. Muratore (Fasano: Schena Editore, Paris: Alain Baudry, 2016), 610.

Chapter 10

"The struggle to Breathe": Narrating the Sick Body in Lorrie Moore's Short Stories

Nadia Boudidah Falfoul

University of Kairouan, Tunisia

Abstract: The attraction of the "medical" body, its diseases and diagnoses, its pain and strain, as a subject of narrative interest, has gained critical and literary ground in the last three decades. Yet amidst this compelling desire to "write the sick body" and to "read the wound" (Geoffrey H. Hartman) lies a challenging urge to express and address the questions of meaning and suffering. Simultaneously invoking and revoking expectations of narrative pleasure through the spectre of communicating pain, illness narratives proliferate through the ambiguous and problematic exploration of the ailing body and/or mind as a reflection of culture, society, and consciousness.

This chapter seeks to bring attention to the great potential that literature possesses to inscribe and shape the cultural meanings and experiences of illness, pain, and suffering. Through a narratological and postmodernist reading of two of Lorrie Moore's collections of short stories (*Like-Life*, 1986 and *Birds of America*, 1998), the chapter contemplates "the seductive entrance of disease into language" (William Osler) and focuses on several ways in which "illness narratives" and "narratives of illness" represent a socio-cultural symptom and symbol of traumatic Post/modernity as they offer to the medical and literary fields a new perspective into art and science, storytelling and medicine. This chapter thus, argues that the discourse of illness challenges and transcends our sense of time, space, continuity, causality, and even language since Pain, as Elaine Scarry asserts, "does not simply resist language but actively destroys it."

Keywords: Illness narrative, language, body, pain, suffering, art, storytelling, medicine.

* * *

The recent emphasis on narrative in cultural studies of illness—together with the drastic changes the meanings of disease or/and illness have undergone for the last three decades— is part of a very deep and broad contemporary current. Indeed, in the late twentieth century, interest in the relationship between medicine, health and narrative focused on studies in the social sciences, on literature, and on medicine. Thus, the emergence of "illness narratives" comes to represent a socio-cultural symptom and symbol of traumatic Post/modernity. Illness narratives offer to the medical and literary fields a new perspective into art and science, storytelling and medicine.

In his book *Discourses of Disease* Howard Y. F. Choy asserts that though illness and disease are used interchangeably nowadays, they do not signify the same thing. In this regard, he refers to Canadian sociologist Arthur W. Frank who points out the distinction between the two concepts "illness" and "disease." He states that illness as a social experience is an experience *in* and *of* disease as a physiological process. Frank's approach is based on the premise that "diseases are historically situated, socially defined, and culturally meaningful," (qtd in Choy, 2), whereas illness taps on the subjective and psychic implications of the disease experience. Consequently, medical literature is rewritten with histories of mental illnesses, studies of psychopathology, and stories of cancer, depression, disabilities and pandemics.

Decades ago, American writer, philosopher, and political activist, Susan Sontag, demonstrated in her book *Illness as Metaphor* (1978) that one of the modern ways to frame diseases is by use of metaphors. Based on the metaphorical approach to disease in literature, her work was fundamental in bringing attention to a new approach to literature and "medical humanities," which explained the way "literature documents and shapes the cultural meaning and experience of illness, pain, and suffering" (Sontag 67). Today, "new discourses have been invented to theorize illness, redefine health, and reconstruct classes and genders" (Choy 2016, 1).

Arthur Kleinman, the American psychiatrist anthropologist of the Harvard Medical School, has changed illness narratives through a literary inquiry towards the system of meanings. His book *The Illness Narratives* offers a pioneering medical narrative approach with a new and distinctive perception "thick with the [patient's] account of the experience of suffering" and rich with the "diversity and stubborn resistance to interpretations of human stories of illness" (Kleinman 1988, 20). Rita Charon, another key figure from this emerging area of study, coined the term "narrative medicine" to refer to "medicine practiced with the narrative skills of recognizing, absorbing, interpreting, and being moved by the stories of illness" (Charon 12). The approach Charon articulates in *Narrative Medicine: Honoring the Stories of Illness* is predicated on a multi-modal and polymorphous notion of narrative as she borrows the literary methods of close reading, reader-response criticism and reception theory to widen the vision of health care. She suggests that "the body is heteroglossic," and doctors need to learn not only "the language of symptom" but also "the language of pleasure, the language of loss, the language of life, and [therefore] come to understand that these discourses, too, speak of health" (Charon 2006, 22).

Neurologist Oliver Sacks follows the same line of thought concerning this new multi-disciplinary narrative trend. He advocates that this medical narrative discourse is extremely significant in bringing the persons, "the human subjects" with their particular experiences of illness, into focus and "To restore the human subject at the center—the suffering, afflicted, fighting human subject—we must deepen a case history to a narrative or tale; only then do we have a 'who' as well as a 'what,' a real person, a patient, in relation to disease—in relation to the physical" (Sacks 1987, viii).

Furthermore, Choy aptly claims, "the narrativization of illness and textualization of the body reveal the politics of disease" (6) since illness narratives do not only provide insight into how pain focuses and transforms lives, but they also demonstrate how illness processes are linked to the broader social and structural contexts of patients, their communities, and their clinicians. Linda C. Garro and Cheryl Mattingly share the same standpoint as they confer in their book *Narrative and the Cultural Construction of Illness and Healing* how illness narrative "foregrounds the human dramas surrounding illness" and creates "alternative" views and visions that would "enhance more fruitful avenues for exploration" (Garro & Mattingly 2000, 8).

However, for literary critics, this genre poses a unique issue in the critical realm as it seeks to draw wider attention to writing about illness and to argue for new approaches to both literary criticism and medical narrative. Several questions might be asked in this regard: How illness narratives—those deeply subjective and painful accounts of confusing and frightening experiences—fit into literary studies as a genre for critical examination? How can we truly "feel" one's reality of such a throbbing experience, while we perfectly know that "physical pain," as Elaine Scarry asserts, "does not simply resist language but actively destroys it" (Scarry 44)? Finally, can illness narrative offer an "enduring contribution to medical narrative"? And does it elucidate, in Elinor Ochs's words, "How personal narrative shapes the architecture of illness and the life course it yields? (1995, 15)

The American writer Lorrie Moore is one of the most outstanding female voices in the American literary scene. Her fictional work has been both popular and critically acclaimed since her debut collection of short-stories entitled *Self-Help* (1985). In her subsequent collections of short fiction, namely *Like Life* (1991) and *Birds of America* (1998), Moore has established her artistic reputation as she tells varied stories about sadness, depression, crisis, disease and death. She is almost exclusively fascinated with broken, suffering and depressed people. She often writes about the dissolution of familial order, the complications and contradictions of contemporary life, and people's multiple physical and psychological afflictions. More importantly, Moore's drive to apply medical diagnoses to literary works, as has been done previously with hysteria, syphilis, tuberculosis, and other illnesses, seems to deepen and complicate our interpretations of her stories. Thus, readers are keenly aware that creating a narrative where characters are grappling with a chronic or fatal disease is an active and constructive process—one that depends on both personal and cultural resources, and push both writer and readers to make meaning of human pain, anguish, and fragility.

If the mind and the body are "the basic constituents of identity," discourses of disease, as Choy argues, "probe into the psychosomatic politics of subjectivity by speaking about the sick person's mental and physical conditions in the sociohistorical context" (Choy 2016, 6). Lorrie Moore is a case in point since she is deeply concerned with the profound impact of illness on her characters' visions of life, society, nature and culture. In so many of Moore's stories, cancer and depression play a crucial role in revealing the underlying suffering of the contemporary American woman. Indeed, these two modern illnesses (cancer and depression) may be symbolic of contemporary society's morals, fears, and hopes. They function as metaphors that enable Moore's characters to bridge gaps, acknowledge their limitations and their strengths, and achieve self-recognition. Moreover, their illnesses often give them a special "stance" and "space" to dream, to love, to hate, to laugh, to cry, to revolt, to enjoy isolation and even to contemplate suicide.

In *Like Life*, depression is depicted both as a real disease and as a symptom of the larger cultural damage inflicted by the postmodern condition. In one of the stories, "To Fill", the thirty-five-year-old depressed narrator, Riva, ends up in a mental institution after stabbing her philandering husband. Her depression is "a vicious cycle" (154) in which she is caught up. It fills her days and nights, recurs when she least expects it.

"Two Boys" is another story about depression. The protagonist, Mary, is a young woman torn between two boyfriends and suffering from a "subtle" nervous collapse. Though she is aware of her impending nervous breakdown, she keeps busy with her work and her two boyfriends and her religious poetry-reading hobby. Yet suddenly in the midst of one of her regular outings in the park, she faces her depression. "How did one's eye-patched rot-toothed life," she wonders, "lead one along so cruelly, like a trick, to the middle of the sea?" (18). Her depression makes her extremely frightened that she will be swallowed by the whiteness and the void of an unknown future, of total isolation and alienation.

In "Go Like This," the narrator, Elizabeth, a writer of children's picture storybooks, is planning her fourth book when she is told she had cancer. Cancer, however, makes her resist and revolt against her illness: she would not allow herself to be subjected to this outside force that has invaded her body: "I am something putrid. I wonder if I smell, decaying from the inside out like fruit, yet able to walk among them like the dead among the living" (75). Elizabeth acknowledges probable death after trying chemotherapy for three weeks, "wearing scarves, hiding hairbrushes" (67) and decides to tell her friends and her husband of her suicidal plans or her "defensive suicide" — "I look around [...] A miracle [...] There appears to be no dissent" (72).

In the title story "Like Life," which concludes Moore's collection *Like Life*, we move into a familiar, yet alien urban world. Mamie is a freelance historical illustrator for children's books. She lives in New York and she regularly drops off throat samples at her doctor's office, preparing herself for cancer and for the pain she is due in the future. "If Mamie ever had surgery, scars in a crisscross up her throat, she would have to know such things. A hat, a scarf, a dot of rouge, mints in the mouth" (153).

Moore's deep and predominant concern with physical suffering and disease permeates her third collection of short stories, *Birds of America* (1998). Much has been said about Moore's own obsession with illness and, though cancer is a recurring subject, Moore is less interested in the grim physical details than in examining how illness changes and transforms the victims' lives. Her stories seem to argue that, out of "plain necessity," men and women inhabiting her fictional world are on the edge of some kind of dissolution. In fact, in more than half the stories in the collection, central characters are stricken with what Flannery O'Connor used to call a "Dread Disease." Most of her characters suffer from cancer, depression, AIDS, etc. They frequently engage in a gripping battle with the disease that has both violent and joyous consequences. Even the children, who inhabit Moore's fictional world, suffer physically; they struggle with Down's syndrome, cystic fibrosis, polio, and cancer. However, many of these aching events and ailments provoke from Moore comic insights into the way pain focuses and transforms lives.

The pillar of *Birds of America* is a short story titled "People Like That Are the Only People Here." It is one of Moore's most celebrated and anthologized works, winning the 1998 O. Henry Award and selected for the Best American Short Stories of 1998. "People Like That Are The Only People Here" is a dramatic work about a couple who learn there's a malignant tumor in their baby's kidney. The "here" of the title is a pediatric oncology ward, in which this baby boy and his parents are forced to inhabit for several weeks. In this story,

Moore takes unprecedented stylistic and formal risks, contemplating "the seductive entrance of disease into language," to use an expression from William Osler. Indeed, Moore's drive to apply medical diagnoses to her literary works seems to deepen and complicate our interpretations of her story, because to speak of illness is to replicate, linguistically, the process of its growth, and its transmission from one subject to another. Once disease enters into language, its transformative and transmissive potential multiplies. "People Like That" offers an excellent example in this regard since the story seems to articulate the "intangible human and emotional factors that surround life when it intersects with the medical field" (Dinty Moore, 28). The power of the story resides not only in the subject matter, dramatic and touching as it is, but also in the narrative style, in the deft, and often ironical, juxtaposition of the tragic and comic, of the poetic and medical discourses. Here is Moore's opening:

> A beginning, an end: there seems to be neither. The whole thing is like a cloud that just lands and everywhere inside it is full of rain. A start: the Mother finds a blood clot in the Baby's diaper. What is the story? Who put this here? It is big and bright, with a broken khaki-colored vein in it. [...] Perhaps it belongs to someone else.... In her mind, the Mother takes this away from his body and attaches it to someone else's. Doesn't that make more sense? (212)

From its opening sentence— "A beginning, an end: there seems to be neither"—the reader is immediately thrown into the family's sense of the surrealism of the situation, the alternating numbness and panic, and the parents' efforts to resist this dreadful fate. Every possible feeling invades the mother when she receives her baby's shocking diagnosis. It is a mistake. It is her own kidney that was accidentally X-rayed. It is a sick joke. It is the end of life. Thus, the narrative in "People Like That" bestows a striking picture of the obscure ghostly new life of parents and children caught in the trauma of pain and suffering and confined within the closed walls of the hospital: "A whole place has been designed and decorated for your nightmare," the desperate mother-narrator says. "Here is where your nightmare will occur" (224).

This sense of the grotesque and the absurd has already been evoked in the very title of the story: "People Like That Are the Only People Here: Canonical Babbling in Peed Onk." Here we notice the incongruous combination of two oddly contradictory expressions "Canonical babblings" and "Peed Onk". "Canonical babblings" is the medical term for the stage in child speech development at around six or seven months when babies move from meaningless sounds to attempts at proper words and speech rhythms. As for "Peed Onk," it is the phonetic spelling of the name given to the Pediatric

Oncology department where the baby is being treated. Ironically, this abbreviation—which means medical knowledge and expertise for doctors and the whole medical staff— means something remotely different for the Mother's distorted perspective; it stands for incomplete dialogue, absurd language, and meaningless sounds. This reminds us of Arthur Frank's view that children's illness narrated by parents is the subgenre of life writing. When the lives of parents are shaped by their children's illness, parents find the life value in it, "the life writing bears the tension of narration" (2000, 136). Parents are inseparable from such illness narrative. Frank also speaks of illness precipitating "[a] self that has become what it never expected to" (2000, 137).

In his article "Fictional Symptoms in Lorrie Moore's "People Like That Are the Only People Here," Tom Ratekin adopts a psychoanalytic approach to focus on "the double reading" of the story through an analysis of Moore's artistic manipulation of both the literary and medical discourses to express the contradictory and paradoxical views concerning a baby's infliction with cancer in a highly-technical and advanced contemporary world. Officially, Moore's story—as she herself repeatedly claims— is fiction, but several elements within the story confirm the autobiographical aspect of the story. Similarly, the Mother in the story ostensibly "follows the official discourse of the hospital" (at one point even joking about the ridiculousness of "alternative" medicine), while at the same time "distancing herself from hospital logic in a way that allows her room to establish an alternative reading" (Ratekin 2016, 19).

In "People Like That Are the Only People Here," Mother (the writer capitalizes all the characters in this story: Mother, Father, Baby, Radiologist, Oncologist, to give the story a universal dimension) resists the medical devices and protests the authority in hospital. Before the operation on Baby, the hospital shows Mother a video about anesthesia. In the video, "the mother holds the baby and fumes are gently waved under the baby's nose until he falls asleep" (233). But the fact is, the mother bitterly realizes, the doctor turns the gas on and "quickly clamps the plastic mouthpiece" (233) over the baby's cheeks and lips. "The Baby is startled. The Baby starts to scream and redden behind the plastic, an odd kidnapping kind of sleep" (233-234). The mother protests, "this is quite different from the video; it is brutal and unforgivable" (234). In face of this unspeakable reality, Mother protects herself from her child's mortality by placing the world of pediatric oncology (the world she cannot and will not accept) into the imaginary world of science fiction. "Without the Baby," the narrator poignantly transmits the mother's baffled situation, "life is something stumbling and unlivable, something mechanical, something for robots, but not life" (217). Thus, the mother's perplexed distinction between the medical use of "symptom" and its psychoanalytic signification is revealed in her strangely grotesque description of the cancer itself: "The Mother wonders what science fiction could begin to compete with the science fiction of cancer itself—a tumor with its differentiated muscle and bone cells, a clump of wild nothing and its mad, ambitious desire to be something: something inside you, instead of you, another organism, but with a monster's architecture, a demon's sabotage and chaos" (Moore 1998, 229).

Here Moore explicitly designates the cancer as a challenge to the symbolic universe. By associating cancer with the monster and the demon, the Mother, in an act of self-defense and resistance, places it outside of her world. "The fantasy of science fiction," Ratekin clarifies, "allows the Mother to enter the world of the hospital while maintaining a safe distance from it" (20).

With her baby's health increasingly deteriorating and his future uncertain, Moore's nameless character is drifting in a strange, despicable world and a disorienting present. "When your child has cancer," the mother sadly relates, "you are instantly whisked away to another planet" (224). In this Pediatric Oncology, "the windows don't open and diesel fumes are leaking into the ventilating system. The air is nauseous and stale" (226). In this Pediatric Oncology, she continues, "you wash your hands for thirty seconds in antibacterial soap before you are allowed to enter through the swinging doors. You put paper slippers on your shoes. You keep your voice down" (224).

What follows can be viscerally difficult to read, we are immersed in the distorted reality of late-twentieth-century life in its purest sense, entirely free of context, reduced to language and vocal impersonation. "Pulling through is what people do around here," she says. "There is a kind of bravery in their lives that isn't bravery at all. It is automatic, unflinching, a mix of man and machine" (230). As the baby enters Pediatric Oncology, "the glassy-eyed parents" enter the "heartbreaking fellowship" of adults passing their days in the Tiny Tim Lounge, "exchanging pale, strenuously hopeful smiles" (227). It is a world where "bald-headed and bandaged citizens smile and wave back," a world where a four-year-old boy is "holding his little deflated rubber ball" (228), which was drawing fluid from his liver.

So many sharp details give the narrative an emotional audacity and provide the action of the story with an immediacy that is brilliant and unbearably clear. The narrative is dazzling: with its mixture of anger and agony, its dead-on depiction of hospital horrors and habits, it offers the reader a compelling account of exterior realism and interior torment of the mother. "The mother began to cry; all of life has led her here, to this moment. After this, there is no more life. There is something else, something stumbling and unlivable, something mechanical, something for robots, but not life" (216).

In the same context of illness narrative and narrative of illness, Laura E. Tanner discusses the image of the sick body in medical waiting rooms. She argues in her insightful article "Bodies in Waiting: Representations of Medical Waiting Rooms in Contemporary American Fiction", that the apparently "empty" space of the medical room, "stages many of our most important cultural assumptions about illness and the body" (Tanner 2002, 117). In her view, although the body always structures our relationship to space, the hospital room "serves as a place in which we are immobilized *in* and *as* our bodies" (Tanner 2002, 116). In radiology, the baby endures an absurd and painful medical experience. He "stands anxiously on the table, naked against the Mother as she holds him still" (213). The radiologist's "cold scanning disc" is moving about the baby's back. "The Baby whimpers, looks up at the Mother. *Let's get out of here*, his eyes beg. *Pick me up*" (italics in original, 213).

If the narrative of a life is structured around a series of experiences and activities that constitute everyday existence, waiting or living in a hospital, definitely "represents the consumption of time without the creation of plot" (Tanner 2002, 118). In this medical space, Tanner explains, "the force of time not only structures but to some extent constitutes experience" (118). "People Like That" serves as a pertinent example here since Moore's representation of the oncology ward points to the way in which its inhabitants, to use Tanner's words, "experience physical and symbolic immobilization as a suspension in time" (117). In the hospital, the confused baby's parents experience an immense void, they feel that "each day… has arrived huge, empty, and unknown, like a spaceship" (231). They are tortured by the stagnant unnerving passage of time: "The synapses between the minutes are unswimmable. An hour is thick as fudge" (235).

More importantly, the narrator depicts the oncology ward as a place that traps her in space and denies her access to the real external world. In the lounge that has no windows, there is no signal to distinguish day from night. Yet, the protagonist of this story tries and fails to "mark" the passage of time. Surrounded by mothers uniformly clad in sweat clothes, she resists, as Tanner says, "the collapse of productivity, subjectivity, and narrative temporality" (118) that the loss of her street (normal) clothes would represent: "This is what the sweatpants are for," she says. "In case the difference between day and night starts to dissolve, and there is no difference at all, so why pretend?" (231).

Again, the language used in "People Like That" powerfully reflects the inability of a collapsing and despairing mind to verbalization: "All that unsayable life!" conveys the difficulty and frustration of the writer's project. A central perception pervades this story and most of Moore's fiction: the inability and failure of language to fully communicate the complexity and complication of lived experience. When the surgeon told the mother that her son had a "Wilm's tumor" in his left kidney and had to go through "radical nephrectomy" before proceeding with chemotherapy, the mother startles: "'*Baby* and *chemo*': they should never even appear in the same sentence together, let alone the same life [...] Chemotherapy. Unthinkable" (italics in original, 216). Mother would rather believe the power of language than accept the surgeon's suggestion. Ironically, in her attempt to resist the surgeon's authority of knowledge, the mother collapses psychologically and verbally. How could she conceive of such a brutally devastating fate for a little, innocent and pure baby? "In someone so tiny, it is frightening and unnatural. She wants to whip out a gun: No, no's, eh? *This whole thing is what I call a no-no*" (italics in original, 237). For the mother, the reality is too grim, and too distressing. Words and their referents have become uncoupled, uncongealed, no longer connected: "It is the unlivable life," the mother bursts, "the strange room tacked on to the house, the extra moon that is circling the earth unbeknownst to science" (235). Therefore, in these stories about cancer, the disorder is more specifically one of telling, of language and narration, and is marked by the attenuation of cause and effect, a slippage between event and narration, the detachment of image from meaning and the complete absence of logic. Thus, one can safely align with Choy's argument that, from "medical practices" of public health to "symptomatic strategies of linguistic interrogation," both scientific language and literary metaphors are "problematized in the contexts of cultural maladies, social disorders, political pangs, and economic epidemics" (Choy 2016, 11).

Another relevant instance of this narrative disturbance and fragmentation occurs in a short story in the same collection, *Birds of America*. "Real Estate" is a terrifying, comic treatment of the disruptive consequences of illness on the female body, focusing particularly on the disintegrating effects of cancer on a woman's body and mind. As she discovers her lung cancer, Ruth, the depressed female protagonist of "Real Estate," feels locked into the prison house of the body, cut off from healthy and normal interactions. Describing Ruth's bewilderment at her lung cancer and her accentuated rage and perplexity at her fate, the narrator revels in word games mixing up the medical discourse of illness and suffering with the emotional discourse of disillusionment and despair: "She felt a twinge in her one lung. 'How does anything get anywhere—that's what I want to know.' She had only ever been the lightest of smokers, never in a high-risk category, but now every pinch, prick, tick, or tock in her ribs, every glitch in the material world anywhere made her want to light up and puff" (191).

In this passage, Ruth's psychological trauma is rendered in a surprisingly poignant and absurdly humorous way, as the narrator betrays the character's "inexplicable desolation" and wild sense of suffering by playing on alliteration and on the onomatopoeic effect of words such as "pinch," "prick," "tick," and "tock" to create a staccato rhythm, which strongly conveys the disturbed and neurotic manifestations of the woman's sense of frustration, absurdity, hopelessness, and helplessness.

"Real Estate" opens with a death-like atmosphere as the third-person omniscient narrator penetrates Ruth's mind, offering a moving image of how disease powerfully and pitilessly distorts one's body and soul: "She was going to die in the spring. She felt such inexplicable desolation then, such sludge in the heart, felt the season's mockery, all that chartreuse humidity in her throat like a gag. How else to explain such a feeling?" (177) Arthur W. Frank proposes the concept of "medical colonization" in his work *The Wounded Storyteller: Body, Illness, and Ethics*. He believes that "colonization was central to the achievement of modernist medicine" (Frank 1995, 5). Modern medicine colonizes the patient's body in the same manner as the colonizers who colonize the land politically and economically. In the same vein, Dan Gottlieb points out that "we stop being people and start being patients. [...] Our identity as people and the world we once knew both are relinquished. We become their patients and we live in their hospital" (Frank, 10). The female protagonist feels that her mind and her whole sense of being are dysfunctional and incompatible with the body, which has endured huge alterations because of illness. Consequently, cancer has made her insecure, disintegrated and dislocated, a stranger to her own body, which "had gone from being a home, to being a house…Nothing about it gave her proper shelter. She no longer felt housed within it" (202).

On another pertinent level, we can refer to Susan Sontag's discussion of the "metaphoric connection" in popular discourse between cancer and pregnancy. The disease, she says, is commonly characterized as "a demonic pregnancy," and a cancerous tumor is seen as "alive, a fetus with its own will." In many of her stories, Moore's female characters engage in precisely this kind of "metaphoric thinking" about cancer or suspected cancer, experiencing it as a malevolent invasion by an alien and hideous organism, an "obscene" mutation of the desired human fetus (several of Moore's middle-aged women long for babies but cannot have them). In many stories where the female protagonists are victims to cancer, the image of a woman's body as host to another organism reprises the theme of motherhood. In a moment of intense psychological crisis, Ruth remembers her body's previous state of health and productivity (when she gave birth to her only daughter) and now she secretly ponders the deteriorating process of her lethal disease: "It seemed her body, so mysterious and apart from her, could only produce illness. Though once, of course, it had produced Mitzy. How had it done that? Mitzy was the only good thing her body had ever been able to grow" ("Real Estate" 203). To use a term Sontag borrows from immunology, a cancerous tumor, or rather, this invader, is a "nonself" that exacerbates the self-arrangement from which Moore's protagonists already suffer. The result is a gradual and painful process of alienation from her material self, which reflects the psychic fracturing that characterize so many of Moore's sick characters: "My body became increasingly strange to me. I became very aware of its edges as I peered out from it" (204).

On another crucial level, the emphasis on the destructive effect of illness on the sufferer's sense of being is intimately related to the character's disruption of the sense of time. Like many ill characters in Moore's short fiction, Ruth's mental world seems to be locked into the present moment. She does not see any horizon or future beyond the present moment of suffering, loss and disintegration. "Ruth began staying inside, drinking tea. She felt tightening, pain and vertigo, but then, was that so new?" ("Real Estate", 203). Moreover, the present itself is composed of discrete, discontinuous moments in which her body and therefore, her sense of herself and the world may not bear any coherence, nor can they establish any cause-effect relationship.

Significantly, such a predicament may have a devastating effect on narrative order. This idea is brilliantly explored by Rimmon-Kenan who contends that tension between a "thematization of disintegration" and a writing that preserves qualities of narrative order may be "a dramatization of the struggle between an acceptance of fragmentation and the need to overcome it by creating a coherent narrative" (Kenan 2006, 243). It may also reflect the oscillation in a patient's life, particularly that of a hospitalized patient, between a strict order of daily routine, tests, and treatments and an internal chaos. In addition, the ill person, as Kenan explains, "has limited control over both the dictated order and the overwhelming inner disorder" (244). The protagonist of "Real Estate" is aware of the irrevocable degeneration of her body by cancer: "She could feel some chaos in her gut—her intestines no longer curled neat and orderly as a French horn but heaped carelessly upon one another like a box of vacuum cleaner parts" (210).

Paradoxically, as the disease reaches a climactic stage, the narrator describes the chaotic condition of the protagonist's sick body in extremely detailed, concrete and grotesque language. Ruth's growing physical and psychological disintegration and her frightening sense of total helplessness are imparted in movingly absurd images and word games: "Her chest ached and all her bones filled with sharp pulsing. She was ill. [...] The cancer, dismantling as it came, had begun its way back. She felt its poison, its tentacular reach and clutch, as a puppet feels a hand" (211).

Hence, the abundance of bodily details clearly emphasizes the materiality of the physical experience, blurred by both medical and metaphoric conceptions of illness. Here, the bodily, visceral level, as Kenan observes, "entertains intimate relations with the sufferer's sense of time and order and hence with the shaping/unshaping of narrative" (247). Put differently, a disintegrating body may threaten the act of telling and the very possibility of narration, considered an essential characteristic of narrative. Indeed, as Miriam Marty Clark assumes, numerous postmodern short stories "hold out not revelation, not a durable or ultimate knowledge, but narrativity itself" (154). Surprisingly, the forces that disrupt narrative are met by and converge for a moment with the need to tell, the power of telling. These stories, as Clark puts it, "do not show the world in a grain of sand", nor do they offer a slice of life, but they "hold out selves in a moment of dispersal: voices before the overwhelmed, beneath the overwhelming" (Clark 1995, 156).

Accordingly, the narrative disruption that typifies the final passage of the short story is concomitant with the protagonist's bodily and mental disintegration. The narrator presents a distressing image of how disease powerfully and pitilessly distorts one's body and soul. Ironically, the story's protagonist seems to speak the unspeakable by over speaking it. The concluding scene—with its truncated, fragmented, and confusing quality—together with the complete disturbance of the narrative structure, epitomize the end of life and the end of any sense of order or harmony. Ultimately, the persistent desire of the body to resist death is counterbalanced by the violence and force of cancer as an invincible, chaotic and fatal reality:

> Though she would have preferred long ago to have died, fled, gotten it all over with the body—Jesus how the body! —took its time. It possessed its own wishes and nostalgias... You couldn't go like that. Within one's own departing but stubborn flesh, there was only the long, sentimental, piecemeal farewell. *Sir? A towel. Is there a towel?* The body, hauling sadness, pursued the soul, hobbled after (emphasis in original, 211).

On the one hand, this passage thematises the collapse of the body, of order, of causality, "sabotaging" the possibility of narrative, at least in its traditional acceptation. On the other hand, the whole text lends coherence to chaos. The disruption of any sense of coherence or order and the blocking of future-oriented continuity make Ruth's speech delirious and mostly unintelligible. As a result, the closing lines of the story evoke a sense of utter confusion and disruption in which the words become ambiguous, the narrative point of view shifts from third-person to second-person, and the body acquires a ubiquitous, ghost-like presence; "its reflection a shrinking charm in the car mirrors as you trundled past the pine grove, past the property line, past every last patch of land, straight down the swallowing road, disappearing and disappearing. Until at last, it was true: you had disappeared" (211).

This is the language of agony, of death and annihilation rendered in a disturbingly poetic and dramatically poignant way. In many stories like this one, the breakdown of narrative and the narration of breakdown are inextricably linked as past and future, time and space, body and mind, tragedy and comedy are drawn into a disorienting and overwhelming present.

In her attempt to "honor the stories of illness", Rita Charon insists on the crucial role of narrative and the significant power of storytelling in conveying new meanings to old human maladies. "As a living thing, narrative has many dimensions and powers," Charon maintains: "The novelist values its creative force; the historian relies on its ordering impulses, the autobiographer redeems its link to identity..." (Charon 2006, 39). In her view, narrative structures are fundamental in telling and retelling stories of illness and suffering. These narratives enable us "to depict characters, represent the passage of time, use metaphor, convey meanings otherwise elusive" and so on. As an instrument for "self-knowledge and communion," Charon concludes: "narrative is irreplaceable" (2006, 55).

In a time where illness pervades society more than ever before, writing about illness is timely, considerate, and thought-provoking. As Anne Fadiman convincingly asserts, writing about medical suffering reveals the fact that "the ailing body points to culture, pain points to philosophy, language points to consciousness, and all point to what is still to be learned about our fragility, our mortality, and how to live a meaningful life" (Fadiman 1997, 131). Indeed, the discourse of illness challenges and transcends our sense of time, space, continuity, causality, and even language since Pain, as Elaine Scarry maintains, "does not simply resist language but actively destroys it" (1985, 4). Hence, the individual consciousness, its illness and malaise are predominant concerns in contemporary short fiction. In such narratives, Love, Bereavement, Disease and Death are now ailments and abstractions, separated from contents or circumstances. They are treated with chemicals or offered other ephemeral salves. However, the despairing tone that pervades these narratives is totally redeemed by haunting accuracy: a fine and careful meditation on the way we live now.

References

Charon, Rita. 2006. *Narrative Medicine: Honoring the Stories of Illness.* New York: Oxford University Press.

Choy, Howard Y. F, ed. 2016. *Discourses of Disease Writing Illness, the Mind and the Body in Modern China.* Leiden: Brill.

Clark, Marty Miriam. 1995. "Contemporary Short Fiction and the Postmodern Condition." *Studies in Short Fiction* 32, no. 2: pp. 116-126.

Fadiman, Anne. 1997. *The Spirit Catches You and You Fall Down: A Hmong Child, Her American Doctors and the Collision of Two Cultures.* New York: Farrar, Straus and Giroux.

Frank, Arthur W. 2000. "Illness and Autobiographical Work: Dialogue as Narrative Destabilisation." *Qualitative Sociology* 23, no. 1: pp. 135–156.

———. 1995. *The Wounded Storyteller: Body, Illness, and Ethics.* London: The University of Chicago Press.

Kleinman, Arthur. 1988. *The Illness Narratives: Suffering, Healing and the Human Condition.* The US: Basic Books.

Mattingly, Cheryl, and Linda C. Garro, eds. 2000. *Narrative and the Cultural Construction of Illness and Healing.* London, University of California Press.

Moore, Dinty W. 2019. *Bodies of Truth: Personal Narratives on Illness, Disability, and Medicine.* Lincoln: University of Nebraska Press.

Moore, Lorrie. 1991. *Like Life: Stories.* New York: Plume.

———. 1998. *Birds of America.* New York: Alfred A. Knopf.

Ochs, Elinor and Lisa Capps. 1996. "Constructing Panic: The Discourse of Agoraphobia." *Anthropological Linguistics* 3, no. 38: pp. 563-566

Ratekin, Tom. 2016. "Fictional Symptoms in Lorrie Moore's 'People Like That Are the Only People Here.'" *International Journal of Žižek Studies* 1, no. 4: pp. 16-32.

Rimmon-Kenan, Shlomith. 2006. "What Can Narrative Theory Learn from Illness Narratives?" *Literature and Medicine* 25, no. 2 (Fall): pp. 241-254.

Sacks, Oliver. 2011. *Awakenings.* London: Pan Macmillan.

Scarry, Elaine. 1985. *The Body in Pain: The Making and Unmaking of the World.* New York: Oxford University Press.

Sontag, Susan. 1977. *Illness as Metaphor.* New York: Farrar Straus Giroux.

Tanner, Laura. E. 2002. "Bodies in Waiting: Representations of Medical Waiting Rooms in Contemporary American Fiction." *American Literary History* 14, no. 1: pp. 115-130.

Chapter 11

Taking Turns in Writing Pain: Comics' Approximation of Pathography

Victoria Lupascu

University of Montréal, Canada

Abstract: This chapter considers the relationship between pathography and the comics genre to examine the ways in which visual representations of illnesses, from the healers' and caregivers' perspective, produce a plurivalent emotional vocabulary for understanding illnesses and grief. I focus on MK Czerwiec's comic book *Taking Turns: Stories from HIV/AIDS Care Unit 371* and Stella Bruzzi's theorisation of approximation as an epistemological tool that highlights a historical fact and "insert[s] it into a narrative, not in order to be collapsed into fiction, but to co-exist in collision with it" (Bruzzi, 2006). As a nurse in an HIV/AIDS special care unit in the 1990s, MK Czerwiec embodies both the professional caregiver and the healer from a biomedical perspective and redefines the concept of boundaries between these roles. By negotiating these two positions, Czerwiec is at a unique junction, portrayed by unbalanced panels and interplay between text and visual representations of patients, and *approximates* the urgency of the epidemic with the slow development of ubiquitous grief in relation to HIV/AIDS in sufferers, healers and caregivers. I claim that the tension between fiction and reality in pathography is firmly apparent in comics such as *Taking Turns* where approximation becomes an underlying hermeneutical means of writing one's own as well as other's pain. Moreover, I believe that comics show the boundaries of language and expand them through colour usage, pagination, panelling and create the physical space of formative silences necessary for the co-existence of illnesses and care. In this expansion that fuels pathography, comics produce epistemological and hermeneutic changes in traditional literary perceptions of illnesses, specifically in relation to HIV/AIDS, by imagining alternative modes of expression and understanding of the epidemic's and illnesses' phenomenological valences.

Keywords: Pathography, Comics, approximation, Iconography of Care, HIV/AIDS, Care Unit 371.

***

"Comics have often been associated with cultural change and are ideal for exploring taboo or forbidden areas of illness and healthcare. We (…) challenge accepted conventions of scholarship, merging the personal with the pedagogical, the subjective with the objective— the image with the text."

(Williams et. al. 2015, 3)

The *Graphic Medicine Manifesto*, as written by Ian Williams, Susan Merrill Squier, Michael Green, Scott Smith and MK Czerwiec, describes these hopes in 2015 and sets forth to visually and textually explore the relationship between healthcare and society. Since then, graphic medicine has been expanding as a field and has, accordingly, proceeded to challenge cultural norms, as well as notions and types of representations of care and health, disability and normativity in bodies. The comics, broadly defined and among many other media, collected under the Graphic Medicine umbrella bring images and texts together to enable different types of literacies and to question our modes of understanding care, illnesses, diseases and the relationship between caregivers and patients.[1] The goal, as the editorial collective expresses it, is a provocation to the status-quo in medicine, visual studies and literature and an invitation for close collaboration.

When it comes to HIV/AIDS, stigma and taboos have never gone away, and kept functioning at lower levels, or were less in the limelight, in the past three decades. Nevertheless, the HIV/AIDS epidemic has revolutionized our understanding of hospice, medical treatments and protocols and has paved the way for new protocols of care and relationships between caregivers and patients. MK Czerwiec, or the Comic Nurse, one of the members of the editorial collective for the *Graphic Medicine Manifesto*,[1] brings forward this exact point in *Taking Turns. Stories from HIV/AIDS Care Unit 371*: the development of a dedicated space of care for the AIDS patients in Chicago in the 1990s and early 2000s where stigma and biased care could not interfere with treatments and valorization of every human life. Czerwiec takes the comics medium as a heuristic not only for "explor[ing] taboo or forbidden areas of illness and healthcare," (Williams et al. 2015, 3) but also for challenging accepted conventions of scholarship. She interweaves autobiography with the oral history genre, the pedagogical with the personal, the factual with the approximated, the images with considerable amounts of text in order to produce a plurivalent emotional vocabulary for understanding illnesses and grief for others and for one's own journey, especially as a healthcare professional during an epidemic. The comic thus created expands the text's linguistic, descriptive capacities and provides us with formative silences in unbalanced panels that allow the readers to sit with the uncomfortable realizations coming from the written text; or to substantiate the questions the characters pose to themselves by taking into consideration the images' texture, composure, pace, lighting, framing and perspective. This becomes a dialogic reading experience in which Czerwiec, the pathographer, constructs an iconography of care through representations of the AIDS Care Unit 371 and her own interactions with the patients there while inviting more intricate modalities of seeing and thinking of and about the act of care, its ethics, motivations and pathways, especially during an epidemic that lessened since the first decade of the 2000s in the US, but has not ended or slowed down significantly in other parts of the world.

The Pathographer

Figure 11.1 The 3Cs. (Czerwiec 2017, 31)

Before starting her preceptorship on Unit 371, MK, the character, is shown around the medical floor and the readers have the opportunity to learn a brief history of the place and of HIV/AIDS as told by patients, nurses, administrative staff, doctors and volunteers. Stretching over the entire first chapter, the tour puts forward the ethos for such a care unit, as well as, importantly for this chapter, the requirements for working there. Specifically, "I don't want anyone to work here because they need a job. You have to want to work in this area, with our patients. And you will need to have the 3 C's: caring, compassion, and competence. We will give you the competence. You must bring the other two" (Czerwiec 2017, 31) (Fig.11.1). Karen Coleman, the person giving MK the tour, and a pivotal member in the Unit, summarizes in the lower left-hand side panel the importance of the job in patients' lives, the connection with anyone admitted there and the openness required to form such relationships, all overseen conceptually by the 3Cs: caring, compassion and competence. The absence of any one of these can be lethal or damaging to already suffering individuals. Moreover, Karen describes working in Unit 371 as a long-term process ("you have to want to work in this area, with our patients") which could provide consistency, sustained compassionate care and grounding to people dying of AIDS-associated illnesses. Underneath this requirement, we can understand Karen explaining the emotional labour and psychological complexity of taking care of patients afflicted by an epidemic with no cure or appropriate medicine at the time.[2]

Karen's incisive insights occupy a large amount of space in the panel and change its balance: the text bubble populates most of it, while Karen's image rests in the corner. MK is not present in the panel and Karen's body stands in relation to a hidden audience ("you") in punctuating these important facts about Unit 371 and the care and compassion protocols developed there. Judging by Karen's and MK's bodies' identical position and orientation in panels two and four (counting from left to right, from the upper part downwards), we can notice a shift in panel three. It does not contain any other elements, but Karen's figure and the text bubble, thus taking away any distractions that could derail our attention from the reading process. The focus zooms in on Karen's upper body and her facial expressions while the amount of text signals for the reader the necessity of a longer time frame to understand and reflect on the information conveyed therein. Also, the color scheme is very neutral, emphasizing the text and directing the eyes into a specific direction. In crafting her words, Karen does not address MK only, although the flow of text on the page would indicate that, but a general audience, "you." The pedagogical aspect becomes clear here, alongside a very subtle critique of public approaches and treatments of the HIV/AIDS epidemic in general and ill people in particular: you will need to have the 2Cs, if you are not in or affiliated with the medical profession: care and compassion. Teachers, mentors, trainers can teach you competence as a professional trait as you practice the other two. Lastly, Karen's figure in the lower right corner, where the speech bubble begins, functions almost like a jumping board, a bridge, to the next panel.

The last panel on the page depicts Karen and MK mirroring the one right above it and regaining part of the balance between text and image. Karen, touching MK's shoulder, reiterates her initial point, "You have to want to make a difference, to help somebody on their journey, whatever that journey may be" (Czerwiec 2017, 31) (Fig. 11.1). Thanks to Karen's hand and body position and MK's presence in the panel, the pronoun "you" reverts to its singular form and refers only to one person. This explains the message's reiteration with different words, especially since MK was a graduate from nursing school by the time she met Karen. In other words, MK surely heard words such as "care" and "compassion" before, in nursing school, so Karen does not utter them directly in the last panel, but emphasizes the diversity of end-of-life choices, as well as the very different path each body declines and influences changes in personality, identity and self-esteem. Additionally, when inviting "[to help] somebody on their journey, whatever that journey might be," Karen acknowledges the biomedical model of care and treatment, but situates it in a multitude of possibilities when it comes to choices available to patients in Unit 371. "Making a difference" with the available medicine in the 1990s and early 2000s could only go so far, while empathy and respect in association with care and compassion made the Unit into what Roger, a patient, describes it in Chapter one, "this is a magnificent place that I'd rather not visit. But they have saved my life. If I have to get better somewhere, I want it to be here" (Czerwiec 2017, 22). After a pause marked by a blank line between two rows of texts, Karen asks MK whether she is ready. MK's facial expression is neutral, as it remains over the entire page, suggesting determination and attentive listening in silence. The written answer, with its difficulties and contradictions, comes on the next page.

Unit 371 offers the space where MK, the healthcare provider, learns the ropes of nursing while writing its oral history that drives the creation of *Taking Turns*. In this context, she interacts with patients and provides support in a myriad of situations, from delivering the correct medicine on time, making sure charts were accurately filled into emphatic conversations and drawing sessions with some of the patients. MK learns to compassionately witness how illnesses and death change one's perspective on the time left to live and, in the comic, she creates a type of pathography that exceeds its initial definition. The most common way of defining pathography comes from Anne Hunsaker Hawkins' 1999 book, *Reconstructing Illness*: "an autobiographical or biographical narrative about an experience of illness" (178), "[pathographies] are authored by particular persons who are directly affected by the events they relate and [...] they provide a corrective to the stark medical procedure" (13). Hawkins takes into consideration the substantial tradition of autobiography in the Western hemisphere that describes experiences related to diseases and illnesses and incorporates biographical works in which the author documents someone else's sufferings and is being directly affected by events which remain vague to the medical profession, yet very important to patients, such as changes in personality or grieving for one's life while still living. In this sense, pathographies formulate epistemological infrastructures which can support the project of reflection on the meaning of life as it approaches its end. Hawkins historicises the practice of pathography in literature in the 20th century, but Joseph Natoli and Mariarosa Laddo posit their generic affiliation with conversion and religious narratives, placing them in an earlier historical period, specifically the 19th century. Natoli argues in favour of considering fiction as pathography and claims that a phenomenological reading of fiction can reveal a great deal of information about the author, as well as about the world view of a specific society. He defines pathography as "a record of phenomenal experiences" (Natoli 1982, 74) closely entangled with the socio-political and cultural milieu of the time. Not all fiction has pathographic characteristics, in Natoli's view, but the ones who do offer unexpected entry points into notions of psychopathology and *weltanschauung*. As a caregiver, MK is part of a specific socio-cultural and political environment where the HIV/AIDS epidemic is a highly sensitive, racialized and politicized topic (Treichler 1999). She records her own and her patients' experiences while putting together text and images for a more comprehensive engagement with an alternative to "stark medical procedures" (Hawkins 13). However, HIV/AIDS Unit 371 was by no means the standard type of care unit in the US or in the world.

HIV/AIDS Care Unit 371 was a firm materialization of the hope for what should have been special care units in the US and in the world before and even after the arrival of H.A.A.R.T.[3] When "no new thing that happened or symptom that showed up turned out to be nothing. It was always the worst thing" (Czerwiec 175), MK proposes the drawing of comics, the mixture of words and images in self-enclosed panels, as pathography in Hawkins' conceptualization as "it concerns attempts of individuals to orient themselves in the world of sickness" (2). Her part is to guide her patients' and her own understanding toward restoring or assembling coherence from and at ontological fault lines opened by the epidemic. This role extends through comics and gains a pedagogical dimension that guides readers in their discovery of Unit 371, as well as in joining in an iconography of care oriented by the 3Cs.[4] MK's book provides readers with competence, not medical in most cases, but in the forms of visual and emotional literacies.

Hawkins, Natoli, Laddo and many others are strong proponents of literature and its potential of reformulating and re-arranging notions of reality, life and selfhood while the physical body declines. Susan M. Squier and Irmela M. Krüger-Fürnhoff open the field wider with a volume on *PathoGraphics*. The introduction explains the conceptual melding between *pathos* and *graphē/graphein* to reassess the tension between word and image which "has historically obscured a broadly shared project of using narrative and aesthetics to serve engagement and activism around the issue of human suffering and pain" (Squier and Krüger-Fürnhoff 2020, 3). AIDS activism has been a prevalent factor in convincing the US government to provide funding for research and infighting against stigma, but the commercialization of highly effective medicine has greatly diminished its power (France 2016). *Taking Turns* proposes an overhaul of the shared project between narrative and aesthetics while showing care for readers and creating a space to engage with suffering and pain while reminding them that the epidemic is not over and is still in need of engagement and activism. In parallel, Adrian Bussone reviews Czerwiec's book and holds that "despite this interweaving of fiction and truth, the story never strays to the fantastical— it is never too grim nor too cheerful, it just *is*" (Bussone 2017, 2, emphasis in the original). In its "being," the book creates the opportunity for readers to connect and react in multifarious ways. But there is a pedagogical nuance through which some panels, such as in Fig. 11.1, create the need for close interaction, for the eyes to rest more on the unbalanced panel and realize it speaks directly to them. Additionally, I take Bussone's remark a step further and contend that this seemingly level ground of text and images provides a conscious choice of balancing the history of AIDS, its political exceptionalisation and instrumentalisation, and its impact on the LGBTQ+ communities with the intent of depicting paradigms of care in times of long-standing crisis. Thus, the *pathos* here appears in steady panels while the *graphein* enhances and explains it in a dialectical motion that assumes pedagogical nuances and redefines MK's position as an author and artist into a pathographer.

Approximating in Colour

The protocols of care implemented in Unit 371 were different than what Nursing Schools or Medical Schools provided for their students. MK learns how different they are at the end of one shift when one patient asks her to hold him since he was really scared (Fig. 11.2). MK gives course to the request and holds him for ten formative minutes, after which she felt "silenced, shaken" and in awe. Four panels, identical in size and shape and having the same green background, capture the moment with writing and no images.

Figure 11.2 Remodeling Boundaries. (Czerwiec 2017, 45)

The choice in colour and writing style, as well as the largely equal amount of writing in each panel, makes them almost interchangeable and problematizes sequential reading (Eisner 2018). The first panel, which sets the circumstances and narratively locks the honouring of the patient's request, can occupy a set position as the first panel on the page, while panels two, three and four (numbered in a traditional order from left to right, top to bottom) can swap places. Reshuffling the panels does not change the meaning, but enhance the emotional intensity of reading about MK's interaction with Stephen, the patient. The close proximity which allows MK to feel "[…] bone, skin, cloth, heartbeat" mitigates a redefinition of professional boundaries. That is not to say that, as a character posits later in the comic, boundaries were not there or that they negatively influenced the course of treatment.[5] It is to say that the awe, defined on the next page as "a feeling of reverential respect mixed with fear or wonder" (Czerwiec 2017, 46), as an affective, all-encompassing response to AIDS patients needed for its manifestation the reinterpretation of medical distance between caregivers and patients. Reshuffling the panels (1, 2, 4, 3 or even 1, 4, 2, 3) as a reading strategy, effaces the causative textual relationship implied by sequential reading between feeling Stephen's heartbeat and being "silenced, shaken" and in awe. In the absence of such textual causation, Stephen's ontological position as a patient in a medical facility changes and the readers witness, guided by the panels' pedagogical intent, the humanizing of "bone, skin, cloth, heartbeat" into a constellation of body, feelings, socio-cultural and political milieus and care protocols exceeding medical directives. The hug Stephen asks for out of fear is indicative of death's and illness' loneliness, as well as of the hospital's perceived environment; MK's waiting for Stephen to end the hug not only reminds us of the 3Cs at the beginning of the comic, but implicitly brings forth one of pathography's missions according to Hawkins, namely to "put the patient back into the medical enterprise—to return the experiencing, suffering human being from the periphery to the center of medicine [...]" (Hawkins 1999, 13). The first step in this direction is, in MK's book, the feeling of awe that redefines medical boundaries.

Although comics traditionally rely on the intermixing between image and text, this page is among the few instances where only writing appears inside panels. The green background brings to prominence the black writing and the panels' borders, which remind us of the familiar pattern ordering the space of the comic repeated seamlessly so far. The green color appears sporadically and in different shades in the entire comic, becoming darker as grief intensifies. While in some Western cultures green is not immediately associated with death or grief, and, in comic books, heroes in green are closer to nature, or the colour becomes associated with growth and the will to life and survive, its use here is intriguing. Lichtenfeld et al. argue for a new interpretation: they see the color green and its different hues as an implicit affective cue. They have concluded through closely controlled experiments that, when shown a big green rectangle in the middle of the page with the word "ideas" written in the middle and then asked to complete a creative task, participants have performed better than the controlled group (Lichtenfeld et al. 2012). Although not rectangles, but squares, the green panels in Fig.11. 2 function as an implicit affective cue in two ways: they draw the readers' attention through the contrasting between the compact background and the opposite page and, secondly, enable a slower engaged reading of repeated actions (the subject-verb construction "I felt" appears three times directly and three times implicitly). Following Lichtenfeld's team, the colour green cues us to understand the words in a more creative modality, allowing thus inherently a multiplicity of ways, depending on each reader, to process, contextualize and reinterpret the affective content.

The panels, the words and the colour enveloping them provide MK and the readers with a way to approximate the pain, loneliness, anxiety, just to name a few, present in Unit 371, in the pre-H.A.A.R.T. era, as well as nowadays for those whose lives are still touched by AIDS-related illnesses. Stella Bruzzi theorizes the *approximation* concept as the insertion of a historical fact "into a narrative, not in order to be collapsed into fiction, but to co-exist in collision with it" (Bruzzi 2006, 44). Approximations, initially defined in relation to documentary films, are multidimensional accounts that contain both the original event they reference, accounts by other people impacted by it, documentaries, stories and "other subsequent narrativizations of it [the historical event] as opposed to [being] merely transparent or mimetic representations" (Ibid., 39). There are a few historical facts present in *Taking Turns*, such as the HIV/AIDS epidemic, the physical existence of Unit 371 and, at a personal level, MK becoming into a nurse. All of them are founding parts of the story, and co-exist in collision with their fictionalized accounts as traits of autobiography and even biography (Nichols 1991). In *Taking Turns*, MK does not offer unilateral representations of grief, interactions or even highly stylized, mimetic renderings of patients or the Unit itself. She provides, instead, implicit affective cues in the forms of colours or through the subtle change in perspective from panel to panel for us to re-form grief (Butler 2010, 97) and expand the use of the extant emotional vocabulary in relation to illnesses and death.

Figure 11.3 Darker Green. (Czerwiec 2017, 131)

Taking Turns in Writing Pain

In an NPR interview on comics and their evolution and relation with canonical works of Western literature, one of the speakers asserts that "comics are a medium that exists in the tension between images and text" (Weldon 2016). While the speakers are preoccupied with asserting once more the importance of both, image and text, in conveying knowledge, their insistence on the medium and its capacious fluidity suggests the pivotal position the said tension occupies in relation to the creation and reproduction of new formulations of knowledge as pain and grief. In Fig.11.2, the comic relies heavily on words, while in Fig. 11.3 it hinges on images. The colour green's intensity deepens with the comic book's progression, as we can see from the darker background in Fig. 11.3. Tim, MK's friend and former patient, is taking his last breaths in the hospital and she and his mother are taking turns accompanying him. Each panel alternates twice between day and night, and the image over the green background becomes smaller as Tim becomes weaker and weaker. In the last panel containing the smallest picture out of the four, MK tells her friend "Tim, it's time," as they had long agreed she would before he lost consciousness. The three words are the only written aspect of the entire page and connect the narrative with an earlier point at which MK and Tim were making friends as the nurse-patient boundaries were becoming more porous. In three panels, MK touches her friend's neck, hand, and chest while the mother appears to stay a little further away. The characters' positions in the panels might suggest their own attitude towards AIDS and dying, but, more convincingly here, their presence stands in for a repetition of sorts. Michael A. Chaney argues that authors drawing themselves in a comic book are not offering us definite representations of themselves. Instead, "it is but one in a series of provisional renderings, none of which may be said to constitute the final, definite version [...]" (Chaney 2016, 123), a draft. MK, just like the mother figure, is transformed by grief as she accompanies the patient towards death. Each self-portrait, as Chaney argues, and each portrait, I argue, are drafts that bring back and perpetuate at the same time a specific event or time period. Each new representation is slightly different in its details, whereas the background remains constant. The repetition of the same frame, albeit in a different size, simultaneously implies the progression and stagnation of personal time. The words, "Tim, it's time," end the background's enveloping of the shrinking image and change the last panel. At the same time, the words stand in tension with Tim's death as they have been uttered, or remembered as uttered, a few pages earlier. The page becomes, thus, an approximation of Tim's death as a symbol for the many lives lost to AIDS, and as a visual narrativisation of pain and grief.

Additionally, the tension palpable here is composite, since the phrase is a graphic reverberation of an earlier conversation between Tim and MK. Tim asks about ways of knowing when death is near and MK promises she will be there to tell him when time comes. A few pages earlier, MK avoids saying these specific words, although maintaining the meaning of the last moments "yes, I do [believe it is time]" (Czerwiec 2017, 127), while the final panel on the page depicts her and Tim's mom at his side. However, in the first panel on the next page, containing no images, we can read "That last page is a lie. It's not what happened. It's what I wished had happened" (Ibid., 128). Afterwards, we find what "really" happened, a much more violent iteration of the preceding page, followed by the same ending panel. The self-portrait, the repeated panels and words form a ritual of mourning, a reverberation of a farewell uttered long beforehand, as well as a draft, or even a rehearsal of sorts, between friends. As one of Unit 371's founding doctors mentioned, "people somehow get the empathy thing that we are all just people taking turns being sick" (Czerwiec 2017, 30), describing thus overarching vulnerability, as well as grounds for compassion and care for each other and for oneself. Drawing on the emotional architecture set in place in the first page with green background (Fig.11.1), this example builds up MK's narrative accountability to Tim by keeping her promise of signaling his death. Moreover, although the images provide a rather stern depiction of the hospice space, the body's presence in the panels conveys the proximity between the caregiver, doctor, nurse, family or friend, and the sufferer (Squier 2015, 49). They enhance the narrative's framing without confining the experience of death to medial paradigms. Meaning emerges, as Johanna Druker suggests in her *Graphesis* (2014), relationally: within the panel and across pages as fragmentary, enwrapped in and challenging professional and personal epistemologies, and at the tension between words and images. The draft, the imperfect image and its repetition, the drawn silences and the black words on green backgrounds become, thus, foundational parts of an always expanding iconography of care that materializes itself through plurivalent emotional vocabularies as seen in the comic.

HIV/AIDS Care Unit 371 incorporated a large number of nurses, specialists, volunteers, friends and family in order to build a support network that could comfort the patient. The caregiver, as any of the network's members, takes turns in supporting and designing care away and in tandem with medical procedures. MK's comic book highlights this constellation of people and their role in Unit 371 in order to dissolve the rigid hierarchies found in hospitals at times and to lay a solid basis for a model of care based on compassionate cooperation. MK, as the pathographer, approximates her colleagues' voices and momentous presence in the Unit and shows, with humour at times, how each patient's journey might change their caregivers' emotional relation with their surroundings in an attempt of balancing pathography. Allowing multiple voices in the comic reminds us of one of the book's main scopes—to create an oral history of Unit 371—, but it also demonstrates how narrative care equally makes us hear these voices and makes room for silent pages where the choice of colour influences affective comprehension and mirrors the caregiver's ethos extending beyond the clinic and onto the page. Christine Hauskeller suggests *mature care* as the proper nomenclature for what MK performs in the comic book, specifically, "[care] which is grounded in knowledge of, and respect for, others—as well as for oneself" (Hauskeller 2020, 153). The last part of the definition is salient, since the comic book develops the autobiographical side of pathography as a commentary on the ontological possibilities of care. In other words, accompanying patients on their journey, "whatever that journey may be," is impossible without respect for oneself and introspection. Boundaries, while heavily altered by the gravity of the AIDS epidemic, can never disappear, but metamorphose into ways that make mature care and the materialization of the 3Cs possible in Unit 371.

Taking Turns shies away from most traditional representations of AIDS patients as there are no characteristics by which we can recognise Kaposi sarcomas or signs of tuberculosis or anything else, for that matter. As a healer and pathographer, MK's main concern regards the existence of the epidemic itself and the ways in which it has affected everyone and everything. The narrative is not sanitized and the emphasis does not fall on gore or the decay of the body. Alternatively, the focus is on providing the readers with a complex visual and textual vocabulary that can be used to simultaneously describe and create silences to allow for grief, friendship, sadness, awe, companionship, care, medical practices and their limits to come into being. This way, the comics medium is resourceful enough to imaginatively engage with the AIDS epidemic while not spectacularizing the sufferers' bodies, but showing how society's entire fabric has been ruptured beyond physical materiality. However, as *Taking Turns* makes clear, there are composite possibilities of honouring and caring for each other and for patients, for building better medical care facilities and for imagining a future despite death's presence. This becomes possible through a vocabulary that substantiates care and is invested in minutely writing individual and collective pain during a crisis and beyond.

Approximations, as techniques of ethical and narrative engagement, give the pathographer freedom to negotiate their own memories and feelings and to present them repeatedly, in multiple drafts through the interweaving of text and image. Using Bruzzi's approach brings to light the accretive nature of illness narratives, as they try to capture the HIV/AIDS' epidemic's multifarious manifestations on the body and on the psyche. The impact diseases and illnesses have on patients and their entire support networks is so vast and complex that only a plurality of literacies can render them legible and intelligible to larger communities. Thus, visual and textual modalities of approaching illnesses and diseases, as well as epidemics and pandemics, from a perspective of pathography creates possibilities of affective engagement with pain and grief that expand our layered emotional vocabulary. Comics, a medium elastic enough to withhold the tension and collaboration between text and image, bridge our understanding of care through their constant drafting of approximations, redesigning of boundaries, traditional literary and visual perceptions of illness, pain and death.

Bibliography

Bruzzi, Stella. "Approximation: Documentary, History and the Staging of Reality." *Moving Image Review & Art Journal* 2, no.1 (2013): pp. 38-52.

Bussone, Adrian. "Experiencing the History of HIV/AIDS: A Review of Taking Turns." *The Comics Grid* 7, no. 1, 2017.

Butler, Judith. *Frames of War: When is Life Grievable?* London and New York: Verso, 2010.

Chaney, Michael. *Reading Lessons in Seeing. Mirrors, Masks, and Mazes in the Autobiographical Graphic Novel.* Jackson: University Press of Mississippi, 2016.

Clough, Patricia Ticineto and Jean Halley, eds. *The Affective Turn. Theorizing the Social.* Durham and London: Duke University Press, 2013.

Czerwiec, MK. *Taking Turns. Stories from HIV/AIDS Care Unit 371.* University Park, Pennsylvania: Pennsylvania University Press, 2017.

Drucker, Johanna. *Graphesis: Visual Forms of Knowledge Production.* Cambridge, Massachusetts: Harvard University Press, 2014.

Eisner, Will. *Comics and Sequential Art: Principles and Practices from Legendary Cartoonist.* New York: W.W. Norton, 2008.

France, David. *How to Survive a Plague: The Inside Story of How Citizens and Science Tamed AIDS.* New York: Alfred A. Knopf, 2016.

Glick, Meghan H. *Infrahumanisms. Science, Culture, and the Making of Modern Non/Personhood.* Durham and London: Duke University Press, 2018.

Hauskeller, Christine. "Care Ethics and Care Contexts: Contributions from Feminist Philosophy." *East Asian Science, Technology and Society: An International Journal. Care in Translation. Care-ful Research in Medical Settings* 14 (Special Issue 2020): pp. 153- 63.

Hawkins, Anne Hunsaker. *Reconstructing Illness: Studies in Pathography.* West Lafayette, Ind.: Purdue University Press, 1999.

Lichtenfeld, Stephanie., Andrew J. Elliot., Markus A. Maier, and Reinhard Pekrun. "Fertile Green: Green Facilitates Creative Performance." *Personality and Social Psychology Bulletin* 38, no. 6 (2012): pp. 784–97.

Loddo, Mariarosa. "Between Sacred and Profane: Pathographies as Renewed Conversion Narratives." *Modern & Contemporary France* 28, no. 4 (2020): pp. 1-15.

MacLeod, Martha. "On Knowing the Patient: Experiences of Nurses Undertaking Care." In *World of Illness. Biographical and Cultural Perspectives on Health and Diseases*, edited by Alan Radley, 179-98. London and New York: Routledge, 1993.

Natoli, Joseph P. "Fiction as Pathography." *Journal of Phenomenological Psychology* 13, no. 1 (1982): pp. 73-84.

Nichols, Bill. *Representing Reality: Issues and Concepts in Documentary.* Bloomington: Indiana University Press, 1991.

Radley, Alan, ed. *World of Illness. Biographical and Cultural Perspectives on Health and Diseases.* London and New York: Routledge, 1993.

Squier, Susan Merrill and Irmela M. Krüger-Fürhoff, eds. *PathoGraphics. Narrative, Aesthetics, Contention, Community.* University Park, Pennsylvania: Pennsylvania State University, 2020.

Treichler, Paula A. *How to Have Theory in an Epidemic. Cultural Chronicles of AIDS.* Durham: Duke University Press, 1999.

Weldon, Glen. "The Term 'Graphic Novel' Has Had a Good Run. We Don't Need it Anymore". NPR, 2016. Accessed June 2, 2020. https://www.npr.org/2016/11/17/502422829/the-term-graphic-novel-has-had-a-good-run-we-don t-need-it-anymore

Williams, Ian., Susan Merrill., Squier., Michael J. Green., Kimberly R. Myers., Scott T. Smith, and MK Czerwiec, eds. *Graphic Medicine Manifesto.* University Park, Pennsylvania: Pennsylvania State University, 2015.

Notes

[1] In the *Graphic Medicine Manifesto*, Scott Smith provides a detailed account of the difference between the terms and the usage of *graphic novels* and *comics*. In graphic medicine, comics appears to be the preferred term and I will employ it in this article as well.

[2] For the emotional labour in healthcare, and pertaining to nurses specifically, see Clough and Halley. 2007. *The Affective Turn. Theorizing the Social.* Durham and London: Duke University Press.

[3] For a larger contextualization of the HIV/AIDS epidemic and H.A.A.R.T. see Glick, Meghan. 2018. *Infrahumanisms. Science, Culture, and the Making of Modern Non/Personhood.* Durham and London: Duke University Press.

[4] I draw on Ian William's conceptualization of the term "iconography of illness" in describing the iconography of care in this article. The later encompasses medical and affective practices that materialize care in a comforting, supporting manner that exceeds the provisions of basic needs to patients or family. See Williams et all. 2015. Graphic Medicine Manifesto. University Park, Pennsylvania: Pennsylvania University Press.

[5] For an in-depth discussion of boundaries in nursing and medicine, see MacLeod, Martha. 1993. "On Knowing the Patient: Experiences of Nurses Undertaking Care." In *World of Illness. Biographical and Cultural Perspectives on Health and Diseases.* Edited by Alan Radley, 179-98. London and New York: Routledge.

III.
Literary Pathographies of the World

Chapter 12

Wopko Jensma as a Pathographer: The Interface between Poetry and Schizophrenia

Ayub Sheik

University of KwaZulu-Natal, South Africa

Abstract: Wopko Jensma's frequent use of neologisms, portmanteau words, fragmentation and experimental topography has often resulted in a private idiomatic language that was seemingly incomprehensible. This difficulty has provoked widely divergent views ranging from accolades to criticism that he had finally "lost it," was "schizophrenic", and that his poetry was nothing more than the confused ramblings of a madman. Jensma's poetry of bizarre pathological motifs and speakers dispersed across multiple subjectivities is a chronicle of personal devastation rooted in the volatile chapter of South Africa's racist past. Image, diction and narrative coalesce in dissonant aesthetic strategies to express the anguish and psychological annihilation emanating from human degradation and despair borne of poverty and political disenfranchisement. Overwhelmed by a repressive society, racism, and insidious materialism, the conflicted speakers in Jensma's poetry retreat into interior psychological spaces and perpetuate pathological acts of self-harm or sadomasochism in response to the bizarre, Orwellian conditions of apartheid existence. The multiple voices which emerge are a startling polyphony of alienation, pathological hate, helplessness and sadomasochism. These voices express the hostility, oppression, and suffering that characterised the apartheid state and his personal torment and anguish. What is especially intriguing is the uncanny coincidence between Jensma's poetry and the aberrations that are present in schizophrenia. Themed by suspicion of persecution, self-mutilation, alienation, hallucinations and manic delusions, Jensma's poetry appropriates the pathological resources of schizophrenia in a surreal critique of racial subjugation and economic oppression. This chapter posits that his affliction from schizophrenia also influenced Jensma's experimental discourse and permeated his work. This is manifest in the use of asocial dialects with highly personal idioms, discordant syntax and substitutes, which make his language extremely difficult to follow at times.

Keywords: Wopko Jensma, schizophrenia, racism, consumer culture, manic, delusion, alienation.

* * *

It is surprising that despite having won the Ad Donker prize for originality of voice and vision in 1983, South African poet and artist, Wopko Jensma, remains relatively obscure. Although Peter Horn, Stephan Gray, and Michael Gardiner amongst others, have attempted critical exposés of Jensma's poetry, Jensma's cryptic and arcane prosody warrants much more critical attention particularly for its innovative aesthetics and surreal portrayal of apartheid cityscapes. This study ambitiously seeks to examine Jensma's intriguing linguistic play and the uncanny coherence between the narratorial voices in his poetry and the aberrations present in schizophrenia.

Jensma's anthologies, *Sing for our Execution* (1973), *Where White is the Colour, Where Black is the Number* (1974), *Have you seen my Clippings* (1977) together with the unpublished, *Blood and more Blood*, constitute an interesting and idiosyncratic response to the strife and turmoil in South Africa in the 1970s. His poetry may be framed within a poetics of resistance, conceived as an antidote to personal and social suffering endured by blacks under apartheid.

Jensma's experimental poetry harnesses the signatures of jazz lyrics, concrete poetry, the avant-garde, as well as African dance forms in bizarre cameos of underclass misery and racial oppression. In lieu of metrical regularity and rhyme the aesthetic experience is simulated by semantic qualities of speech, sound, and rhythmic undulations in a poetry characterized by what Samuel Beckett has called "the withdrawal of semantic crutches" (Schwab 6). Jensma's use of neologisms, portmanteau words, disparate argots, syntactic dislocation, fragmentation, and experimental topography has often resulted in a private idiomatic language that was seemingly incomprehensible at times. This difficulty has provoked widely divergent views ranging from accolades to criticism that he had finally "lost it" and that his poetry was no more than the confused ramblings of a madman. Described by writer and academic, Stephen Gray, as "exceptionally great" and by actor Marcel van Heerden as "way, way ahead of his time" (Blignaut 1996), Jensma is just as commonly referred to as "having lost it" or as "schizophrenic."

Phil du Plessis, a Cape Town physician and friend of Jensma's, was adamant that Jensma's poetry of fragmentation, inverted syntax, seeming incoherence, and recurring motifs of mutilation were symptomatic of schizophrenia. Others such as Michael Gardiner saw Jensma's prosody as a particularly apt representation of the fragmentation and surrealistic nightmare that characterized apartheid South Africa in the sixties and seventies.

In his study, *Mapmakers: Writing in a State of Siege*, Andre Brink (1983) distinguishes between language that is in everyday use and the language used by creative writers:

> The language used by society at large is conditioned by and rooted in convention, since such language is, of necessity, "generalized" and "systematized" within a structure of common denominators. The creative writer's language usage runs counter to that of society. The writer must hone blunted words anew, rekindle the fire of "original inspiration" in them, rediscover original meanings or discover new ones, departing in every respect from the well-known and well-trodden syntactic or semantic structures, exploring whatever territory remains unknown on either side. (Brink 118)

Brink's observation is an apt commentary on Jensma's experimental prosody. By drawing on the delusions, bizarre speech patterns, and narcissism that may be present in schizophrenia, Jensma evoked the delusional, the bizarre, and the narcissism that cloak claims to racial superiority and class elitism. Jensma's poetry transgresses conventional assumptions and definitions of poetry by experiments with syntax, form, topography, rhyme-less verse, and irregular rhythms. Drawing on the influences of the European avant-garde, notably Dadaism, Surrealism, and Expressionism, the imagery is frequently shocking in its references to violence, self-mutilation, and nihilistic despair. The vividness and variety of his language is described by Peter Horn as: "the corrupt sociolect of the slums of Johannesburg and words like 'squadcar' and 'blackjack' presuppose familiarity with life in an apartheid society" (Horn 1994, 24).

Jensma's prosody moves erratically from stark and clear township idioms to the complexity of surrealistic associations, neologisms, semantic dislocation, and syntactic fragmentation which bear a striking resemblance to speech patterns consistent with paranoid schizophrenia. Jensma's diction of private idiomatic language, mixing of dialects, the use of syncopation, ellipsis, and experimental topography have no doubt contributed to the cryptic and arcane aberrations associated with schizophrenia. This seemingly schizoid versification by Jensma's conflicted narratorial voices may be interpreted as a paradoxical wish to protect the core of oneself from communication whilst simultaneously expressing the need to be discovered and acknowledged. Indeed, Jensma himself was diagnosed as schizophrenic and received treatment at the Weskoppies Outpatients Clinic and the Johannesburg General Hospital.

The themes in Jensma's four volumes of poetry range from mutilation, confinement, loss, and conflicted identity to issues of racism, politics, and consumer culture. In adopting a sympathetic perspective to Jensma's seemingly schizoid discourse, this study will endeavour to show that the schizophrenic scrambling of signifiers and spatial disorientation is a quintessential representation of postmodern culture which supersedes the rational and linear narratives that underpin consensual reality. Space-time compression, cognitive dissonance, and surreality find congruent expression in both the schizoid's discourse and in the theatre of signs competing for attention in consumer culture.

This study owes a factual and interpretive debt to the ideas of Roland Barthes, Frederic Jameson, R.D. Laing and Deleuze and Guattari amongst others, an eclectic mix of perspectives that reveal Jensma's poetic craft and insightful social commentary of modernity and oppression by race and class. The alter personalities which abound in Jensma's texts and their flight from reality are read as desperate attempts at self-preservation under alienating and overwhelming circumstances that implode consciousness. Image, diction and story coalesce in innovative aesthetics, which inscribe the anguish and insights of disconnected selves living in multiple realities.

Schizophrenia is one of the most common, enigmatic and disabling mental illnesses. Spitzer's (1992) research indicates that about three in a thousand people suffer from schizophrenia at any given time. As far as is known, schizophrenia exists in all cultures and has been present throughout history. Because of the disorder complexity, few generalizations fit all people diagnosed as schizophrenic. Its most common characteristics are bizarre, irrational beliefs, persecutory delusions, incoherent speech expressed as word salads, thought disorder, and various forms of psychoses. Given the enigma surrounding this disorder, one is inclined to agree with Sass who in his study, *The Paradoxes of Delusion: Wittgenstein, Schreiber and the Schizophrenic Mind* concludes that: "Schizophrenia is a heterogeneous and contested concept which covers a variety of subtypes whose boundaries are still under investigation and perhaps may never be established" (Sass 2002, 15).

No less a mind than Karl Jaspers believed that any attempt at unriddling the enigma of schizophrenia was doomed to failure and that we ought simply to acknowledge a fundamental unknowability (7).

While we often think of schizophrenia as a major departure from normal health, mild symptoms can occur in healthy people and are not associated with illness. This has led to the conclusion that schizophrenia reflects a quantitative rather than qualitative deviation from normality, rather like hypertension or diabetes. Picchioni and Murray's meta-search (2016) suggests that the common perception that schizophrenia has a poor prognosis is not true. More than 80% of patients with their first episode of psychosis will recover, although less than 20% will never have another episode. While many patients with schizophrenia have a lifelong vulnerability to recurrent episodes of illness, a large proportion will have few relapses and make a good functional recovery.

Whilst there is substantial consensus that schizophrenia is a mental illness to be treated by drugs, confinement and therapy, there are also compelling arguments which repudiate this claim. R.D. Laing in *The Divided Self* (1969) and in *Sanity, Madness and the Family* (1990), as well as Deleuze and Guattari's *Anti-Oedipus: Capitalism and Schizophrenia* (1983) are the principal representatives of the anti-psychiatric bloc. These scholars had a sympathetic view of schizophrenia and saw its diagnosis as pathological aberration as a myth. Douglas Kircher points out that Laing held the belief that:

> Schizophrenics (if they wanted to) could produce potentially intelligible communication through their actions. Word salads were red herrings produced to mystify others (they may have also helped to mystify the self). Schizophrenics are deemed by conventional psychiatry to be ill, could be regarded as agents of change whose experiences were potentially understandable and rational when seen as intentional acts within a context. There were using Sartean self-deception as a way of trying to live in what they saw as an unlivable situation. (Mullen 2006, 32)

This perspective gives us insight into the conflicted personas that populate Jensma's texts, personas that are often driven into interior psychological spaces, as well as psychotic and surreal extremes in order to survive an overwhelming and implosive reality. This study will look at Jensma's experimental vignettes which attempt to capture the collapse of space and time in our consumer culture, and then proceed with an analysis of poems reflective of pathological yet incisive responses to the reductive politics of racial essence and cultural crisis.

It is the schizoid's ability to scramble and decode what Deleuze and Guattari associate with contemporary capitalism. Like the schizophrenic, capitalism can insert itself anywhere as a decoder and scrambler. Capitalism breaks down the cultural, symbolic and linguistic barriers that limit exchange. This imperial feature of capitalism is made explicit in Jensma's vignettes of urban cityscapes, which demonstrate the rush of signifiers associated with consumerist culture. One such example is the poem, *suB/BurB/Bia*— "burb" is an expression of disrespect and "sub" is manipulated to suggest a low form of life. In this way, the title presages the sterile images of the decadent city.

> day IN day OUT
> no WAY oUt—
> GENtS/here
> CLOSeD (on a/c
> nOISE...AiR
> cONditioninG
> opium/NicOtiNe
> sHOpSwoPnO
> BLaNKSonlYoR
> F`eLALeGoa
> Fly JetSetoN
> Acid triP to riO
> nOMANhoLes in
> heLL Or FiREeS-
> caPeS to HeaVeN
> SHAKe- 'N-roll't
> BloWbuBBlegUm
> oHBLUeBore
> DaY in DaY out
> NO ExIT – No
> (yACHt 2 FoOk)
> EntrancE here. (Jensma 1977, 40)

Reading the poem stimulates the disorientation and compulsion imposed on consumers by a signification of excess and by the compression of space and time. The poem exposes the power of despotic signifiers and capitalistic reterritorialization.

It creates an impression of the world as a theatre of signs which cannot exclude each other and which exists as a confusion of voices. This schizoid culture has collapsed linear meaning into the compressed time of the perpetual present. The psychosis of modern consumer culture is expressed by experiments with form, topography, fragmentation and condensation. According to Searles: "Condensation is a process in which a variety of meanings/emotions are concentrated in their communicative expression in some comparatively simple statement" (Searles 1998, 393).

The poem is an expression of the urban phenomena of noise, air conditioning, drugs, and bubblegum, artefacts of popular culture which together with the hectic speed of urban life disorientate and overwhelm the speaker. The ontological insecurity of the speaker is expressed as a bizarre sense of engulfment by his surroundings which is manifest in the poem by the parallelism of the syntactic structures in lines 2 and 19:

No WAY oUt-...
NO ExIT-No. (Jensma 1977, 40)

The use of the minimal line and line enjambment enhance the disorientating effect and create a surreal fusion of images. Life is experienced as an overwhelming excess of images compounded by neurotic attempts at escapism. The disorientating and unexpected use of upper and lower case gives the poem a dissonant, clipped rhythm which amplifies the speaker's disenfranchisement and engulfment by urban phenomena. The poem has three parts and is incrementally titled to finally reveal the syndrome of catatonia.

Catatonia is a condition marked by changes in muscle tone or activity associated with a large number of serious mental and physical illnesses. There are two distinct sets of symptoms that are characteristic of this condition. In catatonic stupor, the subject is rendered motionless and initiates no social behaviour. Catatonic excitement, or excessive movement, is associated with violent behaviour directed to oneself or others. In the poem, the subject exhibits both catatonic stupor and hyperactivity.

Interestingly, there is no narrative progression in the poem — this stasis is a synecdoche of the unfolding catatonia in the poem which is characterized by episodes of immobility. The non-metrical line registers the tension between the collage of perceptual experiences in the poem and the subject's attempt at linguistic mediation. The experimental prosody replaces acoustic regularity by emphasizing the graphic visual dimension.

Roland Barthes' study, *Mythologies* (1985) is useful in interpreting the everyday trivia in the poem in a meaningful way. According to Barthes, the signs which appear as natural and expected in the city are in fact an illusionary reality constructed to mask the real structures of power obtained in society. These mythological realities are composed by the "petite bourgeoisie" to encourage conformity to its views and to perpetuate its capitalistic dominance. This cultural ethos promotes beliefs and values congenial to itself. By naturalizing and universalizing such beliefs they are rendered as self-evident and inevitable, excluding rival forms of thoughts and obscuring social reality in ways convenient to itself.

The coded iconic message is the totality of all the messages that are signified by the images. The linguistic message functions in the iconic message by "anchorage" (39), and "relay" (39). With "anchorage": "The text directs the reader through the signifiers of the image...remote-controlling him towards a meaning chosen in advance" (Barthes 1977, 39-40).

The "anchorage" in the poem is the repeated and insistent exhortations to "drink more" (41) and "eat more" (41), and indulges in an orgy of material gratification.

The fragmentary references to catatonia are finally revealed in its entirety in the third part of the poem which is entitled "Catatonia":

> noW screwball!
> SPEEDball, yeS
> HIGHball, send'T
> baby!uP/dOwn
> EscalatoRbaNtu
> Bar/LoUngenO
> siR/YeSboSS?hAf
> yrcHiPs'NeaT'T
> breYten-aL Leen
> iN 'n ruBBersel
> SesmAAndEBrAK
> gRonD/bLoedBaD
> descend dOWn a
> CommOncOLd-O
> BrUshyrteetH
> MoRrOpe/lesTimE
> tHere'SMONeY in
> hOneY/PeanUts/
> piGs/ivory/ebOny
> StoP!no-U-turn. (Jensma 1977, 42)

The repetition of the suffix, "ball" lends an alliterative quality to the staccato rhythm of the poem. The poem is written in a tone of reckless abandon. Its mesmerizing rush of signs is located within a distinctly South African context with references to separate amenities in the apartheid era, the use of snatches of Afrikaans and the imprisonment of the poet, Breton Breytenbach.

The incremental catatonic episodes in the three parts of the poem culminate in a "cul de sac" (1977), which foreground a sense of entrapment and loss of self:

StoP! No-U-turn
CuL De Sac daY
In For daY out! (Jensma 1977, 42)

The staccato rhythm, truncated and dissonant diction, and surreal flow of images make this poem a spectacle of modern confusion and disconcerting haste. The poem is an allegory of a subject caught in a vortex of racial oppression and the paranoia implicit in a constantly changing and bewildering consumerist culture, which reads as an apt description of apartheid's cityscapes and its disenfranchised and impoverished black majority.

The poem may also be critiqued in the context of Jameson's thinking that the media culture of the late twentieth century simulates schizophrenic experience. The rapid succession of signifiers on television and cinema advertisements erodes the viewer's sense of temporal continuity. The images which flash across the screen are: "Isolated, disconnected, discontinuous material signifiers which fail to link up into a coherent sequence" (Jameson 2004, 119).

Wopko Jensma also expresses the disorientation of urban consumer culture by the use of compressed minimal line, the fusion of images and unsettling topography. This links to Fredric Jameson for whom the postmodern montage disorientates the subject and contributes to the egolessness that is characteristic of schizophrenia. By destroying the distinction between low and high art forms, postmodern culture integrates itself into capitalistic mass culture. Jameson links schizophrenia to postmodernism and postmodernism to consumer capitalism. Contemporary capitalism has extended the symptoms of schizophrenia to the masses in the form of postmodern culture. His formulation sees both postmodernism and schizophrenia as cultural forces that decode and scramble and confuse. The schizophrenic confusion destroys the possibility of critical perspectives. In a fragmented cultural milieu, capitalist consumer culture can thrive unopposed. A schizophrenic culture fails to "accede fully into the realm of speech and language" (Jameson 2004, 118). The narratorial voices in Jensma's poetry provide an incisive critique of bourgeois redolence and rampant consumerism, and mediate the crisis in spatial temporal representation brought on by the engulfment of urban phenomena.

By reflecting on the obvious and seemingly natural in the city, Jensma makes explicit the implicit cultural artefacts of consumer culture. These artefacts of mass consumption are false representations that mask the real structures of power in society. In Jensma's poetry, advertising is seen to promote the myth of free choice. A mass culture that encourages conformity to its own views is thus encouraged. Jensma's representations of consumer culture show how the ruling class reproduces its dominance at the level of daily experience. In this process, identity is ensconced in images of sterility and nihilism:

we only hear the clang
we only feel the bite
we only taste the sour pulp of an aimless life....
we are through, we scathed ourselves
down.[1]

Schizophrenia is manifest in Jensma's poetry in the form of delusions, paranoia, and loss of self in his protagonists. Notions of persecution, pathological compulsion, neurotic fantasies, and visual and auditory hallucinations overwhelm Jensma's speakers. These manic reactions arise as a defense against an overwhelming and implosive reality and are desperate attempts at self- preservation.

The poem, "Lo Lull" (1977) is a four-part poem which depicts the anguish and misery of a disconnected self, living in multiple realities. The speaker exercises dominion over the form, shape, and presence of alter personalities as a compensation for his loss of effective control in the real world. The poem is a surreal monologue in which the speaker's identity is threatened as he is overwhelmed by his condition of confinement:

I am a dirty little room
With spiders in the corner of my skull
My mouth a dark pit
Into which human droppings disappear
The speck of rust in my heart worries me

Many people breathe in and out of me
I am at ease with the world
only the speck of rust worries me. (Jensma 1977, 22)

R. D. Laing, in his study *The Divided Self* (1969), points out that in cases of acute alienation and suffering the subject may lapse into a state of "petrification" in order to survive his terror. Petrification is a particular form of terror in which the subject is turned to stone and he regards himself as a thing (Laing 1969, 48). In this instance, words such as "dirty," "dark pit," and "human droppings," (Jensma 1977, 23) indicate an extreme perplexity of identity that has led to the subject projecting his identity upon his room. The subject's alienation and displaced personality is expressed as "the dirty little room" (23) he is confined in. Similarly, "the spiders in the corner of my skull" (22) allude to the walls in his cob-infested cell and the "dark pit into which human droppings disappear" (22) is the toilet pan.

It is clear that self-dehumanization has left the individual with a diminished sense of reality and grossly disorientated. These delusional or hallucinatory perceptions estrange the implied author from the outside world. The speaker considers himself as an isolate, without connection or meaning in the world, like Kafka's character, K in *The Castle* (1969). Walter Benjamin describes K: "For just as K lives in the village on Castle Hill, modern man lives in his body; the body slips away from him, is hostile towards him. It may happen that a man wakes up one day and finds himself transformed into vermin. Exile, his exile, has gained control over him" (Benjamin & Arendt 1986, 26).

In "Lo Lull 3" (1977), the speaker's fragmented psyche has resulted in an alter personality which looks on at his own displaced body:

> I look at myself sleeping
> I look at myself going for a piss
> I look at myself coming out of bed
> I look at myself coming back to bed
> I look at myself having a nightmare
> I look at myself getting up
> I look at myself shaving
> I look at myself going off to work
> I keep looking at myself
> not knowing that I am being watched. (24)

R. D. Laing points out that the disassociation of the self from the body is a response that appears to be available to most people who find themselves enclosed within a threatening experience from which there is no physical escape. An appropriate example is the experiences of prisoners in concentration camps who lapse into a physical withdrawal "into the self" and "out of the body." Despite the unreality of experience, the alter personality is excessively alert and thinks and observes with exceptional lucidity (Laing 1969, 82).

Part 3 of "Only Us" (1977) reflects the depersonalization of the self which is expressed in bizarre images of self-preoccupation.

> The candlestick of my finger
> Burns slowly at the dawn
>
> I have a thousand eyes
> Nine-ninety-nine don't see
> I have a million words to say
> They are all dead in my mouth

but my hands wield an ax
and I know the price is right. (Jensma 1977, 15)

In the first three stanzas, the speaker appears bewildered and clings to his isolation. The absence of punctuation enhances the bizarre effect produced by the intractable delusions of the speaker. These delusions are predicated on manic grandiosity in the form of having a "thousand eyes" (15) and an iridescent finger:

The candlestick of my finger
Burns slowly at the dawn. (15)

Melanie Klein points out that manic grandiosity is discernable by its overvaluations. With this goes the tendency to think of everything on a large scale, to think in large numbers, all this in accordance with imagined omnipotence (Klein 1975, 352).

Paradoxically, the speaker is also confronted by the dread of the dissolution of his schizoid self. This is expressed in the poem by the juxtaposition of overvaluations and devaluations:

I have a thousand eyes
Nine-ninety-nine don't see
I have a million words to say
They are all dead in my mouth. (Jensma 1977, 15)

The images in the poem foreground the delusions of incapacity and deadness of the speaker. Paradoxically, in the last stanza, in spite of the bewildering inertia, the speaker evokes a militant call to arms:

But my hand wields an axe
and I know the price is right. (15)

Part 2 of "Chant of praise for the idi amin dada" (1977) expresses the morbid fascination with destruction:

kiddo smashing a toy
he doesn't destroy
he perceives, percepts
he reconstructs... (Jensma 1977, 48)

The aggressive images and minute attention to acts of destruction are indicative of a narcissistic rage with the object of achieving total control. The aggressive transference of rage underscores the desire for sadistic gratification from destruction and the craving for narcissistic power. The search for power over the object is manifest as a rationalized, intellectualized form of cruelty:

> he doesn't destroy
> he perceives, percepts
> he reconstructs… (48).

The elliptical line ending anticipates the flight from reality and descent into psychoses.

The use of ellipsis in each line foregrounds the alienated and dislocated self of the schizophrenic in part three of "Chant of praise for the idi amin dada" (1977):

> The schizophrenic splits itself, its world………………………..
> Escape voices (yakkity yak) of its conscience……………………...
> Oversensitive nerves, tight as wire sinews……………………..
> Give free reign to its floodlit feelings……………………….....
> It's severe, wild at one, two, one, at once……………………..
> It's unlimited, unrestrained, shows two face……………………
> Unintelligible, cacophonic montages, its dada………………. (Jensma 1977, 49).

The elliptical line endings also underscore the ontological insecurity and threatened identity that characterize schizophrenia. The alter personalities alluded to in the first line of the poem emerge in an attempt to keep terror from imploding consciousness. The schizophrenic "split" is a desperate attempt to preserve existence in the face of extreme trauma.

> The auditory hallucinations in line two:
> Escape voices (yakkity yak) of its conscience…. (49)

They are the most common in schizophrenia and may frequently involve many voices the person may perceive from inside his or her head. These voices may be familiar and may be single or multiple (Bentall 1990, 3). In lines three and four, the schizophrenic is overwhelmed by the manifestations of multiplicity in schizophrenia. The schizophrenic produces what Roland Barthes terms: "The text of bliss…the text that imposes a state of loss…. unsettles the reader's historical, cultural, psychological assumptions, the consistency of his tastes, values, memory, brings to crisis his relations with language" (Glass 1993, 11). This is manifest in the elliptical line endings which is suggestive of the speaker's extreme perplexity about schizophrenia.

The "unlimited, unrestrained, shows two face" (Jensma 1977, 49) nature of the schizoid episode is described by Terry Eagleton as: "The dismantling of our given identities through art," (Eagleton 2011, 191). The "unintelligible, cacophonic montages" (Jensma 1977, 49) in the last line are diagnosed as formal thought disorder in schizophrenia. The most common example of this is when the subject shifts incoherently from one subject to another without displaying that the topics are unconnected. Badcock points out that neologism also abounds in formal thought disorder and are indicative of a tendency to create a private language related to the state of narcissist withdrawal which underlines the disease (Eagleton 2011, 140).

It may also be that Jensma is merely satirizing the way medical discourses speak about schizophrenia in the poem. Jensma is not confirming the truth about medical perceptions of schizophrenia, but transposing elements of the irrational and experimental implicit in "dada" into a new signifying relationship with schizophrenia. Both dada and schizophrenia operate on the premises of the irrational and chance associations in an attempt at liberation from what Lacan notes as: "The use of language as the 'signifier' of the irrational which evolves from a cultural matrix of power, domination, order and regularity" (Glass 1993, 61).

The final part of "Lo Lull" (1977) is a monologue in which the speaker derives masochistic pleasure from an elaborate ritual of mutilation:

> First paint my head in all detail
> Then pluck the eyes out
> Then cut the ears off
> Then strip off the lips
> Then smash the teeth out
> Then burn the hair off
> Then peel off the skin
> Then the nose, the tongue
> First paint my skull in all detail. (Jensma 1977, 25)

The poem is a masochistic ritual in which the subject takes pleasure in pain which culminates in a final loss of self. The compulsive repetitions of painful events betray the speaker's depersonalized view of his body. R. D. Laing points out: "This detachment of the body comes about when the individual regards his body as one object amongst other objects in the world rather than the core of his being. Instead, the body is felt as the core of a false self, which a detached, disembodied self looks upon with tenderness, hatred or amusement as the case may be" (Laing 1969, 71).

Wopko Jenma's poetry of fragmentation, bizarre pathological motifs, and multiple images is a chronicle of personal devastation rooted in the volatile chapter of South Africa's apartheid past. Image, story and diction coalesce in dissonant aesthetic strategies to express the anguish and psychological annihilation emanating from human degradation and despair. Jensma'a poetry also illustrates that meaning and signification do not exhaust poetic function. The text is more than the representation of meaning — the "pheno text," and has to be understood as the engendering of meaning — the "geno-text," (Lechte 1990, 128). This is illustrated by his experimental topography and innovative aesthetics.

Thus, Jensma's experiments with elision, ellipsis, and syncopation also attest to what the poem represses (in the process) that exceeds the subject and his communicative structures. Wopko Jensma's poetry is also an imaginative critique of "constituted realities" and its ambient ideologies, which have exiled the 'other' outside the pale of common humanity. For Jensma, the subject is held together as a fictive and concrete unity by the illusion of misrecognition. Consequently, for Jensma's schizoid speaker's reality, time and personality do not exist. The real world must be invented. In challenging specious bourgeois morality and a repressive political order, Jensma's poetry foregrounds the provocative notion that what society and convention perceive as urbane truth, together with its ideological masks and rites of power, may be fractured, exposed, and satirized by the resources manifest in schizophrenia. Jensma's poetry is significant because it speaks to what society represses, because it cannot control its own unfathomable chaos which is externalized and medicalized as a schizophrenic disease.

References

Barthes, Roland. 1968. *Writing Degree Zero*. Translated by Annette Lavers and Colin Smith. [1st American edition] New York: Hill and Wang.

———. 1985. *Mythologies*. New York: Hill & Wang.

Benjamin, Walter and Hannah Arendt. 1986. *Illuminations*. Translated by Harry Zohn. New York: Schocken.

Bentall, Richard P. 1990. *Reconstructing Schizophrenia*. London: Routledge.

Blignaut, C. 1996. "Revolution in a Shopping Mall". *Mail and Guardian* 25 (July): 12.

Brink André P. 1983. *Mapmakers: Writing in a State of Siege*. London: Faber and Faber.

Deleuze, Gilles and Felix Guattari. 1984. *Anti-Oedipus: Capitalism and Schizophrenia*. London: Athlone.

Eagleton, Terry. 1996. *Literary Theory: An Introduction* (2nd Ed.). Hoboken: John Wiley & Sons.

Glass, J. 1983. *Shattered Lives: Multiple Personality in a Postmodern World.* New York: Cornell University Press.

Horn, Peter. 2004. *Writing My Reading: Essays on Literary Politics in South Africa.* Cross/Cultures: 15. Amsterdam: Rodopi.

Jameson, Frederic. 2004. *Postmodernism and Consumer Society: The Anti-Aesthetic: Essays on Postmodern Culture.* Washington: Bay Press.

Jensma, Wopko Pieter. *Blood and more Blood.* NELM archives: South Africa.

———. 1973. *Sing for Our Execution: Poems and Woodcuts.* Johannesburg: OPHIR/RAVAN, Distributed by Spro-cas Publications.

———. 1974. *Where White Is the Colour, Where Black Is the Number.* Johannesburg: Ravan Press.

———. 1977. *I Must Show You My Clippings.* Johannesburg: Ravan Press.

Klein, M. 1975. "Notes on some Schizoid Mechanisms." In *Developments in Psychoanalysis*, edited by J. Reviere. London: Hogarth Press.

Laing, R. D. 1969. *The Divided Self.* New York: Pantheon Books.

Laing, R. D, and Aaron Esterson. 1990. *Sanity, Madness and the Family: Families of Schizophrenics.* London: Penguin.

Lechte, John. 1990. *Julia Kristeva, Critics of the Twentieth Century.* London: Routledge.

Mullen, Paul E. 2006. "Schizophrenia and violence: From correlations to preventive strategies". *Advances in Psychiatric Treatment*, 12, no. 4: pp. 239–248. doi:10.1192/apt.12.4.239.

Picchioni, M and Robin M Murray. 2007. "Schizophrenia." *Clinical Review*, 335: 1.

Sass, Louis Arnorsson. 2002. *Madness and Modernism: Insanity in the Light of Modern Art, Literature, and Thought.* New York, NY: Basic Books.

———. 1996. *The Paradoxes of Delusion: Wittgenstein, Schreber, and the Schizophrenic Mind.* Ithaca, N.Y.: Cornell University Press.

Schwab, Gabriele. 1994. "Subjects without Selves: Transitional Texts in Modern Fiction". *Harvard Studies in Comparative Literature*, 43. Cambridge, Mass.: Harvard University Press.

Searles, A. 1998. *Schizophrenia: A Modern Perspective.* London: Oxford University Press.

Spitzer, J. 1992. *Understanding Schizophrenia.* Cambridge: McDowell Press.

Notes

[1] The poem has been taken from an unpublished letter to Peter Horn, NELM Archives, Grahamstown, Eastern Cape, South Africa.

Chapter 13

The Black Book as Pathography: Romancing Disease and Decay in the Late Ottoman Empire

Meltem Gürle

University of Cologne, Germany

Abstract: Born to an aristocratic family in Istanbul at the turn of the century and having received an education in French and German, Suat Derviş was one of the leading women writers of her time. Although she is mostly known for her later novels written in the genre of social realism, her first novella, *Kara Kitap* (*The Black Book*), remains as one of the finest examples of decadent literature in Ottoman-Turkish literature with its gloomy setting, the dark theme of illness, and characters at the brink of madness.

Relying on Matei Calinescu's approach that views literary decadence identical with the ideology of progress and on Paul Bourget's treatment of the decadent style as a symptom of cultural breakdown and decay, this chapter reads Derviş's portrayal of disease, decay and death (and the artistic expression she finds to convey these themes) in *The Black Book* in connection with the social and cultural climate of the late Ottoman Empire. In this short novella, where she tells the story of the fall of an aristocratic family through the perspective of a young woman dying of a mysterious disease, Derviş combines the high and the low literature, the philosophical and the popular, and composes a piece that reflects the consciousness of the increasingly weak and decadent Ottoman Empire at the turn of the century.

Keywords: Turkish literature, fin-de-siecle, decadence, Suat Derviş, disease, death, illness.

* * *

In an attempt to define the decadent movement in Europe, the period that extended from the second half of the nineteenth century through the first decades of the twentieth, Romanian literary critic Matei Calinescu suggests reading decadence in line with progress, the dynamo behind the whole rubric of modernity: "Once again, progress *is* decadence and decadence *is* progress" (emphasis original).[1] What Calinescu means by that seemingly paradoxical equation is not that decadence fosters or cherishes the modernist ideology of progress, but that it is not possible to think of one without acknowledging the presence of the other. Similarly, he maintains that modernism as an artistic movement was necessarily decadent, because it was laden with an acute sense of loss and alienation resulting from the high degree of technological development at the turn of the century. Referring to the Goncourt brothers, who speak of a "modern melancholy" in 1864, and Emile Zola, who around the same time writes of "the sickness of progress," Calinescu argues that neurosis, the raw material of decadence, was embedded in modernity from the very beginning.[2]

Literary decadentism, however, while being inseparably conjoined with modernism, is more like an evil twin that challenges equally both the rationalist and the scientific aspects of the idea of progress. Especially vulnerable to the criticism voiced by the Decadent movement is the abstract ideal of humanism that continues through the Enlightenment into modernity and assumes that human beings are inherently good creatures in a constant state of progress toward a better future. Rather than focusing on modernity's narrative of growth based on the constant progress of human development and civilizational maturity, the authors of the decadent tradition, fuelled by the pessimist worldview of Arthur Schopenhauer and the nihilist philosophy of Friedrich Nietzsche, accentuate the miserable aspects of the modern existence foregrounding sickness, degeneration, and decay.

As demonstrated in the works of the French symbolist poet Baudelaire, whose critical view of modernity was inextricably tied with the imagery of "an exhausted civilization in decline, for which artificiality had come to triumph over any life that might be in tune with nature,"[3] the link between decadent society and sickness, especially neurosis and mental instability was sealed very early in decadent literature. In reference to the preface Gautier writes to Baudelaire's *Les Fleurs du mal* (1868), Calinescu maintains that, even though the poet disliked the term decadence and rejected the concept, Baudelaire's work was marked with the subtle awareness of the correlation between the decline of the empires and the imagery of decay and dissolution. While he admits that this connection was especially true for France, possibly because of "the feeling that the nation's power and prestige in the world were declining," Calinescu also underlines the fact that the sense of decadence inherent in the late nineteenth-century literature was not restricted to that country.[4] It was Verlaine, yet another French symbolist poet, who marked the essence of *fin-de-siècle* consciousness with the opening line of his famous sonnet "Langueur" (1884) — *"Je suis l'empire à la fin de la decadence."* This sense of the collapsing civilizations, however, was prevalent all over Europe in the second half of the nineteenth century, which eventually culminated in the outbreak of World War I and destroyed four multinational empires: the Russian Empire in 1917, the German and the Austro-Hungarian in 1918, and the Ottoman in 1922.

Decadence and the Ottomans

As the century was nearing its end, traces of decadent literature became discernible also in the works of the Ottoman novelists and poets. The early novelists of the Ottoman Empire were those of the *Tanzimât*, which was a period of reformation between the years 1839-1876, when the Empire had turned its face to Europe and aspired to embody the social and cultural aspects of Western civilizations. This attempt of modernization was reflected in the novel of the period, which was regarded as a medium to promote the ideas of progress, patriotism, morality and social change.[5] However, a new literary movement was developing in the Ottoman-Turkish novel writing around the 1890s that finally replaced the moralizing, pedagogic, and socially engaged novelistic tradition. This movement, known as *Edebiyat-ı Cedide* (New Literature), was led by a group of authors writing for *Servet-i Fünun* (The Wealth of Sciences), an *avant-garde* literary journal advocating the view that art is for art's sake.[6] Being home to many influential novelists of the time, such as Süleyman Nazif, Mehmet Rauf, and Halit Ziya Uşaklıgil, the journal soon became the heart of the cultural and intellectual life in Istanbul. Turkish historiography traditionally reads the emergence of *Servet-i Fünun* as an outcome of the influence of French literature on Turkish novelists. Şerif Mardin memorably suggests that these authors introduced to the Turkish novel "new psychological analyses in their prose writing under the influence of Paul Bourget."[7] The reference to the French novelist and literary critic is not coincidental: Bourget played a crucial role in the intellectual and literary scene in France at the end of the nineteenth century, and offered arguably the most accurate definition of decadence in his analysis of Baudelaire's poetry: "the moral malady," an existential crisis that is reflected in the literature of the period and had its roots in "dilettantism, nihilism, and cosmopolitanism; the perversions and impotence of modern love; the effects of science; the conflict between democracy and high culture."[8]

While it cannot be denied that *Servet-i Fünun* created a distinctive aesthetic movement under the influence of European, and particularly French, cultural and intellectual circles, one should not overlook the fact that the Empire itself was hit by the turn-of-the-century malaise. The moral sickness that Bourget characterized as part of decadent literature was already intrinsic to the Ottoman consciousness at the end of the nineteenth century, when the Empire was portrayed in its death throes as the "sick man of Europe," which itself was "emblematic of the *fin-de-siècle*."[9] In Istanbul, there emerged a decadent society at the turn of the century ruled over by a corrupt government and a Sultan dominated by fear and hatred. The country was witness to one of the most chaotic periods of Ottoman history marked by autocratic conservatism of Abdulhamid II (1876-1909) as well as the subsequent dramatic transition to constitutionalism that started with the Young Turk revolution of 1908. In the following decade, these rapid changes would lead into the complete dissolution and disintegration of the Ottoman Empire, which would crumble with the occupation of the country by the Allies in the aftermath of World War I.

Suat Derviş: A Child of *fin-de-siècle*

Suat Derviş (1904-1972) was born at the height of this turbulent atmosphere to an aristocratic family in Istanbul. In fact, as she recalls in her memoirs, one of her earliest memories is how she and her sister were rushed to the old family house in Çamlıca at the time of the *31 March Incident* (1909),[10] the counter-coup that attempted to reverse the Young Turk movement and put an end to the Second Constitutional Era in order to re-affirm the position of the Sultan as the absolute monarch. When the counter-coup fails and brings the Young Turks back into power enabling them to form a government, Derviş's parents go back to their lives in the city, where the young Suat gets homeschooled receiving French and German language education from private tutors. As she comes from a liberal family that valued the education of young women, her education continues into her adolescent years. She gets tutored in history, literature, and music, which eventually lands her at Berlin University, where she attended lectures in the Faculty of Letters between the years 1919-1920.[11]

Present literary criticism on her work focuses mostly on exploring the socialist or realist aspects of her later novels,[12] which is understandable when we consider that Derviş wrote most of her notable works in that genre and is regarded as a significant figure in Turkish feminist and socialist movements. Being one of the Ottoman suffragettes and politically active in the early years of the Republic, Suat Derviş was the emblem of the "New Woman" as the free-spirited and independent author and journalist. Focusing on Turkey's social and political problems, she published numerous novellas, short stories and more than ten novels in both Turkish and French. Derviş's early work, on the other hand, especially her first novella *Kara Kitap* (The Black Book, 1920) is written under the influence of the *Servet-i Fünun* movement. In this early stage of her career, Derviş engages in an in-depth analysis of the human psyche, explores the limits of science and nature, and looks for new ways of artistic expression. In *The Black Book*, as she relates the fall of a prominent Ottoman family in a highly symbolic setting, she plays on some distinctive themes of decadent literature reflecting the *fin-de-siècle* malaise that dominated the last years of the Ottoman Empire. Although it was well-received by the literary circles of the time when it was first published [Mehmed Rauf, one of the leading figures of *Servet-i Fünun*, called the author a promising new talent who has introduced "new artistic methods of storytelling"[13]], *The Black Book* remained buried deep under the wave of social realist novelistic tradition for many years. It was not until the late 1990s that Derviş's early novels were discovered again and brought to the attention of the Turkish readers. Fatmagül Berktay, in an article she wrote for the literary journal *Defter* in 1997, draws our attention to the female characters in Derviş's early novels and suggests her to read in the light of feminist criticism. In her own reading, she regards the dark themes of these novels as an indication of the author's choice to remain outside of the "Republican/nationalist ideology,"[14] which was a prevalent theme in the novels of the period.

While crediting this view that reads Derviş's early work in contrast with the nationalist ideology of her time in particular and the modernist fantasy of progress and development in general, in this paper I will focus on the theme of disease and death, and approach it as a metaphor of decay and disintegration of the Ottoman Empire. When *The Black Book* was published in 1920, the Empire had been struggling for more than a century. Its long-standing tradition was challenged by revolts and wars, and most importantly, by modernity and its multifaceted transformations. The nationalist movements were prevailing in the Balkans, because the Ottoman imperial glue was no more able to hold together the ethnic, linguistic, cultural and religious divisions. Ottomans had to live through the devastating years of the First World War followed by the occupation of Istanbul by the Allied Forces as a result of the Armistice of Mudros, which Suat Derviş herself followed as a journalist. The occupation of the capital city was the last straw completely destroying the Sultan's patriarchal authority and ruining the faith in the future of the Empire. While it does not directly engage with the political or social issues of the period, *The Black Book* responds to this gloomy atmosphere with its dark setting, symbolic language, and characters at the brink of madness. In fact, it would not be wide of the mark to suggest that the novella reflects the pathology and the moral crisis that the last members of long-standing Istanbul families go through in the aftermath of the First World War.

The Black Book

With characters suffering both physically and mentally or those that are tormented by watching their loved ones descending into disease and madness, *The Black Book* is a novella saturated with pathos. Şadan, a young Istanbulite, has recently moved with her widowed mother to her uncle's mansion in Çamlıca, a pine forest hill on the Asiatic shore of the Bosphorus with summer cottages and a panoramic view of the city. Şadan is suffering from a mysterious disease (possibly tuberculosis) and is deeply saddened by the fact that she had to leave Istanbul following the death of her father. She is accompanied by her grieving mother, her handicapped and deformed cousin Hasan, her recluse uncle, a frustrated scholar who rarely leaves his study, and her brother Necdet, who we do not see much but hear in the background rhapsodizing on the piano as the family falls apart and the old summer house crumbles into ruins.

Like the melancholy characters, the depiction of the decaying family house adds to the sense of the impending catastrophe. The ancient and picturesque mansion must have seen better days, but now it has succumbed to the wear of time. As a symbol of an obsolete aristocratic class, it is marked by a slow decay rather than a complete ruin: poorly lit rooms with shadows in the corners, the large sofa with its creaking legs, the mysterious library with dusty shelves full of old books, and heavy paintings on the walls constitute the setting of the story. The weather outside does not help to improve the gloomy atmosphere: rough winds blow through the chimneys, the fog constantly seeps through the windows, and the snow slowly covers the pinewood forest in the distance. One should note that the decaying mansion is a recurrent image in the turn-of-the-century Ottoman literature. In reference to the novels of Halit Ziya Uşaklıgil, one of the leading figures of the *Servet-i Fünün* movement, literary critic Zeynep Uysal maintains that the "desolate house" becomes a metaphor of the Ottoman consciousness in the late nineteenth century: "In other words, the human story, the destitution and barrenness of the individual, is told from within, but through the image of a house being shattered because of an impact from outside [...] underlining the fact that the personal sphere belonging to the family is utterly political."[15]

The isolated, dilapidated, windswept mansion introduces also a Gothic element into the story.[16] In addition to the traditional setting of the old house, Derviş uses almost all the conventions of Gothic Romantic literature: The beautiful heroine dying from a mysterious disease, the arrogant and cynical young artist defying both society and God in his reckless pursuit of retribution, and the prevalent imagery of light and dark are all trademarks of that genre. Another subtle but significant Gothic element is the capital at the turn of the century, the uncanny presence of which is felt in the background of the story. Istanbul, seen only from a distance emerges as a monstrous city, which, with its rapidly changing dimensions, poses a threat to the surviving members of this family, who have once witnessed its glorious days, but now have fled its horrors. Derviş prefers to place her characters in an isolated setting as an opposite pole to this "possessed" urban space that is heard and seen from afar as a decadent landscape of uncontrolled madness.

Told in the first person and in the present tense, the story opens in the middle of things, without any proper introduction. When her mother asks whether she is upset, Şadan tries to hide her tears behind the newspaper as she does not want to be discovered crying. "This house is too dark," she says in the hope of changing the subject.[17] This sad remark, however, sets the mood of the story. While at first it seems as if the young woman is talking of her strained eyes because she has been reading in the dark, it soon becomes obvious that she is referring to her own inner darkness, her crippling depression, and her sense of imprisonment in this old mansion. This is how, very early in the text, Derviş walks us into the territory of the Female Gothic, which traditionally explores the entrapment of women within domestic space, the borders of which are drawn by patriarchal authority.[18] Later, when the story unfolds, it comes as no surprise that the plot is based on a desire for movement from "inside" to "outside." Imprisoned in her own body eaten up by the disease, Şadan will strive to go beyond the walls of the old family house governed by impotent and troubled men.

Şadan's cousin Hasan is the most prominent of these troubled male figures. He has spent all his life hiding in this old house and is now secretly pleased that his aunt and cousin have moved in. He has been burdened, from childhood on, with an acute sense of self-consciousness because of his disfigured body. Not only is he a hunchback, but he is also crippled by the sickness of his mind being tortured by the knowledge that he is not pleasing to the eye. Neither is he pleasing to the soul. Şadan is both scared and intrigued by his cousin, who tortures her with his cruel remarks and his poetry of fearful imagery. Watching him sit in the farthest end of the room, lost in thoughts in front of his *secretaire*, she thinks he looks like a wounded animal. She does not notice his crooked body anymore, but she cannot escape his piercing eyes following every move she makes. Hasan picks up the cue when Şadan says the house is dark and takes it as an insult. He responds by saying that his cousin must be bored in the presence of such dull people: his father living like a mouse in the old library surrounded by musty books, his aunt withered with grief and helplessness, and himself, "a freak that you cannot bear to look at twice" (Dervis 2014, 101).

In his rebellion against God, against destiny and against the very nature of things, the red-haired and hot-tempered Hasan emerges as a Byronic character, the well-educated but arrogant and self-destructive outcast. His poetry, the content of which is conveyed to the reader through Şadan's recollection, challenges the divine power that cursed him with his broken body. He warns Şadan that his poems are not meant for the faint-hearted.: "They are like the afreets, like the demons from hell. They would burn your brain, shake your faith, destroy your creed. They are nothing but rhymed and measured words cried against creation, humanity, and nature" (106). With his long cry against the Creator, the creation and His creatures, Derviş's male protagonist also bears traces of Joris-Karl Huysmans' central character Des Esseintes in *À rebours* ("Against Nature").[19] Like Des Esseintes, Hasan is a bizarre, depraved aristocrat, who has left humanity and retreated to a solitary life in the countryside. While this choice is largely due to his physical appearance, we feel that his soul has been possessed by a similar contempt for humanity. Interested only in his art and poetry, he is repulsed by the life outside the mansion. Although he is obsessed with his cousin, Hasan looks down upon Şadan as he suspects that her infatuation with city life is fuelled by her desire for romance. It pains him to imagine that she would have suitors and eventually would become somebody's wife. He mocks her wish to recover ("but poor Şadan, you will never get better, will you?" 107), and regards her as a silly young girl with simple tastes ("ordinary, flat, weak things" 105). Yet he cannot help feeling intimidated by his cousin's sexuality: "If you are leaving the mansion for pleasure and fun, I'd rather see you leave in a coffin" (111). While especially targeting Şadan, Hasan's misogyny knows no boundaries: He hates all the members of the opposite sex, who, in his eyes, are infinitely superficial, immature, and cruel. In fact, Gillespie's comments on Des Esseintes apply to Hasan with equal force: "[he] develops a sense of woman as 'chimera' and 'sphinx' even as his indulgence in the flesh devolves from the actual world into artifices and the imagination."[20] While at the same time craving for their love and attention, Hasan despises women, because he believes that there is no woman "who possesses a heart where inner beauty triumphs over outer appearance" (108). The author presents her antagonist as a broken young man, who has never been loved by a woman and whose wounded heart only a woman could cure — a perspective that saves Hasan from being a plane villain and endows him with psychological depth making him more human. At one point, the young man remembers in pain how his mother used to try in vain to conceal her disgust while holding him in her arms when he was just a child. What stops him from looking into his cousin's face, is the fear that he may see the same pity and contempt in her eyes. This growing shadow of doubt and the possibility of losing Şadan to a healthy young man in the city make Hasan crumble in pain and agony.

As for Şadan, though she respects her cousin, she realizes that she cannot love him back the way he wants to be loved. What she actually wants is to be able to free: She yearns to go back to the city and be a young and careless person again. Living in this dark mansion surrounded by old family furniture, she fears that she will perish "among prescriptions and medicine bottles" before she has lived, loved, and laughed (114). Şadan's melancholy thickens by her awareness of her mental and physical weakness. The city is just out there with all its parties and get-togethers, but it seems miles away from the lonely hill of Çamlıca. It is as if Şadan is paralyzed with grief, which deepens her sense of confinement and helplessness. While she keeps the hope of recovery until the very end, the reader gradually realizes that she will never return home and live "without ever tiring from life and enjoying everything that it has to offer" (114). Life, as she knows it, has already been destroyed. It is not only tuberculosis that she suffers from: Şadan is presented as the victim of the plague of modern progress that has shaken the foundations of the Empire at the turn of the century. This is a time of rapid transformation, manifested in the cities to a greater extent than elsewhere, changing irreversibly the very structure of the society. It is marked by uncertainty and complexity, brought with itself riots and wars as well as disease and despair evoked by the destructive patterns of modernity that have replaced the sense of harmony, which defined the Old World and kept Şadan's family in tune with their social environment.

As the protagonist narrates the fall of the whole family from health, order, and mental balance, we sense that this very same pathology has contaminated the capital city of the Empire. The horror and confusion that emanates from Istanbul is reflected in Hasan's strong repulsion towards the city as well as in Şadan's fascination with it. The post-war Istanbul under the occupation of the Allied Forces, with Italian, French, British and American troops patrolling the streets, with Russian refugees fleeing from the Bolshevik revolution filling cafes and restaurants, is a cosmopolitan place bursting with violent energy. Referring to the night life in İstanbul at the time of the occupation, Carole Woodall mentions elements of debauchery, consumption of substances and alcohol, which, in the 1920s, were part and parcel of the emerging modern culture in the city: "Beyoğlu was the stage of these wayward crossing of peoples that contributed to the existence of decadent cosmopolitanism."[21] Historian Çiğdem Oğuz points out to the fact that Ernest Hemingway, who visited Istanbul in 1922 in order to cover the story of the Greco-Turkish War, deconstructs the exotic image attributed to the Ottoman capital by authors such as Pierre Loti and paints a picture of decay complete with rats and drunken barflies.[22] Yakup Kadri Karaosmanoğlu's novel depicting the same period is called *Sodom and Gommorah* (1928), where Istanbul, in comparison to the biblical city of Sodom, is portrayed as a degenerate and decadent landscape during the occupation. As Erdağ Göknar maintains, this view of the city as a decadent metropolis is generally "linked to the depravity of both the British officers of the occupying forces and the local upper-class women who are romantically involved with them."[23]

Despite her sweet fantasies of romance and strong will to live, Şadan never makes it back to her beloved Istanbul. Held back by her illness and tied up by the possessive love of her cousin, she barely leaves the mansion. Once when she gets out for a short walk in the woods ("I want to feel the wind in my hair. And run and run and run" 109), her condition worsens and she gets bedridden. During the walk outside, hanging onto the arm of her brother, she has talked of going back to the city, "of the first coat she would wear as soon as she gets back to Istanbul, of the lovely and delicate shoes, of the white silk socks, and of leather gloves" (110). Now the dream of the city seems far away. She feels as if the mansion swallows her back: the walls seem to have thickened around her. Hasan is pleased to see her lying in her bed, completely incapacitated, feeble, and shivering with fever. Though worried about her health, he admits that he prefers to lose her to death rather than to the decadent life in Istanbul. In fact, he goes further saying that it would be a relief if she died, at that very instant, which would mean that she would only be his: "Every day I would visit your grave and rest my face on the vault; your tomb would be my personal shrine and your bones my private idols" (111). These semi-erotic encounters with his cousin exhaust Şadan's strength and leave her increasingly confused. Hasan's dark, morbid, and surreal obsession with his cousin gradually takes hold of the young woman's psyche. She is suffocating in the overbearing presence of this devilish figure, who denies her her life and sexuality, and as it turns out to be, literally tries to talk her into her grave. This scene is a textbook example of the *fin-de-siècle* aesthetics, which regards death and beauty inseparable from each other, as it is the case in Baudelaire's many poems focusing on the decay of beautiful things, including the bodies of young women. Hasan's fascination with her cousin's death is not only a romantic fantasy, but also a revenge plot inclined to punish her for her awakening sexuality. Şadan knows that she is beautiful ("I am young and pretty: these two treasures are mine" 114), she craves for the attention of men (" I will perish before I can say I am admired […] dear Lord, did you give me this good looks only to mock me?" 115), and hence is condemned to death by her cousin, who imagines a beautiful death, or a death in beauty, in line with the sublimely aesthetic experience of decadent literature.

The fact that Derviş depicts this controversial character as a crippled figure brings to mind Elaine Showalter's claim that the prevalence of the misshapen offspring in *fin-de-siècle* fiction reflects the conflict between male and female writers over the representation of sexuality: "The syphilitic male became an arch-villain of feminist protest fiction, a carrier of contamination and madness, and a threat to the spiritual evolution of the human race."[24] According to Showalter, "suffering, apish, shriveled, and prematurely aged, these syphilitic children appeared to feminists as living symbols of the devolutionary force of male vice."[25] Derviş's novella, told in the most ambiguous tone, does not give us any clue about the reason why Hasan was born the way he was born, but implies that, as the heir of a long-standing aristocratic family, he pays for the sins of his ancestors.[26] Frustrated, handicapped, and pathetic, Hasan emerges as the embodiment of the damaged virility of the Ottoman Empire. His psychological (and possibly physical) impotence is representative of the injured masculinity of a generation traumatized by political oppression and the humiliation of the occupation. Similarly, rather than engaging in the portrayal of a "hegemonic" model of manhood, Derviş prefers to depict in Hasan's person a troubled, injured masculinity in crisis, haunted by the fear of its own limitations.[27]

The climax of this crisis is presented in the penultimate scene of the novella when Hasan, after finally revealing his feelings to his cousin, rushes out in embarrassment and disappears into the forest. The next day, when his dead body is found buried in the snow, Şadan is overcome by a feeling of finality. Looking at his pale face and the bright red of his hair on the snow, she thinks about the vulnerability of the human existence: "Here are his hands, his head, his chest. Nothing is missing. [...] Yet, he does not exist, is that so?" (121). While she is shattered by the sudden death of her cousin, we know that Şadan is also thinking of her own demise, which, she knows, will eventually come down on her like the thick walls of the mansion that keep her from the world she desires. What she does not know yet is that she will be haunted by this image of his cousin lying lifeless on the snow with "the sun in his red hair framing his head like a flaming halo" (121).

Şadan's anguish in the face of death and the existential notes in the background of the story become more easily discernible in the scenes that take place in the old library, where the young woman tirelessly looks for an answer to her questions and hopes to attach some meaning to her suffering. Though she is an ardent reader (at the beginning of the story, we see her reading Lamartin's *Méditations poétiques*, a book famous for its romantic tone and metaphysical depth), she is not allowed into the library, a private domain of her brooding uncle who does not want to be disturbed while working. When she is finally admitted into that part of the mansion, Şadan feels almost a religious ecstasy in the presence of books. She envies her uncle who has spent all his life in this room surrounded by the knowledge she has been craving for, and is surprised when he says, with a bitter smile on his lips, that he has not found in the books the consolation he was looking for: He has not encountered "any trace of the truth in these volumes;" all he got from his reading is an ever-increasing amount of doubt (113). Yet this does not prevent Şadan from paying regular visits to the library. Every evening, she sneaks into this spacious room and tirelessly walks between the shelves with her eyes on the covers of books in Latin, Greek, Hebrew, Farsi, and Arabic. She wonders whether any of these books contain the truth she is searching for. She feels like going down on her knees and beg them: "I'm sick. I'm dying. Teach me what I need to know in this dark journey" (112).

Şadan's nocturnal visits to the library constitute the backbone of Derviş's narrative. The more she reads, the more crestfallen she gets. As she leafs through the pages in the candlelit room trying to find the answer to one ultimate question, Şadan gradually realizes that death escapes all understanding. She realizes that even if she read all the books in the library in all the languages ever possible, she will not be granted the truth, which one can only gain through the actual experience of death. Şadan's ultimate failure with philosophy ("these wise men slumbering for years in the library" 115) is in line with the anti-rationalist attitude of decadantist literature as it emphasizes the uselessness of reason as a tool in uncovering the mystery of death. Instead of enabling her to come to terms with her own finitude and recognize the pure possibility of her own dying as an inescapable moment, her visits to the library lead her to complete destruction accelerating her fall into madness and disintegration.

An intriguing detail in the library scene is Şadan's encounter with the portrait of a beautiful young man, who, she is told, is her other cousin, now long dead. Hasan's older brother is depicted as a radiant young man with a "large and impressive forehead" and brave piercing eyes that penetrate into the observer's soul. Şadan is captivated by this portrait, which inspires both awe and joy in her. Delirious with fever, she hallucinates that the young man in the portrait comes alive and walks towards her through the shadows in the room. She imagines that his hands will be warm, his chest strong, and his eyes "burning with fires." She hopes to take refuge in his mighty presence from the horrors of the old house, from death and decay: "I just want to trust my whole being to him and say: Brother, I belong to you, help me to live" (114). While Şadan thinks the young man in the painting would have been the brother after her own heart, this scene is loaded with a lot of sexual tension. Through the portrait of the young man, Eros, the life instinct oriented toward sexual desire, enters Şadan's periphery. In her innocence, she instinctively understands that love is what she needs in order to ward off death.

In this ambiguous scene, one can also notice the allusion to Oscar Wilde's *The Picture of Dorian Gray* (1890), which, possibly with the exception of Edgar Allan Poe's brilliant little gem *The Oval Portrait* (1846), is the best rendition of the Gothic theme of "ageless beauty." Affirming once again the aesthetic tastes of the period, Derviş elevates art over nature as she introduces the timeless and beautiful painting as a counterpoint to the imperfect and shadow-like lives of the residents of the old mansion. The *doppelgänger* is unmistakable: Hasan is the evil twin of his bold and beautiful brother in the painting, where we find another echo of our analogy of the dying Empire. While Hasan symbolically represents the "sick man of Europe," the portrait in the library stands for the glorious past of the Ottoman reign. Eternal but frozen in time, the figure of the older brother shines from a frame hanging on the wall. He is as lifeless and barren as the Empire itself. Though she is amazed by the lifelikeness of the portrait, Şadan gradually comes to realize that even this handsome young man, this creature comparable only to a Greek God, had succumbed to the grinding wheels of time. She understands that death will conquer everything – including beauty and glory. There is nothing that can stand in the way of decay. The Empire will fall. The house will disintegrate. Şadan's young and beautiful body will feed the worms. There is no future. No promise of light. No possibility of progress or recovery.

It comes as no surprise when the story ends with Şadan's demise. She fails to overcome the guilt caused by his cousin's sudden death and is eventually taken over by consumption. Haunted to death by the hideous apparition of Hasan, she gets feverish and delusional in her last hours as she gives in to tuberculosis, which seems to have infected her brain. In her delirious last moments, she comes to believe that her cousin has come from the dead to unite with her in hellish eternity as he had promised before he committed suicide.

With its loosely connected scenes that begin and end abruptly without any sense of development or completion, its human figures disappearing in the shadows like ghosts, and its style based on minor narrative fragments, *The Black Book* challenges the temporal order of traditional narration as well as erasing the boundary between imagination and reality. The fact that reality is filtered through the consciousness of the troubled young protagonist adds to the sense of helplessness and confusion that penetrates every line culminating in the deathbed scene where she loses control of everything, both physically and spiritually. All through the story, but especially in this last episode, Derviş keeps her narrative highly ambiguous. She uses fragments of dialogues, broken sentences, and seemingly disconnected passages. There are time lapses between "shots" that remind us of the main character's lapses into fever-induced blackouts. This fragmented structure of the text becomes more apparent as the story nears the end and Şadan is faced with her demons: "I see the phosphorescent green eyes in the darkness. Hasan. He approaches me. I shiver… He is coming closer. He rises on the toes. Kisses me on my forehead. Bring my heart back, he says …

Darkness... Eternal, vertiginous, hellish darkness surrounds me. The pain, the horror, the truth... I'm dying..." (126)

As Şadan slips away before our eyes, the text crumbles and disintegrates losing its logical and grammatical structure. The effect of this technique is that the collage of words and fragments invoke all senses, invite colours and broken images, as in the moment of death. They also produce a *staccato* rhythm in the last part of the story echoing the death rattles of the young woman. However, probably the most important reason behind narrative fragmentation is its organic relation to cultural decay, as found in Bourget's analogy of societal and linguistic evolution. Susan Navarette points to Bourget's treatment of textual decomposition in Decadent style "both as correlative of organismal degeneration and as a symptom of cultural breakdown and decay."[28] Being the pathographer of her time, Derviş's use of language should be read in line with her portrayal of disease, decay, and death. The way she chooses these themes and the artistic expressions she finds to convey those in *The Black Book* cannot be viewed independently from the social and cultural climate of the late Ottoman Empire.

Suat Derviş's portrayal of a young woman's slow descent into madness and death in *The Black Book* can be read in line with the long tradition of European decadent literature. This early piece in her literary career can also be classified under Ottoman decadentism and regarded as one of the last examples of the *Servet-i Fünun* movement. What makes this dark novella unique, however, is its subtle elaboration of the background story. In this ambiguous and symbolic tale structured around the demise of an aristocratic family, Derviş engages with a bigger narrative, namely, the disintegration and fall of the Ottoman Empire. She does this by taking the stark reality of Istanbul under occupation and turning it into a horror story. The decaying house in Çamlıca emerges as an emblem of the old moral and social structure, which is pushed outside the boundaries of the capital city and abandoned to its lonely fate in the woods. It becomes a place of exile, a shrunken space of non-traversable distances, which eventually collapses upon itself destroying the family it hosts. The claustrophobic interior of the house is indicative of not only Şadan's entrapment within the domestic sphere, but also of the diminishing habitat of the Ottoman aristocracy, which, in Derviş's story, is presented as an obsolete and anachronistic entity.

In *The Black Book*, Derviş combines high and low literature, the philosophical and the popular, the political and the personal, and composes a piece that is rich in meaning. With its dramatic tension, psychological complexity, and symbolic ambiguity, Derviş's novella manages to convey to the reader the sense of entrapment and helplessness that the Ottoman upper class felt at the turn of the century. One should not forget that the novella was written at a time when the social framework of the Ottoman Empire had started dissolving, but had not yet been replaced with a national identity. Unlike the earlier novelists of *Tanzimat* period, Derviş presents this breakdown on the symbolic as well as on the linguistic level. What is remarkable though is that while she borrows her style from the canonical French decadent movement, she remains deeply connected to her Ottoman identity. As she observes the fragile balance between the two cultural spheres, she emerges as a significant figure in Turkish literature with her unconventional aesthetic representation of the historical transformation that characterizes the Ottoman Empire at the end of the nineteenth century.

Acknowledgment

The author gratefully acknowledges the support from the Fritz Thyssen Foundation and Trinity Long Room Hub MSCA COFUND Fellowship Programme, which made the writing of this chapter possible.

Bibliography

Aktürk, Şenol. "Toplumcu Gerçekçi Yönüyle Suat Derviş'in Romanlarına Bakış." *International Journal of Social Science* 5, no. 3 (June 2012): pp. 1-33.

Berktay, Fatmagül. "DERVİŞ, Suat (Saadet Baraner) (1905–1972)." In *Biographical Dictionary of Women's Movements and Feminisms: Central, Eastern, and South Eastern Europe, 19th and 20th Centuries*, edited by Francisca de Haan, Krasimira Daskalova, Anna Loutfi. Budapest: Central European University Press, 2006.

———. "İki Söylem Arasında Bir Yazar: Suat Derviş." *Defter* 29 (Kış 1997): pp. 89-100.

Calinescu, Matei. *Five Faces of Modernity: Modernism, Avant-Garde, Decadence, Kitsch, Postmodernism*. Durham, N.C.: Duke University Press, 1987.

Chaitin, Gilbert D. *The Enemy Within: Culture Wars and Political Identity in Novels of the French Third Republic*. Columbus: Ohio State UP, 2009.

Demirci, Tuba. *Body, Disease, and Late Ottoman Literature: Debates on Ottoman Muslim Family in the Tanzimat Period (1839-1908)*. Bilkent University, 2008. Unpublished PhD dissertation.

Derviş, Suat. *Anılar, Paramparça*. İstanbul: İthaki Yayınları, 2017

———. *Kara Kitap*. İstanbul: İthaki Yayınları, 2014.

Evin, Ahmet Ö. *Origins and Development of the Turkish Novel*. Minneapolis: Bibliotheca Islamica, 1983.

Gillespie, Gerald. "Decadence and Modernism." In *Decadence and Literature*, edited by J. Desmarais and D. Weir. Cambridge: Cambridge University Press, 2019.

Göknar, Erdağ. "Reading Occupied Istanbul: Turkish Subject-Formation from Historical Trauma to Literary Trope." *Culture, Theory and Critique* 55, no. 3 (2014): pp. 321-341.

Günay-Erkol, Çimen. *Broken Masculinities: Solitude, Alienation, and Frustration in Turkish Literature after 1970.* Budapest: Central European University Press, 2016.

———. "Toplumcu Gerçekçi Türk Edebiyatında Suat Derviş'in Yeri." Bilkent University Graduate School of Economics and Social Sciences, 2001. Unpublished MA Thesis.

Heffernan, Teresa. *Veiled Figures: Women, Modernity, and the Spectres of Orientalism.* Toronto: University of Toronto Press, 2016.

Huysmans, Joris-Karl. *Against Nature,* trans. Robert Baldick. London: Penguin, 2003.

Mardin, Şerif. *Religion, Society and Modernity in Turkey.* Syracuse, NY: Syracuse University Press, 2006.

Moers, Ellen. *Literary Women.* London: W.H Allen, 1977.

Navarette, Susan Jennifer. *The Shape of Fear: Horror and the Fin de Siècle Culture of Decadence.* Kentucky: The University Press of Kentucky, 1998.

Nissen, Christopher and Marja Härmänmaa, eds. *Decadence, Degeneration, and the End: Studies in the European Fin de Siècle.* New York: Palgrave MacMillan, 2014.

Oğuz, Çiğdem. "'Reality of the Magic of the East:'" Hemingway on the Greco-Turkish War and the Refugee Procession in Eastern Thrace." *Diacronie, Studi di Storia Contemporanea* 40, no. 4 (December 2019) https://www.studi storici.com/2019/12/29/oguz_numero_40/.

Punter, David, *The Literature of Terror: A History of Gothic Fictions from 1765 to the Present Day, Vol 2: The Modern Gothic.* Harlow: Longman, 1996.

Showalter, Elaine. *Sexual Anarchy: Gender and Culture at the fin de siècle.* Viking: New York, 1990.

———. "Syphilis, Sexuality, and the Fiction of the Fin de Siècle." In *Reading Fin de Siècle Fictions,* edited by Lyn Pykett. London: Longman, 1996.

Smith, Andrew and Diana Wallace. "The Female Gothic: Then and Now." *Gothic Studies* 6, no. 1 (2004): 1-7.

Uysal, Zeynep. *Metruk Ev.* İstanbul: İletişim Yayınları, 2014.

Woodall, Carole. "Decadent Nights: A Cocaine-Filled Reading of 1920s Post-Ottoman Istanbul." In *Mediterranean Encounters in the City:* Frameworks of Mediation between East and West, North and South, edited by Michela Ardizzoni and Valerio Ferme. Maryland: Lexington Press, 2015.

Notes

[1] Matei Calinescu, *Five Faces of Modernity: Modernism, Avant-Garde, Decadence, Kitsch, Postmodernism* (Durham, N.C.: Duke University Press, 1987), 156.

[2] *Ibid.*, 167.

[3] Christopher Nissen and Marja Härmänmaa (eds). *Decadence, Degeneration, and the End:* Studies in the European Fin de Siècle (New York: Palgrave MacMillan, 2014), 3.

[4] Calinescu, *Five Faces of Modernity,* 161.

5 Novelists of the Reformation Period, such as İbrahim Şinasi and Namık Kemal believed that literature had a "didactic value" and it had to function properly through the "priority of content over rhetoric." In 1866, Namık Kemal suggested that "meaning ought not to be sacrificed for art," as literature entailed "a great utility of discourse [...] in its service in the proper education of a nation." (qtd. in Evin, 11) (See *Origins and Development of the Turkish Novel*)

6 Servet-i Fünun (ثروتفنون) or Wealth of Knowledge was a famous Ottoman magazine, published between 1891 and 1944. Starting as a magazine with scientific articles and reports, accompanied with humour and literature, it soon turned into a leading literary magazine, publishing modern Ottoman poetry and literature.

7 Şerif Mardin, *Religion, Society and Modernity in Turkey* (Syracuse, NY: Syracuse University Press, 2006) 117.

8 Gilbert D. Chaitin, *The Enemy Within: Culture Wars and Political Identity in Novels of the French Third Republic* (Columbus: Ohio State UP, 2009), 8.

9 Teresa Heffernan, *Veiled Figures: Women, Modernity, and the Spectres of Orientalism* (Toronto: University of Toronto Press, 2016), 66.

10 Suat Derviş, *Anılar, Paramparça* (İstanbul: İthaki Yayınları, 2017), 20-28.

11 Fatmagül Berktay, *Biographical Dictionary of Women's Movements and Feminisms: Central, Eastern, and South Eastern Europe, 19th and 20th Centuries* (Budapest: Central European University Press, 2006), 109.

12 See Şenol Aktürk, "Toplumcu Gerçekçi Yönüyle Suat Derviş'in Romanlarına Bakış," *International Journal of Social Science* 5, no. 3 (June 2012), 1-33; Fatmagül Berktay, "İki Söylem Arasında Bir Yazar: Suat Derviş." *Defter 29* (Kış 1997), 89-100, and Çimen Günay-Erkol, "Toplumcu Gerçekçi Türk Edebiyatında Suat Derviş'in Yeri," Bilkent University Graduate School of Economics and Social Sciences, 2001.

13 Quoted in Günay-Erkol, "Toplumcu Gerçekçi Türk Edebiyatında Suat Derviş'in Yeri," 35.

14 Berktay, "İki Söylem Arasında Bir Yazar: Suat Derviş," 94.

15 Zeynep Uysal, Metruk Ev (İstanbul: İletişim Yayınları, 2014), 15.

16 The old manor house or the secluded castle has been an inseparable part of the rural Gothic from the very early works, such as Walpole's *The Castle of Otranto* and Ann Radcliffe's *The Mysteries of Udolpho*. It is one of the first characteristics that establish the atmosphere of terror in Gothic fiction. Like many other Gothic Romantic conventions, this image continued into the turn-of-the-century literature giving rise to the 'decadent Gothic' of the 1890s, a cross-genre marked by masterpieces as Robert Louis Stevenson's Dr Jekyll and Mr Hyde (1886), Oscar Wilde's *Picture of Dorian Gray* (1891), H. G. Wells' *Island of Dr Moreau* (1896) and Bram Stoker's *Dracula* (1897). (See David Punter, *The Literature of Terror*)

17 Suat Derviş, *Kara Kitap* (İstanbul: İthaki Yayınları, 2014), 101. All translations are my own unless otherwise noted. The following references to *The Black Book* are included as in-text citations in order to facilitate the reading of the text.

[18] The term "Female Gothic" was first employed by Ellen Moers in *Literary Women* (90-91) with reference to female authors writing gothic texts. Yet her analysis of these texts loaded the term with additional meaning as she used it "as a coded expression of women's fears of entrapment within the domestic and within the female body." Though this view provides a significant perspective in Smith and Wallace's 2004 special edition of Gothic Studies, *The Female Gothic*, the editors of this volume also acknowledge that "Moers' definition is too much an umbrella term, and, possibly, too essentialising" (1).

[19] First published in Paris in 1884, *Against Nature* proved to be a major blow to literary realism, which had until then defined the literary and artistic canon in European literature. The novel's protagonist des Esseintes is an aristocrat who seeks to escape from the mediocrity of contemporary society, the capitalist and consumerist society of the bourgeoisie, by withdrawing into a world of his own making, dedicated to realizing his private fantasies and pleasures. The novel is regarded as a literary achievement which almost singlehandedly started the Decadent movement in France. (See, Joris-Karl Huysmans, *Against Nature*, translated by Robert Baldick, (London: Penguin, 2003).

[20] Gerald Gillespie, "Decadence and Modernism," in *Decadence and Literature* edited by J. Desmarais and D. Weir (Cambridge: Cambridge University Press, 2019), 337.

[21] Carol Woodall, "Decadent Nights: A Cocaine-Filled Reading of 1920s Post-Ottoman Istanbul," in *Mediterranean Encounters in the City:* Frameworks of Mediation between East and West, North and South, edited by Michela Ardizzoni and Valerio Ferme (Maryland: Lexington Press, 2015), 19.

[22] Çiğdem Oğuz, "Reality of the Magic of the East:" Hemingway on the Greco-Turkish War and the Refugee Procession in Eastern Thrace," in *Diacronie, Studi di Storia Contemporanea N. 40.4* (December 2019), 7.

[23] Erdağ Göknar, "Reading Occupied Istanbul: Turkish Subject-Formation from Historical Trauma to Literary Trope," *Culture, Theory and Critique* 55:3 (2014), 335.

[24] Elaine Showalter, *Sexual Anarchy. Gender and Culture at the fin de siècle* (Viking: New York, 1990), 198.

[25] Elaine Showalter, "Syphilis, Sexuality, and the Fiction of the Fin de Siècle," in *Reading Fin de Siècle Fictions*, edited by Lyn Pykett (London: Longman, 1996), 170.

[26] As Tuba Demirci argues in her extensive study, *Body, Disease, and Late Ottoman Literature*, in the Ottoman Empire "syphillis was not a contagion reserved for lower classes" (382). According to Demirci, syphillis became a real public health problem during 1870s forcing the Ottoman administration to make the first attempts to prevent the disease. While it was believed that mostly "prostitutes" and "migrant domestic servants, such as cooks and butlers employed in wealthy households" were responsible for the spreading of the disease, at the turn of the century, syphillis was quite common among Muslim men from upper class families (155).

[27] Though in a completely different context and referring to a much later period in Turkey's history, Çimen Günay-Erkol discusses the representation of masculinity by women writers and asks whether they "employed more challenging discourses to explore men's insecurity and inadequacy" (96) at a time of trauma and political oppression. (See *Broken Masculinities*)

[28] Susan J. Navarette, *The Shape of Fear:* Horror and the Fin de Siècle Culture of Decadence (Kentucky: The University Press of Kentucky, 1998), 193-194.

Chapter 14

Dis-eases of the Heart Cured by Magic: Heian *Onmyōji* in Yumemakura Baku's Popular Japanese Fiction

Amy W. S. Lee

Hong Kong Baptist University, Hong Kong

Abstract: Japanese popular fiction writer Yumemakura Baku created a fiction series called *Onmyōji* in the late 1980s, which features the historical court astrologer Abe no Seimei (921-1005), and a courtier of royal blood, Minamoto no Hiromasa (918-980), historically a reputed musician. An *onmyōji* in the Japanese court was responsible for assisting the Emperor in all important matters to do with the state by choosing the most auspicious dates and preparing proper rituals during the festivals. Abe no Seimei was one of the most famous *onmyojis* throughout Japanese history, and this fiction series translates his famed divine power into a more analytical understanding of the human heart and its complex desires. The fiction series is set in the Heian period (794-1185), one of Japan's most glorious cultural and artistic development periods. The stories depict courtiers as well as ordinary citizens coming to seek Abe no Seimei's help when they encountered inexplicable illnesses or suspected intervention from beyond the human world. Adapting the form of modern detective stories, Yumemakura Baku portrays Seimei and Hiromasa as a quasi-Holmes-and-Watson partnership in uncovering the causes of illnesses in these troubled characters. These magical adventures across various worlds of existence juxtapose what is visible in the material world with what cannot be seen in the psychological and emotional realms of the human experience and package those as Abe no Seimei's "magic." In actual fact, the solutions that the court *onmyōji* proposed to his clients were but advice to look into their hearts and acknowledge the reality of their desires and fears. The proposed chapter will read a few of the stories in the series as diagnosis of contemporary illnesses, when the characters were made to face their unfulfilled desires, repressed fears, and challenged sense of identity by the court *onmyōji*, to bring them back to a more comfortable condition with themselves.

Keywords: *Onmyōji*, mediation, psychological dis-eases, repression, depression, emotion.

* * *

Introduction: Japanese Science Fiction and Yumemakura Baku

Yumemakura Baku is undoubtedly one of the most important fiction writers in contemporary Japan, although the volume of scholarly studies on his work is not huge, especially in the English-speaking world. It was thought that the dearth of secondary critical materials on Yumemakura's prolific output was "by simple virtue of its subject matter and genre. Perhaps most damning is its lack of thematic unity, which makes it seem inscrutable to most" (Recchio 2014, 28). Yumemakura started publishing in the mid-1980s, having created works in a range of genres, including science-fiction, horror stories, historical stories, manga, and drama; he had also been involved in stage productions, films and TV shows. Having tried his hand at different genres, he is adept at crossing genre boundaries, no one specific genre seems to be able to contain his work entirely. In a recent paper discussing Sino-Japanese relations, Yumemakura's name appeared in the section "Culture": "While certain areas touching on the history of Sino-Japanese relations remain off-limits, efforts to create friendlier relations are more easily achievable in the soft power/cultural sphere" (Dreyer 2018, 104). An example of such efforts was the film *Legend of the Dragon Cat* (also *Legend of the Demon Cat*), directed by Chen Kaige, based on a "period fantasy novel by Yumemakura Baku" (Dreyer 2018, 104). The novel which inspired this film is a four-volume epic telling the story of a Japanese monk Kūkai (774-835),[1] who went to Changan, capital of Tang China, with the Japanese imperial delegation in 804, and met the famous poet Bai Juyi,[2] with whom he had a miraculous adventure.[3] Even before his collaboration with one of China's most respected film directors, Yumemakura had been a well-loved popular fiction writer with millions of readers across different parts of the world.

Perhaps this discussion of how popular fiction is a diagnosis of contemporary society's diseases can start with the pen name chosen by this Japanese writer.[4] Baku is a spirit in Japanese folklore, it "devours dreams and is sometimes depicted as a supernatural being with an elephant's trunk, rhinoceros eyes, an ox tail, and tiger paws" (Raluca 2012, 134). This hybrid creature was also found in Chinese folklore, people believed that "sleeping on a Baku pelt could protect a person from pestilence and its image was a powerful talisman against the evil" (Raluca 2012, 134). Although it was a non-human being, the "Japanese Baku is a benevolent creature, patterned after a nocturnal animal of the pachyderm family, the tapir, found in the South America and the Malayan Peninsula" (Raluca 2012, 138). Folks believed if someone had a nightmare, he should keep it a secret, face the sun and chant "I cast my last night's dream to Baku" three times to expel the negative images (Raluca 2012, 140). Yumemakura in Japanese literally means "the dream pillow", thus the name of this popular fiction writer is literally "Baku of the Dream Pillow" (Raluca 2012, 140). The namesake of this popular fiction writer is a creature that will absorb our nightmare, always ready by the side of our pillow while we are dreaming.

And indeed, it was through the world of dreams, or fantasies, that Yumemakura Baku first made his successful contact with readers— as a science fiction writer. The first Japanese science fiction was published in the late Edo period in 1857, and toward the end of the century, the apocalyptic science fiction was quite popular. The Expo'70 (World Exposition 1970) held in Osaka helped to increase public interest in science fiction too, as following that "a number of new SF magazines such as *Kisotengai* (Fantastic Idea), *SF adventure*, *SF Hoseko* (SF Jewel), *SF no hon* (SF Book) were published, and through these new magazines some writers debut[ed] as professional SF writers including Yumemakura Baku" (Tanaka 2019, 62). To foreign readers who are familiar with his *Onmyōji* series, it may sound a little strange to see him being referred to as a science fiction writer, as the stories are set in the Heian period (794-1185). However, in Japan, science fiction has a more inclusive identity. It is "understood as fiction based on an imagined future, present, or past, featuring futuristic but often plausible scientific developments and including such tropes as advanced technological achievements, paranormal abilities, and alternate or parallel universes" (Tanaka 2019, 63). That is why even Murakami's *1Q84* (2009)[5] is categorized as science fiction, as it features actions of the same set of characters across parallel universes, albeit situated in a fully recognizable contemporary Japan.

Science fiction's broad inclusiveness has its cause in the circumstantial development of science fiction (and science fiction writers) in Japan. In an interview, veteran science fiction writer Yoshio Aramakire called that "in the mid-eighties, we entered a stagnant period in SF literature. I didn't have a choice and I was writing pseudo-Gothic mysteries for *Kodansha*. But with the emergence of Mr. Hideyuki Kikuchi and Mr. Baku Yumemakura, even the trend of Historical Gothic seemed to have been altered" (Oide 2002, 31). Yumemakura's creative adaptation of historical material, construction of plausible fantasy, and vivid characterization had helped to re-shape the genre.

His first *Onmyōji* story debuted in a youth literary magazine in 1986, and when the manga version came out in 1993, the series, with Abe no Seimei as the protagonist, was already a cultural phenomenon. That is why Tanaka wrote that "since 1990s, it has been often difficult to make a clear distinction between science fiction on the one hand and fantasy based on parallel or alternative time periods featuring magic and other supernatural phenomena as a primary plot element, theme, or setting on the other" (Tanaka 2019, 63). Yumemakura Baku, together with some other popular writers of his time, had changed the scene of science fiction in Japan.

Mass Culture and Popular Fiction:
Reflecting and Resolving Everyday Life Issues

While it has been commonly acknowledged that popular culture is a good source to view the general opinions and emotions of a community, the unique nature and composition of Japanese popular culture has accentuated its role in this respect. Referring to the infiltration of science fiction, Tanaka wrote "science fiction in Japan becomes one of the main genres in visual media culture such as film, manga, and animation" (63). When we look at Yumemakura's popular fiction series *Onmyōji*, its other media spin-offs, as well as the cultural phenomenon it had become, we may realize how much these stories in their different ways have made a connection with the huge body of audiences, not only in speaking to them about things they care for, but also speaking for them in reflecting what they are psychologically and emotionally going through in their individual lives. Therefore, I propose in this chapter to examine a number of stories from the fiction series, and read them as literary maps of the internal dramas that are on-going within the general community. The tremendous success of these stories in appealing to millions of audiences is a good indication of the relevance of these quasi-historical fantasy-detective stories to the current lives in our society.

One of the most remarkable features of Yumemakura Baku's *Onmyōji* series was the wide-ranging fans background. Laura Miller described in her paper the queues of young women waiting outside the number of shrines devoted to Abe no Seimei in Japan,[6] as well as the range of merchandises that had been developed to meet the ever-increasing demands from this group of fans (Miller 2008). She attributed the success of *Onmyōji* to Yumemakura's success in giving Abe no Seimei a complete makeover, which appealed to the "power of the girl market" (Miller 2008, 31). A few years after the first appearance of the stories, Okano Reiko was invited to do a manga version of the stories, which pushed "the novel into explosive popularity with her depiction of Seimei" (Recchio 2014, 27). While Yumemakura had always been very open about his gratitude to Okano, it was not really a surprising result, for the invitation showed a clear understanding of the potential market of the manga - Okano was "a premier girls' manga artist" (Miller 2008, 34). The re-appearance of the Heian court onmōyji "as a young, male beauty recalls the trend beginning in the 1990s in which girls exerted pressure on living men to reproduce *bishonen* aesthetics and style on their own bodies.[7] Now that power is arcing back in time to refashion historical men" (Miller 2008, 36). The female fans' response to the refashioned Seimei was the most direct way that female desires were represented, and later in the discussion of the content, we shall see more of this female desire described and discussed in the narratives themselves.

Besides being an indirect proof of the power of "girl gaze" (Miller 2008, 31), the "Heian onmyōji and Seimei became ideal locations for contemporary girls to situate their interest in divination and occult" (Miller 2008, 41). The young and ambiguously handsome appearance of the court onmyōji may have its power to build a young female fandom, but to have sustained and in fact expanded this fan base over the years, something more than his appearance had been at work. The Heian setting and the divination skills of Seimei together created the perfect site for the female fans to indulge their interest in something which may be considered superstitious or naïve in the modern context. Therefore, Miller referred to the contemporary cultural success of Abe no Seimei as it "gives us a unique perspective from which to consider the role of the culture industry in fueling and buttressing interest in the occult and the possibility of supernatural powers that extend the limits of the human" (Miller 2008, 30-31). For her specific interest, which is the substance of girls' culture, she saw how Yumemakura's reconstruction of Abe no Seimei had fulfilled a few key requirements to become the phenomenon: "Seimei is simultaneously pressed into the service of female subversion when he is so radically reinvented as an aesthetic object of erotic interest" (Miller 2008, 43).

Apparently, the attraction for female fans was not simply young Seimei's erotic appeal, one should not forget Yumemakura's ingenious addition to the Heian onmyōji - Minamoto no Hiromasa (918-980).[8] This is another historical figure at around the same time as Seimei, distantly related to the emperor, allegedly a good musician, but there was no documentation about his friendship with Seimei at all. It was purely the fiction author's artistic decision to have Seimei and Hiromasa as close friends, to have the nobleman's simple-mindedness in contrast to Seimei's perceptive cynicism, and to let their complementary personalities come together in the most fruitful ways when they handled the problems presented to them. In fact, Seimei and Hiromasa were "similar to Sherlock Holmes and Dr. Watson. Since those two were always convening in the Baker Street digs, Yumemakura selected Seimei's mansion as the place where the two Heian gentlemen could always be found sitting and drinking sake" (Miller 2008, 34). The borrowing of the Holmes-Watson dual was deliberate, not only for their famous success in solving mysteries, but also for the ambiguous relationship between the two Victorian gentlemen. Just as fans kept looking for hints of a homoerotic relationship between Holmes and Watson (a common development in contemporary media adaptations), the "homoerotic subtext [in Seimei and Hiromasa's relationship] no doubt was feeding the desires of *yaoi*-hungry girl fans" (Miller 2008, 34).

Born in the middle of the 19th century and flourished at the height of the Victorian era, detective fiction was embraced by people of different classes because of its immediate connection to real life. For the gentler class, it was like an intellectual game whereas for the ordinary people, the locations and life conditions described were very much part of their everyday existence. Their real problems - crimes and deaths - were the main content of these stories, and there was always the intelligent detective (or police) who managed to identify the criminal and restore the community back to safety, a wish that was not often fulfilled in real life. The Seimei-Hiromasa partnership and their adventures appeal to contemporary readers in much the same way as the early detective stories appealed to their original readers, but this component of detection is set in the unique context of Japanese science fiction. Veteran science fiction writer Yoshio Aramaki described SF literature as different from modern literature which merely described problems in life. He said that "people aren't usually mere victims: instead, they solve these problems" (Oide 2002, 34). In his own science fiction, he also dealt with problems in life: "I try to simulate how we can realistically solve them. This is my major theme. Simulation is itself a rather postmodern concept" (Oide 2002, 35). I would like to argue that Yumemakura Baku's Heian-based stories featuring Seimei and Hiromasa are similar to Yoshio Aramaki's "speculative problem-solving" (Oide 2002, 35), only that the problems being featured were real everyday problems - contemporary peoples' diseases.

Contemporary Dis-eases: Seeing the Unseen, Speaking the Unspoken

The historical Abe no Seimei, a government official who was in charge of important ceremonies, rituals and the formulation of the state calendar according to traditional Japanese *onmyōdo* was among the most famous of his kind. There was actual documentation of his work, for example, he was credited to have written *Senjiryakketsu*, a guidebook on how to perform various onmyōdo rituals; but legends about his superhuman abilities were increasingly generated through the centuries. With the newly added stories, descriptions about him also changed over time, "[i]n the Insei period he appears as a middle-aged ritualist of the state. In the Edo period he appears primarily as the young boy - Abe no Doji, abandoned by his fox mother, who has been immortalized in Kabuki performances that are performed to this day" (Recchio 2014, 7). In re-visiting the Heian period and bringing Seimei and Hiromasa to contemporary readers, Yumemakura had "modernized" the characters by skillfully utilizing sex appeal, yet "remaining largely faithful to the material that inspires him, expanding upon the basic narratives of the older texts and adapting them to straddle the line between various genres, such as horror, magical realism, and *jidai shōsetsu*" (Recchio 2014, 5).[9] This Abe no Seimei is a careful construction which simultaneously carries magical power accepted only in his time, and speaks to 21st century readers because the heart of his abilities is his understanding of human nature.

This special quality of the stories to reach out to audiences beyond its own historical setting was also commented upon by Miller, when she tried to understand their popularity among young women. She found "Grant McCracken's concept of 'displaced meaning' especially useful. [...] cultural meaning is said to be removed from daily life and relocated in a safe, distant historical domain, allows me to make sense of onmyōji fixation as more than simple escapist daydreaming of fantasy literature" (Miller 2008, 40). The fantasy fictional space allows contemporary readers to see their own problems being depicted at a safe distance, in the lives of courtiers and ladies or even among ghosts and other non-human creatures. At the end of these adventures, Seimei, with Hiromasa's assistance, would arrive at a conclusion about the root of these problems and how they could be resolved, in many cases using a magic that was perfectly explicable in contemporary language. What I am proposing is that Yumemakura's stories are entertainment which have a diagnostic function; through the creative deployment of Seimei the mediator between the seen world and the unseen world, the stories speak to the readers about their repressed problems and help them find relief in the fictional space.

In the following, three short stories from different periods of Yumemakura's *Onmyōji* fiction series will be discussed, to illustrate them as narratives depicting dis-eases that are consuming the life of contemporary people. The Holmes-Watson type of partnership and story structure adapted makes these stories of detection easy to understand and already assuming a "problem solving" identity in the minds of the readers. Added to this, Seimei's characterization as the all-powerful onmyōji, one who can speak to human and non-human creatures across different lands, puts him in the advantageous position of the pathographer. Often in his conversations with characters who suffered from inexplicable conditions, it was found that the cause was "*oni* as humans whose emotions have taken control of them and transformed them both spiritually and physically" (Recchio 2014, 59).[10] In other words, "the true form of an *oni* in onmyōji's world is overpowering emotion and obsession. Whether or not the *oni* possesses the physical body of the human who harboured those emotions or works through another vessel is a matter of circumstance rather than a qualitative difference" (Recchio 2014, 59). At the end of the stories, often we found that what was causing the diseases in the noble characters were none other than unfulfilled desires, repressed thoughts, and unspeakable yearnings.

A *biwa* called Genjō is stolen by an *oni*: Obsessions personified

This was the first story included in the first *Onmyoji* collection, and one of the most discussed by critics. The story was important in introducing the characters of Seimei and Hiromasa, their personality, and how they worked together. It also set the pattern of Seimei diagnosing the problem and letting Hiromasa the simple-minded gentleman reflects on the meaning of such a problem in the human condition. As usual, Hiromasa came to Seimei's mansion for a chat and a drink, bringing with him news from court, this time, it had to do with a missing *biwa* (a musical instrument) called Genjō. A few nights ago, he heard music played at the Rashō Gate, and recognized the precious instrument's sounds. The *biwa* had been stolen from the imperial palace, and the inhumanly beautiful music confirmed Hiromasa's suspicion that it was an *oni* who had stolen it. He asked for Seimei's help and they both went to the Gate to meet this *oni*. It turned out that the *oni*, named Kandata, was a famous maker of instrument from India in his previous life. Passing by the palace, he recognized his own work the *biwa*, and saw a maid resembling his previous wife. He asked for the maid in exchange for the stolen *biwa*. Seimei agreed to bring what he wanted a few nights later. On the designated night of exchange, the maid's brother tried to trick Kandata but failed. Kandata was angry and killed them both, while Seimei used a spell to protect himself and Hiromasa. Finally, Seimei coaxed the spirit of Kandata to inhabit the precious *biwa* instead, and sent it back to the palace.

Similar to many of the *Onmyōji* stories, this one contains real historical data re-worked to tell a good tale (Recchio 2014). What is of particular interest here is how the author mapped the contemporary human condition onto the historical setting and characters. While Kandata may be seen as the antagonist (he killed the maid and her brother), he was also a victim filled with "rage and anguish, inspired by the course of his life and the things that he lost" (Recchio 2014, 68). His obsession with the *biwa* and his dead wife was understandably human, and his violent reaction to the brother and the maid was only a natural reciprocate to theirs in the first place. As commented by a critic, "[t]he barbarousness of the world in which the *oni* are born and the realization that that world is not so different from our own instills a sense of horror in the reader that is all too intentional" (Recchio 2014, 63). The violence caused by extreme emotions in the story was recognizable because it happened in our world too; Kandata's intense yearning turned it into an *oni*, haunting the palace to look for relief, which again was perfectly recognizable.

The one who translated this story of the *oni* into a conversation with contemporary readers is Seimei, through his compassionate handling of Kandata's spirit, found to have lodged in a dog's body. He "allows the dog's head to tear into his flesh, using the dog as a conduit to channel Kandata's pain into himself through the symbol of the dog's fangs. In so doing, he takes Kandata's pain into himself and redirects Kandata's attention to Genjō" (Recchio 2014, 68). Seimei's action demonstrated a deep understanding of human weaknesses, the pain we feel, as well as his willingness to help ease this pain. His later discussion with Hiromasa confirmed to us his insight into human nature, when he said that the power of the "spell" become stronger if delivered in a gentle and coaxing voice— same as the way lovers' words were the most powerful spells. His gentle encouragement to Kandata's spirit to enter the *biwa* Genjō was delivered in just such a voice. In this interaction with Kandata, an important quality about Seimei was revealed: he was "an objective entity, who views each conscious being as fundamentally equal. His orientation toward other beings, therefore, is one of basic respect for their autonomy, whether they are supernatural or not" (Recchio 2014, 67). This absolute objectiveness puts him beyond any boundaries, and grants him the privileged position to see what cannot be seen, and to say what cannot be said. Abe no Seimei was crafted to be the ultimate pathographer.

The lady of the lute: Decoding the universal language of love

It was early Spring, Hiromasa was at Seimei's drinking wine, surrounded by the fresh scent of plum blossom. Seimei noted his unusual quietness and guessed correctly that it had to do with women. When Hiromasa asked him how he guessed, Seimei answered "because it was written on your face" (Yumemakura 2008, 14). Beginning from five nights ago, Hiromasa was woken up in the middle of the night by a nice flowery scent. When he opened his eyes, a beautiful young lady was sitting by his pillow. The lady was dressed elegantly in a foreign costume, but looked at him with intense sadness, and seemed struggling to tell him something. At first, Hiromasa thought it was only a dream, but the lady appeared for five consecutive nights, and each time struggling to say something. Hiromasa wanted Seimei to help him understand what was going on. Seimei's first response was to tease him, "you must have confessed your love to a lady, and afterwards forgotten her" (Yumemakura 2008, 21). When Hiromasa protested, Seimei became more serious, "perhaps you have unknowingly made a connection somehow" (Yumemakura 2008, 21), and asked Hiromasa to recall what happened five or six days ago.

Six days earlier, he went to the palace to return a precious musical instrument to the Emperor, a wooden *ruan* (of the lute family) that was loaned to him a while ago. The *ruan* was an elegant gem brought by a senior courtier all the way from China, and the music it made impressed Hiromasa so much that he felt "heaven and earth were both resounding with the *ruan*" (Yumemakura 2008, 23). He recalled also the story of the *ruan*, made from one branch of the Sal tree (*Shorearobusta*) under which allegedly Shakyamuni the Buddha went into nirvana. After he returned the instrument, the Emperor himself tried to play it, but no sound came out, and all the courtiers who tried couldn't make any music from the instrument either. The Emperor blamed Hiromasa for having damaged it, and summoned him to court for an explanation. Hiromasa showed them that he had no problem making beautiful music from the *ruan*. Seeing this, the Emperor granted the instrument to Hiromasa as a gift. Seimei asked to see the *ruan*, and when he placed his hand on the wooden surface, he murmured, "so this was the case" (Yumemakura 2008, 28), and started speaking in a foreign language to the *ruan*. In a while, Seimei plucked the strings and music came out! He explained to Hiromasa, "I just told her not to worry, even if other people managed to make some sounds from you, you are already given to Hiromasa" (Yumemakura 2008, 28).

Although the problem of the silent instrument was solved, the appearance of the elegant lady was still a mystery. At this point, Seimei turned to Hiromasa and asked him to confess the rest of the story. Hiromasa admitted that he gave the *ruan* a name "Sal" because it was made from the branch of the Sal tree. He actually spoke to the *ruan*, "Tonight I gave you a name, from now on, you will be called Sal" (Yumemakura 2008, 29), and since then he talked to the instrument as if it was a person, praising its beautiful sounds, and even having a conversation with it. Seimei reminded Hiromasa, "Didn't I tell you before? Giving a name to an object is like casting a spell on the existence of that object…" (Yumemakura 2008, 30)— the name is the most basic form of a spell, for it creates the relationship of owner and possession between the giver of the name and the receiver of the name which is the object. That night, Seimei went home with Hiromasa, expecting to meet the silent lady, because he had told the instrument that he would wait for her there! The lady spoke in a foreign tongue and told Seimei the story of her life— from a branch of the Sal tree. The final mystery was solved: Hiromasa's naming the instrument was symbolically the same as Seimei naming the wisteria in his garden and turning that into his *shikigami*.[11] Returning the *ruan* to the Emperor was, in essence, the same as pledging his love to a lady and then turning his back against her; therefore, Sal (the *ruan*) decided not to make any music, so that the Emperor would send her away to the only person who could play her, Hiromasa.

Interestingly in this story, the one who had actually "cast the spell" was Hiromasa. His genuine admiration for the elegant instrument and the beautiful music caused him to pour his heart out to it, like a friend. It was his pure sincerity and complete devotion that supported the "spell". That was why Seimei said to him in the end, "You have much more distinguished power than I do, only you weren't aware" (Yumemakura 2008, 37). Although Seimei did offer the "help" that Hiromasa asked for, his assistance was the decoding of the communications between the *ruan* (lady) and his honest music-lover friend. Seimei was the supreme decoder: reading Hiromasa's face to know that his problem was related to a lady, reading his nighttime dream as related to something that happened during the day, and reading Hiromasa's love for music to be the root of the whole relationship with the instrument. It was the onmyōji's deep understanding of the human condition, the love, desire, yearning, frustration, sadness, and so on, that allowed him to map what was visible on the surface to the invisible root of these events. The supreme decoder was the perfect pathographer.

Trip to the other world[12] and back: The here and now for the male friends

On a day near the end of autumn, Seimei and Hiromasa were drinking and enjoying the clear weather. They were having a casual conversation about ageing and death, when Hiromasa mentioned the sudden death of the security officer (named "Shan Guangguo" in the Chinese translation) of Fujiwara no Kaneie five days ago.[13] He heard that Seimei went to the funeral but advised the family not to bury nor cremate the body for five days. As Hiromasa talked, a servant of that family came rushing and announced that his dead master had woken up and asked to see Seimei. When Seimei and Hiromasa arrived, Shan related his experience during those five days—when he thought he was in a dream— when everyone except Seimei thought he was dead.

Shan fainted at home (that was why his family thought he was dead) and woke up in a place he had never visited before. Two men, one with a Red Face and one with a Green Face, told him he was dead and was now present in the world of the dead. They brought him to see the King of the dead, who was a dignified old man sitting on a golden throne. He said that Shan was summoned because his wife, who died three years ago, wanted to see him. The wife, who appeared with two iron nails hammered into her head, painfully accused Shan of mistreating her when alive and even after death. Red Face and Green Face, however, reported that she was an unfaithful wife and actually died by her own hands when she accidentally ate the poisoned food that she prepared to kill her husband. Hearing this, the King issued further punishment to the wife and awarded Shan the chance to meet his father who died ten years ago. The King also reminded Shan to hurry back to the world of the living before long.

The father was in an even more terrible state. His body was pierced by thirty-seven nails, and he was beaten with an iron rod nine hundred times every day (Yumemakura 2018a, 148). He told Shan he regretted all the bad things he had done while alive, and begged him to have the Avalokiteśvara sutra copied (Yumemakura 2018a, 149),[14] and to make an offering for him at the local temple. By the merit of the Buddhist sutra, he hoped he could be reborn in the Pure Land. Shan promised to help his father, and with the help of a youth dressed in white, he managed to return to the world of the living before it was too late. He thanked Seimei for his help in keeping his body and "sending" the youth, and as he promised, he commissioned an offering for his father as well as his wife. The matter ended satisfactorily for all as they welcomed the first snow of the year.

As indicated by the title, this story was about someone's experience in the other world. Shan's experience was an illustration of a general Buddhist understanding of death— arriving at the other world, and being assigned different treatments according to the good or bad that one had committed during one's lifetime. While Shan witnessed for himself that both his wife and his father suffered terrible punishment because of the wrong they had committed when they were alive, he also experienced the justice of the King of the dead. The unrepentant wife was further punished, and the wrongly accused Shan was allowed to meet his father. This opportunity also paved the way for his father's redemption because he had the chance to confess his crimes and his remorse. His pleading to Shan was based on a common Buddhist belief— that the copying of sutras was a meritorious act which could help reduce the evilness one had accumulated.

This story is different from the others in the series in two ways. First, Seimei was not actually invited to help find a solution— as the matter was already handled due to Seimei's foresight when he saw the "liveliness" of Shan's supposedly dead body— but only to witness the return of the dead. Second, this narrative featured one of the most explicit "confessions" of love that had ever happened between Seimei and Hiromasa in the long series, although that only took up a very small portion of the entire narrative. The two friends were just enjoying each other's company before and after the incident— an incident that highlighted even more the value of the present moment that they were sharing, with each other. It almost felt as if Shan's long trip to and back from the other world was only the backdrop to put the friendship on centre stage— to celebrate the here and now.

It is in the presentation of the friendship, one that could possibly invite a homoerotic interpretation that we see what critics of Yumemakura referred to as the appeal to contemporary sensibility. The two friends were talking about the passage of time, which could be a depressing topic. Seimei voiced a typically neutral view about this by saying that the passage of time didn't bother him, as he realized that he was "just the same as the scenery around, being also a part of nature" (Yumemakura 2018a, 129). The usually sentimental Hiromasa replied that aging was not so bad when Seimei was still there, when he could still pass moments like that with his friend, drinking. The setting, the occasion, and the language all joined to create an intimate moment of mutual appreciation between two men who had spent a lot of time together. At the end of the story, the readers were once again brought to the two friends, as if to see the effect of the story to the other world on them. Seimei was simply listening to his friend, because "the sound of Hiromasa's speaking voice was just like music, an immense comfort to hear" (Yumemakura 2018a, 153). The subtle but unmistakable underlying same-sex desire is a mark of our time, despite the Heian setting. And the partners were shown to be embracing the Buddhist attitude of appreciating the present moment rather than worrying about the past and the future.

A Soft Psychoanalysis and Psychotherapy in Historical Fantasy

In his evaluation of Yumemakura Baku's *Onmyōji* series, Recchio had written against some of the negative comments by other critics, for example, about Yumemakura's too much fidelity to the original legends, and creating nothing new. His defense of the "original creations" made by the author included the pairing up of Minomoto no Hirosama and Abe no Seimei to become partners in detection very much in the Holmes-Watson mode (Miller 2008; Recchio 2014). This fabrication of the two young men's relationship had created a completely different kind of narrative for the readers, who can find entertainment in the intimate-friendly rapport between the two, and a world in which the visual phenomena are but a reflection of the psychological and emotional landscape inside us. Yumemakura Baku's depiction of Seimei as "a young man at the height of his beauty, who is aloof, self-assured, and most importantly, playful" (Recchio 2014, 41) had opened the doors of the readers' heart to welcome him into our world— as his abilities to transgress boundaries had been demonstrated so amply in the adventures.

Yumemakura's Abe no Seimei is a transgressive being in multiple ways: descendant of human and fox, being trained by the best onmyōji to engage in matters of the other worlds, and having the ability to read the hearts of human and non-human creatures. These qualities put him in an absolutely free position, unbiased by any fear of worldly or unworldly power— thus capable of untainted and fair judgment. Therefore, when he diagnosed the various problems of the Heian noblemen as a manifestation of what was going on in their minds, we defer to his judgment, and follow his curing of these noblemen, to understand that the same things are going on in our minds. In witnessing the way he handled the obsessive Kandata, we understand the destructive power of desire inside us; in seeing how he teased Hiromasa about his love of the lute, we visualize the invisible connections we make in our everyday life with objects and being; and in reading the part he played in the story of Shan, we learn the importance of living in the here and now, and be compassionate to all beings in order to enjoy a full life. The reading experience itself becomes for the readers a second-hand psychoanalysis, which offers us insights to be applied to our own everyday life. More enjoyable than a real psychoanalysis, probably, for on top of the learnings, we can appreciate how two good men, Seimei and Hiromasa, went through fantastic adventures and helped people out of their trouble.

References

Dreyer, June Teufel. 2018. "Japan-China Relations: Warner Words, Continuing Defense Preparations." *Comparative Connections: A Triannual E-Journal on East Asian Bilateral Relations* 20, no. 1: pp. 97-110.

Makoto, Hayashi, and Matthias Hayek. 2013. "Onmyodo in Japanese History." *Japanese Journal of Religious Studies* 40, no.1: pp. 1-18.

Miller, Laura. 2008. "Extreme Makeover for a Heian-Era Wizard." *Mechademia* 3: 30-45.

Oide, Mitsutaka. 2002. "Thinking the Opposite: An Interview with Yoshio Aramaki." *Review of Contemporary Fiction* 22, no.2: pp. 29-35.

Raluca, Nicolae. 2012. "In search for chimeras: three hybrids of Japanese imagination." *Cogito - Multidisciplinary research Journal* 2: pp. 134-147. https://www.ceeol.com/search/article-detail?id=94546.

Recchio, Devin T. 2014. *Constructing Abe no Seimei: Integrating Genre and Disparate Narratives in Yumemakura Baku's Onmyōji*. University of Massachusetts Amherst Masters Theses. 110. https://scholarworks.umass.edu/masters_theses_2/110

Reider, Noriko T. 2003. "Transformation of the Oni: From the Frightening and Diabolical to the Cute and Sexy." *Asian Folklore Studies* 62, no. 1: pp. 133-157.

Reider, Noriko T. 2007. "Onmyoji: Sex, Pathos, and Grotesquery in Yumemakura Baku's Oni." *Asian Folklore Studies* 66, no.1/2: pp. 107-124.

Reider, Noriko T. 2010. *Japanese Demon Lore: Oni, from Ancient Times to the Present*. Logan, Utah: Utah State University Press.

Takayuki, Tatsumi. 2002. "A Soft Time Machine: From Translation to Transfiguration." *Science Fiction Studies* 29, no. 3: pp. 475-484.

Tanaka, Motoko. 2019. "Trajectory of Modern Japanese Science Fiction." *Tamagawa University College of Liberal Arts Journal* 12: pp. 61-64. 玉川大学学術リポジトリ (nii.ac.jp)

Yumemakura, Baku. 2005. *The Monk Kūkai - Ghostly Banquet of the Tang Dynasty [Shamon Kukai To no Kuni nite Oni to Utage su]*. Translated by Jiaobi Lin. Vol. 1. 4 vols. Taipei: Yuan-Liou Publishing Company Limited.

———. 2008. "The Lady of the Lute." In *Onmyoji - Yakou-Hai no Maki*, by Baku Yumemakura, translated by Moro Miya, 9-38. Taipei: Muses Publishing House.

———. 2017. *Legend of the Demon Cat*. Directed by Kaige Chen.

———. 2018a. "Trip to the Other World and Back." In *Onmyoji - Hotarubi no Maki*, by Baku Yumemakura, translated by Miya Moro, 125-154. Teipei: Muses Publishing.

———. 2018b. *The Monk Kūkai - Ghostly Banquet of the Tang Dynasty [Shamon Kukai To no Kuni nite Oni to Utage su]*. Translated by Xiue Xu. Vol. 2. 4 vols. Taipei: ECUS Publishing House.

———. 2018c. *The Monk Kūkai - Ghostly Banquet of the Tang Dynasty [Shamon Kukai To no Kuni nite Oni to Utage su]*. Translated by Xiue Xu. Vol. 3. 4 vols. Taipei: ECUS Publishing House.

———. 2018d. *The Monk Kūkai - Ghostly Banquet of the Tang Dynasty [Shamon Kukai To no Kuni nite Oni to Utage su]*. Translated by Xiue Xu. Vol. 4. 4 vols. Taipei: ECUS Publishing House.

Notes

[1] Kūkai (空海, 774-835) was a Japanese Buddhist monk who went on an imperial expedition at the beginning of the 9th century to Tang China to learn about esoteric Buddhism. He learned from the Chinese monk Huiguo, and when he returned to Japan, he compiled all he learned into a system of doctrines, and he became the eighth Patriarch of Esoteric Buddhism. Ten years later, he founded a Shingon esoteric Buddhist monastic training center on Mount Kōya (高野山).

[2] Bai Juyi (772-846) was a famous Chinese poet in the Tang Dynasty. He was also a government official, therefore his many observations about his society and about life also got into his poems. One of his most famous works is a long narrative poem entitled "Chang Henge" (Song of Everlasting Sorrow), which is about the Emperor's consort Yang Guifei. His works had a great influence over Japanese literature.

[3] The four-volume epic carries the main title *The Monk Kūkai - Ghostly Banquet of the Tang Dynasty*, and each volume has a subtitle. These four subtitles indicate the focus of the monk's adventure in China, they are: (i) Entering Tang, (ii) The Spell of the Terra Cotta, (iii) Foreign Magic, (iv) Not Emptiness. The film directed by Chen Kaige was based on episodes from this epic story.

[4] His real name is Yoneyama Mineo, born in 1951 in Odawara, Japan. Yumemakura Baku is his chosen pen name.

[5] *1Q84* is a three-volume novel by Japanese writer Haruki Murakami, published in 2009-2010. The story was set in a fictional Japan in the year 1984, and depicted events happening around a woman called Aomame, who noticed that there was another world parallel to the real one.

⁶ Abe no Seimei (安倍晴明, 921-1005) was a well-known onmyōji, active during the Heian period in Japan. He worked in the Bureau of Onmyō (陰陽寮Onmyō-ryō), a government body, and was in charge of keeping track of the calendar, divination, and general protection of the capital using his skills in onmyōdō. Although his life was quite well documented, he became the subject of a lot of imaginary stories and fictional constructions.

⁷ *Bishonen* is a Japanese word, literally meaning "beautiful youth (male)". It is a kind of aesthetics prevailing in Japanese popular culture targeting young women's gaze. The ideal image of men for this young feminine fan group has the qualities of androgynous beauty which is not explicitly masculine or feminine.

⁸ Minamoto no Hiromasa (源博雅, 918-980) was a nobleman and was known to be well-versed in a number of musical instruments. Although his mother was a Fujiwara, he was removed from the line of succession, and granted a commoner's name.

⁹ *Jidai shōsetsu* is Japanese, meaning contemporary novels.

¹⁰ *Oni* is a Japanese word usually denoting a special kind of non-human creature. Reider gave an in-depth discussion of the origin of *oni* in her book, *Japanese Demon Lore: Oni, from Ancient Times to the Present*. Logan, Utah: Utah State University Press, 2010. Please also refer to Reider, Noriko T. 2003. "Transformation of the *Oni*: From the Frightening and Diabolical to the Cute and Sexy." *Asian Folklore Studies* 62 (1): 133-157. In Yumemakura Baku's work, *oni* was not used in the most specific sense, but rather a general term to refer to a range of non-human creatures, including "ghosts".

¹¹ *Shikigami* is Japanese, used to refer to a group of beings conjured by the power of someone with supernatural abilities. The strength and abilities of the *shikigami* depends on the power of the master. In Yumemakura Baku's stories, Seimei had a few *shikigami*s, which he conjured from flowers, working for him.

¹² The story title in Chinese translation refers to a trip to "*dunanguo*" (度南國), which is not the name of any proper location. From the content of the story, it is clear that the place referred to is the world of the dead. That is the reason why I choose to use "the other world" to refer to that place.

¹³ Fujiwara no Kaneie (藤原兼家, 929 – 990) was a Japanese statesman, courtier and politician during the Heian period.

¹⁴ In the Chinese translation of the story, the name of the sutra was "guanyinjing" (觀音經). A direct English translation will be "Avalokiteśvara sutra". Since the Lotus Sutra was very popular during the Heian period, I think the author probably was referring to chapter 25 of the Lotus Sutra, which is Avalokiteśvara-vikurvaṇa-nirdeśaḥ. This chapter is popularly known and chanted individually, and often referred to as "guanshiyinjing" (觀世音經).

Chapter 15

Writing Illness: Morbid Humour as a Strategy to Cope with Disease and Pain in Zimbabwean Literature

Nhlanhla Landa, Sindiso Zhou

University of Fort Hare, South Africa

Abstract: The chapter explores how disease and un-wellness in Zimbabwe are subjects of ridicule in NoViolet Bulawayo's *We Need New Names*. Guided by the Freudian concepts of the overt expression of the covert state of the unconscious mind, we do an interpretive analysis of *We Need New Names* to show that Zimbabweans, having endured pain and illness for a long time due to a conspiracy of many issues such as politics, deteriorating economy and a poor health system, resort to morbid humour to cope with it. Bulawayo expertly fuses the subject of disease, specifically HIV and AIDS, and child play to paint a grim picture of the broader socio-economic and socio-political issues bedevilling the postcolonial state in Zimbabwe. She deploys grotesque humour and laughter as coping and resilience strategies to salve postcolonial wounds, disease and pain that stand in the way of everyday survival.

Keywords: NoViolet Bulawayo, postcolonial Zimbabwe, disease, pain, morbid humour.

* * *

The chapter is an interpretive analysis of the depiction of disease and un-wellness in NoViolet Bulawayo's *We Need New Names*.[1] We were interested in how Bulawayo presents disease (of the body, soul and of the mind) in contrast to other forms of un-wellness, such as hunger, poverty and loss of dignity. Our close reading of the novel indicates that Bulawayo deploys morbid humour to cope with socio-economic and other social challenges, including illness. The characters in the novel, who are predominantly children, laugh at myriad ills. They laugh at disease, death, crime, poverty, suffering, the economy and all forms of rot in society. The author harnesses child innocence through the child narrator, thus writing a morbid yet picturesque outline of a moribund society where illness exists in a variety of forms.

Zimbabwe: the context of *We Need New Names*

Zimbabwe is a southern African country, north of South Africa. It is relatively small, with an estimated population of 16 million people in 2016.[2] Zimbabwe shares borders with Botswana, Zambia and Mozambique. The country gained independence from Britain in 1980 and has since then been ruled by the Zimbabwe African National Union Patriotic Front (ZANU PF). The ZANU PF regime has been associated with dictatorship, repression[3] and violence.[4]

Besides the civil unrest between 1980 and 1987, popularly known as *Gukurahundi* (to wipe out dirt or garbage), Zimbabwe has experienced several forms of instability. The three major forms that Bulawayo sets her novel around are *Murambatsvina* (non-tolerance of filth), the socio-economic decline of the state and political instability. *Murambatsvina* "was a clean-up campaign that presumably sought to rid the cities and towns of shack shelters and squatter camps where the poor and other people failing to find affordable accommodation had sought refuge."[5] In reality, the campaign brought more problems for the common citizen, and created even more shacks in the cities. It had devastating effects on women and children,[6] the poor,[7] and the informal sector[8] in general which is a source of livelihood for many in Zimbabwe, although in a survivalist fashion.[9]

In addition, Zimbabwe has faced challenges in relation to disease control and prevention, mainly due to a failing health system caused by the depreciating economy.[10] As a result, diseases such as AIDS and cholera have raged on and disabled families and communities. HIV and AIDS have received a significant portion of attention from both researchers and literary artists. Like all other social problems, attitudes towards AIDS and other diseases and plagues have been transformed by literary texts.[11] In addition, AIDS in particular has remained a problem affecting mostly Sub-Saharan Africa, including Zimbabwe.[12] Zimbabwe has also consistently experienced cholera epidemics over the last three decades,[13] with the 2008 epidemic being one of the most severe.[14]

It is around the above conspiracy of challenges in the post *Murambatsvina* era that Bulawayo sets her novel, *We Need New Names*. As depicted in the novel and in literature in general, there was not much illegality concerning the structures that the government destroyed in 2005. In reality, the campaign, which intended to end illegal housing in the towns, created the illegal structures. Therefore, the campaign was political,[15] and a violation of human rights.[16] It worsened political unrest and drove many into poverty. In addition to the challenges, Bulawayo grapples with the subject of disease, including AIDS, demons and mental illness.

We Need New Names is a 2013 publication that is set around the collapse of the Zimbabwean economy after the government's 2005 Operation *Murambatsvina* (Restore Order). According to our reading of the novel, the operation involved the demolition of proper houses built in places regarded as undesignated, which resulted in the eruption of tin houses in places that did not even have running water. The novel juxtaposes two residential suburbs that are separated by two streets, namely Paradise, a shantytown comprising tin houses, and Budapest, a rich suburb just across. The major characters in the novel are children, whose days are characterised by playing all kinds of games and stealing guavas from the affluent Budapest suburb.

The novel deals with diverse themes, including religion, post-colonial protest, migration, national dysfunction and disease. It also focuses on broken families, immorality, child abuse, political and socio-economic decay, the church and gullibility, the diaspora, violence, displacements, choreographed humanitarian aid, abortion and international relations. This diversity of themes makes the novel a broader reflection of Zimbabwe in what we call literary biographies of the Zimbabwean crisis (2000-2009), a period characterised by economic downturn. Nyambi posits that the Zimbabwean crisis has defined the discourse of the post-colonial trajectory of Zimbabwe.[17]

The chapter employs Freudian concepts of the utility of the unconscious mind in literary analysis drawn from psychoanalytic theory. Freud posits that much of human behaviour is influenced by the unconscious mind.[18] The unconscious mind itself stores much of what we do not want to think of actively as it might not be pleasant, for instance, traumatic experiences and memories. However, these repressed thoughts and experiences usually find their way into daily interactions through humour. Following Freud, we conceptualise an organic and symbiotic link between the unconscious mind, perception of illness of the body and/or mind and morbid humour in *We Need New Names*. We find reference to the unconscious mind's repressed state important especially as we are looking at illness through a child's eyes. However, it becomes complex and imperative to seek insights from a child's perception, when indications are that this particular child is actually an adult in a child's body. To explain this complexity, we refer to the circumstances of stinting poverty, political violence and economic decimation that have forced children to become adults while stripping human beings of every ounce of dignity in the actual lived experiences of Zimbabweans mirrored in the literary work being referenced. Although repressed and stowed away in the unconscious mind, there is a deliberate conglomeration of experiences that force these truths to surface through morbid humour. Our interpretive analysis, therefore, seeks to show that the humour does not reduce in any way the impact or truthfulness of the encounters. Instead, it is a coping and resilience strategy in the face of hardship.

Attention in *We Need New Names* is directed towards illness of the physiological mainly. The author also pays attention to spiritual wellness and mental illness. Therefore, for Bulawayo, health and wellness extend beyond the physical state to the spiritual[19] as well as the mental. More specifically, the author focused considerably on HIV and AIDS. According to the UNAIDS Global Report,[20] about 23.5 million people were living with HIV in Sub Saharan Africa at the end of 2011. We are interested in the 2011-2012 statistics as we presume that this was the period when *We Need New Names* was written. Bulawayo also pays attention to obesity, religious and traditional healing as well as mental illness. The section below discusses Bulawayo's presentation of AIDS.

The AIDS Disease Phenomenon

The subject of AIDS is not new in Zimbabwean literary imaginaries. It has been covered extensively in, especially, literary works produced in the 21st century. For example, Lutanga Shaba's *Secrets of a Woman's Soul*,[21] Brian Chikwava's *Harare North*,[22] and Tendayi Westerhorf's *Unlucky in Love*,[23] are dedicated to the AIDS phenomenon. The subject of AIDS has also been dealt with by Valerie Tagwira in *Uncertainty of Hope*,[24] Charles Mungoshi in *Branching Streams Flow in the Dark*,[25] Virginia Phiri in *Desperate*,[26] and Sharai Mukonoweshuro in *Days of Silence*.[27]

Bulawayo's depiction of AIDS in *We Need New Names* is not different from other literary works of the time in Zimbabwe and elsewhere. Like in Tangwira's *Uncertainty of Hope* in *We Need New Names* AIDS disables and grounds its victims, and leads only to death. In addition, AIDS victims in *We Need New Names* are also subjects of ridicule. Father, the narrator's absentee father who returns home from South Africa after many years of absence, comes home afflicted with AIDS. The narrator caricatures him. Perhaps it is the portrait of illness from the eyes of a child. We read;

> Father comes home after many years of forgetting us, of not sending money, of not visiting us, not anything us, and parks in the shack, unable to move, unable to talk properly, unable to anything, vomiting and vomiting, Jesus, just vomiting and defecating on himself, and it smelling like something dead in there, dead and rotting, his body

a black, terrible stick; I come in from playing Find bin Laden and he is there. (*We Need New Names*, 89)

The physical body is devastated and consumed by the disease to the extent that the individual is merely a shadow of their former self. However, because of the economic woes that the narrator and her mother have suffered in the absence of the breadwinner, the narrator has no kind words for her sick father. The physiological illness, therefore, becomes a subject of bitterness and ridicule. What matters most is that Darling, Mother and Mother of Bones endured years of wanton poverty and abandonment at Father's hands. In essence, when he comes back disabled by the disease, he is a burden and he is invading the new rhythm of their lives; the life they have had to map out in his truancy. Darling, the narrator, comes short of calling Father a *kaka* father. *Kaka* is human excrement and Bulawayo uses this term pervasively in her novel to laugh at everything that is out of order, including *kaka* countries (such as Zimbabwe and others that are not performing well economically and politically), *kaka* churches (that are led by fake prophets) and *kaka* games (those that the children do not like playing).

Returning diseased and helpless provides no solution to the problems of the home, which a father is supposed to solve. After many years of working in South Africa, returning home as a burden is what the family least expected. As aptly put by Chereni, "while cross-border migration provides opportunities for migrant men to fulfil the traditional breadwinner role in the family, it may simultaneously limit their participation in those nurturing roles which require regular contact" (Chereni, 2).[28] However, for some, as the novel shows, cross-border migration represents the end to the breadwinner "burden". The narrator says; "And later, when the pictures and letters and money and clothes and things he had promised didn't come, I tried not to forget him…" (*We Need New Names*, 93). The narrator also states; "because Father does not do anything for us, Mother complains. About our tinned house, Paradise, the food that is not there, the clothes she wants and everything else" (63). This signifies the abandonment of fatherly duties in the midst of socio-economic hardships. In this regard, illness is sketched as not only emasculating and disembodying, but also as alienating, punishing and frightening: a blend of dark experiences usually hidden in the unconscious mind.[29] The section also introduces the subject of women becoming primary breadwinners due to migration, a subject that has received scholarly attention elsewhere.[30]

Family wellness and financial wellness (sending us money), togetherness, love, etc. take precedence to individual (un)wellness. There are other things to worry about, which are more important than the illness of an individual, especially if one is supposed to be taking care of the family in the first place.

Specifically, Mother has to cross the border to fend for the family and Darling has to fend for herself through begging, stealing guavas or other things to sell in order to buy bread for herself and her friends. She also has to go the playground to play with her friends to allow herself to continue being a child. We hold that deprivation of play translates into some form of un-wellness for a child. Mother of Bones has to pray for the family and intercede on their behalf for their spiritual wellness. It does not matter that the church she goes to "… is just *kaka*", meaning fake and deceptive (21).

However, when every member's role in the family is re-evaluated, the 10-year-old has to relinquish her chores and routine to take care of the sick father. Whether this is to show how little importance is attached to the disease in the broader perspective of social problems that the community is faced with such that the caregiver's role can settle on, and become the responsibility of children, or it is to reveal how disease burdens children, Bulawayo protests the disruption of childhood, childhood innocence and several liberties associated with childhood. The narrator says; "Because I have to watch Father now, like he is a baby and I am his mother, it means that when Mother and Mother of Bones are not there, I cannot play with my friends, so I have to lie to them about why" (93). Thus, disease is a disruption of routine and normal life processes. It is an unwanted invader of people's lives. In addition, and as the excerpt above implies, disease turns babies into mothers as they take up daunting tasks of caring for the sick. What makes it worse in this case is that when the children stay home to tend to the sick, they go hungry because at least one of their meals of the day is out there on guava trees in Budapest. Illness is portrayed as humiliating. The child-turned-caregiver has to lie to her friends about why she could not come to play; she is afraid and embarrassed to tell them about a tabooed disease. Otherwise, they may end up avoiding her like a leper. We posit that the author, in this instance, paints a picture of illness as a marginalising force. Once marginalised, the ill individual's identity is slowly erased. Just as the illness is spoken of in hushed tones, the ill becomes interwoven in a dehumanising process leading to death. The shame surfaces to indicate the underlying challenge of accepting illness that is obscured in the unconscious mind.[31]

In *We Need New Names*, disease takes away children's innocence, disrupts child development and interferes with their social connection by piling on them responsibilities that belong to adults. This is because adults are busy trying to survive each day due to the appalling socio-economic conditions that define their lives and those of their families. "She went to the border to sell things so I have to stay with Mother of Bones until she returns. Sometimes Mother comes back after only a few days, sometimes after a week; sometimes she comes back when I don't even know when she is coming" (21). Therefore, the children, who have nothing better to do than play since they do not even go to school anymore, have to pick up adult duties. Therefore, without warning, and especially without being equipped with any relevant skills and information, children are forced to take up adult roles and responsibilities. This exposes them to not only trauma but also to the disease itself. Even for adults, who take up the caregiver responsibility, disease drains and traumatises them. For example, "Mother's eyes are tired and her face is tired. Ever since Father came, she has been busy doing things for him" (97). Thus, disease is draining for all. We view this deterioration of the human condition wherever there is an illness as a reinforcement of the nexus and almost inevitable, logical progression of illness and death. Consequently, the death motif lingers where illness is found.

Probably as a solution to the above challenge and many others, Bulawayo deploys play as a strategy to deal with the different kinds of trauma that confront children, including illness, poverty, starvation, political upheaval, violence and absentee parents. Children devise multiple games to escape from the reality of socio-economic and socio-political conditions of their times. However, when the author introduces the subject of disease, it keeps children away from play. This makes the trauma extremely difficult to deal with. Instead of escaping reality through play, the child is brought into the home-based care arena to take up the duties and responsibilities of adults. Thus, their childhood is stolen as they are forced to improvise and cope with the new kinds of trauma they are exposed to.

Describing the trauma she experienced when her father returned immobilised by disease, the narrator says, "Then he lifts his bones and pushes a claw towards me and I don't want to touch it but Mother is there looking. [...] The claw is hard and sweaty in my hand and I withdraw it fast. Like I've touched fire. Later, I don't want to touch myself with that hand, I don't want to eat with it or do nothing with it, I even wish I could throw the hand away and get another" (90). The physical appearance of the sick is itself traumatising to the child, and then, worse, they have to be the one taking care of the sick, including feeding them. Elsewhere, the narrator describes her father thus; "He is just length and bones. He is crocodile teeth and egg-white eyes, lying there, drowning on the bed. I don't even know its father at the time so I run outside, screaming. Mother meets me with a slap and says, Shhhh..." (90). Once again, illness is sketched as terrifying and conclusive. The stigma and shame are evident. We hold that caring for the sick is the responsibility of the adults, and when children are forced to forgo play and assume adult duties such as facing illness, they are damaged emotionally and their mental development is affected.

Some of the challenges associated with play deprivation are depression, aggression, rigidity in thinking and trauma.[32] In many Zimbabwean families, this adoption of adult duties by children in the light of parental illness progresses, at the demise of both parents, to the concept of child-headed households that have received overwhelming attention from researchers in Zimbabwe.[33]

To cope with the trauma of assuming adult responsibilities like tending to the sick, the children in *We Need New Names* resort to what they know best: play. They bring play into the caring for the sick. In addition, because it is play, it has to be pleasurable and all players have to be actively involved,[34] hence "Stina reaches and takes Father's hand and starts moving it to the song, and Bastard moves the other hand" (103). Even those who are immobilised by sickness are forced to play. Father cannot even easily move his "claws" but when the children bring the play to his bed, they make him play. They laugh and dance, thus making the daunting task much more bearable. Even the stigma associated with disease and "the disease", which elsewhere in the novel (102) leads a woman to commit suicide, seems to disappear when the children call it by name. We read; "It's no use hiding AIDS, Stina says. When he mentions the Sickness by name, I feel a shortness of breath. I look around to see if there are other people within earshot. It's like hiding a thing with horns in a sack. One day the horns will start boring through the sack and come out in the open for everyone to see" (100).

When Darling is instructed not to tell anybody about the presence of the father in the house, Bulawayo introduces the subject of stigma associated with HIV and AIDS. The stigmatisation of those infected as well as those affected by HIV and AIDS is also reflected in the other Zimbabwean literary imaginaries that we listed earlier. However, when Bulawayo introduces play as a mechanism to cope with the trauma of taking care of the sick by the children, stigma falls away. The children start by mentioning the disease by name and go on to discuss it.

In other instances, illness is mentioned in passing, as if to make the subject less important yet the author is highlighting major issues affecting people's well-being. For example, to highlight how the youth were forced to do jobs that involved hard labour that led to illnesses the narrator writes; "Next to Jesus is my cousin Makhosi carrying me when we were little. ... When Makhosi came back, his hands were like decaying logs. He told us about Mdante between bad bouts of raw, painful coughs, how when he was under the earth, he forgot about everything. He said all he knew inside that mine was the terrible pounding of the hammer around him, sometimes even inside him, like he had swallowed..." (23). There is no compensation for the occupational hazards and work-related diseases and trauma highlighted in the novel. Instead, when he returns from the mine, the cousin crosses the border to look for another job. Another example of un-wellness that *We Need New Names* laughs at in passing is obesity. We read;

> Besides that, she is just rolls and rolls of flesh; I cannot help staring, cannot help thinking, But this is not just fatness. In America, the fatness is not the fatness I was used to at home. Over there, the fatness was of bigness, just ordinary fatness you could understand because it meant the person ate well, fatness you could even envy. It was fatness that did not interfere with the body; a neck was still a neck, a stomach a stomach, an arm an arm, a buttock a buttock. But this American fatness takes it to a whole 'nother level: the body is turned into something else - the neck becomes a thigh, the stomach becomes an anthill, an arm a thing, the buttock a I don't even know what. (171)

Elsewhere the bride, the subject of the narrator's words above, is described by two women speaking a Zimbabwean language as "a freaking mountain" (173). Bulawayo's comparison could be based on statistics. According to research, 18.5 percent of children and 39.6 percent of adults had obesity in 2015–2016, which is an increase from 13.9 percent of children and 30.5 adults who had obesity in 1999–2000.[35] By contrast, a recent study by Amugsi et al.[36] placed Zimbabwean adult females, the group at the highest risk of obesity, at 13 percent of the population having obesity. However, excessive thinness is also considered unattractive. On the television screen are two pictures of a woman, "a before one, when she was bigger and looked like a real person, and an after one, where she is thin and looks like a beautiful thing" (190). Thin is beautiful but it makes the woman look like a thing and not a real person. Here we discuss obesity as a red flag in a continuum in which illness and death share space. Physical and mental illness punctuate the events in *We Need New Names* conveniently to indicate the intricate link between the individual and the nation, the physical and the spiritual, and between life and death.

Mental illness is also only mentioned in passing. Tshaka Zulu, an old Zimbabwean living in the US is a patient at Shadybrook, an institution for the mentally ill. He occasionally comes out to perform at ceremonies organised by Zimbabweans. Quite often, he gets out of hand and threatens other patients at the psychiatric home. The narrator too describes his sickness as madness that grips him, and he starts speaking in a particular Zimbabwean language, and the only medicine is to speak to him in that particular Zimbabwean language.

Compared to Andrew, a co-inmate at Shadybrook who would hack into websites and post nude pictures of himself, or to another mentally sick person who chased Darling and her friends all the way from Budapest to Paradise half-naked, Tshaka Zulu was not dangerous. He was also not as dangerous as the groom at a wedding back in Paradise who "just upped and picked up a log and started clobbering people, including his own bride" and he "never got better; wherever he went people were always fleeing for their lives" (236). However, as time goes on and as there seems to be no solution to his hallucinations, Tshaka Zulu's mental state worsens. He even visits the airport and demands a flight to take him to Buckingham Palace "so he could go and talk to the queen about the things she owes him" (271). At last, when they realise that the talk of spears he has been doing all along referred to real spears tucked away in his room, and when he goes out to attack imaginary colonialists, the police shoots him.

Spiritual Un-wellness

Bulawayo presents two strands to spiritual wellness in the novel, and these are Christianity and African Traditional Religion. On the way to Fambeki hill where the HOLY CHARIOT CHURCH OF CHRIST led by Prophet Revelations Bitchington Mborro, the road that Darling and Mother of Bones use passes next to a traditional healer's house. Vodloza, the healer, attends many of the people's problems. In a queue outside;

> They are waiting for Vodloza to divine with their ancestors because that's his job. A large white sign says in bold red English words: VODLOZA, BESTEST HEALER IN ALL OF THIS PARADISE AND BEYOND WILL PROPER FIX ALL THESE PROBLEMSOME THINGS THAT YOU MAY ENCOUNTER IN YOUR LIFE: BEWITCHEDNESS, CURSES, BAD LUCK, WHORING SPOUSES, CHILDRENLESSNESS, POVERTY, JOBLESSNESS, AIDS, MADNESS, SMALL PENISES, EPILEPSY, BAD DREAMS, BAD MARRIAGE/MARIIAGELESSNESS, COMPETITION AT WORK, DEAD PEOPLE TERRORIZING YOU, BAD LUCK WITH GETTING VISAS ESPECIALLY TO USA AND BRITAIN, NONSENSEFUL PEOPLE IN YOUR LIFE. THINGS DISAPPEARING IN YOUR HOUSE ETC. ETC. ETC. PLEASE PAYMENT IN FOREX ONLY. (Bulawayo 2013, 27)

This way, Bulawayo summarises some of the major challenges seeking the intervention of the ancestors. There is a long queue of people waiting on Vodloza "to divine with their ancestors" (27).

The above lines reflect the infantilisation of the citizenry, as they are made to believe religion is a solution to all their problems. Even those suffering from poverty are asked to pay in forex only if they want to eradicate their poverty. Religion and faith healing are commercialised due to increased stressors in the society as well as due to more people turning to religion and faith for answers to otherwise economic challenges. The turning to religion for all kinds of un-wellness has been linked to poverty and the loss of faith in the socio-political and socio-economic systems of the country.[37] However, research shows a substantial link between disease and economic conditions of a country. For example, it shows there is a link between mental illness and levels of violence, poor socio-economic status, poverty, and low levels of education among other issues.[38]

Bulawayo's presentation of disease and traditional healing is not different from her presentation of the prophet and healing. To start with, congregants often consult the diviner for some of their problems, even though the church considers the healer pagan. Furthermore, when the prophet is performing a healing session, the evangelists and women pray. "This is what they must do in order for the Holy Spirit to come properly, but they have to keep their voices kind of controlled so they don't sound like the pagans at Vodloza's shack. I have seen them calling the ancestors behind Vodloza's shack, the pagans— drums bark and men roar and women shriek, bodies leap in the air, bodies writhe, and sometimes clothes fall off" (39). This way, the only difference between the healing at the *kaka* church (21) and at the pagan healer's shack described in the above excerpt is that at the church voices are controlled and at the healer's shack, all caution falls away.

The lack of contradistinction between the church and the diviner's place seems to be Bulawayo's way of showing how the actions of different social actors conspire to make the lives of ordinary citizens, especially the poor, very difficult. In *We Need New Names*, religious social actors use what Landa, Zhou and Tshotsho call "spiritually elevated placement" to benefit financially.[39] For example, after praying for Father, the prophet declares that the spirit of the narrator's long-dead grandfather that had long been troubling the narrator had finally left her. However, the prophet adds that it "does not mean the spirit is gone because it has now got into Father and is devouring his blood and body, making him all bony and sick and taking his strength away" (99). The narrator adds that the prophet said in order to avenge the spirit and heal the sick man, "We had to find two fat white virgin goats to be brought up the mountain for sacrifice, and that father has to be bathed in the goats' blood. In addition, Prophet Revelations Bitchington Mborro says he will need "five hundred U.S. dollars as payment, and if there are no U.S. dollars, Euros will do. When he says this, Mother gets up angry-like and boils out of the shack, slamming the door behind her" (99). When the mother shows her displeasure at the actions of the clergyman, he declares that, "God also told me that the wife is possessed too, by three demons" (99). With this satire, we laugh at both disease and sickness. The demands in payment for services rendered are just ridiculous in the light of the appalling economic conditions in which they find themselves.

The entire healing session becomes a joke when the healer demands of the poor family living in a one-room shack payment of a large sum (five hundred

US dollars) in either American dollars or Euros, over and above sourcing two goats. In addition, those who show that they are not gullible are dismissed as demon-possessed. This way, those that are gullible, like Mother of Bones, strengthen their resolve to support the activities of the bogus clergyman and seek their prayers for sickness and other forms of un-wellness. Bulawayo is showing here how the religious leaders (both at the church and at the traditional diver's), for the reason that there are "no doctors or nurses at the hospital because they are always on strike", make a large profit off the poor and needy (99).

Bulawayo also presents the subject of spiritual healing, at least the church side of it, as a center for sexual abuse of troubled women. Indecent assault happens even at the altar. The narrator reports that the prophet "leaps onto the woman like maybe he is Hulkogen, squashing her mountains beneath him" (40). He "prays for the woman like that, pinning her down and calling to Jesus and screaming bible verses. He places his hands on her stomach, on her thighs, then he puts his hands on her thing and starts rubbing and praying hard for it, like there is something wrong with it. His face is alight, glowing" (40). On seeing the prophet praying for the woman like this, Chipo, the pregnant teenager, tells her friend that what the prophet is doing to the woman is what her grandfather did to her when he raped her. The healing process is ridiculed and dismissed in its entirety as indecent assault right at the altar. While we can perhaps laugh at the childlike description of the incident, we do not lose sight of the grave and problematic issue of abuse of women by the clergy, an issue in Zimbabwe that Landa, Zhou and Tshotsho have addressed in detail.

The chapter was interested in how disease and un-wellness in Zimbabwe are a subject of ridicule in NoViolet Bulawayo's *We Need New Names*. Illness is coextensive with pain and suffering. The synonymous relationship therefore, presupposes death as the ultimate destination and consequence of illness, hence this tendency to subject the ill individual to a continuum of discriminative practices. It is this problematic framing of illness that automatically presents a skewed trajectory that predominantly isolates and stigmatises the ill and the illness. Through interpretive analysis, we established that *We Need New Names* attempts to write the reality of illness by venturing into the unconscious terrains where all the unpleasant and traumatic events and truths are suppressed. In that regard, we demonstrate that morbid humour does not reduce in any way the impact or truthfulness of the scenes and encounters that give us a view into the grim nature of illness. Instead, morbid humour is a coping and resilience strategy in the face of adversity resulting from pain and disease.

Bibliography

Ahmed Sirajuddin., Pradip Kuma Bardin., Anwaral Iqbal., Ramendra Nath Mazumder., Azharul Islam Khan., M Sirajul Islam., Abul Kasem Siddique, and Alejandro Cravioto. "The 2008 Cholera Epidemic in Zimbabwe: Experience of the icddr, b Team in the Field." *Journal of Health, Population and Nutrition* 29, no. 5 (2011): pp. 541-546. doi: 10.3329/jhpn.v29i5.8909

Amugsi, Dickson Abanimi., Zacharie T Dimbuene., Blessing Mberu., Stella Muthuri, and Alex C Ezeh. "Prevalence and time trends in overweight and obesity among urban women: an analysis of demographic and health surveys data from 24 African countries, 1991-2014." *BMJ Open* 7, no. 10 (2017): e017344.

Benyera, Everisto and Chidochashe Nyere. "An Exploration of the Impact of Zimbabwe's 2005 Operation Murambatsvina on Women and Children." *Gender & Behaviour* 13, no. 1 (2015): pp. 6522-6534.

Bibi Islam., Tariq Khan, and Akbar Ali. "AIDS discourse in Nikita Lalwani's essay "Mister X versus Hospital Y." *Pakistan Journal of Society, Education and Language* (**PJSEL**) 2, no. 1 (2016): pp. 2521-8123.

Bratton, Michael and Masunungure Eldred. "Popular reactions to state repression: Operation Murambatsvina in Zimbabwe." *African Affairs* 106, no. 422 (2006): pp. 21–45. https://doi:10.1093/afraf/adl0

Bulawayo, NoViolet. *We Need New Names.* London: Chatto & Windus, 2013.

Chereni, Admire. "Fathering and Gender Transformation in Zimbabwean Transnational Families." *Forum: Qualitative Social Research* 16, no. 2 (2015): Art. 20. http://www.qualitative-research.net/

Chibisa, P and C. Sigauke. "Impact of Operation Murambatsvina (Restore Order) on flea markets in Mutare: Implications for achieving Mdg 1 and sustainable urban livelihoods." *Journal of Sustainable Development in Africa* 10, no. 1 (2008): pp. 31-65.

Chikwava, Brian. *Harare North.* London: Jonathan Cape, 2009.

Ciganda, D., A. Gagnon, and E. Y. Tenkorang. "Child and young adult-headed households in the context of the AIDS epidemic in Zimbabwe, 1988–2006." *AIDS Care (AIDS CARE)* 24, no. 10 (2006): pp. 1211-1218.

Desiree, R. Fitzpatrick. "From Paradise to Destroyedmichgen: An Analysis of the Function of Names in We Need New Names by No violet Bulawayo." Undergraduate Honors Thesis. 2015. Available at: https://scholar.colorado.edu

Freud, Sigmund. *Character and Culture.* New York: Collier, 1963.

Gray, Peter. "The value of play: The definition of play provides clues to its purposes. Psychology Today", 1-5 (2008). http://www.psychologytoday.com/blog/freedom-learn/200811/the-value-play-i-the-definiti.

Hales Craig M., Margaret D Carroll., Cheryl D Fryar, and Cynthia L Odgen. "Prevalence of obesity among adults and youth: United States, 2015–2016". *National Center for Health Statistics,* Data Brief 288, 2017. https://www.cdc.gov/nchs/products/databriefs/db288.htm (accessed July12, 2020).

Hammerschlag, Carl. "The Spirit of Healing in Groups". *Monograph from a Modified Text of the Presidential Address Delivered to the Arizona Group of*

Psychotherapy Society in Oracle, Arizona, April. Phoenix, AZ: The Phoenix Indian Medical Center, 1985.

Hoang, Lan Ahn & Brenad SA Yeoh. "Breadwinning wives and "left-behind" husbands: Men and masculinities in the Vietnamese transnational family". *Gender & Society* 25, no. 6 (2011): pp. 717-739.

Hove-Musekwa Senelani D., Farai Nyabadza., Christinah Chiyaka., Prasenjit Das., Agraj Tripathi, and Zindoga Mukandavire. "Modelling and analysis of the effects of malnutrition in the spread of cholera". *Mathematical and Computer Modelling* 53 nos. 9-10 (2011): pp. 1583-1595. DOI: 10.1016/j.mcm.2010.11.060.

Hughes, Bob. *Insights and understandings: Developments in Playwork Theory.* Cornwall: PLAY-ADD, 2003a.

Kadlec, Alison. "Play and public life". *Wiley Interscience*, Winter nos. 3-11 (2009). Retrieved from http://www.ncl.org/publications/ncr/98-4/Kadlec.pdf

Kidia, Khameer. K. "The future of health in Zimbabwe". *Global Health Action* 11, no. 1 (2018): 1496888. DOI: 10.1080/16549716.2018.1496888

Landa, Nhlanhla & Sindiso Zhou. "A Critical Discourse Analysis of 'Religious Othering' in Pentecostalism: A Case of the Apostolic Faith Mission in Zimbabwe." In *Pentecostalism and human rights in contemporary Zimbabwe*, edited by Francis Machingura, Lovemore Togarasei & Ezra Chitando, 39-55. Cambridge: Cambridge Scholars Publishing, 2018.

Landa Nhlanhla., Sindiso Zhou, and Baba Tshotsho. "Interrogating the Role of Language in Clergy Sexual Abuse of Women and Girls in Zimbabwe." *Journal for the Study of Religion* 32, no. 2 (2019): pp. 1-20. DOI: http://dx.doi.org/10.17159/2413-3027/2019/v32n2a5

Masunungure, Eldred. "Zimbabwe's Agonising but Irreversible Political Transition." *European Conference on African Studies*, June 4-7, Leipzig, 2009.

Maushe, Francis and Jacob Mugumbate. "'We are on our own': Challenges facing child headed households (CHH), a case of Seke rural area in Zimbabwe." *African Journal of Social Work* 5, no. 1 (2015): pp. 33-60.

Mukonoweshuro, Sharai. *Days of Silence.* Harare: Wonder Book Publishers, 2000.

Mungoshi, Charles. *Branching Streams Flow in the Dark.* Harare: Mungoshi Press, 2013.

New York Times. 'U.N. condemns Zimbabwe for bulldozing urban slums', 23 July 2005. Available at: https://www.nytimes.com/2005/07/23/world/africa/un-condemns-zimbabwe-for-bulldozing-urban-slums.html

Njaya, Tavonga. "Informal Sector, Panacea to the High Unemployment in Zimbabwe? Case of Informal Sector Enterprises of Harare Metropolitan." *International Journal of Research in Humanities and Social Studies* 2, no. 2 (2015): pp. 97-106.

Nyambi, Oliver. *Life-Writing from the Margins in Zimbabwe: Versions and Subversions of Crisis.* London: Routledge, 2019.

Nyoni, Thabani and Wellington G Bonga. "Population growth in Zimbabwe: A threat to economic growth?" *Journal of Economics and Finance (DRJ-JEF)* 2, no. 6 (2017): pp. 29-39.

Pasura, Dominic. "Re-gendering the Zimbabwean diaspora in Britain." In *Zimbabwe's exodus: Crisis, migration, survival*, edited by Jonathan Crush & Daniel Tevera, 207-222. Cape Town: Southern African Migration Project, 2010.

Patel, Vikram and Arthur Kleinman. "Poverty and common mental disorders in developing countries." *Bulletin of the World Health Organization* 81, no. 8 (2003): pp. 609–615.

Phiri, Virginia. *Desperate*. Harare: Xavier F. Carelse, 2002.

Potts, Deborah. "'Restoring Order?' Operation Murambatsvina and the Urban Crisis in Zimbabwe." *Journal of Southern African Studies* 32, no. 2 (2006): pp. 273-29.

Shaba, Lutanga. *Secrets of a Woman's Soul*. Harare: Weaver Press, 2005.

Shangvi, Siddharth. *Hello Darling*. India: Random House publishers, 2008.

Tagwira, Valerie. *The Uncertainty of hope*. Harare: Weaver Press, 2006.

Takaza, S., K. Nyikahadzoi., B.K. Chikwaiwa., A.B Matsika., G. Muchinako., and E. Ndlovu. "A comparative analysis of impact of alternative care approaches on psychosocial wellbeing of orphans and other vulnerable children (OVC) in Zimbabwe." *Journal of Social Development in Africa* 28, no. 2 (2013): pp. 9-30.

UNAIDS report on the global AIDS epidemic. Joint United Nations Programme on HIV/AIDS (UNAIDS), 2012. https://www.hst.org.za/publications/NonHST%20Publications/20121120_UNAIDS_Global_Report_2012_en.pdf

Westerhorf, Tendayi. *Unlucky in Love*. Harare: Public Personalities Against Aids Trust, 2005.

Zhou, Sindiso & Nhlanhla, Landa. "Life narratives mirroring the feminization of HIV and AIDS Trauma: Zimbabwean Perspectives of Coping and Resilience." In *Perspectives on Coping and Resilience*, edited by Venkat Pulla, Andrew Shatte and Shane Warren, 399-418. Nepal: Authors Press, 2013.

Notes

[1] Bulawayo, NoViolet. *We Need New Names*. London: Chatto & Windus, 2013.

[2] Nyoni, Thabani & Wellington, Bonga G. "Population growth in Zimbabwe: A threat to economic growth?" *Journal of Economics and Finance (DRJ-JEF)* 2, no. 6 (2017): 29-39.

[3] Moyo, Simbarashe. Regime survival strategies in Zimbabwe in the 21st Century. African Journal of Political Science and International Relations 7, no. 2 (2013, May): 67 – 78.

[4] Masunungure, Eldred. Zimbabwe's Agonising but Irreversible Political Transition. A Paper presented at the European Conference on African Studies, June 4-7, Leipzig, 2009

[5] Zhou, Sindiso & Nhlanhla, Landa. "Life narratives mirroring the feminization of HIV and AIDS Trauma: Zimbabwean Perspectives of Coping and Resilience". In *Perspectives on Coping and Resilience*, edited by Venkat Pulla, Andrew Shatte and Shane Warren, 399-418. Nepal: Authors Press, 2013.

[6] Benyera, Everisto & Chidochashe, Nyere. "An Exploration of the Impact of Zimbabwe's 2005 Operation Murambatsvina on Women and Children." *Gender & Behaviour* 13, no. 1 (2015): 6522-6534.

[7] Potts, Deborah. "Restoring Order'? Operation Murambatsvina and the Urban Crisis in Zimbabwe". *Journal of Southern African Studies* 32, no. 2 (2006): 273-29.

[8] Chibisa, P & Sigauke, C. "Impact of Operation Murambatsvina (Restore Order) on flea markets in Mutare: Implications for achieving Mdg 1 and sustainable urban livelihoods." *Journal of Sustainable Development in Africa* 10, no. 1 (2008): 31-65.

[9] Njaya, Njaya, Tavonga. "Informal Sector, Panacea to the High Unemployment in Zimbabwe? Case of Informal Sector Enterprises of Harare Metropolitan". *International Journal of Research in Humanities and Social Studies* 2, no. 2 (2015): 97-106.

[10] Kidia, Khameer, K. "The future of health in Zimbabwe". *Global Health Action* 11, no. 1 (2018): 1496888. DOI: 10.1080/16549716.2018.1496888

[11] Bibi, Islam, Tariq Khan & Akbar Ali. "AIDS discourse in Nikita Lalwani's essay "Mister X versus Hospital Y." *Pakistan Journal of Society, Education and Language* (**PJSEL**) 2, no. 1 (2016): 2521-8123.

[12] UNAIDS, report on the global AIDS epidemic. Joint United Nations Programme on HIV/AIDS (UNAIDS), 2012. Available at: https://www.hst.org.za/publications/NonHST%20Publications/20121120_UNAIDS_Global_Report_2012_en.pdf

[13] Hove-Musekwa, D., Farai Nyabadza, Christinah Chiyaka, Prasenjit Das, Agraj Tripathi & Zindoga Mukandavire "Modelling and analysis of the effects of malnutrition in the spread of cholera". *Mathematical and Computer Modelling* 53 nos. 9-10 (2011): 1583-1595. DOI: 10.1016/j.mcm.2010.11.060

[14] Ahmed Sirajuddin, Pradip Kuma Bardin, Anwaral Iqbal, Ramendra Nath Mazumder, Azharul Islam Khan, M Sirajul Islam, Abul Kasem Siddique and Alejandro Cravioto. "The 2008 Cholera Epidemic in Zimbabwe: Experience of the icddr, b Team in the Field." *Journal of Health, Population and Nutrition* 29, no. 5 (2011): 541-546. doi: 10.3329/jhpn.v29i5.8909

[15] Bratton Michael & Eldred, Masunungure. "Popular reactions to state repression: Operation Murambatsvina in Zimbabwe." *African Affairs* 106, no. 422 (2006). 21–45. https://doi:10.1093/afraf/adl0

[16] New York Times, *'U.N. condemns Zimbabwe.* New York Times. 'U.N. condemns Zimbabwe for bulldozing urban slums', 23 July 2005. Available at: https://www.nytimes.com/2005/07/23/world/africa/un-condemns-zimbabwe-for-bulldozing-urban-slums.html

[17] Nyambi, Oliver. *Life-Writing from the Margins in Zimbabwe: Versions and Subversions of Crisis.* London: Routledge, 2019.

[18] Freud, Sigmund. *Character and Culture.* New York: Collier, 1963.

[19] Hammerschlag, Carl. "The Spirit of Healing in Groups". *Monograph from a Modified Text of the Presidential Address Delivered to the Arizona Group of Psychotherapy Society in Oracle,* Arizona, April". Phoenix, AZ: The Phoenix Indian Medical Center, 1985.

[20] UNAIDS, *Report on the global AIDS epidemic.*

[21] Shaba, Lutanga. *Secrets of a Woman's Soul.* Harare: Weaver Press, 2005.

[22] Chikwava, Brian. *Harare North.* London: Jonathan Cape, 2009.

[23] Westerhorf, Tendayi. *Unlucky in Love.* Harare: Public Personalities Against Aids Trust, 2005.

[24] Tagwira, Valerie. *Uncertainty of Hope.* Harare: Weaver Press, 2006.

[25] Mungoshi, Charles. *Branching Streams Flow in the Dark.* Harare: Mungoshi Press, 2013.

[26] Phiri, Virginia. *Desperate.* Harare: Xavier F. Carelse, 2002.

[27] Mukonoweshuro, Sharai. *Days of Silence.* Harare: Wonder Book Publishers, 2000.

[28] Chereni, Fathering and Gender Transformation, 1-20.

29 Freud, Character and culture, 1-320.
30 Chereni, Fathering and Gender Transformation, 1-20; Pasura, Dominic. Re-gendering the Zimbabwean diaspora in Britain. In *Zimbabwe's exodus: Crisis, migration, survival*, edited by Jonathan Crush & Daniel Tevera, 207-222). Cape Town: Southern African Migration Project, 2010.
31 Freud, Character and culture, 1-320.
32 Kadlec, Alison. "Play and public life". Wiley Interscience, Winter nos. 3-11 (2009). Retrieved from http://www.ncl.org/publications/ncr/98-4/Kadlec.pdf
33 Maushe and Mugumbate, Francis & Jacob Mugumbate. "We are on our own": Challenges facing child headed households (CHH), a case of Seke rural area in Zimbabwe". *African Journal of Social Work* 5, no. 1 (2015): 33-60. Takaza, S. Nyikahadzoi, K., Chikwaiwa, B., Matsika, A, B., Muchinako, G, &Ndlovu, E. "A comparative analysis of impact of alternative care approaches on psychosocial wellbeing of orphans and other vulnerable children (OVC) in Zimbabwe". *Journal of Social Development in Africa* 28, no. 2 (2013): 30. 22.; Ciganda, D., Gagnon, A. and Tenkorang, E. Y. "Child and young adult-headed households in the context of the AIDS epidemic in Zimbabwe, 1988–2006." *AIDS Care (AIDS CARE)* 24, no. 10 (2006): 1211-1218.
34 Gray, Peter. "The value of play: The definition of play provides clues to its purposes. Psychology Today", 1-5 (2008). http://www.psychologytoday.com/blog/freedom-learn/200811/the-value-play-i-the-definiti.
35 Hales Craig M, Margaret D Carroll, Cheryl D Fryar and Cynthia L Odgen. "Prevalence of obesity among adults and youth: United States, 2015–2016". *National Center for Health Statistics*, Data Brief 288, 2017. https://www.cdc.gov/nchs/products/databriefs/db288.htm (accessed July12, 2020).
36 Amugsi, Dickson Abanimi, Zacharie T Dimbuene, Blessing Mberu, Stella Muthuri and Alex C Ezeh. "Prevalence and time trends in overweight and obesity among urban women: an analysis of demographic and health surveys data from 24 African countries, 1991-2014." *BMJ Open* 7, no. 10 (2017): e017344.
37 Landa, Nhlanhla & Sindiso Zhou. A critical discourse analysis of 'religious othering' in Pentecostalism: A case of the Apostolic Faith Mission in Zimbabwe. In *Pentecostalism and human rights in contemporary Zimbabwe*, edited by Francis Machingura, Lovemore Togarasei & Ezra Chitando, 39-55. Cambridge: Cambridge Scholars Publishing, 2018.
38 Patel, Vikram & Arthur Kleinman. "Poverty and common mental disorders in developing countries". *Bulletin of the World Health Organization* 81, no. 8 (2003): 609–615.
39 Landa Nhlanhla, Sindiso Zhou and Baba Tshotsho. Interrogating the Role of Language in Clergy Sexual Abuse of Women and Girls in Zimbabwe. *Journal for the Study of Religion* 32, no. 2 (2019): 20 pages. DOI: http://dx.doi.org/10.17159/2413-3027/2019/v32n2a5

Chapter 16

"Back from the Shades of Death": The Pleasures and Pains of Convalescence in the Nineteenth-Century City

Edward Grimble

Lancing College, UK

Abstract: "There are many excellent books for the sick whilst they are ill. I have, myself, felt a want of a distinct and separate book for those who are recovering," asserted Rev. Robert Milman in his 1865 examination of the spiritual and religious state of convalescing. His views could be extended to literary scholarship more broadly: I would like to re-examine the precarious, peculiar and intellectually provocative states of convalescence as examined by nineteenth and early twentieth-century writers. Inhabiting a hinterland between illness and wellness and isolation and sociability, the recovering subject provides a vitally important way of examining the relationship between the private and public aspects of metropolitan life: how the city, its streets, and its crowds are encountered and experienced by the individual. Sustained study of the convalescent across a number of urban texts permits the uncovering of one of the marginalised "doubles" of the ubiquitous *flâneur*, a figure who has become amorphous through endless reformulation and reshaping. The cities of Baudelaire, Poe, Dickens, Whitman and others are populated by these liminal figures whose experiences of the metropolis are fuelled by the convalescent's unique combination of curiosity, childlike wonder at the urban spectacle, acute susceptibility to impressions, mental and pedestrian febrility, and mania.

Keywords: *Flâneur*, urban walking, urban writing, urban space, convalescence, relapse.

* * *

In his work on the rhythms of urban space, *Rhythmanalysis*, the celebrated Marxist sociologist Henri Lefebvre, who pioneered thoughts on the right to the city and the production of social space, writes that "in order to grasp and analyse rhythms," and in particular those of the street, "it is necessary to get outside them, but not completely: be it through illness or a technique."[1] He continues, asserting that "to grasp a rhythm it is necessary to have been *grasped* by it; one must *let oneself go*, give oneself over, abandon oneself to its duration." Cities are contrapuntal, paradoxical and endlessly protean spaces. For Lefebvre, one can only understand the urban experience through this process of "situat[ing] oneself simultaneously inside and outside" of it—the contradictory nature of the city demands a similar contradiction in the practice of how it is experienced. The writer, almost ninety when he wrote *Rhythmanalysis* (it would be published posthumously in 1992) and with his days of wandering and *flânerie* behind him, found this liminal site on his balcony on the Rue Rambuteau, overlooking the Le Centre Pompidou, and from which he could hear "the noises [below] distinguish themselves, the flows separate out, rhythms respond to one another." Lefebvre's liminality, and specifically the relationship between "illness" and "technique" in the manner individuals experience the city, illustrates a crucial intersection of how cities are experienced: as at once topographical, psychological and physiological. This essay will apply pressure to Lefebvre's conjunction by examining not the way that the city has been imagined by writers of the nineteenth and early twentieth centuries through "illness or technique," but through illness *as* technique. In particular, I will focus on the figure of the urban convalescent—one who stands, precariously on slightly shaken legs perhaps, between those states of illness and wellness—and in so doing offer a mutually illuminating examination of writing, illness, and the city, while challenging the tendency amongst literary scholarship to allow the figure of *flâneur* (often in a sometimes warped guise) to monopolise the role of "hero" of modernity, and of the modern city.

These are city experiences at street level, rather than from the balcony or the omnibus; before entering into a more sustained examination of the urban convalescent, bracing his or her shot nerves before taking those first steps out into the urban throng, I would like to address the ubiquitous figure of the *flâneur*. "Definitions," writes Keith Tester in the introduction to his companion compilation to *flânerie* and the *flâneur*, "are at best difficult and, at worst, a contradiction of what the *flâneur* means. In himself, the *flâneur* is, in fact, a very obscure thing."[2] Despite his own rich and rewarding cultural and literary legacy, the *flâneur* has, I would suggest, suffered from a ceaseless process of reconception and often misconception, and who since he began walking the Parisian boulevards and arcades has been subject to incessant translations, transformations and transpositions. He—and it is more often than not, a "he"—

is the wandering urban type whom Charles Baudelaire in his seminal essay "The Painter of Modern Life" (1863) describes as being akin to "a mirror as vast as this crowd; to a kaleidoscope endowed with consciousness."[3] Indeed, the critical history of the *flâneur* echoes this shifting, kaleidoscopic status, and displays these similar traits of resisting the stationary or the inert. He is a product of the city, the quintessentially "modern" space in which spontaneity and inconsistency reign supreme; he necessarily resists the imposition of a stable set of traits or requisite patterns of behaviour (Tester's difficult definitions), instead remaining alluringly polymorphous.

On the page, as much as in the street, the *flâneur* is always altering, turning and deviating, and whilst in many instances, the emergence of a *flâneur* figure in a particular city or genre has helped to elucidate the ways in which a work interrogates what it means to experience "modernity"—for Baudelaire, "the ephemeral, the fleeting forms of beauty"—in many more cases what occurs is a process akin to a coagulation of a far more varied parade of urban types.[4] The convalescent is a member of this gallery, alongside such figures as the nightwalker, the criminal, the *flâneuse*, the detective, the stalker, addict, daydreamer, or window-shopper. Commodification, control and composure are, I would suggest, the three points of departure between the wandering *flâneur* and his equally dilatory relative, the convalescent.

Languid, Passive and Receptive

"There are many excellent books for the sick whilst they are ill. I have, myself, felt a want of a distinct and separate book for those who are recovering", writes the Reverend Robert Milman at the beginning of his didactic treatise on the spiritual, religious and moral condition of convalescence.[5] Indeed, Milman is only one of many religious writers in the nineteenth century who argued that the interstitial space between illness and health was underrepresented in literature on the subject: three decades later, for instance, the Reverend Somerset Lowry asserted in strikingly similar prose that "it is strange that while so much has been written for the invalid in the time of sickness, there are but few books which deal with the special needs of Convalescence"—the problem of a perceived absence of literature relating to convalescence seems, then, to have been a chronic one.[6] Their vigorous interest in the spiritual state of convalesce is rooted in a belief that it is, fundamentally, a precarious one, and both men are conscious of what Milman calls the "dangers of recovery" as one emerges from illness: namely those of carelessness, shallowness and worldliness.[7] As the convalescent "gradually [comes] out into the world again," they worry that the humility and knowledge of God that they received in the seclusion of the sick bed will be calamitously lost.[8] Taking those first steps out into society again is therefore to run the very real risk of falling not simply back into illness, but into irreparable sin in which "Satan snatches the word away at once" and the corrupting power of "recurr[ing] worldliness slowly but surely chok[es] the word."⁹ Here, then, as they are in texts to which I will turn later, the convalescent subject is the site of a struggle not simply between heath and sickness, but between redemption and diabolism.

Although stripped of the trappings of the church, salvation and the state of the soul, voices from the medical profession during the course of the century *also* sought to refocus attention on this transitional period of recovery, during which the patient languishes in what Charles Lamb, in his essay "The Convalescent" (1825), calls "this flat swamp of convalescence, left by the ebb of sickness, yet far enough from the *terra firma* of established health."¹⁰ An article in the *Boston Medical Intelligencer* (1826) even suggests that "no period of disease is so fraught with danger as that of convalescence."¹¹ Indeed, the attitude expressed in the article's opening remarks, that "again and again would we caution the profession against a custom that prevails too commonly among us [...] we mean the habit of leaving our patients the moment their disease does," could just as well be extended to the realm of literary criticism, I would contend.¹² The critic ministers most diligently to the sick and ailing: Athena Vrettos, for example, assembles a convincing "poetics of illness" rooted in the assertion that, simply put, "it is difficult to find many Victorian novels that *do not* participate in a general dialogue about sickness and health."¹³ However, Vrettos makes too sharp a distinction between the two states of "sickness and health" by abruptly "mov[ing] from disease to health" between the book's third and fourth chapters: the interstitial space of convalescence (and the precariousness of the recovering subject) is therefore shrunk to the point of disappearance.¹⁴ Indeed, Susan Sontag's influential work in *Illness as Metaphor* (1978) also propagates this binary distinction between illness and wellness in her discussion of "the kingdom of the sick" and "the kingdom of the well."¹⁵ What is required, therefore, is the recognition that the separation between illness and wellness is neither fixed nor stable: convalescence is not a border line to be crossed, but a disorienting and largely unmapped hinterland to be gradually, dangerously negotiated before we can consider ourselves safely back on Lamb's *terra firma* of health.¹⁶

This liminality which is integral to the idea of convalescence is found across several attempts in the nineteenth century to define the term in medical discourse—although Tester's warning on the *flâneur* that 'definitions are at best difficult' is equally pertinent here.¹⁷ Two medical theses presented to the *Faculté de Médecine de Paris* in 1837 by Hyacinthe Dubranle and Edmond Marc Hermel offer a foundation for discussion. In the opening of his thesis, Dubranle suggests the following: "La convalescence est un état intermédiaire à la maladie à laquelle il succède et à la santé à laquelle il conduit. Ella commence à l'époque où les symptômes qui caractérisent la maladie ont disparu, et fini à l'époque où l'exercise libre et régulier qui constituent la santé est pleinement rétabli."[18]

Hermel, meanwhile, makes a slightly more rigorous attempt to regulate this fundamentally transitional state between illness and health, asserting that it is:

> [C]et état dans lequel l'homme, après avoir souffert la maladie, tend à recouvrer la santé ou l'état qui lui est propre. C'est une dernière phase de la maladie qui forme sa transition à la santé. Ella a plusieurs périodes: la première est le décroissement graduel ou rapide de la maladie; la seconde, l'état intermédiaire, caractérisé d'un ou de plusieurs organes, l'insuffisance ou la prédominance des fonctions isolées ou réunies; la troisième, celle où le convalescent commence à braver impunément les vicissitudes auxquelles il est exposé.[19]

Reading these two definitions raises more questions than it answers: when, for instance, can the convalescent be said to be no longer simply "braving" the vicissitudes of ordinary life, but coping with them in a condition of restored health? Can one identify the moment at which the symptoms of a disease disappear? What is the full restoration of the abilities in free and regular exercise which constitute healthiness? These definitions, in making admirable attempts to address the state of convalescence with concision and simplicity, identify its most provocative and integral quality: that it is a state which *resists* and *disrupts* any notion of hard distinctions, oppositions or condensed definitions. In linguistic terms, it is something of a diagnostic enigma.

Vitally, it is specifically the *city* which poses a particularly insidious danger to the recovering subject that far outweighs the pastoral. Hermel comments on the fact that "l air des villes et de leurs alentours," full as it is of "la respiration, les émanations de tout les êtres qui y sont renfermés, par les debris des substances alimentaires, les établissements insalubres, les combustions considérables, les exhalaisons de tout espèce," is actively hostile to the convalescent, who should instead be relocated to the countryside.[20] One vignette in particular serves as an effective confluence for the sensations and shocks, pains and pleasures that constitute the convalescent state. In his "Meditations of a Painter" (1912), the Italian surrealist artist Giorgio de Chirico narrates the perplexing and provocative experience which inspired his *Enigma of an Autumn Afternoon* (1910):

> One clear autumnal afternoon I was sitting on a bench in the middle of the Piazza Santa Croce in Florence. It was of course not the first time I

had seen the square. I had just come out of a long and painful intestinal illness, and I was in a nearly morbid state of sensitivity. The whole world, down to the marble of the buildings and foundations, seemed to me to be convalescent.[21]

This moment of painful epiphany is one of at once re-emergence, reimagining and re-apprehension, in which the urban quotidian is seen as if through new eyes. There is something revelatory in this almost Platonic moment of startled "coming out," both out of illness and of the sick room into the streets once more. "All things long for you [...] step out of your cave! All things want to be your physician!," writes Friedrich Nietzsche in a section of *Thus Spoke Zarathustra* titled simply "The Convalescent."[22]

Crucially, however, according to De Chirico it is both subject *and* city that appear to be experiencing this regenerative state of convalescence. The recovering subject views his urban environment in physiological terms as an extension or duplication of his own stuttering health. "The history of London as a human body is striking and singular," writes Peter Ackroyd in the introduction to his magisterial biography of the capital, but equally striking are those depositions which, like that of De Chirico, see the city in a state of frail and precarious health that mirrors that of the observer.[23] When in her poem "A March Day in London," Amy Levy writes of "the east wind" which blows through the streets, "which chills the flesh to aches and pains / and sends a fever through all the veins" she seems to be giving voice as much to the ailing streets as to the shivering speaker.[24] In his essay "Night Walks" (1860) Charles Dickens, like De Chirico, finds this unstable elision between city and subject. The essay is a "confront[ation]" with the nocturnal city which examines a series of attempts to exorcise the trauma, grief and subsequent insomnia caused by the death of his father, John Dickens: the result of a feverish infection brought on by an appalling operation—the "most terrible [...] known in surgery," Dickens recalled in a letter to his wife—for the removal of bladder stones.[25] Impelled into the streets in the dead of night, between midnight and dawn, Dickens's speaker comments on "the restlessness of a great city, and the way in which it tumbles and tosses before it can get to sleep."[26] Although this tumbling and tossing may, according to the speaker, constitute "one of the first entertainments offered to the contemplation of us houseless people," in reality, it is a moment of self-projection. This individual dissociation, in which the walker loses a solid sense of self continues as London, "as if in imitation of individual citizens belonging to it, ha[s] expiring fits and starts of restlessness." The city itself, as well as the wandering speaker, becomes a study of the volatility and fitfulness of attempted recovery and insomnia. This protean sense of identity which darkness affords lingers firstly in Dickens's unsettled use of pronouns. "A temporary inability to sleep," he writes, "caused *me* to walk about the streets all night [emphasis added]," which is followed immediately by a shift towards an identification with the collective in "*us* homeless people [emphasis added]," as the narrator now extends his experiences to the unacknowledged community of isolated nocturnal wanderers. Dickens then simply adopts the third-person "Houselessness," the persona who, nightly, "would walk and walk and walk, seeing nothing but the interminable tangle of streets": in the midst of the throes of London's "fits and starts," the subject's sense of self is destabilised. These questions are also apparent in the title of the essay; Jeremy Tambling perceptively comments that "night walks" can function either adjectively or as a noun—and if the latter, then it is night itself that walks, "ghost-like," in a hinterland between illness and wellness.[27] Uncovered here is what Walter Benjamin, writing about the relationship between Baudelaire and Paris in his series of fragmentary reflections titled "Central Park", calls the "infirmity and decrepitude of a great city," in which the whole metropolis shudders and convulses in time with the recovering subject who has returned tentatively to its maze of streets.[28]

De Chirico writes of this revelatory convalescent state of bringing with it a "nearly morbid state of sensitivity," and in doing so he captures both the vulnerability and helplessness of the convalescent, but also his receptiveness to sensory stimulation.[29] This sense of delicacy but also of imaginative potency is present in the literature of convalescence before the idea is urbanised in the middle of the nineteenth-century, and in particular, the convalescent is said to see the world as though through the eyes of the *child*: somebody for whom even the most ordinary forms and occurrences are imbued with wonder and novelty. Samuel Taylor Coleridge, in his *Biographia Literaria*, writes of genius as the ability "to combine the child's sense of wonder and novelty with the appearances which every day for perhaps forty years had rendered familiar."[30] The "prime merit of genius," he continues, is "so to represent familiar objects as to awaken in the minds of others a kindred feeling concerning them and that freshness of sensation which is the constant accompaniment of mental, no less than of bodily, convalescence."[31] The heir to this Romantic conception of the state of convalescence as it moves from pastoral to urban is Baudelaire, who like Coleridge recognised the poetic possibilities of this highly sensitive and receptive state of apprehension and observation.

"Convalescence," writes Baudelaire in "The Painter of Modern Life," "is like a return to childhood" in which "the convalescent, like the child, enjoys to the highest degree the faculty of taking a lively interest in things, even the most trivial in appearance."[32] Indeed, De Chirico himself saw this receptive state of childishness in which one sees the world anew as nothing short of a vital component to originality and aesthetic potential, and he writes after his description of the bench in the Florentine square that "a truly immortal work of art can only be born through revelation," citing Schopenhauer's assertion that: "to have original, extraordinary, and perhaps even immortal ideas, one has but to isolate oneself from the world for a few moments so completely that the most commonplace happenings appear to be new and unfamiliar, and in this way reveal their true essence."[33]

In this formulation, then, the mundanity of the everyday anaesthetises the urban subject, dulling their surroundings and in doing so closing down their aesthetic potential—this is the state of "spleen" which Benjamin, discussing Baudelaire's *Les Fleurs du Mal* (1857), "kills interest and receptiveness."[34] The hypersensitive convalescent state shows, then, Lefebvre's "illness" and "technique" at work, whereby the individual lingers in what could be called a privileged (precarious and painful though it may also be) state of receptiveness to his environment.[35] In his thesis, Dubranle writes that "bien que les sensations soient moins parfaites, les convalescents sont plus *impressionnables* [emphasis added]."[36] This impressionable state brings with it a less discriminating gaze, suggests Baudelaire, in which "even the most trivial" of subjects can be of the greatest interest—convalescents and children, it would seem, are spectators devoid of aesthetic prejudice.[37] Robert Louis Stevenson, himself an almost perpetual convalescent, writes in his own study of illness and recovery "Ordered South" that although "we may have passed a place a thousand times and one," the helplessly susceptible convalescent state means that "on the thousand and second it will be transfigured, and stand forth in a certain splendour of reality from the dull circle of surroundings; so that we see it with a child's first pleasure."[38] Indeed, in Baudelaire's boldest declaration of the importance of the value of convalescence in allowing the artist to replicate—or regress to—his childlike view of the world in which "everything [is seen] as a novelty" and in which one is "always 'drunk'" on one's environment, he suggests that *genius itself* "is no more than childhood recaptured at will, childhood equipped now with man's physical means to express itself, and with the analytical mind that enables it to bring order into the sum of experience, involuntarily amassed."[39] In essence, the metropolis' aesthetic genius is someone who can be endlessly receptive to what Benjamin calls the incessant "shocks" and stimulation of urban living, but who can also *cope* with them and bring an organising power to bear on that wealth of "experience, involuntarily amassed."[40] This is the reason why Baudelaire so reveres the artist Constantin Guys, who "loves mixing with the crowds, loves being incognito," and who is "perpetually in the spiritual condition of the convalescent."[41]

It is the extent of the convalescent's ability to withstand the impact of the city in this sensitive state that makes him a figure in crisis. The "returning strength" and receptiveness to stimulation after so long a period of isolation can seem, according to an 1877 article in the *Saturday Review of Politics, Literature, Science and Art* "almost too rough and rude a friend for the poor weak body."[42] "Our bodies during convalescence," the writer argues, "become bones of contention between strength and weakness, each of which struggles hard for mastery," and in doing so they capture perfectly this fact that convalescence is fundamentally a state of both crisis *and* contradiction.[43] As Virginia Woolf writes in her novel *Jacob's Room* (1922), "the body after long illness is languid, passive, receptive of sweetness, but too weak to contain it."[44]

Shades of Death

Although indebted to a Romantic tradition with Coleridgean roots, the convalescent state examined in this essay is a fundamentally urban one, and in turning now to Edgar Allan Poe's "The Man of the Crowd" (perhaps the archetypal myth of urban convalescence) and then to Walt Whitman's "The Sleepers", I will interrogate this perilous moment when the fragile individual must once again enter the public space of the city. This is the point at which the carapace against which he must bear the shocks and stimuli of metropolitan life is tested most painfully and relentlessly. After all, to return to Hermel's 1837 thesis: "de tous les dangers auxquels l'homme est exposé pendant la maladie, il n'y a pas de plus insidieux que ceux de la convalescence"—despite the suspicion of youthful hyperbole, there is certainly truth in what the young doctor has to say.[45] Both texts dramatise the aforementioned "struggle for mastery" to which the mind and body of the newly emerging walker is subject, and it is the endurance of these stresses and pressures that elevates the aesthetically minded convalescent to a point at which he can offer a spluttered or wheezed challenge to the *flâneur* as the hero of nineteenth-century modernity.[46]

Cities and those individuals who walk and wander their streets are reimagined and encountered as if anew by the recovering subject who occupies at once this febrile and fertile state situated between both illness and wellness. His hypersensitive state and tendency to view the world as if seen through the wondering eyes of a child makes the convalescent a fascinating medium for examining the aesthetic potentials of the endless series of encounters, shocks and stimuli that comprise urban experience. Poe's vignette is not only a sustained examination of how the convalescent responds to these shocks and vibrant stimuli of the city, however. It is also something of a warning: it alerts us to what Lowry and Milman have identified as the dangers of convalescence, in which "worldliness"—a term which seems to evoke metropolitan and cosmopolitan, rather than rural, excitement—threatens to destabilise the subject's fragile state.[47]

Poe's short story opens thusly:

> Not long ago, about the closing in of an evening in autumn, I sat at the large bow window of the D— Coffee-House in London. For some months I had been ill in health, but was now convalescent, and, with returning strength, found myself in one of those happy moods which are so precisely the converse of ennui—moods of the keenest appetency, when the film from the mental vision departs [...] and the intellect, electrified, surpasses as greatly its every-day condition [...] Merely to breathe was enjoyment; and I derived positive pleasure even from many of the legitimate sources of pain. I felt a calm but inquisitive interest in everything. With a cigar in my mouth and a newspaper in my lap, I had been amusing myself for the greater part of the afternoon, now in poring over advertisements, now in observing the promiscuous company in the room, and now in peering through the smoky panes into the street.[48]

These "smoky panes" are what Michel de Certeau would later call "transparent caesura[e]," and they offer for the convalescent narrator a necessary disconnection from the immediate action of the streets.[49] They shelter the fragile subject from what Leigh Hunt had, in 1825, called the relentless "thrusting commercial and imperial spirit of the times": the convalescent sits ensconced in the café window, prohibited by his lingering illness from once again having to rejoin the "two dense and continuous tides of population were rushing past the door [...] and the tumultuous sea of human heads" which make up the dehumanised, circulating traffic of commuters, employees and city-dwellers.[50] This is the almost ecstatic position of being able to spectate on the life of metropolis whilst not yet having to contribute to the efficacy of the urban capitalist system which R. L. Gentles articulates in his essay, "Convalescence." He notes that during recovery one is able to "shake off all speculation as to what you are to do when take up the thread again" of professional obligations.[51] Instead, he continues, the "soul is satisfied with [...] commonplace surroundings"—this, he suggests, "is the true luxury of convalescence, and is as necessary for the physical well-being of the sufferer as [...] medicaments."[52] It is a sentiment echoed by Charles Lamb, who suggests that in the sick bed the convalescent finds a "regal solitude" because, in short: "to the world's business he is dead."[53]

Initially, his "observations took an abstract and generalising turn," but, we are told, the narrator soon "descended to details, and regarded with minute interest the innumerable varieties of figure, dress, air, gait, visage, and expression of countenance."[54] Crucially, the gaze of Poe's narrator lingers on those figures who show some sign of decrepitude themselves:

Others, still a numerous class, were restless in their movements, had flushed faces, and talked and gesticulated to themselves, as if feeling in solitude on account of the very denseness of the company around. When impeded in their progress, these people suddenly ceased muttering, but re-doubled their gesticulations, and awaited, with an absent and overdone smile upon the lips, the course of the persons impeding them.[55]

There is a perverse communion between the narrator, and those with whom he shares both the city but also this state of perpetual decrepitude. As Hermel writes in his thesis, "l'attitude, la marche, les mouvements, le repos meme du convalescent, sont l'image active de sa faiblesse. Tout ce qu'il fait trahit en lui la diminution de la contractilité musculaire, le défaut d'énergie de l'énervatio": the ambulating convalescent also betrays himself.[56] (Indeed, this is another reason why the convalescent could never attain the cool, anonymous detachment of the *flâneur*, as due to the lingering presence of his infirmity he is simply too conspicuous.) What is given is a frenzied and febrile *physiologie*, as the narrator "descend[s] in the scale of what is termed gentility', and in doing so finds "darker and deeper themes for speculation."[57] To the restless, flushed and muttering figures in the crowd he adds "feeble and ghastly invalids, upon whom death had placed a sure hand."[58] These poor souls "sidled and tottered through the mob" in a tortured ambulation that mirrors that of De Chirico in Florence, who writes that "in the street I was afraid I would succumb to fainting and always walked close to the walls," as if the stimulation of the streets was always threatening to overwhelm him.[59]

As night falls, the "fitful and garish lustre" of the gas lamps throws the city into shadowy chiaroscuro and the "wild effects of the light enchained me to an examination of individual faces;" it is "thus occupied in scrutinising the mob" that the convalescent catches sight of "a decrepit old man, some sixty-five or seventy years of age [with] a countenance which at once arrested and absorbed my whole attention."[60] To the hypersensitive spectator intent on rapidly and feverishly deciphering and taxonomising each face in the nocturnal crowd which passes endlessly beyond the glass planes, this man leaves the narrator "singularly aroused, startled, fascinated." His efforts to read the man end only in an irritating fragmentation of his character, in which his analysis yields only "the ideas of vast mental power, of caution, of penuriousness, of avarice, of coolness, of malice, of blood-thirstiness, of triumph, of merriment, of excessive terror, of intense—of supreme despair." Dissatisfied and energised by this wildly enumerative failure to understand the old man, the narrator makes his way out into the street driven by "a craving desire to keep the man in view—to know more of him." Here, then, the convalescent sacrifices the sanctuary of the café and yields himself up to the jostling crowd, and in doing so, he appears to morph ever so slightly from recovering patient to detective, or even stalker. "For my own part I did not much regard the rain—the lurking of an old fever in my system rendering the moisture somewhat too dangerously pleasant. Tying a handkerchief about my mouth, I kept on." In Lefebvre's formulation, Poe's narrator has been "*grasped*" by the city, and he "give[s] [him]self over" to it in his monomaniacal pursuit of the stranger.[61]

And keep on he does: throughout the night and the following day, the narrator tails the old man through the labyrinthine streets, until on the evening of the second day, they return to the same coffee house in which the story opens. By this point, the narrator says despondently, he "grew wearied unto death," and looking the old man straight in the face is resolved to abandon a pursuit that appears to have escalated beyond idle or even febrile curiosity to an almost self-destructive monomaniacal obsession: "This old man [...] refuses to be alone. He is the man of the crowd. It will be in vain to follow; for I shall learn no more of him, nor of his deeds."[62]

In his discussion of the short story, Baudelaire describes the narrator's initial convalescent state as being that of a man who has "only recently come back from the shades of death."[63] Back at the D— Hotel and "wearied unto death," it would seem as though the narrative has a kind of pathological as well as topographical circularity: in recklessly plunging into the streets in an attempt to satisfy what Baudelaire calls the "compelling, irresistible passion" that has supplanted what was initially the receptive curiosity of the convalescent, their wild circumambulation of the city seems to push the narrator into a kind of relapse.[64] Matthew Beaumont, in his thrilling *Nightwalking*, argues that the old man is "simply the repository of popular suspicions about solitary individuals who occupy the metropolitan streets at night," whilst William Sharpe goes a step further, suggesting that the Man of the Crowd is himself the Devil, "not only because his diabolic features surpass any 'pictural incarnations of the fiend,'" but also because his way of striding "'to and fro' in the city echoes Satan's motion in the Book of Job."[65] Poe's man of the crowd, "gasp[ing] as if for breath while he thr[ows] himself amid the crowd" with "intense agony" and "mad energy" is not simply the perpetually manic double of the convalescent narrator, but an incarnation of the diabolical urban "worldliness" that Lowry, Milman, Dubranle and Hermel identify as posing the greatest threat to the fragile health of the convalescent.[66] The old man, his spirits flickering up "as a lamp which is near its death-hour," is the spectral reminder of the dangers of convalescence and of the city's ability to obliterate the precariously returning health of the convalescent.[67] He is a reminder that, as Mary Ethel Granger writes in her instructional work *Life Renewed: A*

Manual for Convalescents Arranged for Daily Reading, "long Convalescence, ending in relapse and death, is by no means unfrequent."[68]

An episode in Bram Stoker's *Dracula* (1897), which despite the critical attention that has been paid to the importance of illness and disease in the novel has been often overlooked, further illustrates this perilously fragile state in which the convalescent must negotiate the city. The sudden death of Hawkins forces the couple to return to London for the funeral, a trip that Mina "dread[s]."[69] Taking an omnibus to Hyde Park Corner before strolling through Piccadilly, Mina sees "a very beautiful girl, in a big cart-wheel hat, sitting in a victoria outside Guiliano's." Harker, at the same moment, clutches Mina's arm with a sudden tightness:

> He was very pale, and his eyes seemed bulging out as, half in terror and half in amazement, he gazed at a tall, thin man, with a beaky nose and black moustache and pointed beard, who was also observing the pretty girl. [...] His face was not a good face; it was hard, and cruel, and sensual, and his big white teeth, that looked all the whiter because his lips were so red, were pointed like an animal's. Jonathan kept staring at him, till I was afraid he would notice. (Stoker 2003, 183)

Unnoticed by all but Harker, the Count comes to London in order that he might, as he had told Harker at his castle, "be in the midst of the whirl and rush of humanity, to share its life" and, of course, prey on its population. The Count is, on the one hand, an image of the Baudelairean *flâneur* in his most predatory and insidious incarnation: he may be the "prince enjoying his incognito wherever he goes," but rather then "an ego athirst for the non-ego," Dracula is the ego athirst for blood.[70] "I do believe that if he had not had me to lean on and to support him he would have sunk down," says Mina as Harker slips into unconsciousness on a bench in Green Park to which they have staggered, the Count had plunged back into the throng in pursuit of the young woman.[71] The experience of the crowd is to be in the midst of "the ebb and flow, the bustle, the fleeting and the infinite," writes Baudelaire; it is to be subject to an incessant series of shocks and chance encounters.[72] Poe and Stoker illustrate the danger of this endlessly stimulating space for the convalescent, whose lingering infirmity renders him ill-equipped to parry the city's blows even as he heroically re-emerges onto its streets, pursued as he always is by the possibility of slipping back towards sickness and the morbid "shades of death."[73]

The Fevers Stop

Many of the writers examined here—Poe, Baudelaire, De Chirico and others—have shown that the incessant shocks and stimuli that constitute urban experience pose to the convalescent a dangerous threat to their precarious position between illness and health. The urban convalescent, making his first unsteady steps through the city's streets, has been in turns vulnerable, volatile, nervous, neurotic, feverish and febrile, and plagued, as I have suggested by the spectre of relapse in which his fragile condition may no longer be able to withstand the pressure placed upon it by the energetic city and its crowds. These cities too, seem to vibrate in a strange convalescence, as architecture and infrastructure themselves appear "restless," "fitful" and "feverish"—or even in the state articulated by De Chirico in his "Meditations of a Painter" in which "the whole world, down to the marble of the buildings and foundations, seemed [...] to be convalescent."[74] To close this examination of urban convalescence, I would like to turn finally to Walt Whitman's poem "The Sleepers," suggesting that it offers a rare and therefore valuable dramatisation, not of the atomising, anaesthetising nor isolating ebb and flow of illness and health, but instead of a kind of individual and collective restoration or recovery.

Whitman's verse begins in the same familiar state which has been encountered time and again here, as the speaker declares that he "wander[s] all night in my vision":

> Stepping with light feet, swiftly and noiselessly stepping and stopping,
>
> Bending with open eyes over the shut eyes of sleepers,
>
> Wandering and confused, lost to myself, ill-assorted, contradictory,
>
> Pausing, gazing, bending, and stopping.[75]

Patterns of sibilance and consonance simultaneously register hurried and staggered steps, and the footfall of Whitman's speaker is erratic and jolting in these sequences of "pausing, gazing, bending, and stopping." Here, movement and mindset share the same fitfulness, and in this dissociative state in which the speaker is "lost" even to himself Whitman is conjuring a sense of ailing directionless in which rather than enjoy the confident strolling of the *flâneur* he treads only with the feeling that, as Stevenson writes in "Ordered South," these excursions and walks will "prove too long or too arduous for [this] feeble body."[76] He suffers too from the same compulsion to categorise and taxonomise his fellow city-dwellers that monopolised Poe's convalescent narrator, flitting his restless and imaginative gaze in turn from "the little children in their cradles" to the "married couple [who] sleep calmly in their bed, he with his palm on the hip of the wife, and she with her palm on the hip of the husband"—a perhaps surprisingly tender image devoid of any sort of scandalous, Asmodean voyeurism.[77] Caught in his own oneiric, esoteric solipsism, the speaker is alone among these intimately connected groups and couples, stumbling in his quasi-convalescent state. His impulse to catalogue does not, or cannot, discriminate, however, and these images jostle alongside those of the "wretched features of ennuyés, the white features of corpses, the livid faces of drunkards," as well as "prisoners," "the murderer that is to be hung" and even "the murder'd person." As Poe and Baudelaire had done in their short fiction and poetry, respectively, Whitman's speaker seems to encounter the slumbering city as somehow legible as he gazes on sleeping figures of "the female that loves unrequited" and "the male that loves unrequited."

In a moment of self-recognition, it is however the city's ill and ailing to whom the speaker seems closest:

> I stand in the dark with drooping eyes by the worst-suffering and the most restless,
>
> I pass my hands soothingly to and fro a few inches from them,
>
> The restless sink in their beds, they fitfully sleep. (Whitman 2002, 357)

The poem here seems to be edging towards a moment of more tender communion, where the sweep and scope of the speaker's gaze takes on a greater degree of intimacy and intensity, and the act of looking approaches or almost gives way to the act of touching. Whitman's speaker therefore treads a fine line when he goes "from bedside to bedside" and "dream[s] in my dream all the dreams of the other dreamers" (eventually "becom[ing] the other dreamers," he says) because he seems at once to exhibit the same form of compulsive curiosity and speculation about the crowd examined earlier, and also a kinder, gentler ministering approach to his fellow men and women that is very often replaced in the urban stroller by the carapace of a kind of disinterested aloofness. Detached physiognomising is now supplanted by a fluidity and endless reformulation of the speaker's own personality in which he is:

> the actor, the actress, the voter, the politician,
>
> The emigrant and the exile, the criminal that stood in the box,
>
> He who has been famous and he who shall be famous after to-day,
>
> The stammerer, the well-form'd person, the wasted or feeble person. (Whitman 2002, 358)

This compulsion to read the city's inhabitants and re-invent the self again and again is febrile and intoxicating: "I am a dance—play up there! the fit is whirling me fast!," he cries, and this "wasted and feeble" speaker whirls in a state that with every utterance seems to mirror more and more accurately the "compelling, irresistible passion" which Baudelaire ascribes to Poe's convalescent narrator.[78]

If the poem's opening stanzas dramatise the way in which the fragile individual who teeters worryingly in the liminal position between wellness and illness, composure and compulsion, then its subsequent sections show signs of hope: in the second half of "The Sleepers" Whitman deviates from his antecedents and offers a vision of recovery, reparation and even redemption for his feverish speaker. Now "elements merge in the night" and "the exile returns home, / The fugitive returns unharmed [...] the immigrant is back beyond months and years," and the speaker sees this urban convergence—rather than fragmentation or alienation—as an immensely aesthetic vision: "I swear they are all beautiful," he muses, as "the wildest and bloodiest is over, and all is peace."[79] What is at peace here is not simply this serene harmonising of the disparate elements of the nocturnal metropolis, however, but the physiologies of city and speaker: the "wildest" fits and throes subside and:

> The breath of the boy goes with the breath of the man, friend is inarm'd by friend [...]
>
> The felon steps forth from the prison—the insane becomes sane—the suffering of sick persons is reliev'd,
>
> The sweatings and fevers stop—the throat that was unsound is
>
> sound—the lungs of the consumptive are resumed—the poor distress'd head is free,
>
> The joints of the rheumatic move as smoothly as ever, and smoother than ever,
>
> Stiflings and passages open—the paralyzed become supple,
>
> The swell'd and convuls'd and congested awake to themselves in condition,
>
> They pass the invigoration of the night, and the chemistry of the night, and awake.[80]

The fitful city and the convalescent nightwalker seem cleansed and healed in this moment of spiritual and bodily restoration, awakening from sleep and sickness. It is a significant moment of resistance to the apparently chronic state in which most city dwellers exist: from the "restless" and "worst-suffering" of Whitman's American metropolis to Poe's flushed, muttering and stumbling Londoners. To exist in the city seems to necessarily place one in a perpetual state of transition from sickness to health—the febrility of city life is almost irrepressible. The drama of Whitman's verse here is a far cry from the flippant and blasé suggestion made by Charles Lamb in his earlier essay "The Londoner," in which he writes that whilst "I am naturally inclined to hypochondria [...] in London it vanishes, like all other ills".[81] Rather than simply vanishing, Whitman's malaise has been thrillingly felt, wrestled with, and finally exorcised. After this transformative convalescence in which "night and sleep have liken'd [...] and restored," Whitman speaks of the urban night in affectionate, intimate terms: the speaker first "returns to [it] again and love[s] it" as a mate, but then shifts again and "returns to you," the nocturnal metropolis, "O my mother," nurtured and fulfilled.[82]

Bibliography

Ackroyd, Peter. *London: The Biography*. London: Chatto and Windus, 2000.

Baudelaire, Charles. *The Painter of Modern Life*, translated by P. E. Charvet. London: Penguin, 2010.

Beaumont, Matthew. *Nightwalking: A Nocturnal History of London*. London: Verso, 2016.

Benjamin, Walter. *The Writer of Modern Life*, edited by Michael W. Jennings. Trans. Howard Eiland et al. Cambridge, MA: Belknap Press, 2006.

Coleridge, Samuel Taylor. *Biographia Literaria*, edited by Adam Roberts. Edinburgh: Edinburgh University Press, 2014.

Colter, Hattie. *Medoline Selwyn's Work*. Boston, MA: Ira Bradley & Co, 1889.

———. "Convalescence." *Boston Medical Intelligencer* I, no. 45 (March 1826): 179.

———. "Convalescence." *Saturday Review of Politics, Literature, Science and Art* 44 (October 1877): pp. 417–418.

De Certeau, Michel. *The Practice of Everyday Life*, translated by Steven F. Rendall. Berkely, CA: University of California Press, 2011.

De Chirico, Giorgio. 'Meditations of a Painter," translated by Louise Bourgeois and RobertGoldwater. In *Theories of Modern Art: A Source Book for Artists and Critics*, edited by Herschel B. Chipp, 397–401. Berkeley: University of California Press, 1969.

———. *Memoirs of Giorgio de Chirico*, tanslated by Margaret Crosland. New York: Da Capo Press, 1994.

Dickens, Charles. *Dickens' Journalism*. Vol 4, edited by John Drew and Michael Slater. London: J.M. Dent, 2000.

———. *The Pilgrim Edition of the Letters of Charles Dickens: Volume* 6, edited by Graham Storey et al. Oxford: Oxford University Press, 1988.

Dubranle, Hyacinthe. *Essai sur la convalescence: Thèse*. Paris: Rignoux, 1837.

Ford, Mark, ed. *London: A History in Verse*. Cambridge, MA / London: Belknap Press, 2012.

Gentles, R. L. "Convalescence." *The Saint Pauls Magazine* 12 (April 1873): pp. 458–463.

Granger, Mary Ethel. *Life Renewed: A Manual for Convalescents Arranged for Daily Reading*. London: Longmans, 1891.

Hermel, Edmond Marc. *Essai sur le traitement de la convalescence par l'hygiène: Thèse*. Paris: Rignoux, 1837.

Holden, Anthony. *The Wit in the Dungeon: A Life of Leigh Hunt*. London: Little, Brown, 2005.

Hopkins, Jane Ellice. *Sick-Bed Vows, and How to Keep Them: A Book for Convalescents*. London: J. Nisbet, 1869.

Lamb, Charles. "The Londoner". In *Poems and Essays of Charles Lamb*, 485–487. London: Frederick Warne & Co., 1879.

———. "The Convalescent." In *The Essays of Elia*, 246–250. London: Macmillan, 1910.

Lefebvre, Henri. *Rhythmanalysis: Space, Time and Everyday Life*, translated by Stuart Elden and Gerald Moore. New York: Continuum, 2004.

Lowry, Somerset. *Convalescence: Its Blessings, Trials, Duties, and Dangers*. London: Skeffington & Sons, 1895.

Milman, Robert. *Convalescence: Thoughts for Those who are Recovering from Sickness*. London: Whittaker, 1865.

Nietzsche, Friedrich. *Thus Spoke Zarathustra*, edited by Adrian del Caro and Robert B. Pippin. Trans. Adrian del Caro. New York: Cambridge University Press, 2006.

Poe, Edgar Allan. *Selected Tales*, edited by David van Leer. Oxford: Oxford University Press, 1998.

Sharpe, William. *New York Nocturne: The City After Dark in Literature Painting, and Photography, 1850–1950*. Princeton, NJ: Princeton University Press, 2008.

Sontag, Susan. *Illness as Metaphor*. New York: Farrar, Straus and Giroux, 1978.

Stevenson, Robert Louis. "Ordered South." In *Virginibus Puerisque and Other Papers*, 137–163. London: C. Kegan Paul & Co, 1861.

Stoker, Bram. *Dracula*. London: Penguin, 2003.

Tambling, Jeremy. *Dickens' Novels as Poetry*. New York: Routledge, 2015.

Tester, Keith, ed. *The Flâneur*. London: Routledge, 1994.

Vrettos, Athena. *Somatic Fictions: Imagining Illness in Victorian Culture*. Stanford, CA: Stanford University Press, 1995.

Whitman, Walt. *Leaves of Grass and Other Works*, edited by Michael Moon. New York, W. W. Norton & Co, 2002.

Woolf, Virginia. *Jacob's Room*. Oxford: Oxford University Press, 2008.

Notes

[1] Henri Lefebvre, *Rhythmanalysis*, trans. Stuart Elden and Gerald Moore (New York: Continuum, 2004), 27.
[2] Keith Tester, "Introduction," in *The Flâneur*, ed. Tester (London: Routledge, 1994), 7.
[3] Charles Baudelaire, *The Painter of Modern Life*, trans. P. E. Charvet (London: Penguin, 2010), 13.
[4] Ibid., 56.
[5] Robert Milman, "Notice," in *Convalescence: Thoughts for Those who are Recovering from Sickness* (London: Whittaker, 1865).
[6] See Somerset Lowry, *Convalescence* (London: Skeffington & Sons, 1895) and Jane Ellice Hopkins, *Sick-Bed Vows* (London: J. Nisbet, 1869).
[7] Milman, *Convalescence*, 61.
[8] Ibid., 75.
[9] Ibid., 61.
[10] Charles Lamb, "The Convalescent," in *The Essays of Elia* (London: Macmillan, 1910), 250.
[11] Anon., "Convalescence," *Boston Medical Intelligencer*, Volume III, Issue 45 (1826), 179.
[12] Ibid., 179.
[13] Athena Vrettos, *Somatic Fictions* (Stanford, CA: Stanford University Press, 1995), 1.
[14] Ibid., 16.
[15] Susan Sontag, *Illness as Metaphor* (New York: Farrar, Straus and Giroux, 1978), 3.
[16] In *Medoline Selwyn's Work* (Boston, MA: Ira Bradley & Co, 1889), 375, Hattie Colter, like Lamb in "The Convalescent," discusses recovery in geographical terms when she describes the convalescent as "one who had been visiting dim, mysterious shores, and had got safely back from those outlying regions." Of course, what the religious and medical writers examined here have shown is the danger of using such an almost foolhardy adverb as "safely," which ignores the spectre of relapse.
[17] Tester, *The Flâneur*, 7.
[18] Hyacinthe Dubranle, *Essai sur la convalescence: Thèse* (Paris: Rignoux, 1837), 5.
[19] Edmond Marc Hermel, *Essai sur le traitement de la convalescence par l'hygiène: Thèse* (Paris: Rignoux, 1837), 9.
[20] Ibid., 10.
[21] Giorgio de Chirico, "Meditations of a Painter," translated by Louise Bourgeois and Robert Goldwater, in *Theories of Modern Art: A Source Book for Artists and Critics*, ed. Herschel B. Chipp (Berkeley, CA: University of California Press, 1969), 397.
[22] Friedrich Nietzsche, *Thus Spoke Zarathustra*, translated by Adrian del Caro, ed. Adrian del Caro and Robert B Pippin (New York: Cambridge University Press, 2006), 174.
[23] Peter Ackroyd, *London* (London: Chatto and Windus, 2000), 1.
[24] Amy Levy, "A March Day in London," in *London*, ed. Mark Ford (Cambridge, MA: Belknap Press, 2012), 465.
[25] Dickens, "Night Walks," in *Dickens' Journalism*, Vol 4, ed. John Drew and Michael Slater (London: J. M. Dent, 2000), 150; Dickens, to Catherine Dickens, 25 March 1851, in *The Pilgrim Edition of the Letters of Charles Dickens*, Vol 6, ed. Graham Storey, Kathleen Mary Tillotson, and Nina Burgis (Oxford: Oxford University Press, 1988), 333.
[26] Dickens, "Night Walks", in *Dickens' Journalism*, 150.

²⁷ Jeremy Tambling, *Dickens' Novels as Poetry* (New York: Routledge, 2015), 16.
²⁸ Walter Benjamin, *The Writer of Modern Life*, ed. Michael W Jennings, trans. Howard Eiland et al. (Cambridge, MA: Belknap Press 2006), 152.
²⁹ De Chirico, "Meditations of a Painter", 397.
³⁰ Samuel Taylor Coleridge, *Biographia Literaria*, ed. Adam Roberts (Edinburgh: Edinburgh University Press, 2014), 62.
³¹ Ibid., 62.
³² Baudelaire, *The Painter of Modern Life*, 10.
³³ Arthur Schopenhauer, quoted in De Chirico, "Meditations of a Painter", 397.
³⁴ Benjamin, *The Writer of Modern Life*, 170.
³⁵ Lefebvre, *Rythmanalysis*, 27.
³⁶ Dubranle, *Essai sur la Convalescence*, 13.
³⁷ Baudelaire, *The Painter of Modern Life*, 10.
³⁸ Robert Louis Stevenson, "Ordered South", in *Virginibus Puerisque and Other Papers* (London: C Kegan Paul & Co, 1861), 153.
³⁹ Baudelaire, *The Painter of Modern Life*, 11.
⁴⁰ Ibid., 11.
⁴¹ Ibid., 7, 10.
⁴² "Convalescence", *Saturday Review of Politics, Literature, Science and Art* Volume 44 (October 1877), 417.
⁴³ Ibid., 417.
⁴⁴ Virginia Woolf, *Jacob's Room* (Oxford: Oxford University Press, 2008), 162.
⁴⁵ Hermel, *Essai sur le traitement de la convalescence*, 7.
⁴⁶ 'Convalescence', *Saturday Review*, 417.
⁴⁷ Milman, *Convalescence*, 61.
⁴⁸ Edgar Allan Poe, "The Man of the Crowd", in *Selected Tales*, ed. David van Leer (Oxford: Oxford University Press, 1998), 84.
⁴⁹ Michel de Certeau, *The Practice of Everyday Life*, translated by Steven F. Rendall (Berkely, CA: University of California Press), 112.
⁵⁰ Leigh Hunt, quoted in Anthony Holden, *The Wit in the Dungeon* (London: Little Brown, 2005), 205;
Poe, "The Man of the Crowd," 84.
⁵¹ R. L. Gentles, "Convalescence," in *The Saint Pauls Magazine* Volume 12 (April 1873), 458.
⁵² Ibid., 458–459.
⁵³ Lamb, "The Convalescent,", 246.
⁵⁴ Poe, "The Man of the Crowd," 85.
⁵⁵ Ibid., 85.
⁵⁶ Hermel, *Essai sur le traitement de la convalescence*, 28.
⁵⁷ Poe, "The Man of the Crowd," 86.
⁵⁸ Ibid., 86.
⁵⁹ Ibid., 86; Giorgio de Chirico, *Memoirs of Giorgio de Chirico*, translated by Margaret Crosland (New York: Da Capo Press, 1994), 60–61.
⁶⁰ Poe, "The Man of the Crowd," 87–88.
⁶¹ Lefebvre, *Rhythmanalysis*, 27.
⁶² Poe, "The Man of the Crowd," 91.
⁶³ Baudelaire, *The Painter of Modern Life*, 10.

64 Ibid., 10.
65 Matthew Beaumont, *Nightwalking* (London: Verso, 2016), 410;
William Sharpe, *New York Nocturne: The City After Dark in Literature Painting, and Photography, 1850–1950* (Princeton, NJ: Princeton University Press, 2008), 72. Sharpe adds that 'in eighteenth– and early nineteenth–century English literature, "d———" usually stands for "damned". The two men of the crowd are fellow fiends, incarnations of the modern night, unable to exist apart from the throng'.
66 Poe, "The Man of the Crowd," 90–91;
Milman, *Convalescence*, 61.
67 Poe, "The Man of the Crowd," 91.
68 Mary Ethel Granger, *Life Renewed: A Manual for Convalescents Arranged for Daily Reading* (London: Longmans, 1891), 12.
69 Bram Stoker, *Dracula* (London: Penguin, 2003), 169.
70 Baudelaire, *The Painter of Modern Life*, 13.
71 Stoker, *Dracula*, 184.
72 Baudelaire, *The Painter of Modern Life*, 13.
73 Ibid., 10.
74 De Chirico, "Meditations of a Painter," 397.
75 Walt Whitman, "The Sleepers," in *Leaves of Grass and Other Works*, ed. Michael Moon (New York, W. W. Norton & Co, 2002), 356.
76 Stevenson, "Ordered South," 153.
77 Whitman, "The Sleepers," 357.
78 Ibid., 357;
Baudelaire, *The Painter of Modern Life*, 10.
79 Whitman, "The Sleepers," 363.
80 Ibid., 363.
81 Lamb, "The Londoner," in *Poems and Essays of Charles Lamb* (London: Frederick Warne & Co., 1879), 486.
82 Whitman, "The Sleepers," 363–364.

Chapter 17

The Lessons (Not) Learned: Literary Bioethics and Biopolitics from Stoker to Atwood

Ronja Tripp-Bodola

Louisiana State University, USA

Abstract: This chapter discusses biopolitics and bioethics as a broader epistemological framework that transverses a number of topics. It takes a look at narratives, from Stoker's *Dracula* to Atwood's *The Handmaid's Tale*, and traces bioethics and the Foucauldian concept of biopolitics in these narratives to argue that these concepts are at the core of the literature/medicine interactions in the long twentieth century. By offering an exemplary overview that illustrates the overarching socio-political take of literature biopolitics and bioethics and its ramifications for contemporary bio-social concerns, this chapter ultimately contributes to the discussion of literature's importance for the field of medical humanities and argues for an integration of literary biopolitics into medical education.

Keywords: Michel Foucault, biopolitics, bioethics, docile bodies, literature and medicine, medical humanities.

* * *

In his study on *Biopolitics and the Novel,* Arne de Boever writes "while much has been said about Foucault and literature and about literature's relation to disciplinary power, the connection between literature and biopolitics remains relatively unexplored" (2013, 9). This contribution would like to continue this exploration in more historical depth. It argues that both, bioethics and the Foucauldian concept of biopolitics are the main trajectory of literary-medical interactions in the long twentieth century, and that their broader epistemological framework transverses a number of topics discussed in this collection. This chapter offers exemplary readings of medical ethics as well as the connection between bacteriology and colonial racism in Bram Stoker's *Dracula* (1897), substance use and psychiatric biopower in Aldous Huxley's *Brave New World* (1932) and *Brave New World Revisited* (1958), as well as the ethics of pain and care in Samuel Beckett's *Malone Dies* (1956). The fictional academic response in Margaret Atwood's *The Handmaid's Tale* (1985) will serve as a springboard for my concluding remarks. I hope to illustrate that the overarching socio-political take of literature on matters of biopower offers not just a representation of biopolitics or ethics, but a critical view on healthcare, its practices, discourse and institutions that is central to medical humanities, and that it should become part of the medical education as it reverberates in contemporary discussions of systemic inequities in healthcare, exacerbated by the COVID -19 pandemic.

Biopolitics and Bioethics

In early May 2020, President Trump was visiting a factory that was commissioned to make protective equipment, specifically N95 masks, to address shortage and meet heightened demand (Keith 2020). The president, himself not wearing a mask, was shown around the facility while the PA blasted the Guns N' Roses song, "Live and let Die." He told the workers, "'You're part of this incredible industrial mobilization— the biggest since World War II, [...] you make America proud'" (Keith 2020). This anecdote illustrates the basic principles of biopower, and points to the topicality of the concept. At the same time, it demonstrates how a simple lyrical comment can underscore and at the same time challenge and expose Trump's agenda.

Biopolitics, biopower and governmentality are terms that were coined by the historian Michel Foucault and developed over two lecture series and in several of his book-length studies. It received much attention in more contemporary debates on genetics, ethics, and totalitarianism (Agamben 1998, Malabou 2008). Biopolitics, according to Foucault, emerged during the nineteenth century as a new form of governmental power:

> [W]e now have the emergence, with this technology of biopower, of this technology of power over 'the' population as such, over men insofar as they *are living beings*. It is continuous scientific, and it is the power *to make live*. Sovereignty took life and let live. And now we have the emergence of a power that I would call the power of regularization and it, in contrast, consists in making live and letting die. (Foucault 2003, 247)

According to Foucault, we have two modes of power-relation: "the body-organism-discipline-institutions series," and the "population-biological processes-regulatory mechanism-State" (250). An example for the first series would be corporeal punishment and imprisonment. The second series doesn't need coercion or force; people gladly practice hygiene to prevent infections or take birth control measures. Foucault calls the notion of governing on the basis of willing participation "governmentality."

And thus, the "biological came under State control" (240). It was controlling "birth, death, production, illness, and so on" (242-243) with certain techniques (and technologies) of power, for instance: demographic surveys and statistics, birth control, hygiene, vaccination and other medical improvements. With the shift in focus onto living, death became a taboo, the "most private thing of all" (248). Furthermore, the attempt to eliminate accidents or epidemics means that "[p]ower has no control over death, but it can control mortality" (Ibid.). Hence, these biopolitical techniques aim to regulate the biological processes of humankind in order to subtly secure stability, an "equilibrium" (240) which rests on the normalization of biological processes. But the measures also include working-class housing, education, child care, and other "[a]ttempts [...] to increase their productive force" (242). This illustrates that biopolitics did not — and does not — replace sovereignty completely, but still employed at least the "disciplinary technology of labor" (Ibid.), connecting biopolitics to neoliberalism.

Medicine, of course, is essential to a biopower, as Foucault writes,

> because of the link it establishes between scientific knowledge of both biological and organic processes [and] medicine becomes a political intervention-technique with specific power-effects. Medicine is a power-knowledge that can be applied to both the body and the population [...] and it will therefore have both disciplinary effects and regulatory effects. (252)

Medicine and particularly the practices, discourses and episteme of what later became public health have been intricately linked to regulatory practices and institutions such as insurance, urban planning, etc. Herein lies the root of health disparities and inequities in the outcome because at the same time, racism as well as war against the "Other" are "inscribed as the basic mechanism of power." As Foucault explains, both war and racism are necessary means to the biopolitical end — justified by biological or scientific reasoning, such as eugenics, and linked to the logic of war: my enemy must die so that I can live. Moreover, "[t]he fact that the other dies does not mean simply that I live in the sense that his death guarantees my safety; the death of the other, the death of the bad race, of the inferior race (or the degenerate, the abnormal) is something that will make life in general healthier: healthier and purer" (255). Especially the link between race and the "degenerate" once again brings to the fore the role of medical discourse and the power of the physician in determining what is normal, and that the degenerate madman and the racial are posing a similar threat to the biopolitical state.

As Foucault pointed out in another lecture from the same series, gothic novels are both political novels and science fiction. As "politics fiction" (Foucault 2003, 212), they focus essentially "on the abuse of power," and as science fiction "their function is to reactivate [...] a whole knowledge about feudalism" and its governing principles. These categories apply to Bram Stoker´s late Victorian novel *Dracula*.

Fighting Contagious Otherness — Bram Stoker's *Dracula* (1897)

The disease— for not to be all well is a disease— interest me.

— Stoker, *Dracula*

Jørgensen calls Stoker "a seismograph of late Victorian science and culture (2015, 41), and *Dracula* certainly was the product of scientific as well as political *zeitgeist*. The socio-cultural and medical changes that had taken place over the previous few decades had profound and long-lasting effects on modern medicine as well as Victorian literature. They were biopolitical in nature, and steeped in bioethical debates: Darwinism, evolutionism, bacteriology as a new, emerging field alongside an early biologist psychiatry. The Contagious Diseases Act and the law that prohibited vivisection were just passed, and the medical profession dominated the scientific discourse, its gaze and its politics.

Late Victorian sensed the pending decline of the British Empire and a backlash of centuries of unchecked colonial exploitation and terror. In his seminal article "The Occidental Tourist," Arata (1990) discusses how closely Stoker's novel is linked to the fear of counter-colonialism. The novel has frequently been read as the clash of old order of pre-enlightenment feudalism still haunting the modern, science-based and progress-oriented democratic power. What makes *Dracula* stand out among other novels of the 1890s is the extent to which medicine, bioethics and doctors are involved in the plot. More than that, *Dracula* exemplifies the deployment of biopower in response to the racial, dehumanized Other, the counter-colonial invader. And who would be better suited to represent this governmentality than the two doctors.

Significantly, in his rewriting of the established tradition of vampiric literature, Stoker added the lunatic asylum, the degenerate madman and the doctor (Pedlar 2006, 136), elements central to his novel. The notorious, eccentric Abraham Van Helsing "M.D., D. Ph., D. Lit. etc. etc." (Stoker 1997, 106) became synonymous with vampire hunters in the cultural imaginary. Dr. Seward, on the other hand, is less known despite the fact that it is his medical voice that dominates the discourse — as literally his voice, as he keeps his diary with a phonograph.

The use of this ground-breaking recording device marks him as the modern man of science and technology. His first entry, however, presents him to the reader as a patient, a man who is suffering from unrequited love. Lucy Westenra, the first London victim of the Count, had just rejected Seward's courtship. He tries to "cure" his lovesickness by dealing with his patients, regaining control and power:

> Since my rebuff of yesterday I have a sort of empty feeling [...] As I knew that the only cure for this sort of thing was work, I went down amongst the patients. I picked out one who has afforded me a study of much interest. [...] I questioned him more fully than I had ever done, with a view to making myself master of the facts of his hallucination. In my manner of doing it there was, I now see, something of cruelty. I seemed to wish to keep him to the point of his madness— [...]. (61)

After a blow to his masculinity, his response is to empower himself through dominating his patient as he wants to become the "master" of his case while "keeping" him where he is. From the very beginning, Dr. Seward's character points to the power relations involved in psychiatric patient care and exacerbates them to the point of abuse. The "lunatic" or degenerate is conceived of as a subhuman subject for study, a problem to be solved; he is not regarded as a suffering individual to be cured (Pedlar 2006, 156). In this regard, Steward and Van Helsing are physicians very typical of their times (Groom 2018, 135).

Van Helsing is, according to Seward, a "philosopher and a metaphysician, and one of the most advanced scientists of his day; and he has [...] an absolutely open mind" (Stoker 1997, 106). Seward, on the contrary, is a representative of narrow-minded rationality, he is ill-equipped to understand the concepts that Van Helsing brings up, so he labels them abnormal (Pedlar 2006, 145): "'Dr. Van Helsing, are you mad?' He raised his head and looked at me [...]. 'Would I were!' he said" (Stoker 1997, 173). Accordingly, his diagnoses, particularly psychiatric diagnoses, are inherently unethical:

> I gave Renfield a strong opiate to-night, enough to make even him sleep, and took away his pocket-book to look at it. [...] My homicidal maniac is of a peculiar kind. I shall have to invent a new classification for him, and call him a zoöphagous (life-eating) maniac; [...] He gave many flies to one spider and many spiders to one bird, and then wanted a cat to eat the many birds. What would have been his later steps? It would almost be worthwhile to complete the experiment. [...] Men sneered at vivisection, and yet look at its results to-day! [...] Had I even the secret of one such mind—did I hold the key to the fancy of even one lunatic—I might advance my own branch of science to a pitch compared with which Burdon-Sanderson's physiology or Ferrier's brain-knowledge would be as nothing. (Stoker 1997, 71)

The "Cruelty to Animals Act" (1876) and the anti-vivisection movement that Dr Seward is referring had raised questions about medical bioethics, specifically about research motives and cruelty (Groom 2018, 136–137). While Renfield is treated as a specimen that the scientist collects, observes and then classifies, quite in concordance with the scientific methods of his time, the animals are worth being sacrificed for the greater good.[1]

The novel exposes the ethical implications of categorization, diagnosing and patient care by making the inherent abuse more pronounced. In addition to Dr. Seward's motivations, he sedates the patient for no medical reason but to steal his notebook. This is a significant detail because it points to the relation of writing, recording and classifying in colonial and biopolitical discourse, and Renfield's notes challenge the power relation of the doctor-patient interaction Butler (2002, 18); therefore, suggesting to call Renfield a "graphomaniac patient." The raw data of numbers and charts that he creates is closely connected to the colonial practices and therefore points to the counter-colonization, as Renfield acts as an executive clerk who writes more when Dracula is near.

Dracula's counter-colonization (Arata 1990) is not just feared because of potential racial contamination or his uncontrolled, unregulated reproduction.[2] His procreation and "aristocratic immortality" (Pedlar 2006, 140) aims at "colonis[ing] the world with his own kind" (139) that is neither alive nor dead and therefore outside of the biopolitical control. As a sovereign power, Count Dracula is killing and letting select few live who then continue his mission. Thus, he threatens the subversion of the entire biopower, so vampires are constructed to represent the Other that they can "let die":

> [E]volution, degeneration, socio-biology and eugenics were appropriated to legitimate and expand imperial hegemony in their identification of

symptoms of degeneration in marginalized individuals and communities of different sexualities, classes and 'races' or national identities and their promotion of health and fitness for the imperial body and the perpetuation of the Empire. (Mousoutzanis 2011, 61)

The vampires are killed by the doctors because they are conceptualised not simply as an inferior, but as a different species. This also ties in with the history of colonization, since it had been intertwined with bacteriology and the fear of uncontrollable epidemics (Jørgensen 2015, 36) which led to the introduction of tropical medicine into the colonial apparatus. Obstacles to the colonial endeavour were often "pathogenic, hitherto unidentified microorganisms" (39). Bacteria were thought of as more aggressive and destructive than other pathogenic factors. Their procreative qualities made them more powerful, and their invisibility an object of fear. Furthermore, the medical discourse explicitly compared bacteria to demons, while the surging spiritualism movement "found scientific legitimacy in its reference to bacteria" (Jørgensen 2015, 41).

Accordingly, Jørgensen (2015, 40) links late-nineteenth-century narratives of vampiric epidemics directly to the advent of bacteriology, and points out that some of the cures offered by Van Helsing are directly rooted in the notion of hygienic, antiseptic prevention of contagion, such as sterilizing the earth or using garlic, a natural antibiotic. Also, the disease or illness that Lucy is suffering from is described in terms of symptoms of tuberculosis. And finally, Dracula himself is characterized by "bacteria-like features. The count is polymorphic, and one of the forms he adopts is infinitesimal dust particles [...]. In this shape, he is capable of entering even hermetically sealed rooms" (Jørgensen 2015, 41).

Vampires are conceptualized into an invasive subhuman species that challenges the biopower and brings its ethical structures to light. And while biopower and governmentality triumphs in the end, the questions of ethics in *Dracula* remain ambiguous. The physician's role as a representative of biopower is brought to light. They all are dominating the narrative and the discourse with their diagnoses of degeneration. "Madness," as Pedlar writes, "is a focal point" (2006, 156). Not only does Seward defend vivisectors who were demonised by society (Groom 2018, 136), but the way Seward treats Renfield hints at a "sinister [sign] that the doctor is aligned with Dracula; and the lunatic is one locus of their struggle for mastery" (Pedlar 2006, 142).

Chemical Persuasion and Docile Bodies — Huxley, *Brave New World* (1932)

Many of Aldous Huxley's works are all based on cutting-edge medical and scientific research at the times they were written. His family had a scientific legacy: his grandfather T.H. Huxley was an eminent biologist who shaped Victorian modern medicine significantly and was nicknamed "Darwin's Bulldog" for being an outspoken evolutionist. His brother Julian was an award-winning biologist and populariser of science, as was Huxley himself.

Brave New World is a biopolitical dystopian vision that takes the developments of nineteenth-century biopolitics to its fictional extreme (Tripp 2014). One of the most pronounced and widely discussed biopolitical aspects of Huxley's dystopian novel is gene-technology and reproduction politics. Substance use is an aspect that might be less obvious to a critique of biopower because it is associated with addiction. In Huxley's novel, it foregrounds the nexus of biopolitical discourse, practices and something Foucault referred to as the "docile body" (Foucault 1979, 135-169).

The world depicted in Huxley's 1932 dystopia is divided into two parts, the civilized world and the so-called savages. The savages practice and represent everything that the *Brave New World* tries to exclude, they represent the Other to the new world order. They are riddled by a number of maladies including alcoholism— a nasty, dirty habit, while the civilized world uses soma, a clean synthetic new drug. It does not cause any physical dependency, nor is it stigmatised as an addiction. On the contrary, using this substance is widely accepted and even expected of the citizens. It becomes part of the governmentality. As Huxley later wrote in *Brave New World Revisited*, "[w]henever anyone felt depressed or below par, he would swallow a tablet or two of a chemical compound called soma" (2007, 296).

A common propagandistic saying in the novel is, "[e]verybody's happy now," "now" indicating the contrast to previous social orders. Accordingly, the status quo must be preserved at all costs. Its stability, according to the government, is endangered by emotions in general and emotional relationships in particular. Thus, society depends on the social stability and equilibrium of the castes, the uninterrupted consumption and the pleasure principle of "happiness." And if ever anything unpleasant should somehow happen, there's always *soma*: "to calm your anger, to reconcile you to your enemies, to make you patient and long suffering. [...] Now, you swallow two or three half-gramme tablets, and there you are. Anybody can be virtuous now. You can carry at least half your morality about in a bottle. Christianity without tears— that's what *soma* is" (213).

The chemical substance *soma*, the Greek word for "body," is another indication of the biopolitical "processes-regulatory" mechanisms of power. Alcohol, still drunk by the "savages," would "incapacitate [someone] as a citizen," it "marks the disintegration of personality" (Stankiewicz 2001, 35) and renders them less productive, effective and useful to the state. Alcohol is directed at *zoe*, soma operates as the life-style drug on the level of *bios*.

Furthermore, it suggests a substitution for the Eucharist tradition. Thus, it not only becomes the new hedonistic "religion" — "Christianity without tears" — but, in replacing the body of Christ (his *soma*), it becomes a substitute for life itself and thus the epitome of the biopolitical agenda.

In his chapter "Chemical Persuasion" in *Brave New World Revisited*, Huxley points out how much the substance use policy was part of a totalitarian regime aimed to control the masses:

> In the *Brave New World* the soma habit was not a private vice; it was a political institution, it was the very essence of the Life, Liberty and Pursuit of Happiness guaranteed by the Bill of Rights. But this most precious of the subjects' inalienable privileges was at the same time one of the most powerful instruments of rule in the dictator's armory. (Huxley 2007, 297)

The aim is to create "both happy and docile" citizens in this fictional world (Ibid.). The "docile bodies" in a biopolitical setup are different from those Foucault described at a time of sovereign power as these are steeled by a rigorous self-discipline that expresses the internalized anticipation of punishment. That body is the body of a soldier that "is manipulated, shaped, trained, [it] obeys, responds, becomes skilful and increases its forces" (Foucault 1979, 136).

Via the nineteenth-century factory worker, this leads to Huxley's biopolitical dystopias where bodies become mostly consumers to propel the neo-liberalist economy. These bodies are docile not by means of discipline and punishment, but by psychological and chemical "persuasion" on a reward-based logic to decrease resistance. Yet, this is only one use of substances that are not stigmatized as addictions. As Huxley is pointing out, a:

> dictator could [...] ensure himself against political unrest by changing the chemistry of his subjects' brains and so making them content with their servile condition. He could use tranquillizers to calm the excited, stimulants to arouse enthusiasm in the indifferent, hallucinants to distract the attention of the wretched from their miseries. But how, it may be asked, will the dictator get his subjects to take the pills that will make them think, feel and behave in the ways he finds desirable? In all probability it will be enough merely to make the pills available. (2007, 301)

Governmentality in its extreme! Looking back and re-evaluating his own dystopian novel almost three decades later, he observes that the "non-existent ripple of 1931 has become a tidal wave of biochemical and psychopharmacological research" (Huxley 2007, 298). In the 1960s at the latest, it became clear that pills were made readily available and could be easily be attached the proverb "mother's little helpers." Substance use is only one means among many by which the novel utilizes the contemporary developments in psychopharmacology and recreational drugs to drive its socio-critical message. It points to bioethics and systems of diagnosing that has the power to sanction or stigmatise behaviour what is considered a medicinal substance use and what is considered as a substance use disorder? What constitutes a physical dependency and what an addiction? And, above all, what purpose does that diagnosis serve in the larger biopolitical framework of a society? Huxley has several suggestions:

> Meanwhile pharmacology, biochemistry and neurology are on the march, and we can be quite certain that, in the course of the next few years, new and better chemical methods for increasing suggestibility and lowering psychological resistance will be discovered. [...] They may help the psychiatrist in his battle against mental illness, or they may help the dictator in his battle against freedom. More probably [...] will both enslave and make free, heal and at the same time destroy. (Huxley 2007, 303)

Huxley's comparison of the psychiatrist to a dictator suggests that their power-relations are comparable, moreover, that their means are analogous and geared towards similar ends. Their care is ambiguous, and care taking always inherently a power-relation, as we have seen above in regards to Dr. Seward and his patient, and we shall reencounter later in Beckett's uncared for, and uncaring characters.

Letting Oneself Die and Ethics of Pain — Beckett, *Malone Dies* (1956)

> I didn't understand women at that period. [...] Nor men either. Nor animals either. What I understand best, which is not saying much, are my pains.
>
> — Beckett, "First Love"

From his early prose to the late plays, Beckett's characters have been in physical pain. They suffer from accidents, violence or simply physical decline. Regardless of the cause, acuity or chronicity, they talk about it even if something is just "unspeakably painful" (Beckett 2010, 50). The trilogy of novels that were all published in the 1950s — *Molloy, Malone Dies* and *The*

Unnamable— are no exceptions. Molloy walks on crutches, and in *The Unnamable*, "Beckett goes inside of verbal consciousness and probes the tormenting experience of speaking" (Tsushima 2012, 225). In the following, I will focus on the dying Malone who suffers from pains "deep down in my trunk, I cannot be more explicit" (Beckett 2010, 192).

Pain in Beckett's work has been looked at in several ways, as the most recent collection by Tanaka et al. (2012) illustrates. However, the pervasive approach is still one that sees "pain" as a phenomenological proof of an existence that falls short of representation, one that is literally outside, *ek-sistent*, of the subject constituted by and through language. Accordingly, pain could be read as pain the subject feels when faced with the limits and shortcomings of language (Tsushima 2012). However, as I have argued elsewhere in regard to *Endgame* (Bodola 2020), Beckett's aesthetics was one of the "un-word" that calls for linguistic, performative and medial violence, destruction rather than deconstruction. Accordingly, pain is a necessary by-product. The characters are not in pain because everything is meaningless, it is their mode of existence.

Malone is bedridden, he can only move his head and hand. He is completely "impotent" (Beckett 2010, 178). He thinks that with "a little effort" (173) he could kill himself, "[b]ut it is just as well to let myself die" (173) — transposing the sovereign power to end his own life (the only potency that is left) onto the biopolitical sphere. Instead, he uses a pencil and his exercise book to tell his own story lying naked in his bed in a room that he never leaves. His frame narrative is intermingled with that of a boy, Sapo, who turns into Macmann growing up. Both characters are probably Malone at a younger age.

As he doesn't remember how he got there, Malone is not sure where he is, but he is sure it is "not a room in a hospital, or a madhouse" because he had "listened at different hours of the day and night and never heard anything suspicious" (177), though he said he is "looked after" (178). The same is true for Macmann who "came to again [...] in a kind of asylum" (248) called Saint John of God. Words like keeper, inmates and the fact that they don't have names but numbers "Let one hundred and sixty-six get up and go out," (260) suggest a forensic institution of sorts. This is supported by Malone telling us about how many people he killed and his frequent violent thoughts. Malone is completely alone while Macmann still interacts with his keeper:

> When asked for example to state whether Saint John of God's was a private institution or run by the State, a hospice for the aged and infirm or a madhouse, if once in one might entertain the hope of one day getting out and, in the affirmative, by means of what steps, Lemuel remained for a long time plunged in thought, sometimes for as long as ten minutes or a quarter of an hour, motionless [...]. It usually ended

by his saying he did not know. [...] Then he would add, But I'll enquire. And taking out a notebook as fat as a ship's log he made note, murmuring, Private or state, mad or like me, how out, etc. Macmann could then be sure he would never hear any more about it. (259-260)

This Kafkaesque atmosphere underscores the opaqueness of institutional power as an underlying principle. Without revealing its control mechanisms, it physically and mentally disciplines and abuses the subjects, if only through neglect or abandonment. Malone on his death bed, therefore, is the incarnation of the docile body which gradually internalized the external abuse.[3] The setting, on the other hand, represents what Foucault called heterotopia– literally the "other spaces" outside of our society where we exile undesired bodies, everything that poses a biopolitical threat and made into a taboo such as death, sickness and "degeneracy": cemeteries, hospitals, prisons and mental institutions.

As Kennedy (2019, 5) argues, "from *More Pricks than Kicks* to *Malone Dies*" Beckett's engagement with biopower was directed at "Irish psychiatric power" and how it "produced its object for the purposes of social regulation in the guise of care/cure." Whether it is a mental institution that Malone is in or not, the care (or lack thereof) that he receives is a prominent aspect in the novel. Not only are the caretakers actually keepers, they are abusive. Malone remembers that at first, he was looked after by an "old women" (Beckett 2010, 149) who was "good" to him, inquired about his needs but now all he sees is "the gaunt hand and part of the sleeve" (149) when his soup is brought. Eventually, this ceases to happen as well, and he finds himself left in his room without food or care. In contrast to that, Macmann starts out with an assigned keeper Moll, who despite being very strict on regulations engages in an intimate, grotesque affair with him. At first, she takes very good care of him, but then falls violently ill, deteriorating right in front of his eyes. The tables have turned, now he is the careless caretaker. As suggested by his other keeper Lemuel in the quote above ("mad or like me?"), the lines are blurred between inmate and keeper.

Macmann/Malone is literally and figuratively impotent, and passively exposed to the abuse. The only thing that Macmann does is ask questions, the only thing that Malone does is write questions down for the "visitor" who comes in to beat him (Beckett 2010, 265). Asking what ails the infirmed, what their needs are, just like his caretaker does at the very beginning, is the ethical thing to do. That has been a literary trope for centuries and is rooted in the notion of *caritas*, charity, in Christian Middle Ages. Parceval, the Red Knight, fails not because he loses a battle, but because he fails to ask the infirmed Fisher King what is wrong with him.

As writing is all that is left to Malone, it is his only means of communication and at the very beginning, he significantly refers to it as "playing the game" (174). This is reminiscent of the language game, a concept Wittgenstein uses to describe how members of a life form engage with one another to behave responsibly, that is ethically. Wittgenstein's example is that of pain. Taking "I am in pain" both as a statement and as a physical expression, Wittgenstein thinks about the question of how to respond responsibly, literally: to avoid "generaliz[ing] the one case so *irresponsibly*" (italics my emphasis, Wittgenstein 2009, 293) and behaving like an "inhuman brute" (Wittgenstein 1982, 242):

> Suppose that everyone had a box with something in it which we call a "beetle". No one can ever look into anyone else's box, and everyone says he knows what a beetle is only by looking at his beetle. — Here it would be quite possible for everyone to have something different in his box. One might even imagine such a thing constantly changing. — But what if these people's word "beetle" had a use nonetheless? — If so, it would not be as the name of a thing. The thing in the box doesn't belong to the language-game at all; not even as a *Something*: for the box might even be empty. (Wittgenstein 2009, 293)

It doesn't matter what is in the box and if I will ever be able to see (understand) it, it doesn't matter whether the person is just pretending to have pain in the end. What matters is that we play the game: I assume the other person is like me, that she is playing the same game, and that her use of the word pain bears a "family resemblance," in Wittgensteinian terms, to mine, and then asks further questions. That is the responsible, ethical thing to do, not a "brutish" generalisation, a one-fits-all approach that excludes certain bodies — which is the guiding principle of biopolitics, interested only in governing the masses instead of curing and caring for the individual.

Responding to *The Handmaid's Tale* (1985) — in lieu of a conclusion

> Our responsibility begins with the power to imagine.
>
> — Murakami, *Kafka on the Shore*

Murakami's statement was certainly not the first to stress the importance of imagination for ethical behaviour. Universalist approaches to ethics, from Kant to Hare, have argued that the ability to put oneself in somebody else's shoes lies at the foundation of moral actions. Two questions are raised: of what quality is this empathic imagination, and: how can we arrive at ethical behaviour through imagination?

One simplistic answer is literature, and cognitive studies have tried to provide a scientific basis for that claim, which implicitly suggests that English Departments are the most ethical places on Earth. Reading, apparently, is not enough. Moreover, as de Boever argues, the rise of the novel and the rise of biopolitics conspicuously overlap. Literary biopolitics are challenging the politics and policies but they are at the same time complicit in propagating the biopolitical narratives. An extended history of literary biopolitics, that de Boever finds lacking, is not going to change the literary narratives from turning into ethical *pharmaka* (de Boever 2013, 4-5). We can agree on the notion that literary biopolitics matter, but how and to whom?

Margaret Atwood's *The Handmaids Tale* is a powerful biopolitical dystopia with a focus on reproductive rights and feminist suppression in a theocratic totalitarian regime. Adami (2011) reads Atwood's novel as a bioethical comment that extrapolates, imagines if you will, the consequences of our contemporary actions. While this is not wrong, it is literally not the whole story. Atwood's novel is also a cautionary tale about academia missing an opportunity to act on the tale's moral. They don't take Offred's tale or her pains seriously because her story doesn't fit into their historical narrative. They discredit the female source and relativise the totalitarian anti-feminist practices of Gilead. The academic conference that is satirised in the fictional addendum titled "Historical Notes" (Atwood 2010/1985, 311-324) remains ironically ignorant of their own sexism. In Wittgenstein's words, their *brutish* generalisations and their warnings of "caution to pass moral judgment" (Ibid., 15) on the system that reduces human beings to a reproductive organ exposes how unethical the pseudo-objective response is and how impotent this renders the academic discourse.

Recently, the attention has turned to systems and institutions, rather than individual responses and response-abilities. Raising awareness is a zero-sum game, if it doesn't lead to action items that change policies, institutional policies and practices. And it takes a clear understanding of the historical developments that informed these systems. Accordingly, now more than ever, humanities have to follow Ette's call for action and take on *their* responsibility as part of the life sciences (Ette 2010). They need to take their knowledge and skills to places where changes are needed, and not pass on a historical opportunity for change.

This takes us back to the beginning, to the topicality of biopolitics in general and its ramifications for twenty-first-century societies in which (not) wearing a protective mask becomes a political event while the rhetoric is that of war: The idea to invoke the Defence Production Act to make protective gear and the fight against COVID on the "front lines" begs the rhetorical question of who would be the equivalent of disposable cannon fodder. "Black Lives

Matter" point out what should be obvious, but is not a given. Systemic inequities are deeply rooted in nineteenth-century industrialization, urbanization, neoliberalism, and the overarching biopolitical setup. If we don't consider that in our discussions of systemic racism, particularly with regard to the health care system, we will continue to remedy symptoms, instead of causes. Thus, ultimately, this article contributes to the discussion of literature's importance in the field of medical humanities, as much as it points to the importance of the history of medicine and biopolitics that has never been more topical or pressing to integrate into undergraduate, graduate and continued medical education.

Bibliography

Adami, Valentina. *Bioethics Through Literature: Margaret Atwood's Cautionary Tales*. Trier: WVT, 2011.

Agamben, Giorgio. *Homo Sacer. Sovereign Power and Bare Life*, translated by Daniel Heller-Roazen. Stanford: Stanford UP, 1998.

Arata, Stephen D. "The Occidental Tourist: *Dracula* and the Anxiety of Reverse Colonization." *Victorian Studies* 33, no. 4 (Summer 1990): pp. 621–645.

Atwood, Margaret. *The Handmaid's Tale*. London: Vintage, 2010/1985.

Beckett, Samuel. "First Love." (1946). *The Complete Short Prose*. New York: Grove Press, 1995: pp. 25–45.

Beckett, Samuel. *Three Novels*. (1955-1957). New York: Grove Press, 2010.

Bodola, Ronja. "Samuel Beckett, *Endgame*: Die Literatur des Unworts und die Aufgabe des Kritikers." In *Handbuch Literatur und Philosophie*, edited by Andrea Allerkamp and Sarah Schmidt, no pag. Berlin: de Guyter. 2021.

Boever, Arne de. *Narrative Care: Biopolitics and the Novel*. London: Bloomsbury Publishing, 2013.

Bryden, Mary. "'That or Groan.' Paining and De-paining in Beckett." In *Samuel Beckett and Pain*, edited by Tanaka, Mariko Hori, Yoshiki Tajiri et al., 201-215. Amsterdam, New York: Rodopi, 2012.

Butler, Erik. "Writing and Vampiric Contagion in Dracula." *Iowa Journal of Cultural Studies*, no. 2 (2002): pp. 13–32.

Ette, Ottmar. Literature as Knowledge for Living, Literary Studies as Science for Living. *PMLA* 125, no. 4 (2010): pp. 977-993.

Evans, Parker. "Beckett and Bare Life: Post-War Political Subjectivity in *Molloy*." *Estudios Irlandeses: Journal of Irish Studies* 14, no. 2 (2019): pp. 65–77.

Foucault, Michel. *Discipline and Punish: The Birth of the Prison*. London: Vintage, 1979.

Foucault, Michel. *Society Must Be Defended: Lectures at the Collège De France, 1975-76*, edited by Mauro Bertani and Alessandro Fontana, translated by David Macey. New York: Picador, 2003.

Groom, Nick. *The Vampire: A New History*. New Haven: Yale University Press, 2018.

Huxley, Aldous. *Brave New World, including Brave New World Revisited* (1932/1958). New York: Harper Collins, 2007.

Jørgensen, Jens Lohfert. "Bacillophobia: Man and Microbes in *Dracula*, the *War of the Worlds*, and the *Nigger of the 'Narcissus'*." *Critical Survey* 27, no. 2 (2015): pp. 36–49.

Keith, Tamara. "Trump Returns to the Road with Arizona Trip to Mask-Maker." *NPR*, May 5, 2020. Accessed August 15, 2020. https://www.npr.org/2020/05/05/850102811/trump-returns-to-the-road-with-arizona-trip-to-mask-maker.

Kennedy, Seán. "Samuel Beckett and Biopolitics [Special Issue]." *Estudios Irlandeses: Journal of Irish Studies* 14, no. 2 (2019): pp. 1–114.

Malabou, Catherine. *What Should We Do With Our Brain*. New York: Fordham, 2008.

Mousoutzanis, Aris. "'Death Is Irrelevant': Gothic Science Fiction and the Biopolitics of Empire." In *Gothic Science Fiction 1980-2010*, edited by Sara Wasson and Emily Alder, 57–72. Liverpool: Liverpool University Press, 2011.

Murakami, Haruki. *Kafka on the Shore*. New York: Alfred A. Knopf, 2005.

Pedlar, Valerie. "The Zoophagous Maniac: Madness and Degeneracy in Dracula." In *The Most Dreadful Visitation: Male Madness in Victorian Fiction*, edited by Valerie Pedlar, 134–158. Liverpool: Liverpool University Press, 2006.

Sparks, Tabitha. "Medical Gothic and the Return of the Contagious Diseases Acts in Stoker and Machen." *Nineteenth-Century Feminisms*, no. 6 (2002): pp. 87–102.

Stankiewicz, W.J. "Aldous Huxley Our Contemporary (A Political Theorist's View)." *Aldous Huxley Annual*, no. 1 (2001): pp. 31-41.

Stoker, Bram. *Dracula (1897), Authoritative Text, Contexts, Reviews and Reactions, Dramatic and Film Variations, Criticism*, edited by Nina Auerbach and David J. Skal. New York, London: W.W. Norton, 1997.

Tanaka, Mariko Hori, Yoshiki Tajiri, and Michiko Tsushima, eds. *Samuel Beckett and Pain*. Amsterdam, New York NY: Rodopi, 2012.

Tripp, Ronja. "Biopolitical Dystopia: Aldous Huxley, Brave New World (1932)." In *Dystopia, Science Fiction, Post-Apocalypse*, edited by Eckart Voigts and Alessandra Boller, 29–45. Trier: WVT, 2015.

Tsushima, Michiko. "The Appearance of the Human at the Limit of Representation Beckett and Pain in the Experience of Language," In *Samuel Beckett and Pain*, edited by Mariko Tanaka et al., 217-235. Amsterdam, New York: Rodopi, 2012.

Wittgenstein, Ludwig. *Last Writings on the Philosophy of Psychology*. Chicago: University of Chicago Press, 1982.

Wittgenstein, Ludwig. *Philosophical Investigations. The German text with an English translation, fourth revised edition*, edited by P.M.A. Hacker and Joachim Schulte. West Sussex: Wiley Blackwell, 2009.

Notes

[1] Killing the vampires – Lucy, for instance – raises much less concern. The Vampire is even less than an animal, I disagree with Groom (2018, 135) that the Vampires were the ones vivisecting live donors. They were rather portrait as dead beasts that not only can be killed but also can be experimented on without the trace of an ethical conundrum. On the findings of Ferrier, his influence on early biological psychiatry and how this relates to Dr. Seward, see Pedlar (2006, 142).

[2] The novel has received significant attention from feminist critics, and has been discussed extensively in terms of its gender issues, including a reading of Dracula's mating in terms of the contentious Contagious Diseases Act (Sparks 2002).

[3] Evans (2019) reads Molloy with both Foucault and Agamben, a reading that would be rewarding for all three novels. Compare also with Bryden (2012).

Coda:
"How is the pain?"

Mohona Banerjee

Amity University, Noida, India

"How is the pain?"
A simple question
Sets off torrid confusion
Words stumble over each other
Trying to get out
Right.
It is difficult to sieve an answer
Difficult to put thoughts in a straight line
Knowing they will be shot dead
The moment they are out.
Cells mutate and grow into clusters
While you sleep
You wake up to find yourself morphed
Into a nightmare
And you cannot see yourself
In the mirror anymore.
There is no room for reflection.
All there is room for
Is isolation that breeds humiliation
As you feel yourself change
Into something you cannot recognise.
Needles push into your body
You scream in agony
Regret every moment in your past
When you did not worship
What you used to be.
Steel scalpel scrape away
The nightmare,
And the whole of you is held together

By stitches and mind numbing pain.
It is only the pain
That reminds you a nightmare
Has the capacity to walk out
Your imagination
Eat, breathe and be alive.
It is only the pain
That reminds you
You can never be whole
While pieces of you lay abjected
In sterile surgical trays.
Ask me again
How is the pain?
I shall wade through my confusion
And tell you
"I am fine".

Notes on Contributors

Amy W. S. Lee has a background in comparative literature and cultural studies. She has published creative non-fiction as well as critical studies in the area of contemporary feminist fiction, autobiographical writing, witchcraft and magic, and using literature for creative learning experiences. She recently completed an M.A. in Buddhist Studies and is seeking new insights into the autobiographies of Buddhist monks and how the self is presented in such writings. She is an Associate Professor in the Department of Humanities and Creative Writing at Hong Kong Baptist University where she takes advantage of narratives to create interactive and interdisciplinary learning experiences for students.

Anda Pleniceanu is a Ph.D candidate at the Centre for the Study of Theory and Criticism at Western University in Ontario, Canada. She obtained her MA from Western University in Comparative Literature and a BA in Classics from the University of Toronto. Her dissertation attempts to rethink the modern subject in light of the notion of radical negativity. Aside from her dissertation, she does research on texts and concepts that can destabilize our linear and systematic/categorical understanding of the world and ourselves.

Anik Sarkar is an Assistant Professor of English at Salesian College, India. He is currently pursuing his Ph.D from the Department of English, University of North Bengal. His latest publications include "Subjugation and Resilience in the Poems of Meena Kandasamy" in an edited volume, *Perspectives on Indian Dalit Literature* (2020) and "I am a Tree Leaning" in *Environment and Postcolonialism: A Literary Response* (forthcoming, Lexington Books). His novella, *The Man Who Sold Diseases* was published by Juggernaut in 2018.

Ayub Sheik is Associate Professor at the University of Kwazulu-Natal in South Africa. He was previously a Mellon Postdoctoral Fellow at the University of Kwazulu-Natal and a DAAD scholar at the University of Essen, Germany. He has also taught at several universities in Dubai. His research preoccupations are poetry, postgraduate literacy and narrative studies.

Chloe Leung is currently a PhD candidate in English Literature at The University of Edinburgh. Her research interests include Modernism, especially

Virginia Woolf, D.H. Lawrence, and E.M. Forster; Stoic Philosophy; the medical humanities; and the performing arts. She has been awarded a MPhil thesis in September 2019 on Virginia Woolf and Russian ballet in the early 20th century, examining the underexplored physical gestures of Woolf's characters and how their balletic movements stylize emotions.

Edward Grimble lives, writes and teaches in West Sussex, England, having recently obtained degrees from Balliol College, Oxford and the University of Bristol. His research focuses on the depiction and experience of cities in art and literature, and on the literature of both urban and rural walking.

Gabriel Quigley is a PhD candidate in Comparative Literature at New York University. His research interests include interwar modernism, postcolonial theory, critical race theory, disability studies, and twentieth-century philosophy. Amongst other venues, his work has been published in *Samuel Beckett Today / Aujourd'hui* and he is the Special Issues Supervisor for *Interventions* journal of postcolonial studies. His current research project examines how degeneration theory and scientific racism shaped the works of central writers of anglophone modernism, including James Joyce, Samuel Beckett, Djuna Barnes, and Ezra Pound.

Jamil Ahmed, B.A. (Hons.) Philosophy, PG Diploma in Occupational Therapy, is a Doctoral candidate at Middlesex University in London. His research is currently on culture-bound syndromes in the therapeutic context.

With advanced degrees in philosophy and literature, **Meltem Gürle** is a comparative literature scholar from Istanbul. Her research interests are modernity and modernism, the theory of the novel, and the Bildungsroman. Meltem Gürle worked as a lecturer at Boğaziçi University (Istanbul) between 2001- 2016. She continued her research on contemporary Irish and Turkish novel as Marie Skłodowska-Curie Fellow at Trinity College Dublin (2017-2018) and as Fritz Thyssen Fellow at the University of Cologne (2018-2020). Presently, she is working as a guest professor at the University Duisburg-Essen, where she both teaches at the Institute of Turkish Studies and writes her book on the Turkish Bildungsroman.

Mohona Banerjee loves reading and writing poetry. She teaches in Amity University, Noida, India.

Nadia Boudidah Falfoul is an Assistant Professor at the Faculty of Arts and Human Sciences, University of Kairouan, Tunisia. She holds a Ph.D on the discourse of humour in the fiction of contemporary American women writers. She participated in many international conferences organized by Oxford University, The College of London, University of Virginia, University of Texas, etc. Her articles are published in Tunisia and abroad (USA, Britain, Germany).

Nhlanhla Landa and **Sindiso Zhou** are senior lecturers in the Department of English and Comparative Literature in the faculty of Social Sciences and Humanities at the University of Fort Hare in South Africa.

Nina Muždeka is an Associate Professor of Anglophone literature and culture at the University of Novi Sad, Serbia. Her areas of interest include contemporary literatures in English with a special focus on gender theory, genre theory, narratology and media studies. She has published on a broad number of topics including identity construction in fiction, feminist ideology in contemporary British women's fiction, dialogic features of postmodernist fiction, narratological aspects of the construction of news stories, and socio-political and ideological positioning in Nordic Noir. Most notable are her two monographs, one on the issue of genre in Julian Barnes's novels (2006) and the other on magical realism in the novels of Angela Carter (2016).

Ricardo Rato Rodrigues is currently Assistant Professor of Portuguese Studies at UMCS (Uniwersytet Marii Curie-Skłodowskiej w Lublinie), Poland. In 2016, he obtained his PhD in Lusophone Studies from the University of Nottingham, with a thesis entitled *A Silent Scream: Madness and Trauma in the early works of António Lobo Antunes*. Between 2016 and 2018, he worked as Camões Instructor at the Queen Mary, University of London. Currently, a member of several research groups, such as the *International Consortium for the Study of Post Conflict Societies* (University of Nottingham), *International Health Humanities Network* and he also serves an external researcher at Centro de Estudos Humanísticos (CEHUM). His research interests are varied, from trauma and madness in literature and the arts, health humanities, comparative literature (especially in between the lusophone and anglophone contexts), psychiatry, suicide studies, politics in literature, applied drama and gender studies (with a special focus on masculinities).

Ronja Tripp-Bodola, PhD, has published on literature and biopolitics, ethics as well as medicine. She is currently working at LSU Health Sciences Center,

New Orleans, where she is developing a medical humanities curriculum for the Department of Psychiatry. Her publications include "Biopolitical Dystopia. Aldous Huxley, Brave New World (1932)," Dystopia, Science Fiction, Post-Apocalypse, eds. E. Voigts, A. Boller, 2015, pp. 29-46; Picturing Life: Wittgenstein's Visual Ethics, 2016 (co-ed. with K. Schoellner); "Biopower and Docile Bodies: Psychiatry", in Palgrave Encyclopedia of Health Humanities, eds. Paul Crawford and Paul Kadetz, 2020.

Seunghyun Shin is a graduate student in the Department of English at the University of Vermont, USA. He received his Bachelor's degree in English from the University at Albany, SUNY. His research interests include 20th and 21st century American literature, modernism, contemporary poetry, and critical theory. His current research is on William Carlos Williams and contemporary poetry.

Tatiana Prorokova-Konrad is a postdoctoral researcher in the Department of English and American Studies at the University of Vienna, Austria. She holds a PhD in American Studies from the University of Marburg, Germany. She was a Visiting Researcher at the Forest History Society (2019), an Ebeling Fellow at the American Antiquarian Society (2018), and a Visiting Scholar at the University of South Alabama, USA (2016). She is the author of *Docu-Fictions of War: U.S. Interventionism in Film and Literature* (University of Nebraska Press, 2019), the editor of *Transportation and the Culture of Climate Change: Accelerating Ride to Global Crisis* (West Virginia University Press, 2020) and *Cold War II: Hollywood's Renewed Obsession with Russia* (University Press of Mississippi, 2020), and a coeditor of *Cultures of War in Graphic Novels: Violence, Trauma, and Memory* (Rutgers University Press, 2018).

Victoria Lupascu is an Assistant Professor of Comparative Literature and Asian Studies at the University of Montréal. Her areas of interest include medical humanities, visual art, 20th and 21st Chinese literature and Global South studies. Her work explores how writers and artists engage with and produce medical narratives to unveil hidden histories of suffering and marginalization. The current research has a comparative framework and juxtaposes works by authors and artists such as Yan Lianke, DrauzioVarella, Liu Bolin and Cristi Puiu; it examines how their works theorize *disease* and *disposability* as means of cultural and social critique.

Index

A

Abject, xix, 33
Adorno, Theodor, 45
Aeschylus, xvii, xviii, 3, 4, 5, 6, 7, 8, 11, 12, 14, 15, 17
Africa, xviii, xxiv, 19, 20, 21, 24, 25, 28, 105, 108, 109, 177, 178, 179, 191, 192, 227, 228, 230, 231, 239, 241, 242, 243, 287, 289
Al Que Quiere, 114, 121, 122, 125, 126
alienation, xxi, xxiv, 41, 43, 81, 92, 105, 128, 129, 147, 154, 177, 178, 186, 194, 260
Antunes, António Lobo, xvii, xxi, 95, 97, 98, 104, 109, 110, 289
approximation, xxiii, 159, 160, 168, 169
atopia, xviii, 3, 4, 5, 7, 10, 12, 14
Atwood, Margaret, xviii, 268, 280, 281

B

Baku, Yumemakura, xvii, xviii, xxv, 211, 212, 213, 214, 216, 223, 224, 225, 226
Baudelaire, Charles, 247, 263
Beckett, Samuel, xvii, xix, 33, 34, 39, 45, 46, 47, 178, 268, 281, 282, 288
Benjamin, Walter, xviii, xxviii, 3, 5, 187, 251, 264
bioethics, xviii, xxvii, 267, 270, 272, 276
biopolitics, xviii, xxvii, 267, 269, 274, 279, 280, 289
Birds of America, xxiii, 143, 145, 147, 152, 157
body, ix, xii, xiv, xv, xx, xxi, xxii, xxiii, 15, 16, 24, 25, 35, 36, 43, 52, 54, 59, 65, 66, 68, 69, 74, 78, 81, 88, 95, 97, 103, 115, 135, 137, 143, 145, 146, 147, 148, 151, 152, 153, 154, 155, 156, 162, 163, 165, 167, 170, 171, 187, 190, 199, 200, 203, 205, 210, 214, 217, 219, 221, 222, 226, 227, 229, 230, 231, 235, 237, 250, 253, 258, 269, 273, 274, 275, 278, 285
Brave New World, xviii, 268, 273, 274, 275, 282, 290
Brave New World Revisited, xviii, 268, 274, 275, 282
Bulawayo, NoViolet, xviii, xxvi, 227, 238

C

Capitalism, 33, 36, 181, 191
care, xv, xviii, xix, xxiii, xxiv, 22, 30, 33, 34, 35, 36, 37, 38, 39, 40, 42, 44, 45, 46, 47, 58, 70, 78, 89, 97, 100, 131, 132, 133, 145, 159, 160, 161, 162, 163, 164, 165, 167, 170, 171, 172, 173, 214, 231, 232, 233, 234, 239, 241, 243, 268, 269, 271, 272, 276, 278, 281
Care Unit 371, xviii, xxiii, 159, 160, 161, 164, 170
Comics, xxiii, 159, 160, 172

community, xviii, 3, 4, 10, 11, 12, 13, 14, 15, 42, 103, 116, 129, 214, 216, 232, 251
Conrad, Joseph, xvii, xix, 19, 20, 30, 31
Consciousness, 49
consumer culture, 178, 180, 181, 182, 185
convalescence, xxvi, 245, 247, 248, 249, 250, 251, 252, 253, 254, 256, 258, 261, 262, 263, 264
Critical Medical Humanities, 49, 62, 63
Czerwiec, MK, xviii, xxiii, 159, 160, 173

D

decadence, xxv, 73, 193, 194, 195
delusion, 178
depression, xx, 49, 50, 52, 106, 144, 146, 147, 199, 212, 233
Derviş, Suat, xviii, xxv, 193, 196, 197, 206, 207, 208, 209
Dickens, Charles, 250, 262, 263
disability, xix, xx, xxii, 33, 36, 37, 38, 41, 43, 44, 45, 49, 51, 52, 54, 55, 56, 58, 127, 129, 130, 136, 137, 160, 288
Disability Studies, 36, 37, 46, 47, 49, 139, 141
disease, xi, xiii, xv, xxiii, xxv, xxvi, 9, 14, 15, 20, 21, 25, 26, 29, 51, 57, 61, 69, 103, 114, 115, 137, 143, 144, 145, 146, 147, 148, 153, 154, 155, 190, 191, 193, 197, 198, 199, 201, 206, 210, 227, 228, 229, 231, 232, 233, 234, 237, 238, 248, 249, 257, 270, 273, 290
docile bodies, 267, 275
doctor, xxi, 28, 50, 58, 60, 61, 95, 98, 99, 100, 101, 102, 103, 105, 107, 114, 116, 117, 121, 122, 124, 132, 147, 149, 170, 253, 271, 272, 273
Dracula, xviii, xxvii, 209, 257, 262, 265, 267, 268, 270, 272, 273, 281, 282, 283

E

emotion, 78, 212, 217
empathy, xvii, xxii, 34, 69, 113, 114, 116, 117, 119, 163, 170
Endgame, xix, 33, 34, 39, 40, 41, 43, 45, 47, 277, 281
Esposito, Roberto, xviii, 3, 4, 10, 11, 12, 13, 15, 16, 17

F

Federici, Silvia, xix, 33, 35, 46, 47
Feminism, 38, 124, 130, 207, 209, 282
fin-de-siecle, 193
flâneur, xxvii, 245, 246, 247, 248, 253, 255, 257, 258
Foucault, Michel, 109, 126, 267, 268
Fraser, Nancy, xix, 33, 36, 46

G

gender, xxii, 36, 39, 42, 127, 128, 129, 130, 137, 283, 289

H

Heart of Darkness, xvii, xviii, 19, 20, 21, 25, 30
Hiromasa, Minamoto no, xxv, 211, 215, 226
HIV/AIDS, xviii, xxiii, 159, 160, 162, 164, 168, 170, 171, 172, 173, 241, 242

Index 293

Holub, Miroslav, xvii, xx, xxviii, 65, 66, 79
homophobia, xxiii, 127, 137
Huxley, Aldous, xviii, 268, 273, 282, 290

I

illness, ix, xi, xii, xiii, xiv, xv, xvi, xvii, xviii, xx, xxi, xxiii, xxv, xxvi, 15, 19, 20, 21, 22, 23, 24, 25, 26, 27, 28, 29, 30, 33, 49, 50, 51, 52, 53, 54, 55, 56, 57, 58, 59, 60, 61, 62, 64, 65, 66, 69, 71, 76, 78, 81, 92, 95, 100, 101, 103, 104, 105, 107, 108, 109, 115, 116, 121, 128, 137, 143, 144, 145, 146, 147, 148, 149, 151, 152, 153, 154, 156, 160, 163, 167, 171, 173, 181, 193, 202, 227, 229, 230, 231, 232, 233, 234, 235, 237, 238, 245, 246, 247, 248, 249, 250, 251, 252, 253, 254, 257, 258, 260, 269, 273, 276
Illness as Metaphor, 26, 31, 63, 108, 109, 110, 144, 157, 248, 262, 263
illness narrative, xv, xx, xxiii, 49, 81, 115, 116, 143, 144, 145, 149, 151, 171
immunity, xviii, 3, 4, 12, 14, 15, 17
isolation, xxiii, xxvi, 68, 127, 130, 136, 137, 146, 147, 188, 245, 253, 285

J

Jackson, Shirley, xviii, xxii, 127, 128, 138, 139, 140, 141
Jensma, Wopko, xvii, xviii, xxiv, 177, 178, 185, 191

K

Kittay, Eva Feder, xix, 33, 37, 45, 46, 47

L

labour, xix, 33, 34, 35, 36, 37, 38, 39, 45, 162, 173, 234
lesbian, xxii, 127, 130, 133, 134, 136
Like Life, 145, 146, 147, 157
love, xxiii, 5, 87, 89, 123, 127, 130, 132, 133, 146, 195, 200, 201, 202, 204, 219, 220, 221, 222, 224, 231, 261, 271

M

madness, xxv, 9, 16, 26, 28, 50, 81, 82, 83, 91, 92, 103, 106, 128, 136, 137, 193, 197, 198, 199, 203, 204, 206, 235, 271, 289
Malone Dies, xviii, xxvii, 268, 276, 278
manic, xxiv, 50, 177, 178, 186, 188, 256
mediation, 183, 212
medical humanities, ix, xxvii, 50, 51, 58, 144, 267, 268, 281, 288, 290
medical poems, xxi, 65
medicine, xv, xvi, xvii, xx, xxii, xxiii, xxvii, 20, 49, 50, 51, 52, 54, 58, 62, 79, 96, 97, 98, 104, 106, 109, 113, 114, 115, 116, 117, 122, 124, 143, 144, 149, 153, 160, 162, 163, 165, 167, 173, 201, 235, 267, 269, 270, 273, 274, 281, 289
Microorganisms, 66
Modernist, 114

Moore, Lorrie, xviii, xxiii, 143, 145, 146, 149, 157
morbid humour, xxvi, 227, 229, 238
Murambatsvina, 228, 229, 239, 241, 242

N

Nano-poetics, 70, 79
narrative structure, 20, 29, 155, 156
Nijinsky, Vaslav, xvii, xxi, 81, 93

O

Objectivist, 114, 121
Onmyōji, xxv, 211, 212, 213, 214, 217, 218, 223, 224

P

pain, ix, x, xiv, xv, xvi, xvii, xx, xxii, xxiii, xxiv, xxvi, 7, 8, 9, 10, 15, 16, 27, 41, 49, 50, 52, 57, 58, 59, 60, 61, 62, 63, 65, 66, 68, 69, 71, 75, 77, 78, 99, 101, 113, 114, 115, 116, 117, 119, 120, 121, 122, 124, 143, 144, 145, 146, 147, 148, 154, 156, 159, 165, 167, 169, 171, 172, 190, 200, 206, 219, 227, 238, 254, 268, 276, 277, 279, 285, 286
Pathography, xiii, xv, xix, xxii, xxiii, xxv, xxviii, 19, 21, 24, 27, 31, 95, 103, 108, 109, 113, 114, 115, 125, 127, 159, 160, 172, 173, 193
Pathology, 66, 69, 77
patriarchy, xxii, 127, 128, 129, 130, 131, 132, 134, 136, 137
phenomenology, 81
Physician-writer, 114
Poe, Edgar Allan, 204, 253, 264

Poetics, 79
post-colonial Zimbabwe, xxvi, 229
Prometheus Bound, xvii, xviii, 3, 4, 6, 11, 14, 17
psychological dis-eases, 212
psychosis, xxi, 81, 83, 84, 91, 92, 181, 182
psychotherapy, 81

R

racism, xxiv, 20, 177, 178, 180, 268, 269, 281, 288
relapse, 245, 256, 258, 263
repression, 51, 212, 228, 239, 242
Rhythmanalysis, 246, 262, 263, 264
Ricoeur, Paul, xvi, 83

S

Scarry, Elaine, xxiii, 59, 143, 145, 156
Schizophrenia, xxv, 83, 86, 87, 177, 180, 181, 186, 191, 192
Seimei, Abe no, xxv, 211, 214, 215, 216, 219, 223, 224, 226
Self-Help, 145
Sontag, Susan, 26, 57, 107, 109, 144, 153, 248, 263
Spring and All, 114, 121, 123, 125, 126
Stoker, Bram, xviii, 209, 257, 265, 268, 270
storytelling, xxiii, 143, 144, 156, 197
suffering, ix, xiv, xv, xvii, xviii, xix, xx, xxi, xxiii, xxiv, 3, 6, 7, 8, 9, 10, 12, 14, 15, 16, 19, 20, 30, 43, 55, 58, 61, 65, 66, 68, 69, 71, 78, 79, 95, 98, 99, 101, 104, 105, 106, 107, 143, 144, 145, 146, 147, 148, 152, 154, 156, 162, 165, 167, 177,

178, 186, 198, 203, 228, 236, 238, 259, 260, 261, 271, 273, 274, 290

T

Taking Turns. Stories from HIV/AIDS Care Unit 371, 160, 172
The Black Book, xviii, xxv, 193, 197, 198, 205, 206, 209
The Diary of Vaslav Nijinsky, xxi, 81, 82, 92, 93
The Handmaid's Tale, xviii, xxvii, 267, 268, 279, 281
The Voyage Out, xvii, xx, 49, 50, 52, 56, 57, 59, 60, 61, 63
Therapy, 288
Thomson, Garland, 38
Turkish literature, xxv, 193, 207
tyranny, 6

U

urban space, 199, 245, 246
urban walking, 245
urban writing, 245

V

violence, xiii, xviii, 3, 4, 5, 6, 7, 13, 14, 15, 16, 25, 50, 68, 155, 179, 192, 218, 228, 229, 233, 237, 276, 277

W

Waiting for Godot, xix, 33, 34, 39, 40, 41, 45, 46, 47
We Have Always Lived in the Castle, xviii, xxii, 127, 128, 129, 130, 137, 138, 139, 140, 141
We Need New Names, xviii, xxvi, 227, 228, 229, 230, 231, 232, 234, 235, 237, 238, 239, 241
Whitman, Walt, 253, 258, 265
Williams, William Carlos, xi, xvii, xviii, xxii, 113, 114, 117, 125, 290
Woolf, Virginia, xii, xiv, xvii, xx, 49, 50, 62, 63, 64, 115, 253, 264, 288

www.ingramcontent.com/pod-product-compliance
Lightning Source LLC
Chambersburg PA
CBHW072123290426
44111CB00012B/1750